Social Theory of International Politics

Drawing upon philosophy and social theory, *Social Theory of International Politics* develops a theory of the international system as a social construction. Alexander Wendt clarifies the central claims of the constructivist approach, presenting a structural and idealist worldview which contrasts with the individualism and materialism which underpins much mainstream international relations theory. He builds a cultural theory of international politics, which takes whether states view each other as enemies, rivals, or friends as a fundamental determinant. Wendt characterizes these roles as "cultures of anarchy," described as Hobbesian, Lockean, and Kantian respectively. These cultures are shared ideas which help shape state interests and capabilities, and generate tendencies in the international system. The book describes four factors which can drive structural change from one culture to another – interdependence, common fate, homogenization, and self-restraint – and examines the effects of capitalism and democracy in the emergence of a Kantian culture in the West.

ALEXANDER WENDT is an Associate Professor at the University of Chicago. He has previously taught at Yale University and Dartmouth College. He is the author of several articles in leading journals on international relations theory.

CAMBRIDGE STUDIES IN INTERNATIONAL RELATIONS: 67

Social Theory of International Politics

CAMBRIDGE STUDIES IN INTERNATIONAL RELATIONS

Series list continues after index

Social Theory of International Politics

Alexander Wendt

CAMBRIDGE
UNIVERSITY PRESS

PUBLISHED BY THE PRESS SYNDICATE OF THE UNIVERSITY OF CAMBRIDGE
The Pitt Building, Trumpington Street, Cambridge, United Kingdom

CAMBRIDGE UNIVERSITY PRESS
The Edinburgh Building, Cambridge CB2 2RU, UK
40 West 20th Street, New York, NY 10011-4211, USA
477 Williamstown Road, Port Melbourne, VIC 3207, Australia
Ruiz de Alarcón 13, 28014 Madrid, Spain
Dock House, The Waterfront, Cape Town 8001, South Africa

http://www.cambridge.org

First published 1999
Reprinted 2000, 2001 (twice), 2003

Printed in the United Kingdom at the University Press, Cambridge

Typeset in Palatino 10/12$\frac{1}{2}$ pt [CE]

A catalogue record for this book is available from the British Library

ISBN 0 521 46557 5 hardback
ISBN 0 521 46960 0 paperback

For Bud Duvall

Contents

Analytical Table of Contents

Acknowledgements

In this book I develop a theory of the international system as a social construction. Since the term is used in many ways, the first half of the book is a conceptual analysis of what I mean by "social construction." The issues here are philosophical and may be unfamiliar to some students of international politics. However, I have tried throughout to be as clear as possible, keeping in mind a comment James Caporaso made about my first publication in 1987, that "there is nothing so profound here that it cannot be said in ordinary language." I cannot really say that what follows is "ordinary language," but his plea for clarity has become for me an important demand of this kind of work. The other half of the book is a theory of international politics based on that philosophical analysis. Juxtaposed to the Realisms that tend to dominate at least North American IR scholarship, this theory is a kind of Idealism, a Structural Idealism, although I refer to it only as a constructivist approach to international politics. As such, the book might be seen overall as a work of applied social theory. While not reducible to social theory, many debates in IR have a social theory aspect. My hope is that even when the arguments below prove problematic, the contours of those issues will have been brought into sharper relief.

I approach this material as a political scientist, which is to say that I have little formal training in social theory, the primary analytical tool of this study. To address this problem I have read broadly but without much guidance, in mostly contemporary philosophy and sociology. To credit these sources I have followed a generous citation policy, even if specialists – in IR and social theory alike – will still find much that is missing. By the same token, however, it was not possible here to properly address all of that scholarship. The bibliography should be seen as a resource for further reading rather than as a measure of what I have seriously engaged.

Over the long course of writing this book I have acquired a number of significant debts.

The book is descended from a dissertation done at the University of Minnesota, was mostly written at Yale University, and then completed at Dartmouth College. I am grateful for the time and support provided by all of these institution. Among many esteemed colleagues I have benefitted especially from the advice and role models of David Lumsdaine, Ian Shapiro, and Rogers Smith.

The most sustained debt is to my classmates in the "Minnesota School" of constructivism, and especially Mike Barnett, Mark Laffey, Rhona Leibel, and Jutta Weldes. Although their thicker constructivisms should not be identified with the thin one on offer below, this book is in a real sense a joint product of our conversations over the past 15 years.

For most of the book's writing my graduate students at Yale were my primary intellectual community and reality check, particularly the "third year class" of Janice Bially, Steve Brooks, Ian Cooper, Ian Hurd, and Roland Paris. Many of the formulations below, and many more that failed, were first tried on them.

I am especially grateful to the following individuals.

My parents, Hans and Martha, who constructed me to write such a book.

Charles Green, of Macalester College, who first showed me the value of taking a philosophical approach to politics.

David Sylvan, who taught me about constitution and told me to read Mead; the book would have been better had I read Simmel as well.

Steve Smith, of Aberystwyth, who first suggested I write the book, gave me a venue to publish it, and provided invaluable support throughout the process.

Nina Tannenwald, who when my enthusiasm waned impressed upon me the need to keep going.

Mike Barnett (again), whose unflagging humor and regular phone calls helped keep me in perspective.

Mlada Bukovansky, who talked me through the first draft and gave me a life in the second. Whatever dialectical elements there are below – and there are not enough – are due to her.

Jennifer Mitzen, who gave the book its finish. The trust I had in her critical eye made it possible to let the book go.

Most of those named above also provided comments on one or more chapters. Many other people provided helpful and sometimes extensive input as well. They include Badredine Arfi, Tom Banchoff, David Dessler, Marty Finnemore, Rod Hall, Martin Hollis, Pat Jackson, Ron Jepperson, Peter Katzenstein, Bob Keohane, Jeff Legro, Andy Moravcsik, Bill McSweeny, Himadeep Muppidi, Henry Nau, Brad Westerfield, and probably others, to whom I can only apologize for the state of my records. Finally, there are the many now anonymous individuals at the numerous seminars where this material has been presented, who asked questions that forced me to think harder. The book is much better for all of this help.

The book is dedicated to Raymond (Bud) Duvall, dissertation advisor and father of the Minnesota School. He cannot be blamed for all of what follows, but without him the book would not have been written.

No science can be more secure than the unconscious metaphysics which tacitly it presupposes.

Alfred North Whitehead

1   Four sociologies of international politics

In recent academic scholarship it has become commonplace to see international politics described as "socially constructed." Drawing on a variety of social theories – critical theory, postmodernism, feminist theory, historical institutionalism, sociological institutionalism, symbolic interactionism, structuration theory, and the like – students of international politics have increasingly accepted two basic tenets of "constructivism":[1] (1) that the structures of human association are determined primarily by shared ideas rather than material forces, and (2) that the identities and interests of purposive actors are constructed by these shared ideas rather than given by nature. The first represents an "idealist" approach to social life, and in its emphasis on the sharing of ideas it is also "social" in a way which the opposing "materialist" view's emphasis on biology, technology, or the environment, is not. The second is a "holist" or "structuralist" approach because of its emphasis on the emergent powers of social structures, which opposes the "individualist" view that social structures are reducible to individuals. Constructivism could therefore be seen as a kind of "structural idealism."

As the list above suggests there are many forms of constructivism. In this book I defend one form and use it to theorize about the international system. The version of constructivism that I defend is a moderate one that draws especially on structurationist and symbolic interactionist sociology. As such it concedes important points to materialist and individualist perspectives and endorses a scientific approach to social inquiry. For these reasons it may be rejected by more radical constructivists for not going far enough; indeed it is a

---

[1] A term first used in International Relations scholarship by Nicholas Onuf (1989).

thin constructivism. It goes much farther than most mainstream International Relations (IR)[2] scholars today, however, who sometimes dismiss any talk of social construction as "postmodernism." Between these extremes I hope to find a philosophically principled middle way. I then show that this makes a difference for thinking about international politics.

The international system is a hard case for constructivism on both the social and construction counts. On the social side, while norms and law govern most domestic politics, self-interest and coercion seem to rule international politics. International law and institutions exist, but the ability of this superstructure to counter the material base of power and interest seems limited. This suggests that the international system is not a very "social" place, and so provides intuitive support for materialism in that domain. On the construction side, while the dependence of individuals on society makes the claim that their identities are constructed by society relatively uncontroversial, the primary actors in international politics, states, are much more autonomous from the social system in which they are embedded. Their foreign policy behavior is often determined primarily by domestic politics, the analogue to individual personality, rather than by the international system (society). Some states, like Albania or Burma, have interacted so little with others that they have been called "autistic."[3] This suggests that the international system does not do much "constructing" of states, and so provides intuitive support for individualism in that domain (assuming states are "individuals"). The underlying problem here is that the social structure of the international system is not very thick or dense, which seems to reduce substantially the scope for constructivist arguments.

Mainstream IR scholarship today largely accepts these individualist and materialist conclusions about the states system. It is dominated by *Theory of International Politics*, Kenneth Waltz's powerful statement of "Neorealism," which combines a micro-economic approach to the international system (individualism) with the Classical Realist emphasis on power and interest (materialism).[4] Waltz's book helped

---

[2] Following Onuf (1989), capital letters denote the academic field, lower case the phenomenon of international relations itself.

[3] Buzan (1993: 341).

[4] Waltz (1979). I will use capital letters to designate theories of international relations in order to distinguish them from social theories.

2

generate a partially competing theory, "Neoliberalism," stated most systematically by Robert Keohane in *After Hegemony*, which accepted much of Neorealism's individualism but argued that international institutions could dampen, if not entirely displace, the effects of power and interest.[5] The fact that Neorealists and Neoliberals agree on so much has contributed to progress in their conversation, but has also substantially narrowed it. At times the debate seems to come down to no more than a discussion about the frequency with which states pursue relative rather than absolute gains.[6]

Despite the intuitive plausibility and dominance of materialist and individualist approaches to international politics, there is a long and varied tradition of what, from the standpoint of social theory, might be considered constructivist thinking on the subject. A constructivist worldview underlies the classical international theories of Grotius, Kant, and Hegel, and was briefly dominant in IR between the world wars, in the form of what IR scholars now, often disparagingly, call "Idealism."[7] In the post-war period important constructivist approaches to international politics were advanced by Karl Deutsch, Ernst Haas, and Hedley Bull.[8] And constructivist assumptions underlie the phenomenological tradition in the study of foreign policy, starting with the work of Snyder, Bruck, and Sapin, and continuing on with Robert Jervis and Ned Lebow.[9] In the 1980s ideas from these and other lineages were synthesized into three main streams of constructivist IR theory:[10] a modernist stream associated with John Ruggie and Friedrich Kratochwil,[11] a postmodernist stream associated with

---

[5] Keohane (1984).

[6] See, for example, Grieco (1988), Baldwin, ed. (1993), Kegley, ed. (1995), and Schweller and Priess (1997).

[7] On inter-war idealism see Long and Wilson, eds. (1995).

[8] Deutsch (1954, 1963), Haas (1964, 1983, 1990), Bull (1977). Less widely cited, Andrews (1975) comes as close as any to anticipating contemporary constructivist IR scholarship. Keohane and Nye's (1977/1989) work on interdependence can also be seen as a precursor.

[9] Snyder, Bruck, and Sapin (1954), Jervis (1970, 1976, 1978), Lebow (1981).

[10] The work of neo-Gramscians like Robert Cox (1987) and Stephen Gill (1993, ed.) also could be put into this category, although this is complicated by their relationship to Marxism, a "materialist" social theory. Additionally, Hayward Alker deserves special mention. Impossible to classify, his ideas, often circulating in unpublished manuscripts, were an important part of the revival of constructivist thinking about international politics in the 1980s. He has recently published a number of these papers (Alker, 1996).

[11] Ruggie (1983a, b), Kratochwil (1989).

;hard Ashley and Rob Walker,[12] and a feminist stream associated
ith Spike Peterson and Ann Tickner.[13] The differences among and
within these three streams are significant, but they share the view that
Neorealism and Neoliberalism are "undersocialized" in the sense that
they pay insufficient attention to the ways in which the actors in
world politics are socially constructed.[14] This common thread has
enabled a three-cornered debate with Neorealists and Neoliberals to
emerge.[15]

The revival of constructivist thinking about international politics
was accelerated by the end of the Cold War, which caught scholars on
all sides off guard but left orthodoxies looking particularly exposed.
Mainstream IR theory simply had difficulty explaining the end of the
Cold War,[16] or systemic change more generally. It seemed to many
that these difficulties stemmed from IR's materialist and individualist
orientation, such that a more ideational and holistic view of international politics might do better. The resulting wave of constructivist
IR theorizing was initially slow to develop a program of empirical
research,[17] and epistemological and substantive variations within it
continue to encourage a broad but thin pattern of empirical cumulation. But in recent years the quality and depth of empirical work has
grown considerably, and this trend shows every sign of continuing.[18]
This is crucial for the success of constructivist thinking in IR, since the
ability to shed interesting light on concrete problems of world politics
must ultimately be the test of a method's worth. In addition, however,
alongside and as a contribution to those empirical efforts it also seems
important to clarify what constructivism is, how it differs from its
materialist and individualist rivals, and what those differences might
mean for theories of international politics.

Building on existing constructivist IR scholarship, in this book I
address these issues on two levels: at the level of foundational or
second-order questions about what there is and how we can explain

[12] Ashley (1984, 1987), R. Walker (1987, 1993).
[13] Peterson, ed. (1992), Tickner (1993).   [14] Cf. Wrong (1961).
[15] See Mearsheimer (1994/5), Keohane and Martin (1995), Wendt (1995), and Walt
(1998).
[16] For a good overview of recent efforts see Lebow and Risse-Kappen, eds. (1995).
[17] Keohane (1988a).
[18] See, for example, Campbell (1992), Klotz (1995), Price (1995), Biersteker and Weber,
eds. (1996), Finnemore (1996a), Katzenstein, ed. (1996), Bukovansky (1997, 1999a, b),
Adler and Barnett, eds. (1998), Barnett (1998), Hall (1999), Weldes (1999), and Weldes,
et al., eds. (1999), Reus-Smit (1999), and Tannenwald (1999).

4

or understand it – ontology, epistemology and method; and at the level of substantive, domain-specific, or first-order questions.

Second-order questions are questions of social theory. Social theory is concerned with the fundamental assumptions of social inquiry: the nature of human agency and its relationship to social structures, the role of ideas and material forces in social life, the proper form of social explanations, and so on. Such questions of ontology and epistemology can be asked of any human association, not just international politics, and so our answers do not explain international politics in particular. Yet students of international politics must answer these questions, at least implicitly, since they cannot do their business without making powerful assumptions about what kinds of things are to be found in international life, how they are related, and how they can be known. These assumptions are particularly important because no one can "see" the state or international system. International politics does not present itself directly to the senses, and theories of international politics often are contested on the basis of ontology and epistemology, i.e., what the theorist "sees." Neorealists see the structure of the international system as a distribution of material capabilities because they approach their subject with a materialist lens; Neoliberals see it as capabilities plus institutions because they have added to the material base an institutional superstructure; and constructivists see it as a distribution of ideas because they have an idealist ontology. In the long run empirical work may help us decide which conceptualization is best, but the "observation" of unobservables is always theory-laden, involving an inherent gap between theory and reality (the "underdetermination of theory by data"). Under these conditions empirical questions will be tightly bound up with ontological and epistemological ones; how we answer "what causes what?" will depend in important part on how we first answer "what is there?" and "how should we study it?" Students of international politics could perhaps ignore these questions if they agreed on their answers, as economists often seem to,[19] but they do not. I suggest below that there are at least four "sociologies" of international politics, each with many adherents. I believe many ostensibly substantive debates about the nature of international politics are in part philosophical debates about these sociologies. In part I of this book I attempt to clarify these second-order debates and advance a constructivist approach.

---

[19] Though see Glass and Johnson (1988).

Social theories are not theories of international politics. Clarifying the differences and relative virtues of constructivist, materialist, and individualist ontologies ultimately may help us better explain international politics, but the contribution is indirect. A more direct role is played by substantive theory, which is the second concern of this book. Such first-order theorizing is domain-specific. It involves choosing a social system (family, Congress, international system), identifying the relevant actors and how they are structured, and developing propositions about what is going on. Substantive theory is based on social theory but cannot be "read off" of it. In part II of the book I outline a substantive, first-order theory of international politics. The theory starts from many of the same premises as Waltz's, which means that some of the same criticisms commonly directed at his work will have equal force here. But the basic thrust and conclusions of my argument are at odds with Neorealism, in part because of different ontological or second-order commitments. Materialist and individualist commitments lead Waltz to conclude that anarchy makes international politics a necessarily conflictual, "self-help" world. Idealist and holist commitments lead me to the view that "anarchy is what states make of it."[20] Neither theory follows directly from its ontology, but ontologies contribute significantly to their differences.

Even with respect to substantive theorizing, however, the level of abstraction and generality in this book are high. Readers looking for detailed propositions about the international system, let alone empirical tests, will be disappointed. The book is about the *ontology* of the states system, and so is more about international *theory* than about international politics as such. The central question is: given a similar substantive concern as Waltz, i.e., states systemic theory and explanation, but a different ontology, what is the resulting theory of international politics? In that sense, this is a case study in social theory or applied philosophy. After laying out a social constructivist ontology, I build a theory of "international" politics. This is not the only theory that follows from that ontology, but my primary goal in building it is to show that the different ontological starting point has substantive import for how we explain the real world. In most places that import is merely to reinforce or provide ontological foundations for what at least some segment of the IR community already knew. On the

---

[20] Wendt (1992).

substantive level IR scholars will find much that is familiar below. But in some places it suggests a rethinking of important substantive issues, and in a few cases, I hope, new lines of inquiry.

In sum, the title of this book contains a double reference: the book is about "social theory" in general and, more specifically, about a more "social" theory of international politics than Neorealism or Neoliberalism. This chapter makes two passes through these issues, emphasizing international and social theory respectively. In the first section I discuss the state-centric IR theory project, offer a diagnosis of what is currently wrong with it, and summarize my own approach. In a sense, this section presents the puzzle that animates the argument of the book overall. In the second section I begin to develop the conceptual tools that allow us to rethink the ontology of the international system. I draw a "map" of the four sociologies involved in the debate over social construction (individualism, holism, materialism, and idealism), locate major lines of international theory on it, and address three interpretations of what the debate is about (methodology, ontology, and empirics). The chapter concludes with an overview of the book as a whole.

The states systemic project

Constructivism is not a theory of international politics.[21] Constructivist sensibilities encourage us to look at how actors are socially constructed, but they do not tell us which actors to study or where they are constructed. Before we can be a constructivist about anything we have to choose "units" and "levels" of analysis, or "agents" and the "structures" in which they are embedded.[22]

The discipline of International Relations requires that these choices have some kind of "international" dimension, but beyond that it does not dictate units or levels of analysis. The "states systemic project" reflects one set of choices within a broader field of possibilities. Its units are states, as opposed to non-state actors like individuals,

---

[21] I have been unclear about this in my previous work (e.g., 1992, 1994). I now wish to draw a sharper distinction between constructivism and the theory of international politics that I sketch in this book. One can accept constructivism without embracing that theory.

[22] On levels of analysis see Singer (1961), Moul (1973), and Onuf (1995). In much of IR scholarship units and levels of analysis are conflated. I follow Moul (1973: 512) in distinguishing them, and map them onto agents and structures respectively.

transnational social movements, or multinational corporations. The level of analysis on which it tries to explain the behavior of these units is the international system, as opposed to the personality of foreign policy decision-makers or domestic political structures. Waltz was one of the first to articulate the states systemic project systematically,[23] and the particular theory he helped erect on that basis, Neorealism, is so influential in the field today that project and theory are often equated. There is no question that the assumptions of the states systemic project significantly shape, and limit, our thinking about world politics. These assumptions are controversial and there are other theories of the states system besides Neorealism. I am offering a theory of the states system critical of Waltz's. Given my critical intent, one might wonder why I choose such a mainstream, controversial starting point. In this section I first address this question, and then discuss what I think is wrong with current states systemic theorizing and how it might be fixed.

State-centrism

Regulating violence is one of the most fundamental problems of order in social life, because the nature of violence technology, who controls it, and how it is used deeply affect all other social relations. This is not to say other social relations, like the economy or the family, are *reducible* to the structures by which violence is regulated, such that we could explain all social relations solely by reference to structures of violence. Nor is it to say that the most interesting issue in any given setting concerns the regulation of violence. The point is only that other social relations could not exist in the forms they do unless they are compatible with the "forces" and especially "relations of destruction."[24] If people are determined to kill or conquer each other they will not cooperate on trade or human rights. Power may be everywhere these days, but its forms vary in importance, and the power to engage in organized violence is one of the most basic. How it is distributed and regulated is a crucial problem. That is the aspect of world politics in which I am interested in this book. Since the state is a structure of political authority with a monopoly on the legitimate use of organized violence, when it comes to the regulation of violence internationally it is states one ultimately has to control.

---

[23] Waltz (1959).   [24] Cf. Deudney (1999).

States have not always dominated the regulation of violence, nor do they dominate unproblematically today. In pre-modern times states in Europe competed with two other organizational forms, city-states and city-leagues,[25] and outside Europe they competed with all manner of forms. These alternatives eventually were eliminated. But states have continued to struggle to assert their monopoly on violence, facing challenges from mercenaries and pirates well into the nineteenth century,[26] and from terrorists and guerrilla groups in the twentieth. Under these and other pressures, some states have even "failed."[27] This suggests that the state can be seen as a "project" in the Gramscian sense, an on-going political program designed to produce and reproduce a monopoly on the potential for organized violence. Still, overall this project has been quite successful. The potential for organized violence has been highly concentrated in the hands of states for some time, a fact which states have helped bring about by recognizing each other as the sole legitimate bearers of organized violence potential, in effect colluding to sustain an oligopoly. My premise is that since states are the dominant form of subjectivity in contemporary world politics this means that they should be the primary unit of analysis for thinking about the global regulation of violence.

It should be emphasized that "state-centrism" in this sense does not preclude the possibility that non-state actors, whether domestic or transnational, have important, even decisive, effects on the frequency and/or manner in which states engage in organized violence. "State-centrism" does not mean that the causal chain in explaining war and peace stops with states, or even that states are the "most important" links in that chain, whatever that might mean. Particularly with the spread of liberalism in the twentieth century this is clearly not the case, since liberal states are heavily constrained by non-state actors in both civil society and the economy. The point is merely that states are still the primary medium through which the effects of other actors on the regulation of violence are channeled into the world system. It may be that non-state actors are becoming more important than states as initiators of change, but system change ultimately happens *through* states. In that sense states still are at the center of the international system, and as such it makes no more sense to criticize a theory of international politics as "state-centric" than it does to criticize a theory of forests for being "tree-centric."

---

[25] Spruyt (1994).   [26] Thomson (1994).   [27] Helman and Ratner (1992/1993).

9

This state-centric focus is not politically innocent. Critics might argue that its insights are inherently conservative, good only for "problem-solving" rather than radical change.[28] That is not my view. Neorealism might not be able to explain structural change, but I think there is potential in IR to develop state-centric theories that can. A key first step in developing such theory is to accept the assumption that states are actors with more or less human qualities: intentionality, rationality, interests, etc. This is a debatable assumption. Many scholars see talk of state "actors" as an illegitimate reification or anthropomorphization of what are in fact structures or institutions.[29] On their view the idea of state agency is at most a useful fiction or metaphor. I shall argue that states *really are* agents. Decision-makers routinely speak in terms of national "interests," "needs," "responsibilities," "rationality," and so on, and it is through such talk that states constitute themselves and each other as agents. International politics as we know it today would be impossible without attributions of corporate agency, a fact recognized by international law, which explicitly grants legal "personality" to states. The assumption of real corporate agency enables states actively to participate in structural transformation.

In sum, for critical IR theorists to eschew state-centric theorizing is to concede much of international politics to Neorealism. I show that state-centric IR theory can generate insights that might help move the international system from the law of the jungle toward the rule of law. It is true that knowledge always is more useful for some purposes than for others,[30] and knowledge gained from an analysis of states and organized violence might do little to empower non-state actors interested in trade or human rights. But that simply means that state-centered IR theory can only be one element of a larger progressive agenda in world politics, not that it cannot be an element at all.

Systems theory

States are rarely found in complete isolation from each other. Most inhabit relatively stable systems of other independent states which impinge on their behavior. In the contemporary states system states recognize each other's right to sovereignty, and so the state-centric "project" includes an effort to reproduce not only their own identity,

---

[28] Cox (1986); also see Fay (1975).
[29] For example, Ferguson and Mansbach (1991: 370).   [30] Cox (1986).

but that of the system of which they are parts: states in the *plural*. In this book I am interested in the structure and effects of states (or "international") systems, which means that I will be taking a "systems theory" approach to IR. In order to avoid confusion it is important to distinguish two senses in which a theory might be considered "systemic": when it makes the international system the dependent variable, and when it makes the international system the independent variable.[31] My argument is systemic in both senses.

A theory is systemic in the first, dependent variable sense when it takes as its object of explanation patterns of state behavior at the aggregate or population level, i.e., the states system. This is what Waltz calls a "theory of international politics." Theories of international politics are distinguished from those that have as their object explaining the behavior of individual states, or "theories of foreign policy."[32] It is important that IR do both kinds of theorizing, but their dependent variables, aggregate behavior versus unit behavior, are on different levels of analysis and so their explanations are not comparable. Their relationship is complementary rather than competitive. Like Waltz, I am interested in international politics, not foreign policy. Most of the substantive theories discussed in this book are systemic in this sense, and so the question of the appropriate object of explanation, the explanandum, does not really come up. One implication of this systemic orientation is that although I criticize Neorealism and Neoliberalism for not recognizing the ways in which the system shapes state identities and interests, which might be seen as in the domain of theories of foreign policy, in fact explaining state identities and interests is not my main goal either. This is a book about the international system, not about state identity formation. I show that the former bears on the latter in ways that are consequential for thinking about international politics, but state identities are also heavily influenced by domestic factors that I do not address.

The second, independent variable, sense in which IR theories are commonly called systemic is more at stake here. In this sense, which is due to Waltz,[33] a theory is considered "systemic" (or, sometimes, "structural") when it emphasizes the causal powers of the structure of the international system in explaining state behavior. This is distinguished from "reductionist" theories of state behavior that emphasize

---

[31] This framing is due to Steve Brooks. [32] Waltz (1979: 121–122).
[33] Ibid.: 38–59.

"unit-level" factors like decision-makers' psychology and domestic politics. The behavior in question might be unit or aggregate; the systemic–reductionist distinction is usually only invoked among theories of international politics, but it could also be applied to theories of foreign policy.[34] Systemic theories explain international politics by reference to "structure" (of the international system), while reductionist theories explain international politics by reference to the properties and interactions of "agents" (states). The relationship between the two kinds of theory is competitive, over the relative weight of causal forces at different levels of analysis. Neorealism is a systemic theory in this second sense because it locates the key causes of international life in the system-level properties of anarchy and the distribution of capabilities. Liberalism is sometimes considered a competing, reductionist theory because it locates the key causes in the attributes and interactions of states.[35]

Like Waltz, I aim to develop a systemic as opposed to reductionist theory of international politics. However, in taking this stance I take issue with his exclusion of unit-level factors from systemic theorizing, on the grounds that he has misconstrued what divides the two kinds of theory. I argue that it is impossible for structures to have effects apart from the attributes and interactions of agents. If that is right, then the challenge of "systemic" theory is not to show that "structure" has more explanatory power than "agents," as if the two were separate, but to show how agents are differently structured by the system so as to produce different effects. Waltz's two kinds of theory *both* do this; both make predictions based on assumptions about the relationship of structure to agents. The debate, therefore, is not between "systemic" theories that focus on structure and "reductionist" theories that focus on agents, but between *different theories of system structure* and of how structure relates to agents. To capture this shift in the understanding of "systemic" it may be best to abandon Waltz's terminology, which is not in line with contemporary philosophical practice anyway. In chapter 4 I argue that what he calls "systemic" theory is about the "macro-structure" of international politics, and "reductionist" theory is about its "micro-structure." Both kinds of theory invoke the structure of the system to explain patterns

---

[34] For discussion of how Neorealism might be adapted to explain foreign policy see Elman (1996).

[35] Keohane (1990), Moravcsik (1997).

of state behavior and as such both are systemic in Waltz's sense, but both also invoke unit-level properties and interactions – just in different ways because their respective structures are on different levels of analysis.

The possibility of systems theory, of whatever kind, assumes that the domestic or unit and systemic levels of analysis can be separated. Some might disagree. They might argue that international inter-dependence is eroding the boundary between state and system, making domestic policy increasingly a matter of foreign policy and vice-versa,[36] or that the boundary between state and system is a social construction in the first place which needs to be problematized rather than taken as given.[37] For them, "levels" thinking is a *problem* with IR theory, not a solution.

There are at least two responses to such criticism. One is to argue on empirical grounds that international interdependence is not rising, or that the density of interactions remains much higher within states than between them.[38] If so, we can continue to speak of domestic and systemic politics as distinct domains. This is not a particularly strong defense of the systemic project, however, since it means the probable growth of interdependence in the future will erode the utility of systemic theorizing. Moreover, because it assumes low systemic density, this response also paradoxically suggests that systemic factors may not be very important relative to unit-level ones in the first place.

Juridical grounds offer a stronger rationale for systems theory. Regardless of the extent to which interdependence blurs the *de facto* boundary between domestic and foreign policies, in the contemporary international system political authority is organized formally in a bifurcated fashion: vertically within states ("hierarchy"), horizontally between ("anarchy").[39] This is partly due to the nature of states, and partly to the international institution of sovereignty, in which states recognize each other as having exclusive political authority within separate territories. As long as global political space is organized in this way, states will behave differently toward each other than they do toward their own societies. At home states are bound by a thick structure of rules that holds their power accountable to society. Abroad they are bound by a different set of rules, the logic, or as I shall argue, logics, of anarchy.

[36] Hanrieder (1978).   [37] Campbell (1992).
[38] Waltz (1979: 129–160), Thomson and Krasner (1989).   [39] Waltz (1979: 114–116).

Even if we agree that the unit and system levels can be separated, there is still the question of whether the international *political* system is a separate domain. Is it fair to assume institutional differentiation within the international system between political, economic, and perhaps other functional sub-systems? States are the core of any international system, since they constitute the distinct entities without which an "inter"national system by definition cannot exist. In international systems that are institutionally *un*differentiated the logic of inter-state relations is the only logic, and historically this has been the dominant modality of international politics.[40] In such worlds there might still be distinct "sectors" of economic, political, or military interaction,[41] but as long as these are not institutionally distinct they will not constitute distinct logics. States have interacted in the economic issue area for centuries, for example, but usually through mercantilist policies that reflected the logic of their military competition. In the past two centuries and especially since World War II, however, the international system has experienced substantial institutional differentiation, first into political and economic spheres, and more recently, arguably, into a nascent sphere of global civil society as well. The ultimate cause of these changes is the spread of capitalism, which unlike other modes of production is constituted by institutional separations between spheres of social life.[42] The transposition of this structure to the global level is far from complete, but already it is transforming the nature of international life. This does not vitiate systemic theorizing, which has a distinct role as long as states are constitutionally independent, but it does mean that the content of "the international" is not constant.

In sum, the states systemic project assumes that its object can be studied relatively autonomously from other units and levels of analysis in world politics. We cannot study everything at once, and there are good reasons for marking off the states system as a distinct phenomenon. This does not make one a Realist. Systemic theorizing is sometimes equated with Realism, but this is a mistake. Nor does it mean that the states system is the only thing that IR scholars should be studying. IR scholars have sometimes neglected non-state units and non-systemic levels, but that is hardly an argument against also

[40] Cf. Chase-Dunn (1981).   [41] Buzan, Jones, and Little (1993: 30–33).
[42] Wood (1981); cf. Walzer (1984). See Rosenberg (1994) for a provocative exploration of some of the effects on international relations of the capitalist separation of economy and polity.

studying the states system. There are many things in world politics that states systemic theorizing cannot explain, but this does not mean the things which it does explain should be lost.

Neorealism and its critics[43]

The states systemic project does not commit us to any particular theory of how that system works. In principle there are many systemic theories. One of the basic issues that divides them is how they conceptualize the "structure" of the system. Neorealism offers one such conceptualization, one so dominant today that systemic IR theory is often equated with it. Earlier systemic theories contained at least implicit conceptualizations of structure,[44] but *Theory of International Politics* was the first to think in self-consciously structural terms. Since its publication in 1979 it has probably been cited more than any other book in the field, and it is today one of IR's foundational texts. There are few such works in social science, and in an academic world given to fads it is easy to forget them in the rush to catch the next wave of theory. If parsimony is over-rated as a theoretical virtue,[45] then cumulation is surely under-rated. With that in mind I shall take Waltz's structuralism – and Ashley and Ruggie's conversation with it – as my starting point, but from there engage in some substantial "conceptual reorganization"[46] that will ultimately yield a structural theory different in both kind and content from Neorealism. This theory competes with Waltz's argument in some ways, and supports it in others. But I see it primarily as trying to explain the latter's cultural conditions of possibility, and in so doing the basis for alternative, "non-Realist" cultures of anarchy.[47] Because I wrestle with Neorealism throughout this book I will not present it in detail here. Instead, I summarize three of its key features, identify some of its problems and principal responses to those problems, and then outline my own approach.

Despite Waltz's professed structuralism, ultimately he is an individualist. This is manifest most clearly in his reliance on the analogy to neoclassical micro-economic theory. States are likened to firms, and

---

[43] The phrase is Keohane's, ed. (1986).
[44] See Kaplan (1957), Scott (1967), and Bull (1977).   [45] Lebow (1998).
[46] Denis (1989: 347).
[47] On some possible relationships among theories see Jepperson, Wendt, and Katzenstein (1996: 68–72).

the international system to a market within which states compete. "International-political systems, like economic markets, are individualist in origin, spontaneously generated and unintended."[48] From the standpoint of structural theorizing in the social sciences more generally this analogy is surprising, since most structuralists are holists. Yet Waltz goes further than traditional economic theory in emphasizing the feedback effects of international structure on state agents. Competition eliminates states who perform badly, and the international system socializes states to behave in certain ways.[49] Thus, the top–down story that holists tell about agents and structures seems on the surface to get equal billing in Waltz's framework with the bottom–up story told by individualists. Nevertheless, I argue that his top–down story is considerably weaker than it should be because of the micro-economic analogy. Economists are uninterested in the construction of actors, which is one of the most important things a structure can explain, and this neglect is largely mirrored in Neorealism.

A micro-economic approach to structure does not tell us what structure is made of. Some economists see the market as an institution constituted by shared ideas, others see only material forces. A second feature of Neorealist structuralism, therefore, is its materialism: the structure of the international system is defined as the distribution of material capabilities under anarchy. The kinds of ideational attributes or relationships that might constitute a *social* structure, like patterns of friendship or enmity, or institutions, are specifically excluded from the definition.[50] Variation in system structure is constituted solely by material differences in polarity (number of major powers), and structural change therefore is measured solely by transitions from one polarity distribution to another.

Finally, writing at a time when the autonomy of the systemic project was not clearly recognized, Waltz is also very concerned to maintain a clear distinction between systemic and unit-level theorizing. To this end he argues that the study of interaction between states, or what is sometimes called "process," should be seen as the province of unit-level rather than systemic theory. In his view this follows from a concern with international politics rather than foreign policy. He seeks to explain aggregate constraints and tendencies in the system rather than the actions of particular states. Since theories of interaction have particular actions as their explanatory object, this seems to place them

---

[48] Waltz (1979: 91).   [49] Ibid.: 74–77.   [50] Ibid.: 98–99.

outside the concern of systemic theory. Waltz's neglect of international interaction has left it in something of a theoretical limbo: consigned by Neorealism to the purgatory of unit-level theory, students of foreign policy decision-making tend to be equally uninterested because of its apparent systemic dimension.[51]

Individualism, materialism, and neglect of interaction form the core of Neorealist structuralism, and to many in IR this simply "is" what a structural theory of international politics looks like. Over the years it has come in for substantial criticism, but critics sometimes throw the systemic theory baby out with the Neorealist bathwater. That is, much of the criticism is aimed at the Neorealist *version* of systemic theory, i.e., at its individualism, its materialism, and/or its neglect of inter- action processes. Since a proper review of this literature would take an entire chapter, let me simply mention three important criticisms that animate my own search for an alternative.

One is that Neorealism cannot explain structural change.[52] To be sure, Neorealism acknowledges the possibility of structural change in one sense – namely transitions from one distribution of power to another.[53] But the kind of structural change the critics have in mind is less material than *social*: the transition from feudalism to sovereign states, the end of the Cold War, the emergence of peace among democratic states, and so on. Neorealists do not consider such changes "structural" because they do not change the distribution of power or transcend anarchy. As a result, while no doubt conceding the importance of something like the end of the Cold War for foreign policy, their emphasis in thinking about such change returns always to the macro-level logic of "plus ça change . . . ." The logic of anarchy is constant.[54]

A second problem is that Neorealism's theory of structure is too underspecified to generate falsifiable hypotheses. For example, vir- tually any foreign policy behavior can be construed as evidence of balancing. Neorealists could argue that during the Cold War confron- tational policies were evidence of Soviet balancing of the West, and that after the Cold War conciliatory policies were. Similarly, in the old days states balanced militarily, now they do so through economic

---

[51] Though see Herrmann and Fischerkeller (1995).
[52] See, for example, Ruggie (1983a), Ashley (1984), R. Walker (1987), Wendt (1992), and Kratochwil (1993).
[53] For a Realist approach to structural change see Gilpin (1981).
[54] For example, Mearsheimer (1990a), Fischer (1992), and Layne (1993).

means. Given this suppleness, it is not clear what would count as evidence against the balancing hypothesis. Perhaps the "bandwagoning" behavior of the post-Cold War period, but on this point Neorealists have given themselves a generous time frame. Christopher Layne, for example, argues that it may take fifty years before Germany and Japan adjust to the collapse of the Soviet Union by balancing militarily against the United States.[55] Neorealism admittedly is not designed to explain foreign policy. But if any policy short of national suicide is compatible with balancing, then it is not clear in what sense "states balance" is a scientific claim.

Finally, there is doubt that Neorealism adequately explains even the "small number of big and important things" claimed on its behalf.[56] I am thinking in particular of power politics and again of balancing, tendencies which Waltz argues are explained by the structural fact of anarchy alone. In 1992 I argued that what is really doing the explanatory work here is the assumption that anarchy is a self-help system, which follows from states being egoists about their security and not from anarchy.[57] Sometimes states are egoists and other times they are not, and this variation can change the "logic" of anarchy. I take that argument further in chapter 6. The "sauve qui peut" egoism of a Hobbesian anarchy has a different logic than the more self-restrained egoism of a Lockean anarchy, which differs still from the Kantian anarchy based on collective security interests, which is no longer "self-help" in any interesting sense. This suggests that even when the character of the international system conforms to Neorealist predictions, it does so for reasons other than Neorealism is able to specify.

These and other problems have contributed to a widespread sense of crisis in the systemic project. Few scholars today call themselves Neorealists. Simplifying hugely, we can group IR scholars' responses to this situation into two categories. One is to set aside states and the states system and focus instead on new units of analysis (non-state actors) or new levels (individuals or domestic politics). This has generated much interesting work in recent IR scholarship, but it is no substitute for systemic theorizing. Non-state actors may be increasingly significant, but this does not mean we no longer need a theory of the states system. Similarly, individuals and domestic politics may be important causes of foreign policy, but ignoring systemic structures

---

[55] Layne (1993).   [56] Waltz (1979).   [57] Wendt (1992).

assumes that states are autistic, which usually is not the case. This first response changes the subject rather than deals with the problem.

The second response might be called reformist: broaden Neorealism to include more variables, without changing its core assumptions about system structure. Simplifying again, here we see two main directions, post-Waltzian (my term) and Neoliberal. The former retains a focus on material power as the key factor in world politics, but supplements it with ideational or other unit-level variables. Stephen Walt argues that perceptions of threat are necessary to fill out Waltz's theory, and that these stem from assessments of intentions and ideology.[58] Randall Schweller looks at variation in state interests, and especially the distinction between status quo and revisionist states.[59] Buzan, Jones, and Little extend the purview of systemic theory to include the study of interaction.[60] And so on. In developing these insights post-Waltzians have often turned to Classical Realism, which has a richer menu of variables than its leaner Neorealist cousin. Neoliberals, on the other hand, have capitalized on Waltz's micro-economic analogy, which has rich conceptual resources of its own. By focusing on the evolution of expectations during interaction, they have shown how states can develop international regimes that promote cooperation even after the distribution of power that initially sustained them has gone.[61] And more recently Neoliberals have turned to "ideas" as an additional intervening variable between power/interest and outcomes.[62]

Although their portrayals of international politics differ in important ways, post-Waltzians and Neoliberals share a basic premise: Waltz's definition of structure. Post-Waltzians are less wedded to micro-economic analogies, but have not fundamentally abandoned Waltz's materialist assumptions. Neoliberals have exploited his micro-economic analogies in ways that attenuate those assumptions, but have been reluctant to abandon materialism altogether. They acknowledge that "ideas matter," but they do not see power and interest themselves as effects of ideas. This has left Neoliberals vulnerable to the charge that their theory is not distinct from, or that it is subsumed by, Neorealism.[63] As noted above, the latter is heavily underspecified

---

[58] Walt (1987).   [59] Schweller (1994).
[60] Buzan, Jones, and Little (1993); also see Snyder (1996).
[61] Krasner, ed. (1983), Keohane (1984), Oye, ed. (1986).
[62] Goldstein (1993), Goldstein and Keohane, eds. (1993).
[63] See Mearsheimer (1994/1995).

and so the significance of this charge is unclear. However, what is important from my perspective is what is *not* being talked about. That is, whatever the outcome of their debate, it is unlikely to yield a substantial rethinking of structure – certainly, talk of social construction is anathema to them all.

It would be useful to consider whether the efforts to reform Neorealism are all compatible with the "hard core" of the Neorealist research program, and particularly its ontology, or whether some of these efforts might constitute "degenerating problem shifts."[64] Rather than challenge the ontological coherence of Neorealist-Neoliberalism, however, let me just stipulate the core of an alternative. The basic intuition is that the problem in the states systemic project today lies in the Neorealist conceptualization of structure and structural theory, and that what is therefore needed is a conceptual reorganization of the whole enterprise. More specifically, I shall make three moves.

The most important move is to reconceptualize what international structure is made of. In my view it is exactly what Waltz says it is not: a social rather than material phenomenon. And since the basis of sociality is shared knowledge, this leads to an idealist view of structure as a "distribution of knowledge" or "ideas all the way down" (or almost anyway). This conceptualization of structure may seem odd to a generation of IR scholars weaned on Neorealism, but it is common in both sociology and anthropology. Chapters 3 and 4 explain this proposal, but the intuition is straightforward: the character of international life is determined by the beliefs and expectations that states have about each other, and these are constituted largely by social rather than material structures. This does not mean that material power and interests are unimportant, but rather that their meaning and effects depend on the social structure of the system, and specifically on which of three "cultures" of anarchy is dominant – Hobbesian, Lockean, or Kantian. Bipolarity in a Hobbesian culture is one thing, in a Lockean or a Kantian culture quite another. On a social definition of structure, the concept of structural change refers to changes in these cultures – like the end of the Cold War in 1989 – and not to changes in material polarity – like the end of bipolarity in 1991.

A sociological turn is also evident in the second move, which is to argue that state identities and interests are more constructed by the

---

[64] Lakatos (1970). For a good discussion of this issue see Vasquez (1997) and subsequent rejoinders.

international system than can be seen by an economic approach to structure. If we adopt a holist conceptualization of structure we can see two aspects of state construction that an individualist approach ignores: the ways in which state identities rather than just behavior are affected by the international system, and the ways in which those identities are constituted rather than just caused by the system (I explain these distinctions below). Because of the low density of international society I do not claim that states are constructed *primarily* by international structures. Much of the construction is at the domestic level, as Liberals have emphasized, and a complete theory of state identity needs to have a large domestic component. But these identities are made possible by and embedded in a systemic context.

My last move follows Buzan, Jones, and Little in arguing that interaction or process is a proper concern of systemic theory, but takes the argument considerably further.[65] Buzan, Jones, and Little's innovation is important for showing that more outcomes are possible in anarchic systems than are suggested by Waltz's model. But like him they assume that anarchies have a certain "logic" independent of process (hence their title, *The Logic of Anarchy*), and that interaction is not itself "structured." Against this I shall argue that anarchy has no logic apart from process and that interaction *is* structured, albeit not at the macro-level. Neorealists may worry that this move undermines the autonomy of systemic theory. I disagree. The distinctiveness of the systemic project lies not in its ostensible independence from unit-level properties, but in its concern with the effects of how *inter*-national relations are structured, which cannot be explained by theories that treat states as autistic. Recognizing this allows us to broaden systemic theorizing to include structures of interaction, and opens up the possibility of explaining changes in the logic of anarchy by processes within the international system.

My concern with interaction also has a practico-ethical motivation. The daily life of international politics is an on-going process of states taking identities in relation to Others, casting them into corresponding counter-identities, and playing out the result. These identities may be hard to change, but they are not carved in stone, and indeed sometimes are the only variable actors can manipulate in a situation. Managing this process is the basic practical problem of foreign policy, and its ethical dimension is the question of how we *should* treat the

---

[65] Buzan, Jones, and Little (1993).

Other. I shall not say very much about these practical and ethical issues in this book, but they motivate my project insofar as managing relationships and determining how we ought to act depend in part on answers to the explanatory question of how certain representations of Self and Other get created. This cannot be answered by unit-level theorizing alone.

These three moves are an attempt to rethink the dominant ontology of international structure. IR scholars often unnecessarily disparage ontology talk. In our daily lives we all have ontologies, since we all make assumptions about what exists in the world: dogs, cats, and trees. Normally we do not think of these assumptions as an ontology, much less as problematic, because most of their referents present themselves directly to our senses. If we can stub our toe against it, it must be real. Ontology gets more controversial when it invokes unobservables. Physicists legitimately disagree about whether quarks exist. Compared to physicists, however, who can test their ontological intuitions in sophisticated experiments, IR scholars have virtually no direct empirical access to the deep structure of the reality they study. Waltz's theory is based on a particular ontology of international politics. This ontology may be wrong, but it cannot be overturned by a few anomalies, overlooked events, or strained interpretations, since it is difficult to separate what we "see" in international life from our conceptual lenses. By the same token, however, it is useful for IR scholarship to contemplate more than one ontology. Constructivism is one such alternative, and my aim is to articulate it and explore its substantive implications.

A map of structural theorizing[66]

The previous section showed that saying that one's theory is "structural," as Neorealists do, tells us little until we have specified what kind of structuralism we are talking about. Systemic theories of international politics conceptualize structure in different ways. In this section I interpret different forms of structural IR theory in light of two debates in social theory. One is about the extent to which structures are material or social, the other about the relationship of

---

[66] I want to thank Ron Jepperson for his contribution to my thinking in this section. Earlier versions of this map appeared in Wendt and Friedheim (1995) and Jepperson, Wendt, and Katzenstein (1996).

structure to agents. Each debate contains two basic positions, which yields four sociologies of structure (materialist, idealist, individualist, and holist) and a 2×2 "map" of combinations (materialist–individualist, materialist–holist, and so on). This map is applicable to any domain of social inquiry, from the family to the world system. It is important for me because it sets up the choices we have in thinking about the ontology of international structure. I sort out and identify types of structural theorizing and show the implications of these choices for the types of questions we ask and answers we can find.

Four sociologies

I'll begin by explaining each pair of sociologies of structure, making a continuum for each. The first pair is material–ideational. The debate over the relative importance of material forces and ideas in social life is an old one in IR scholarship. For purposes of creating a single continuum, let us define its central question as: "what difference do ideas make in social life?" or, alternatively, "to what extent are structures made of ideas?" It is possible to hold positions anywhere along this continuum, but in practice social theorists cluster into two views, *materialist* and *idealist*. Both acknowledge a role for ideas, but they disagree about how deep these effects go.

Materialists believe the most fundamental fact about society is the nature and organization of material forces. At least five material factors recur in materialist discourse: (1) human nature; (2) natural resources; (3) geography; (4) forces of production; and (5) forces of destruction. These can matter in various ways: by permitting the manipulation of the world, by empowering some actors over others, by disposing people toward aggression, by creating threats, and so on. These possibilities do not preclude ideas also having some effects (perhaps as an intervening variable), but the materialist claim is that effects of non-material forces are secondary. This is a strong claim, and in assessing it it is crucial that the hypothesized effects of material forces be strictly separated from the effects of ideas. Unfortunately this often is not done. In contemporary political science, for example, it has become commonplace to juxtapose "power and interest" to "ideas" as causes of outcomes, and to call the former "material" forces. I agree that power and interest are a distinct and important set of social causes, but this only supports materialism if their effects are not constituted by ideas. The materialist hypothesis must be that material forces *as such* – what might be called "brute" material forces – drive social forms. I argue in chapter 3 that understood in this way material forces explain relatively little of international politics.

Idealists believe the most fundamental fact about society is the nature and structure of social consciousness (what I later call the distribution of ideas or knowledge). Sometimes this structure is shared among actors in the form of norms, rules, or institutions; sometimes it is not. Either way, social structure can matter in various ways: by constituting identities and interests, by helping actors find common solutions to problems, by defining expectations for behavior, by constituting threats, and so on. These possibilities need not deny a role for material forces, but the idealist claim is that material forces are secondary, significant insofar as they are constituted with particular meanings for actors. The material polarity of the international system matters, for example, but *how* it matters depends on whether the poles are friends or enemies, which is a function of shared ideas. In contrast to the materialist tendency to treat ideas in strictly causal terms, therefore, idealists tend to emphasize what I call the constitutive effects of ideas.

Given that the term "idealism" also refers to a theory of international politics, it should be noted that idealism in social theory does not entail Idealism in IR. Indeed, there are so many potential misunderstandings of idealist social theory that it might be useful to summarize briefly what it is NOT. (1) It is not a normative view of how the world ought to be, but a scientific view of how it is. Idealism aims to be just as realistic as materialism. (2) It does not assume that human nature is inherently good or social life inherently cooperative. There are bleak idealist theories as well as optimistic ones. Materialists do not have a monopoly on pessimism or conflict. (3) It does not assume that shared ideas have no objective reality. Shared beliefs and the practices to which they give rise confront individual actors as external social facts, even though they are not external to actors collectively. Social structures are no less real than material ones. (4) It does not assume that social change is easy or even possible in a given, socially constructed context. Actors must still overcome institutionalization, power asymmetries, and collective action problems to generate social change, and, indeed, sometimes this is *more* difficult in social structures than material ones. (5) Finally, it does not mean that power and interest are unimportant, but rather that their meaning and effects depend on actors' ideas. US military power means one thing to Canada, another to a communist Cuba. Idealist social theory embodies a very minimal claim: that the deep structure of society is constituted by ideas rather than material forces. Although most mainstream IR scholarship is materialist, most modern social theory is idealist in this sense.

Materialists and idealists tend to understand the impact of ideas differently. Materialists privilege causal relationships, effects, and questions; idealists privilege constitutive relationships, effects, and questions. Since I address this distinction at some length in chapter 2, let me just preview here. In a causal relationship an antecedent condition X generates an effect Y. This assumes that X is temporally prior to and thus exists independently of Y. In a constitutive relationship X is what it is in virtue of its relation to Y. X presupposes Y, and as such there is no temporal disjunction; their relationship is necessary rather than contingent. Causal and constitutive effects are different but not mutually exclusive. Water is caused by joining independently existing hydrogen and oxygen atoms; it is constituted by the molecular structure known as H_2O. H_2O does not "cause" water because without it something cannot *be* water, but this does not mean that that structure has no effects. Similarly, masters and slaves are caused by the contingent interactions of human beings; they are constituted by the social structure known as slavery. Masters do not "cause" slaves because without slaves they cannot *be* masters in the first place, but this does not mean the institution of slavery has no effects. The distinction is an old one, but poorly appreciated today. I think the blurring of causal and constitutive relationships has helped generate much of the current confusion in IR scholarship about the relationship between ideas and material forces. Resurrecting the distinction will probably not end these debates, but may help clarify what is at stake.

These broad-gauge definitions of materialism and idealism constitute the hard cores of alternative research programs, ontologies, or "sociologies," and as such are not specific to IR. To some extent each can accommodate the insights of the other, but only on its own terms. Some materialists concede that shared beliefs can affect behavior, and some idealists concede that material forces can affect social possibilities, which move both toward the center. A truly synthetic position is hard to sustain, however, because materialists will always object to arguments in which the ideational superstructure bears no determinate relation to the material base, and idealists will always object to arguments in which it does. This reflects the competing directives of the two sociologies: "start with material factors and account as much as possible for the role of ideas in those terms," and vice-versa. This tends to create a bimodal distribution of substantive theories along the continuum, with no true middle ground.[67]

The second debate concerns the relationship between agents and structures. The "agent–structure problem" has become a cottage industry in sociology, and increasingly in IR.[68] For purposes of defining a continuum let me frame its central question as: "what difference does structure make in social life?" *Individualism* and *holism* (or "structuralism" in the Continental sense)[69] are the two main answers. Both acknowledge an explanatory role for structure, but they disagree about its ontological status and about how deep its effects go. Individualism holds that social scientific explanations should be reducible to the properties or interactions of independently existing individuals. Holism holds that the effects of social structures cannot be reduced to independently existing agents and their interactions, and that these effects include the construction of agents in both causal and constitutive senses. People cannot be professors apart from students, nor can they become professors apart from the structures through which they are socialized. Holism implies a top–down conception of social life in contrast to individualism's bottom–up view. Whereas the latter aggregates upward from ontologically primitive agents, the former works downward from irreducible social structures.

The disagreement between individualists and holists turns in important part on the extent to which structures "construct" agents. In order to understand this idea we need two distinctions: the one made above between causal and constitutive effects, and a second one between the effects of structures on agents' *properties*, especially their identities and interests, and effects on agents' *behavior*.[70] To say that a structure "constrains" actors is to say that it only has behavioral effects. To say that a structure "constructs" actors is to say that it has

---

[67] Cf. Adler (1997b).

[68] On the latter see Wendt (1987), Dessler (1989), Hollis and Smith (1990), Carlsnaes (1992), Buzan, Jones, and Little (1993), Doty (1996) and Clark (1998).

[69] Given that all sides claim the concept of structure as their own it seems better to use "holism" here and then let the protagonists argue about the nature of structure.

[70] Robert Powell's (1994) distinction between "preference over outcomes" and over "strategies" makes the same point.

property effects. In systemic IR, theories that emphasize such effects have become known as "second image reversed" theories.[71] Property effects are deeper because they usually have behavioral effects but not vice-versa. Both property and behavioral effects, in turn, can be either caused or constituted by structures. Since constitutive effects imply a greater dependence of agents on structures, I shall treat them as deeper as well.

Individualism tends to be associated with causal effects on behavior, but I shall argue that the individualist view is compatible in principle with more possibilities than its critics (or even proponents) typically acknowledge, most notably with structures having causal effects on agents' properties, for example through a socialization process. I say "in principle," however, because in *practice* it is holists and not individualists who have been most active in theorizing about the causal construction of agents. Most individualists treat identities and interests as exogenously given and address only behavioral effects.[72] This is particularly true of the form of individualism that dominates mainstream IR scholarship, namely rationalism (rational choice and game theory), which studies the logic of choice under constraints. In a particularly clear statement of this view, George Stigler and Gary Becker argue that we should explain outcomes by reference to changing "prices" in the environment, not by changing "tastes" (identities and interests).[73]

Rationalist theory's restricted focus has been the object of much of the holist critique of individualism. Still, individualism in principle is compatible with a theory of how structures cause agents' properties. What it rules out is the possibility that social structures have constitutive effects on agents, since this would mean that structures cannot be reduced to the properties or interactions of ontologically primitive individuals. The constitutive possibility is the distinctively holist hypothesis.

As I indicated at the beginning of this chapter, the international system is a hard case for a holist argument, since its low density means that the identities and interests of states may be more dependent on

---

71 Gourevitch (1978).

72 This may stem from the fact that while the "denotation" of individualism is compatible with the structural determination of interests, its "connotation" is that given individuals must be the starting point for theory. On the connotative and denotative aspects of theories see Krasner (1991).

73 Stigler and Becker (1977); Becker's (1996) later work relaxes this assumption.

domestic than systemic structures. The challenge for holists in IR becomes even more acute if we grant that individualism is compatible at least in principle with the *causal* construction of states by systemic structures. Perhaps under the influence of rationalism, however, in practice individualists in IR have neglected that possibility, and they do not acknowledge even in principle any *constitutive* effects that systemic structures might have on states. I believe the structure of the international system exerts both kinds of effects on state identities. These may be less than the effects of domestic structures, and certainly a complete theory of state identity would have a substantial domestic component. But explaining state identity is not my primary objective in this book – it is to clarify the nature and effects of international structure, which is a different question.

This discussion, and the behavior-property distinction, may shed some light on the confusion in IR about the character of Waltz's theory, which is seen as structuralist by some,[74] and individualist by others.[75] What is going on here, I think, is that different scholars are focusing on different senses in which his theory is structural. On the one hand, Waltz argues that the international system selects and socializes states to become "like units."[76] This is a construction argument – not merely state behavior but also state properties are seen as effects of international structure. On the other hand, the effects of structure to which Waltz is pointing are all causal rather than constitutive, which supports an individualist interpretation of his approach. And while arguing that the structure of the system tends to produce like units, in most of his book Waltz treats state identities and interests in rationalist fashion as given, which supports that reading even more strongly. In the end, therefore, Waltz's structuralism is mixed, though tending toward the individualist view that there is relatively little construction of states going on in the international system.

As with materialism and idealism, individualism and holism constitute the ontological hard cores of research programs in which certain propositions are treated as axiomatic and inquiry is directed at reconciling reality with them. This creates the same kind of limited flexibility with bimodal tendencies that we saw before. Some individualists are interested in identity and interest ("preference") for-

---

[74] R. Walker (1987), Hollis and Smith (1990), Buzan, Jones, and Little (1993).
[75] Ashley (1984), Wendt (1987), Dessler (1989).   [76] Waltz (1979: 95, 128).

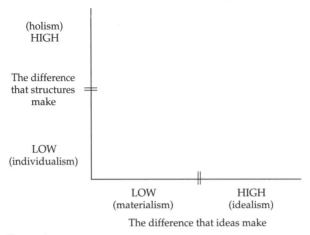

Figure 1

mation, and some holists concede that agents have intrinsic attributes. Yet, even as they struggle toward the center of the continuum, both sides cling to foundational claims that constrain their efforts. Individualist theories of preference formation typically focus on agents rather than structures, and holistic theories of intrinsic attributes typically minimize these as much as they can. Here too, in other words, we get a clustering of substantive theories around two basic poles.

If we put the materialism–idealism debate on the x-axis, and individualism-holism on the y-, then we get the picture as shown in Figure 1. If one purpose of this book is to clarify the concept of "social construction," then the x-axis is about the first term in this phrase, the y- about the second.

Locating international theories

Figure 1 provides a framework for thinking about the second-order differences among IR theories that are considered "structural." Each sociology constitutes the ontological core of a research program that exerts a centripetal force on substantive theorizing along the portion of the spectrum which it occupies, which undermines the continuous nature of each dimension in favor of a dichotomous one. What I mean is, research programs have specific ontological centers of gravity, so that even as they reach outward to incorporate the concerns of others – as materialists incorporate ideas, as holists incorporate agency – the resulting theories or arguments remain somewhat truncated.

In this section I suggest where different theories of international politics might fall on the map, including my own. My purpose is only illustrative; I will not make much further use of this classification. It should also be emphasized that the map, while applicable to any level of analysis, is applicable to only one level at a time. This will affect how we classify theories. If the designated level is the international system, then a theory which assumes states are constructed entirely by domestic structures will be classified as individualist. If we move to the domestic level of analysis, that same theory might be holist relative to a theory of the state which emphasizes individual people. The latter may itself be holist relative to one which emphasizes brain chemistry. And so on. What follows, therefore, is a map of *systemic* IR theory.

Theories in the lower-left quadrant have a materialist and individualist attitude toward social life. (1) *Classical Realism* holds that human nature is a crucial determinant of the national interest, which is an individualist argument because it implies state interests are not constructed by the international system.[77] Classical Realists vary in the extent to which they are materialists, with some like E.H. Carr granting a significant role to "power over opinion,"[78] but their focus on human nature and material capabilities place them generally in this category. (2) *Neorealism* is more clearly materialist than Classical Realism, and attaches more explanatory weight to the structure of the international system. But insofar as it relies on micro-economic analogies it assumes this structure only regulates behavior, not constructs identities. (3) *Neoliberalism* shares with Neorealism an individualist approach to structure, and most Neoliberals have not challenged Waltz's view that power and interest are the material base of the system. But unlike Neorealists they see a relatively autonomous role for institutional superstructure.

Theories in the upper-left quadrant hypothesize that the properties of state agents are constructed in large part by material structures at the international level. At least three schools of thought can be found here. (1) *Neorealism* bleeds into this corner to the extent that it emphasizes the production of like units, although in practice most Neorealists take state identities as given, and the absence of constitu-

---

[77] See especially Morgenthau (1946, 1948/1973).   [78] Carr (1939).

tive effects from its conceptualization of structure in my view makes it ultimately compatible with individualism. (2) *World-Systems Theory* is more clearly holist,[79] although its materialism must be qualified to the extent that it emphasizes the relations rather than forces of production (see chapter 3). (3) *Neo-Gramscian Marxism* is more concerned than other Marxisms with the role of ideology, pushing it toward the eastern hemisphere, but it remains rooted in the material base.[80]

Theories in the lower-right quadrant hold that state identities and interests are constructed largely by domestic politics (so individualism at the systemic level), but have a more social view of what the structure of the international system is made of. (1) *Liberalism* emphasizes the role of domestic factors in shaping state interests, the realization of which is then constrained at the systemic level by institutions.[81] (2) And *Neoliberalism* moves into this corner insofar as it emphasizes the role of expectations rather than power and interest. But to my knowledge no Neoliberal has explicitly advocated an idealist view of structure, and I shall argue in chapter 3 that at the end of the day it is based on a Neorealist ontology.

The Neorealist–Neoliberal debate that has dominated mainstream IR theory in recent years has been basically a debate between the bottom-left and bottom-right quadrants: agreeing on an individualist approach to system structure, the two sides have focused instead on the relative importance of power and interest vs. ideas and institutions.

The principal challenge to this debate has come from scholars in the upper-right quadrant, who believe that international structure consists fundamentally in shared knowledge, and that this affects not only state behavior, but state identities and interests as well. I shall call any theory in this quadrant "constructivist." In addition to the work of John Ruggie and Friedrich Kratochwil, which has not become associated with a particular label, at least four schools might fit here. (1) The *English School* does not explicitly address state identity formation, but it does treat the international system as a society governed by shared norms, and Timothy Dunne has argued convincingly that it is a forerunner of contemporary constructivist IR theory.[82] (2) The *World Society* school focuses on the role of global culture in constructing

---

[79] See Wallerstein (1974), Bach (1982), and Wendt (1987).
[80] Cox (1987), Gill, ed. (1993).   [81] Doyle (1983), Russett (1993), Moravcsik (1997).
[82] Bull (1977), Dunne (1995); also see Wendt and Duvall (1989).

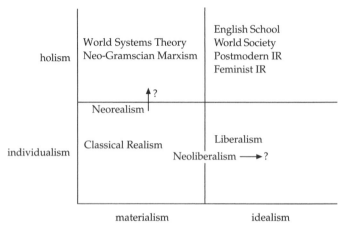

Figure 2

states.[83] (3) *Postmodernists* were the first to introduce contemporary constructivist social theory to IR, and continue to be the most thorough-going critics of materialism and rationalism. (4) And, finally, *Feminist* theory has recently made important inroads into IR, arguing that state identities are constructed by gendered structures at both the national and global levels. Summing up, then, we get something like Figure 2.

The argument of this book falls in the upper-right quadrant, and within that domain it is particularly indebted to the work of Ashley, Bull, and Ruggie. IR today being a discipline where theoretical allegiances are important, this raises a question about what the argument should be called. I do not know other than a "constructivist approach to the international system." In general opposed to method-driven social science,[84] I have in effect written a book arguing that a new method can advance our thinking about international politics. This is justified insofar as social theory methods shape the theories with which we in turn observe the world, but it means that the argument is rooted more in social theory than in IR. Despite the author's training as a political scientist, in other words, the book is written from a philosopher's point of view. As a result, its substantive argument cuts across the traditional cleavages in IR between Realists,

---

[83] Meyer (1980), Thomas, *et al.* (1987), Meyer, *et al.* (1997); for a good overview see Finnemore (1996b).

[84] See Shapiro and Wendt (1992), Wendt and Shapiro (1997).

Liberals, and Marxists, supporting and challenging parts of each as the case may be. Readers will find much below that is associated usually with Realism:[85] state-centrism, the concern with national interests and the consequences of anarchy, the commitment to science. There is also much associated with Liberalism: the possibility of progress, the importance of ideas, institutions, and domestic politics. There is a Marxian sensibility in the discussion of the state. If I knew more about Hegel and the Idealism of the inter-war period perhaps that would be an appropriate affiliation, but ever since Carr's devastating critique "Idealist" has functioned in IR primarily as an epithet for naivete and utopianism, connotations which naturally I want to avoid.[86] In any event, however, these connections should be seen not as evidence of some desire for grand synthesis, but simply of a starting point outside the traditional categories of IR theory. "A constructivist approach to the international system" is the best description of the theory presented in this book.

Three interpretations

Now that I have positioned IR theories within my map of social theory assumptions, the question is: what is at stake with their second-order commitments? We can approach the answer from three perspectives, methodology, ontology, or empirics. Since these affect how we subsequently think about the differences among systemic IR theories, each bears at least brief scrutiny. For purposes of illustration I will focus on the debate along the y-axis between those who take identities and interests as given (rationalists) and those who do not (constructivists). A similar illustration could be developed along the x-axis.

A methodological difference

On one level the difference between rationalism and constructivism is merely that they ask different questions, and different questions need not involve substantive conflict. All theories have to take something

---

[85] Apart from Waltz, among Realists I see particular affinities to the work of Arnold Wolfers (1962).

[86] Carr (1939). For an overview of Hegel's views on international relations see Vincent (1983); cf. Fukuyama (1989). On inter-war Idealism, see Long and Wilson, eds. (1995). With the end of the Cold War Kegley (1993) has suggested that we are now in a "neoidealist moment."

as given, and in so doing "bracket" issues that may be problematized by others.[87] Rationalists are interested in how incentives in the environment affect the price of behavior. To answer this question they treat identities and interests as if they were given, but this is perfectly consistent with the constructivist question of where those identities and interests come from – and vice-versa. If the issue is no more than methodological, in other words, identities and interests can be seen as endogenous or exogenous to structure *with respect to theory only*, not reality. Neither approach is intrinsically "better" than the other, any more than it is "better" to inquire into the causes of malaria than smallpox; they are simply different. It is important to keep this in mind in view of the polemics that surround rational choice theory. On one level the theory is nothing more than a method for answering certain questions, and as such it makes no more sense to reject it than it did for early Marxist economists to reject mathematics because it was used by "bourgeois" economists.

While questions and methods do not determine substantive theory, however, they are not always substantively innocent. There are at least two ways in which our questions and methods can affect the content of first-order theorizing, particularly if one set of questions comes to dominate a field.

First, whether we take identities and interests as given can affect the debate along the *x*-axis about the importance of ideas and material forces. Neorealists, for example, argue that state interests stem from the material structure of anarchy. If we start with this assumption, then ideas are reduced a priori to an intervening variable between material forces and outcomes. Ideas may still play a role in social life, for example by determining choices among multiple equilibria, but to take the Neorealist analysis of identity and interest as given is nevertheless implicitly to concede that the fundamental structure of international politics is material rather than social. This is what Neoliberal regime theory did in the 1980s when it defined the theoretical problem as showing that international institutions (which are shared ideas) explained additional variance beyond that explained by material power and interest alone – as if institutions did not also constitute power and interest. The pattern is repeating itself in recent Neoliberal scholarship on ideas, in which the null hypothesis is that "actions . . . can be understood on the basis of egoistic interests, in the

---

[87] Giddens (1979: 80–81).

context of power realities"[88] – as if ideas did not also constitute power and interest. That is, Neoliberalism concedes too much to Neorealism a priori, reducing itself to the secondary status of cleaning up residual variance left unexplained by a primary theory. A theory to challenge Neorealism must show how intersubjective conditions constitute material power and interests in the first place, not treat the latter as an idea-less starting point.

A second danger, as noted by Ruggie, is that a methodology can turn into a tacit ontology.[89] Rationalist methodology is not designed to explain identities and interests. It does not rule out explanations, but neither does it offer one itself. However, Neoliberals increasingly acknowledge that we need a theory of state interests. Where should we look for one? One place would be the international system; another, domestic politics. Neoliberals overwhelmingly favor the latter. This may be because state interests *really are* determined by domestic politics, but it may also be because Neoliberals have so internalized a rationalist view of the international system that they automatically assume that the causes of state interests must be exogenous to the system. By conditioning how rationalists think about the world, in other words, exogeneity in *theory* is tacitly transformed into an assumption of exogeneity in *reality*. The latter ultimately may be the right conclusion empirically, but that conclusion should be reached only after comparing the explanatory power of domestic and systemic theories of state identity formation. It should not be presumed as part of a method-driven social science.[90]

In sum, legitimate methodological differences may generate different substantive conclusions. The dependence of theory on method is an occupational hazard in all scientific inquiry, but it becomes especially problematic if one method comes to dominate a field. To some extent this has happened with rationalism in mainstream systemic IR theory. In such a context certain questions never get asked, certain possibilities never considered.

An ontological difference

Perhaps the most common interpretation of the dispute between rationalists and constructivists is that it is about ontology, about what kind of "stuff" the international system is made of. Two early

---

[88] Goldstein and Keohane (1993: 37).   [89] Ruggie (1983a: 285).
[90] On the latter see Shapiro and Wendt (1992).

expressions of this view in IR came from Ashley and from Kratochwil and Ruggie.[91] Ashley was one of the first to problematize Waltz's micro-economic analogy, which he argued was based on an individualist ontology, while Kratochwil and Ruggie argued that there was a contradiction in regime theory between the intersubjectivist epistemology implied by the concept of regime and the individualist ontology of regime theory's rationalist basis. The subsequent discussion of the agent–structure problem in IR followed these leads and also focused on ontology, notably on whether systemic structures are reducible to preexisting agents or have a relatively autonomous life of their own. I explore the latter question in some detail in chapters 4 and 6 below.

A related ontological issue, which is the frame for chapter 7, concerns how we should think about "what's going on" when actors interact, and in particular about what it means to take identities and interests as "given." Taking *something* as given is necessary in any explanatory endeavor by virtue of the simple fact that it is humanly impossible to problematize everything at once. Even postmodernists who want to problematize agents "all the way down" will end up taking certain things as given. This inescapable fact points back toward the methodological difference noted above. However, in taking identities and interests as methodologically given there is also an implicit ontological question of whether they are seen themselves as processes that need to be socially sustained (but which we just happen not to be interested in today), or as fixed objects that are in some sense outside of social space and time. In the latter view, the production and reproduction of identities and interests is not going on, not at stake, in social interaction. If that is true then how states treat each other in interaction does not matter for how they define who they are: by acting selfishly nothing more is going on than the attempt to realize selfish ends. In the constructivist view, in contrast, actions continually produce and reproduce conceptions of Self and Other, and as such identities and interests are always in process, even if those processes are sometimes stable enough that – for certain purposes – we plausibly can take them as given.

The difference matters for the perceived nature of international politics and for the possibilities of structural change. In chapter 7 I ask how egoistic states might transform the culture of the international

---

[91] Ashley (1983, 1984), Kratochwil and Ruggie (1986).

system from a balance of power to a collective security system. One possibility is that they learn to cooperate while their egoistic identities remain constant. It is hard to be optimistic about this given the collective action problems that confront egoists, but it could happen. On the other hand, if certain foreign policy practices undermine egoistic identities and generate collective ones, then structural change might be easier. It all depends on what is going on when states interact. This is a matter of ontology because differences of opinion cannot easily be settled by appeals to "the facts," since any facts we collect will be shot through with ontological assumptions about what we are looking at that are not easily falsified.

This book is based on the conviction that despite their seeming intractability, ontological issues are crucial to how we do and should think about international life, and that IR scholarship today is insufficiently self-conscious about them. Having said this, however, I also want to inject this concern with ontology with an empirical sensibility. One might conclude from the ontological interpretation of their debate that rationalists and constructivists face a situation of radical incommensurability, such that we should simply pay our money and take our choice. This is unwarranted. Different ontologies often have different implications for what we should observe in the world.[92] Empirical evidence telling against these ontologies might not be decisive, since defenders can argue that the problem lies with the particular theory being tested rather than the underlying ontology, but it may still be instructive. The possibility that different ontologies are incommensurable should not be treated as an excuse to avoid comparison.[93] Ontology-talk is necessary, but we should also look for ways to translate it into propositions that might be adjudicated empirically.

An empirical difference

There are at least two empirical issues at stake in the debate between rationalists and constructivists. First, to what extent are state identities and interests constructed by domestic vs. systemic structures? To the extent that the answer is domestic, state interests will in fact be exogenous to the international system (not just "as if" exogenous), and systemic IR theorists would therefore be justified in being rationalists about the international system. This is basically the

---

[92] Kincaid (1993).   [93] Wight (1996).

Neoliberal approach. To the extent that the answer is systemic, however, interests will be endogenous to the international system. Rationalist theories are not well equipped to analyze endogenous preference formation, and thus a constructivist approach would be called for. Second, to what extent are state identities and interests constant? Rationalism typically assumes constancy, and if this is empirically warranted we would have an independent reason for being rationalists about the international system regardless of how the first question was answered. Even if states identities and interests are constructed within the international system, if the results of that process are highly stable then we lose little by treating them as given.

Answering these questions would require an extensive program of theory building and empirical research, which is not the goal of this book. My point is that these questions are useful for IR because they are amenable to substantive inquiry in a way that ontological debates are not. Of course, I still maintain that IR scholars cannot escape ontological issues entirely, since what we observe in world politics is closely bound up with the concepts through which we observe it. In sum, then, my attitude toward these debates, to quote Hacking paraphrasing Popper, is that "it is not all that bad to be pre-scientifically metaphysical, for unfalsifiable metaphysics is often the speculative parent of falsifiable science."[94]

Epistemology and the via media

Figure 2 is meant to capture second-order differences among systemic IR theories about the nature and effects of international structure. The rest of this book is an attempt to clarify these differences and advocate one particular ontology of international life.

However, if asked on a survey to name the most divisive issue in IR today, a majority of scholars would probably say *epistemology*, not ontology. The importance of the epistemological issue in IR as a discipline is reflected in the fact that it is considered one of our Great Debates. In this "Third Debate"[95] the field has polarized into two main camps: (1) a majority who think science is an epistemically privileged discourse through which we can gain a progressively truer understanding of the world, and (2) a large minority who do not recognize a privileged epistemic status for science in explaining the

[94] Hacking (1983: 3).   [95] Lapid (1989).

world out there. The former have become known as "positivists" and the latter as "post-positivists," although this terminology is not particularly clarifying, since strictly speaking "positivism" is an early twentieth-century philosophy of science that probably few contemporary "positivists" would endorse. Given that an important part of what divides the two camps is whether they think the methods of natural science are appropriate in social inquiry, it might be better to call them "naturalists" and "anti-naturalists," or advocates of "Explanation" and "Understanding" respectively.[96] In any case, the two sides are barely on speaking terms today, and seem to see little point in changing this situation.

There are many – going back to Kratochwil and Ruggie's influential analysis of the supposed contradictions between Neoliberal regime theory's ontology and epistemology[97] – who might argue that the ontological debates of concern to me can be subsumed by this epistemological divide. The rationale begins with positivism's assumption of a distinction between subject and object. Such a distinction is relatively easy to sustain if the objects of inquiry are material, like rocks and trees, and perhaps even tanks and aircraft carriers, since these do not depend on ideas for their existence. Tanks have certain causal powers whether or not anyone knows it, just as a tree falling in the forest makes a sound whether or not anyone hears it. This seems to line up a materialist ontology with a positivist epistemology, and indeed most materialists in IR are positivists. Conversely, it is harder to sustain the subject–object distinction if society is ideas all the way down, since that means that human subjects in some sense create the objects their theories purport to explain. This seems to line up idealist ontologies with a post-positivist epistemology, and indeed many idealists in IR are post-positivists. From this standpoint the ontological choices in Figure 2 come down to an epistemological choice between two views of social inquiry.

Given my idealist ontological commitments, therefore, one might think that I should be firmly on the post-positivist side of this divide, talking about discourse and interpretation rather than hypothesis testing and objective reality. Yet, in fact, when it comes to the epistemology of social inquiry I am a strong believer in science – a pluralistic science to be sure, in which there is a significant role for "Understanding," but science just the same. I am a "positivist." In

---

[96] Hollis and Smith (1990).   [97] Kratochwil and Ruggie (1986).

some sense this puts me in the middle of the Third Debate, not because I want to find an eclectic epistemology, which I do not, but because I do not think an idealist ontology implies a post-positivist epistemology. Contrary to Kratochwil and Ruggie, I see no contradiction in Neoliberal regime theory. Rather than reduce ontological differences to epistemological ones, in my view the latter should be seen as a third, independent axis of debate.

In effect, therefore, I hope to find a "via media"[98] through the Third Debate by reconciling what many take to be incompatible ontological and epistemological positions. This effort, which I make in chapter 2, injects significant tensions into the argument of this book. Some will say that no via media exists. They may be right, but I nevertheless press two arguments: (1) that what really matters is what there is rather than how we know it, and (2) that science should be question-rather than method-driven, and the importance of constitutive questions creates an essential role in social science for interpretive methods. Put more bluntly, I think that post-positivists put too much emphasis on epistemology, and that positivists should be more open-minded about questions and methodology. No one can force positivists and post-positivists to talk to each other, but in trying to construct a via media I hope to show that at least there is something to talk about.

Plan of the book

The book is written so that it may be read "à la carte." Each chapter is a relatively freestanding discussion of a particular theoretical issue, and although they follow a clear progression, by building in some redundancy I hope to have made it possible to see the larger picture without reading everything at once. To this end the book is organized into two parts, "Social theory" and "International politics."

Part I lays out the version of constructivism that I think is most plausible. I focus on epistemology and ontology, but examples from international politics and IR theory ground the discussion.

Chapter 2, "Scientific realism and social kinds," develops the epistemological basis for the argument. This chapter asks: how can we be both positivist and constructivist? Using a realist philosophy of science (no relation to Political Realism) I make three main arguments.

---

[98] This description was suggested to me by Steve Smith.

On one flank, I attempt to block post-positivist critiques by defending the view that constructivist social theory is compatible with a scientific approach to social inquiry. Constructivism should be construed narrowly as an ontology, not broadly as an epistemology. On another flank, I use scientific realism to block empiricist claims that we should not make ontological claims about unobservables. On the surface this does not change how we practice science, but it has implications for how we think about the objects of social science, "social kinds." Scientific realism legitimates a critical social science committed to discovering the deep structure of international life. Finally, the chapter develops the distinction between causal and constitutive questions and effects, which is crucial to understanding the difference that ideas and social structures make in international politics.

Chapters 3 and 4 shift the focus to ontology. Chapter 3, " 'Ideas all the way down?': on the constitution of power and interest," examines the idealist–materialist debate along the x-axis of figure 1. I show that two ostensibly materialist explanations associated particularly with Realism – explanations by reference to power and interest – actually achieve most of their explanatory power through tacit assumptions about the distribution of ideas in the system. My argument here posits a distinction between two kinds of stuff in the world, brute material forces and ideas, which means that the answer to the question posed by the chapter's title is actually negative – it is *not* ideas *all* the way down. Brute material forces like biological needs, the physical environment, and technological artifacts do have intrinsic causal powers. However, once we have properly separated material forces and ideas we can see that the former explain relatively little in social life. Using Waltz's theory of structure as a foil I first show that the meaning and thus explanatory power of the distribution of capabilities is constituted by the distribution of interests in the system. Then, shifting my focus to rational choice theory, I argue that those interests, in turn, are ideas. The argument that interests are themselves ideas (of a particular kind) raises the question of whether rational choice theory is ultimately a materialist or idealist theory. It is usually seen as materialist, but I argue that the theory is actually better seen as a form of idealism. Understood in this way it is fully compatible with – if subsumed by – a constructivist perspective. Power and interest are important factors in international life, but since their effects are a function of culturally constituted ideas the latter should be our starting point.

Chapter 4, "Structure, agency, and culture," addresses the onto-logical debate between individualists and holists along the *y*-axis of figure 1, with particular reference to how a constructivist approach to analyzing the structure of culture differs from an individualist, game-theoretic one. Again using Waltz as a launching point, this time focusing on his definition of structure, I distinguish between two effects of structure, causal and constitutive, and between two levels of structure, micro and macro. Individualist theories are useful for understanding causal effects at the micro-level, and, construed flex-ibly, can be stretched to cover macro-level causal effects as well. As in chapter 3, therefore, I argue that mainstream approaches have con-siderable validity as far as they go; they just do not go far enough. My argument is that an individualist ontology is not equipped to deal with the *constitutive* effects of cultural structure. As such rational choice theory is incomplete as an account of social life. Holist theories capture these constitutive effects, and since these effects are a con-dition of possibility for rationalist arguments, the latter should be seen as depending on the former. This synthetic position is made possible by the essentialist proposition that individuals are self-organizing creatures. This step concedes a crucial point to individualism, but I argue that most of the attributes we normally associate with indi-viduals have to do with the social *terms* of their individuality rather than their individuality per se, and these are culturally constituted. Up to this point the argument focuses on agents and structures separately; a concluding section focuses on system process. Here I argue that culture is a self-fulfilling prophecy, i.e., actors act on the basis of shared expectations, and this tends to reproduce those expectations. Still, it is in these processes of reproduction that we also find transformative potential. Under certain conditions the processes underlying cultural reproduction can generate structural change. This argument is the basis for the claim that "anarchy is what states make of it."

In part II I turn to a substantive argument about the nature of the international system which is conditioned but not determined by the social constructivist approach outlined in part I. This is the part of the book that can be considered a case study in social theory. I organize it around the three main elements of the agent–structure problematique, with chapters on state agency, international structure, and systemic process respectively.

Chapter 5, "The state and the problem of corporate agency," has two main objectives. The first is to defend the assumption that states are unitary actors to which we legitimately can attribute anthropomorphic qualities like identities, interests, and intentionality. This assumption, much maligned in recent IR scholarship, is a precondition for using the tools of social theory to analyze the behavior of corporate agents in the international system, since social theory was designed to explain the behavior of individuals, not states. Drawing on both Weberian and Marxian forms of state theory, I argue that states are self-organizing entities whose internal structures confer capacities for institutionalized collective action – corporate agency – on their members. Having established that states are unitary actors, my other objective is to show that many of the qualities that Realists think are essential to these actors, including most importantly their self-interested and power-seeking character, are contingent and socially constructed. States' essential qualities matter because they impose transhistorical limits on world politics that can only be escaped by transcending the state. But offering a more stripped down conceptualization of the essential state and its national interests reveals possibilities for new forms of international politics within a state-centric world that would otherwise be hidden. This argument is developed through a conceptual analysis of four concepts of "identity" – personal/corporate, type, role, and collective – which includes a brief discussion of "self-interest" that attempts to make that concept useful by clearly delimiting its referential scope.

Chapter 6, "Three cultures of anarchy," uses the framework developed in chapter 4 to explicate the deep structure of anarchy as a cultural or ideational rather than material phenomenon, and to show that once understood in this way, we can see that the logic of anarchy can vary. After clearing the ground by arguing that even highly conflictual anarchies can be based on shared ideas, I begin with the proposition that different cultures of anarchy are based on different kinds of roles in terms of which states represent Self and Other. I identify three roles, enemy, rival, and friend, and argue that they are constituted by, and constitute, three distinct, macro-level cultures of international politics, Hobbesian, Lockean, and Kantian respectively. These cultures have different rules of engagement, interaction logics, and systemic tendencies. The contemporary international system is mostly Lockean, with increasing Kantian elements. Most of the chapter is taken up with an analysis of the three cultures. I make the argument that they can be internalized to three different "degrees" in state identities, which correspond to different reasons for why states might comply with systemic norms – coercion, self-interest, and legitimacy. These different reasons for compliance generate different pathways by which a given culture can be realized, and correspond roughly to how Neorealists, Neoliberals, and constructivists explain rule-following. Since the more deeply that cultural norms are internalized the more difficult they are to change, the chapter shows – perhaps counter-intuitively given the association of constructivism with ease of social change – that the more that culture matters in international politics the more stable the international system becomes.

Chapter 7, "Process and structural change," looks at how processes of interaction reproduce and transform systemic structures. I begin by distinguishing two models of what is going on when states interact – a rationalist model which treats identities and interests as exogenously given and constant, and a constructivist model, drawing on symbolic interactionism, which treats them as endogenous and potentially changeable. Developing the latter suggestion, I argue that identities evolve through two basic processes, natural and cultural selection, the latter consisting of mechanisms of imitation and social learning. In the rest of the chapter I apply this framework to the explanation of structural change in international politics, which, building on chapter 6, I define as a change from one culture of anarchy to another (and in particular, for purposes of illustration, from a Lockean to Kantian culture), rather than in the Neorealist fashion as a change in the distribution of material capabilities. Cultural change involves the emergence of new forms of collective identity, and so it is on the determinants of the latter that I focus. I discuss four "master variables" or causes of collective identity formation: interdependence, common fate, homogenization, and self-restraint, each of which can be instantiated or realized concretely in multiple ways. The result is a model of structural change that provides the social theory underpinnings for Liberal arguments about the consequences of a proliferation of liberal democratic states, while leaving open the possibility that other pathways might achieve the same result.

In a brief concluding chapter I summarize the central themes of the book and raise questions about the practice of IR and the potential for reflexivity in international society.

Part I Social theory

2 Scientific realism and social kinds

How is it possible to adopt an idealist and holist ontology while maintaining a commitment to science, or positivism broadly understood? This chapter constructs the "via media" that grounds my modernist constructivism.

The state and states system are real structures whose nature can be approximated through science. Acceptance of this proposition entails "scientific realism" (in this chapter simply "realism"), a philosophy of science which assumes that the world exists independent of human beings, that mature scientific theories typically refer to this world, and that they do so even when the objects of science are unobservable. Theory reflects reality, not the other way around; as realists like to say, they want to "put ontology before epistemology."

Most IR scholarship, mainstream and critical alike, seems to presuppose these assumptions, which means that most IR scholars are at least tacit realists. When they make their philosophical views explicit, however, they often take *anti*-realist positions. An exchange in 1985 among prominent mainstream IR scholars on matters of philosophy of science featured apparent consensus on the empiricist view that in order to be scientific explanations must ultimately be deductive in form, a characteristic form of anti-realism.[1] The dominance of empiricist philosophy of science in IR is being challenged today by another strand of anti-realism, "post-positivism," in what has become known in IR theory as the Third Debate.[2] Throughout this debate references to realist philosophy of science have been remarkably rare, David

---

[1] Bueno de Mesquita, Krasner, and Jervis (1985).
[2] See, for example, Lapid (1989), Neufeld (1995), and Vasquez (1995).

47

Dessler's work being a notable exception.[3] This neglect is surprising, since as one critic put it, "[t]here is little doubt that realism has come to be the predominant ontological position among contemporary philosophers of science."[4]

Why should it matter whether IR scholars call themselves realists? After all, realist and anti-realist physicists disagree about the ontological status of quarks, but this does not affect their research. The reason is that social scientists are less confident than physicists about what their practice should look like, and often have turned to philosophers for methodological guidance. In mainstream IR theory they have turned to empiricists. For example, the rise of quantitative methods during the behavioral revolution of the 1950s reflected the then dominant logical empiricist belief that behavioral laws must be the basis of scientific explanations.[5] Similarly, in the 1960s IR behavioralists criticized the Political Realist concern with the "national interest" because it was unobservable and therefore unscientific.[6] The deductivism of rational choice theorists, in turn, reflects the other, "logical," half of logical empiricism, that "we must not be lulled by apparent empirical success into believing that scientific knowledge can be attained without the abstract, rigorous exercise of logical proof."[7] Moving away from the mainstream, the interest of some contemporary IR scholars in discourse analysis reflects the interpretivist view that social life is not amenable to causal explanation. And so on. In each of these cases anti-realist epistemologies are being invoked to privilege or reject certain methods a priori.

I think that IR scholars have been too worried about epistemology and have not sufficiently let the nature of their problems and questions dictate their methods. This, in turn, has distorted the content of substantive IR theory. But to make the argument that we need to shift from epistemology to ontology, I need first to counter anti-realist anxieties. For this an epistemological argument is required. In this chapter I provide the foundation for the realist claim that states and the states system are real (ontology) and knowable (epistemology), despite being unobservable.

To do so I address two anti-realist criticisms. One critique concerns whether scientific theories refer to, and thus provide knowledge

---

[3] Dessler (1989, 1991).   [4] Rouse (1987: 130).
[5] Gunnell (1975: 147); see Dessler (1991) for a realist critique of how empiricism has shaped the scientific study of war.
[6] Hollis and Smith (1990: 28–32).   [7] Bueno de Mesquita (1985: 129).

about, reality "out there," as claimed by most scientists and scientific realists. This doubt comes in two forms. Its moderate, empiricist, variant focuses on unobservable entities. Whether or not scientific theories actually refer to unobservables, empiricists argue we cannot *know* this because we cannot see them, and we therefore have no warrant for claiming they exist. This is putting epistemology before ontology. This stance affects the study of IR because neither the state nor states system is observable. We might point to a speeding police car and say "there goes the state," but that is not "the" state, which consists of thousands of people, the structure of which cannot be seen. Similarly, we cannot see the structure of the international system, whether conceptualized in material or social terms. According to empiricists, in this situation the most we are warranted in saying is that the concepts of state and states system are useful fictions or instruments for organizing our experience, not that they refer to real structures. The second, more radical critique is the postmodernist view that we cannot even know if seemingly *observable* entities, like cats and dogs, exist out there in the world. While empiricists at least think that observable reality exists independent of discourse and can be known through science, postmodernists argue that even cats and dogs are effects of discourse and as such science offers no privileged insight into how they work. For postmodernists, "constructivism" is an epistemology as well as an ontology because theories quite literally "construct" the world. Despite this difference, empiricists and post-modernists would both reject the realist claim that IR theory can know the deep structure of international reality. Epistemological anxiety makes for strange bedfellows, as we shall see. As a realist I argue against both empiricists and postmoderns that IR theory can get at deep structure.

The other challenge to a realist interpretation of international politics is that, even if science can know nature, it cannot know *society*. Scientific realism assumes that reality exists independent of human beings – that subject and object are distinct – and can be discovered through science. To that extent realist philosophy of science, like empiricism, is "positivist." This poses no special problems for materialists, who think society is not fundamentally different than nature. Positivism is more problematic for constructivists, who think that social kinds are made mostly of ideas.

The problem for constructivists is twofold. First, if social kinds are made of ideas then they do not exist independent of human beings.

Post-positivists think this collapses the distinction between subject and object upon which a realist interpretation of science depends.[8] Unfortunately, the issue is not settled even within the realist camp, with many realists about *natural* science arguing that the dependence of society on ideas makes a realist *social* science impossible.[9] Second, if idealism is true then the most important effect of ideas is constitutive rather than causal. This suggests to some that the methods of natural science, with their emphasis on causal mechanisms, must be replaced in social inquiry with the methods of interpretation and discourse analysis – Understanding rather than Explanation.[10] These two problems pose a particularly serious challenge to a realist view of social science because they are an immanent critique, using the nature of society (ontology) to vitiate a naturalistic or positivistic epistemology. On this view, even if we can be realists about nature, a "realism about ideas" is incoherent, and as such there can be no via media between positivist and post-positivist approaches to social science.

This chapter responds to these anti-realist challenges in four parts. The first two sections defend the view that mature scientific theories provide knowledge of reality, even when reality is unobservable. The first section defines realism and examines its debate with empiricism and postmodernism on how (or whether) theories "hook on to" reality, while section 2 takes up what has been called the "Ultimate Argument" for realism. The rest of the chapter deals with the tension between realism and the idealist basis of social kinds. In section 3 I show that idealism about social kinds does not vitiate the subject–object distinction or a positivist approach. Finally, I reframe the Explanation–Understanding debate around a distinction between causal and constitutive questions. This helps transform apparently intractable epistemological issues into more benign methodological ones, and will subsequently prove crucial to understanding the "difference that ideas make" in international life.

---

[8] For example, Neufeld (1995).

[9] See Devitt and Sterelny (1987: 72–79), Hacking (1986, 1991), Currie (1988), Nelson (1990), and Little (1993). Among realist philosophers of natural science of whom I am aware, only Putnam (1975) and Boyd (1991) advocate realism about social kinds. Arguments in favor of realism in the social realm include Bhaskar (1979, 1986), Keat and Urry (1982), Sayer (1984), Dessler (1989, 1991), Layder (1990), Greenwood (1991), New (1995), Searle (1995), and Lane (1996).

[10] Von Wright (1971), Hollis and Smith (1990).

1 Scientific realism and theories of reference

The core of scientific realism is opposition to the view, held in various forms by its skeptical critics, that what there is in the world is somehow dependent on what we know or believe. Under this heading a variety of principles have been said to define realism. Michael Devitt finds one, Joseph Rouse five, Geoffrey Hellman seven, and Jarrett Leplin ten.[11] Rather than address these complexities let me stipulate three:

1 the world is independent of the mind and language of individual observers;
2 mature scientific theories typically refer to this world,
3 even when it is not directly observable.

It should be noted that these principles say nothing about the nature or structure of society. Some social scientific realists think that realism entails particular social and/or substantive theories, usually structuration theory and Marxism respectively.[12] I do not share that view. Realism is a philosophy of science, not a theory of society, and as such does not answer first-order, empirical questions. *Any* theory of society or international politics can be interpreted in realist terms. Realism makes it possible to conceive of states and states systems as real and knowable, but it does not tell us that they exist, what they are made of, or how they behave. That is a job for social scientists, not philosophers.

In what follows I discuss and justify the three realist principles in the light of empiricist and postmodern skepticism. I focus on the realist philosophy of *natural* science. Society is not reducible to nature, but nature is its material foundation and as such it is important to establish realism about natural science first. Also, since realism is at its most intuitive in this domain it is a useful starting point for those not familiar with it. It is true that, as I mentioned above, not all realists agree that we can be realists about society. But I first want to discuss realism in ways that make clear the realist common ground.

---

[11] Devitt (1991), Rouse (1987: 132), Hellman (1983), and Leplin (1984).
[12] This view can be traced to Bhaskar (1979, 1986), although in his work no explicit conflation is made. For discussion, see Wendt and Shapiro (1997).

World independence

This is the starting point for all versions of scientific realism, embodying the implicit ontology of science and common sense. As Devitt puts it, "it is not just that our experiences are *as if* there are cats, there are cats. It is not just that the observable world is *as if* there are atoms, there are atoms."[13] The world is what it is whether we see it or not; ontology before epistemology (much less method). This implies philosophical materialism or physicalism, which means that the world ultimately is made up of the sub-atomic particles studied by particle physicists. The belief that observables like cats exist independent of human beings is usually called "common-sense" realism, while the view that unobservables like atoms exist is called "scientific" realism. All scientific realists are common-sense realists, and the two together are sometimes known as "epistemic" realists. But not all common-sense realists are also scientific realists. Empiricists are admitted common-sense realists, and I shall argue that interpretivists and postmodernists are tacit common-sense realists, but they all reject scientific realism because they reject the reality of unobservables. Since the state and states system are unobservable, scientific realism is my primary concern here.

The assumption that the material world exists independent of our knowledge would be trivial were it not so often called into question. The traditional source of skepticism was the view of classical empiricists like Locke, Berkeley, and Hume that the only things which we can be *certain* exist are our perceptions or "sense-data." This view shifts the question of what exists in the world to what exists in our minds, and creates the conundrum of how we can know what is "out there" in reality. Note that the classical empiricists did not deny the existence of cats and dogs; rather, the claim was that their ontological status was dependent on what we could know about them from sense-data because only the latter were epistemically secure. In Berkeley's dictum, "esse est percipi" ("to be is to be perceived"). Few today would openly endorse such a statement, but its anti-realist spirit lives on in contemporary empiricism and postmodernism. The hard-bitten empiricists of the behavioral revolution exhibit anti-realism when they eschew talk of unobservable structures as "unscientific" or "metaphysical." And postmodernists are equally skeptical about world independence, and

---

[13] Devitt (1991: 45); emphasis in the original.

treat the world as an effect of discourses from which we have no access to an objective reality, a view anticipated by Thomas Kuhn's view that paradigms create "different worlds."[14] In different ways, both are suggesting that what is in the world depends upon us. To that extent their ontologies are anthropocentric or "human chauvinist,"[15] although the label is somewhat ironic, since the underlying rationale is premised on a sense of human limitation.

Mature theories refer to the world

This claim of scientific realism aims to solve the epistemological problem of how mind and language hook on to the world by advocating a particular theory of reference. Theories of reference are concerned with how the meaning of terms like "dog" or "state" is fixed. They determine how we think about knowledge and truth, since truth always implies successful reference, although, as we shall see, the reverse is not necessarily true: successful reference does not necessarily imply truth. Three theories dominate contemporary debates about reference: the *description* theory favored by empiricists, the *relational* theory of postmodernists, and the *causal* theory advocated by realists.[16] The first two have important affinities that form an unholy alliance against realism.

The description theory was long the orthodoxy. It gained prominence in response to the problems facing the "naive" or "picture" theory of reference held by early realists, who argued that meaning was determined directly by objects. The picture theory has difficulty accounting for the arbitrariness of the words we associate with objects as well as the difference in meaning between different descriptions of the same object. For example, it cannot explain the difference between "Taiwan is a renegade province of China" and "Taiwan is an independent state." Gottlob Frege, the father of modern description theories, introduced the notion of "sense" to solve these problems.[17] According

---

[14] Kuhn (1962). Also see Nelson Goodman's (1978) discussion of "worldmaking," on which Nick Onuf's (1989: 37–38) IR constructivism builds. In the terms here, Onuf is an anti-realist.

[15] Musgrave (1988: 245).

[16] Mitchell (1983) and Devitt and Sterelny (1987) are good introductions to the debates; many of the important contributions are collected in Schwartz, ed. (1977) and Moore, ed. (1993).

[17] Frege (1892/1993).

to Frege, the sense of a term is determined by the properties we associate with it, and "sense determines reference." The sense of "dog," for example, is given by the descriptions "four-legged barking canine . . .," and these in turn determine reference to dogs. On this view, therefore, meaning and truth are a function of descriptions within language, not a relation between words and reality.[18]

This creates a worry about how descriptions are determined, since if not by objects in the world then how do we know they are not inventions of our mind? Description theorists deal with this problem in empiricist fashion by basing descriptions on observation, which in their view has an epistemically privileged status because it is the only thing apart from analytic truths about which we can be certain. We include "barking" in the sense of "dog" because in our perceptions dogs bark. In keeping with empiricism's skeptical epistemology, however, description theorists treat these perceptions as sense-data in the mind rather than as effects of an entity "out there" in the world. This failure to base reference ultimately in the external world is what led Hilary Putnam, a realist critic of the description theory, to see it as a form of epistemological idealism.[19]

The key problem with the description theory is that it does not allow us to refer successfully to something if we have a mistaken description of it. If our descriptions change so must the putative entities to which they refer.[20] Did pre-Copernicans refer to the same sun as we, even though they described it one way and we another? Description theorists would have to say no. A science fiction fantasy devised by Putnam reveals the problem clearly.[21] Twin Earth is a planet in a parallel universe in every way identical to our own, but whose residents are ignorant of us. Thus, when Twin Earthers say "Tony Blair" they are referring to the individual who lives on their planet, while we mean the one who lives here. Yet, on the description theory the referents of these two statements must be identical, since they have identical senses, and sense determines reference. Putnam concludes that, "[c]ut the pie any way you like, 'meanings' just ain't in the *head*."[22] Meanings must have something to do with the relationship of words to the external world.

As opposed to the description theory's empiricism, the relational

---

[18] Devitt and Sterelny (1987: 51–52).   [19] Putnam (1975: 208–209).
[20] See especially Kripke (1971) and Putnam (1975).
[21] Putnam (1975: 223–227); for a good overview see Devitt and Sterelny (1987: 51–52).
[22] Putnam (1975: 227).

theory of reference is rooted in Saussure's structural linguistics and forms the basis of postmodern epistemology.[23] It rejects empiricism's view that meaning is immediately present to the mind when a word is understood ("logocentrism"), and holds instead that meaning is produced by relations of difference within a discourse. "An object is defined not by what it is in itself – not by its essential properties – but by its relationship in a structure."[24] When we learn the meaning of "dog," we do not acquire knowledge of an entity beyond discourse, but of its role or "signifying disposition" within our language.[25] As Terence Hawkes puts it, "[t]he word 'dog' exists, and functions within the structure of the English language, without reference to any four-legged barking creature's real existence."[26] Given the ease with which this view can be misinterpreted, it should be emphasized that it does not require a denial of reality "out there," an issue about which postmodernists are (or should be) agnostic. The claim is merely that reality has nothing to do with the determination of meaning and truth, which are governed instead by power relations and other sociological factors within discourse.[27] Postmoderns often think of their view as an abandonment of epistemology. But as with the description theory, critics see the relational theory as a form of epistemological idealism, since on this view reference to the material world effectively drops out altogether, leaving us with only "difference" within language.[28]

The effects of holding a relational theory of meaning on theorizing about world politics are apparent in David Campbell's provocative study of US foreign policy, which shows how the threats posed by the Soviets, immigration, drugs, and so on, were constructed out of US national security discourse.[29] The book clearly shows that material things in the world did not force US decision-makers to have particular representations of them – the picture theory of reference does not hold. In so doing it highlights the discursive aspects of truth and reference, the sense in which objects are relationally "constructed."[30] On the other hand, while emphasizing several times that he is not denying the reality of, for example, Soviet actions, he

---

[23] See Hawkes (1977: 19–28).   [24] Devitt and Sterelny (1987: 212).
[25] Mitchell (1983: 74).   [26] Hawkes (1977: 17).
[27] Foucault (1980); see Nola (1994) for a useful, if unsympathetic, attempt to clarify this proposition.
[28] Mitchell (1983), Devitt and Sterelny (1987: 215–220); cf. Alcoff (1993).
[29] Campbell (1992).   [30] Cf. Weldes (1999).

specifically eschews (p. 4) any attempt to assess the extent to which they *caused* US representations. Thus he cannot address the extent to which US representations of the Soviet threat were accurate or true (questions of correspondence). He can only focus on the nature and consequences of the representations.[31] Of course, there is nothing in the social science rule book which requires an interest in causal questions, and the nature and consequences of representations are important questions. In the terms discussed below he is engaging in a constitutive rather than causal inquiry. However, I suspect Campbell thinks that any attempt to assess the correspondence of discourse to reality is inherently pointless. According to the relational theory of reference we simply *have* no access to what the Soviet threat "really" was, and as such its truth is established entirely within discourse, not by the latter's correspondence to an extra-discursive reality.[32]

The main problem with the relational theory of reference is that it cannot account for the resistance of the world to certain representations, and thus for representational failures or *mis*interpretations. Worldly resistance is most obvious in nature: whether our discourse says so or not, pigs *can't* fly. But examples abound in society too. In 1519 Montezuma faced the same kind of epistemological problem facing social scientists today: how to refer to people who, in his case, called themselves Spaniards. Many representations were conceivable, and no doubt the one he chose – that they were gods – drew on the discursive materials available to him. So why was he killed and his empire destroyed by an army hundreds of times smaller than his own? The realist answer is that Montezuma was simply wrong: the Spaniards were not gods, and had come instead to conquer his empire. Had Montezuma adopted this alternative representation of what the Spanish were, he might have prevented this outcome because that representation would have corresponded more to reality. The reality of the conquistadores did not force him to have a true representation, as the picture theory of reference would claim, but it did have certain effects – whether his discourse allowed them or not. The external world to which we ostensibly lack access, in other words,

---

[31] See Jussim (1991) on the radical constructivist neglect of questions of accuracy and correspondence.

[32] A similar paragraph might have been written about Arturo Escobar's (1995) very interesting book on development theory, in which the question of the extent to which representations of Third World development are constrained by the objective conditions is not addressed.

often frustrates or penalizes representations. Postmodernism gives us no insight into why this is so, and indeed, rejects the question altogether.[33]

The description theory of reference favored by empiricists focuses on sense-data in the mind while the relational theory of the postmoderns emphasizes relations among words, but they are similar in at least one crucial respect: neither grounds meaning and truth in an external world that regulates their content.[34] Both privilege epistemology over ontology. What is needed is a theory of reference that takes account of the contribution of mind and language yet is anchored to external reality.

The realist answer is the causal theory of reference. According to the causal theory the meaning of terms is determined by a two-stage process.[35] First there is a "baptism," in which some new referent in the environment (say, a previously unknown animal) is given a name; then this connection of thing-to-term is handed down a chain of speakers to contemporary speakers. Both stages are causal, the first because the referent impressed itself upon someone's senses in such a way that they were induced to give it a name, the second because the handing down of meanings is a causal process of imitation and social learning. Both stages allow discourse to affect meaning, and as such do not preclude a role for "difference" as posited by the relational theory. Theory is underdetermined by reality, and as such the causal theory is not a picture theory of reference. However, conceding these points does not mean that meaning is entirely socially or mentally constructed. In the realist view beliefs are determined by discourse *and* nature.[36] This solves the key problems of the description and relational theories: our ability to refer to the same object even if our descriptions are different or change, and the resistance of the world to certain representations. Mind and language help determine meaning, but meaning is also regulated by a mind-independent, extra-linguistic world.

---

[33] Alcoff (1993: 99).

[34] On this and other similarities between empiricism and postmodernism see Boyd (1992: 164–169) and D'Amico (1992).

[35] See Kripke (1971), Putnam (1975), and Boyd (1979). While Saul Kripke is usually credited with the first statement, this has recently been challenged by Quentin Smith, who argues that Ruth Barcan Marcus had the original ideas. For a review of the ensuing controversy, as well as a clear summary of the causal theory, see Holt (1996).

[36] Kitcher (1993: 164–167).

Underlying the causal theory is an ontological assumption that the world contains "natural kinds" like water, atoms, or dogs.[37] Natural kinds are self-organizing, material entities whose causal powers are constituted by intrinsic, mind-independent structures rather than by human social convention. These material entities exert a reality constraint on us, such that if we want to succeed in the world our theories should conform to them as much as possible. If we want to cure AIDS, we need to know how the AIDS virus works. Bringing knowledge into conformity with natural kinds is the main task of science. Our knowledge of natural kinds is always fallible, of course, and so science may fail to "carve nature at its joints." But it is a feature of natural kinds that they produce certain effects whether we like it or not. Human beings have long wanted to fly, but only succeeded once they learned how to overcome gravity. Pigs will never fly because it is not in their nature.

In pure form the causal theory of reference is most applicable to natural kinds, and I argue later in this chapter that elements from the description and relational theory need to be incorporated when dealing with social kinds. However, in the realist view social life is continuous with nature, and as such science must be anchored to the world via the mechanisms described by the causal theory.

The causal theory has gained a considerable following,[38] in part because it solves important problems faced by its rivals. It has also been subject to criticism.[39] Let me address two concerns.

The first is the relationship between reference and truth. Realism entails a correspondence theory of truth, which means that theories are true or false in virtue of their relationship to states of the world. Still, realists agree with Quine, Kuhn, and Lakatos that all observation is theory-laden. Theory to some extent constructs its own facts.[40] This means that *realism is anti-foundationalist.*[41] Thus, although it is common to conflate the two, the correspondence theory of truth does not entail epistemological foundationalism. What makes a theory true is the extent to which it reflects the causal structure of the world, but

---

[37] See Boyd (1991), Hacking (1991), Kornblith (1993), and Haslam (1998).

[38] There is growing evidence that people have a genetic predisposition to identify natural kinds (Kornblith, 1993: 83–107), and the same is probably true of other animals, for whom the ability to distinguish predators and prey seems essential to survival.

[39] For example, Dupre (1993).   [40] As Waltz (1979: 5–12) seems to agree.

[41] Boyd (1989: 11–13), Kitcher (1993: 162).

theories are always tested against other theories, not against some pre-theoretical "foundation" for correspondence. This raises the question of how we can know for certain that a claim of reference is true.[42] The answer is that we cannot, and so we should have confidence only in the referents of "mature" theories that have proven successful in the world. Even then we can speak only of "approximate" truth,[43] but this does not matter. A key virtue of the causal theory is that it separates truth from reference. Truth presupposes reference, but reference does not presuppose truth. The causal theory allows us to refer successfully to an entity even if we have a mistaken view of its nature. Realists believe that through science we are gradually gaining a better understanding of the world (see below), but all knowledge claims are fallible and as such "The Truth" does not do any interesting work in their philosophy of science.

A second problem for the causal theory is that the boundaries of many natural kinds are hard to specify, which seems to suggest they do not have any essential properties at all. This concern goes back to Locke, who argued that differences in nature are all matters of degree rather than kind.[44] Echoing Locke's empiricist sentiments, in recent years postmodernists and radical feminists have used the existence of ambiguous boundaries to argue that things which society previously took as natural, like gender differences, are actually social constructions and thus politically negotiable.

The problem is acknowledged by contemporary realists. As Richard Boyd points out, indeterminacy of reference is even an implication of the theory of evolution, since speciation depends on deviant cases intermediate between parent and emerging species.[45] Rather than conclude that species are mere conventions, however, Boyd suggests a realist solution. He argues that species and other natural kinds are constituted by homeostatic *clusters* of properties. Individual elements in these clusters might not be essential, in which case we will have to settle for kind-definitions in terms of "fuzzy sets" and "stereotypes" rather than necessary and sufficient conditions.[46] But this does not damage realism about natural kinds. There are many differences between Labrador retrievers and collies, but a causally significant gap exists between them and cats. How we classify borderline cases can be

---

[42] On the implications of the theory-ladenness of observation for testing theories see Greenwood (1990), Hudson (1994), and Hunt (1994).
[43] Boyd (1990).   [44] See Kornblith (1993: 13–34).   [45] Boyd (1991: 142).
[46] Putnam (1975: 217), Boyd (1989: 18), Sayer (1997: 456–457).

important, especially in social life, but this does not mean the classification of natural kinds is *merely* a power play. Dogs cannot breed with cats no matter how we classify them. This says something about their nature, not about discourse.

Theories provide knowledge of unobservables

The epistemological anxieties of empiricists and postmodernists become even more acute when scientists start talking as if terms that have no observable referent (what are usually called "theoretical terms"), like electrons, preferences, or states, really do refer to unobservable entities or structures. Only the most determined skeptic will worry about whether "table" or "chair" refer to objects in the world, although such skeptics still exist.[47] But compared to observables, our knowledge of unobservables is much more dependent on what our *theories* rather than our senses tell us, so that we will have to abandon this knowledge as soon as we abandon the theories which give support to the unobservables.[48] This challenges the realist claim that reality (ontology) conditions theory (epistemology), since when it comes to unobservables we cannot know what is there apart from theory. In so doing it risks opening the floodgates to the social construction of meaning and truth. Waltz baptized the structure of the states system in one way and Bull did so in another, but for all we know it does not even exist.

The empiricist response to this problem is to treat theories in which unobservables appear "instrumentally" rather than "realistically," that is, as devices for organizing experience rather than as referring to hidden structures. This assumes a foundationalist epistemology in which observation has a privileged epistemic status relative to theory, such that whenever a theory cannot be reduced to observation statements, it should be treated in only instrumental terms. Even more than the description theory, instrumentalism about unobservables puts epistemology squarely before ontology. What we can claim to exist depends on what we can know, and we can only know what we can see. This view goes back at least to Hume, who treated causation as "constant conjunctions" of events because he thought we could never have certain knowledge of unobservable causal mechanisms.

---

[47] See Edwards, *et al.* (1995), and for a realist response, O'Neill (1995).
[48] Kroon (1985).

Instrumentalism was the philosophical orthodoxy in the heyday of logical positivism and empiricism, and gained widespread acceptance in the social sciences through an influential essay by Milton Friedman.[49]

In principle it should not matter to their conduct whether scientists adopt an instrumentalist or realist interpretation of unobservables. Admittedly, natural scientists routinely conduct expensive experiments designed to manipulate the putative referents of theoretical terms, which would be odd if they did not believe such entities really existed. But instrumentalism is intended only as a reconstruction of scientific practice, as a philosophical analysis of what kinds of scientific claims can be epistemically justified, not as a description of valid scientific practice. It is not meant as a warning to scientists to stop consorting with unobservables. As Herbert Feigl put it, "[n]o philosopher of science in his right mind considers this sort of analysis [logical empiricism] as a recipe for the construction of theories."[50] Beginning with the behavioral revolution, however, social scientists have done just that, basing their efforts to find lawlike generalizations and build deductive theories on empiricist reconstructions of science. This has two dangers.

The first is to encourage "as if" thinking. If theories are merely instruments for organizing experience, then it does not matter whether their assumptions are realistic. The task of theory becomes merely to predict successfully or "save the phenomena."[51] The problem is that just because a process can be modeled "as if" it works a certain way does not mean that it in fact works that way. If our view of science makes successful explanation dependent on successful prediction (see below), and nothing else, then insofar as we believe that there is a world independent of thought we may never get around to explaining how it really works. Even some sympathetic to empiricism have doubted whether "as if" theorizing is science.[52]

The second danger of instrumentalism is specific to realism about social kinds. Empiricist social scientists may conclude that instrumen-

---

[49] Friedman (1953). Instrumentalism's most important advocate today is probably Bas van Fraassen (1980). See Churchland and Hooker, eds. (1985) for realist commentary on van Fraassen and his reply, and Lagueux (1994) for an updating of Friedman's essay in light of van Fraassen's work.

[50] Feigl (1970: 13).   [51] Van Fraassen (1980); also see Waltz (1979: 10).

[52] Moe (1979).

talism's injunctions pertain to the study of society as much as nature, and so dismiss a priori as "metaphysical" any theory that invokes unobservables. Individualists have long used just such a tactic to attack as "ideological" the positing by holist theories like Marxism of unobservable deep structures.[53] This would vitiate as well any talk of the state and states system as real and knowable.

Pointing out that philosophical arguments should not be conflated with injunctions for research still does not solve the realists' problem, however, of how we can know unobservables. The response is two part, one negative and one positive.

The negative case is directed at the empiricist claim that observation provides an incorrigible foundation for knowledge. Realists argue that no rigid distinction between theory and observation can be sustained because all observation is theory-laden.[54] Theory-language may differ from observation-language in the degree to which it presupposes background beliefs, but it does not differ in kind. Unobservables therefore pose no unique problem for the causal theory of reference. Taken alone, this argument does not warrant belief in unobservables, however, and if anything puts us on the slippery slope of the epistemological relativist who argues that observation is not just theory-laden but theory-*determined*. To halt this slide the realist needs a positive argument that we have access to unobservables beyond the theories in which they are embedded.

It should be emphasized at the outset that there is no dispute between realists and empiricists that theories which include theoretical terms can be explanatory. The dispute is over what this fact entails for the ontological status of unobservables. The question comes down to this: Is it *reasonable* to infer the existence of electrons as the cause of certain observable effects, given that electron theory is our best satisfactory explanation for those effects yet might turn out later to be wrong? Is it *reasonable* to infer the existence of the state from the activities of people calling themselves customs officials, soldiers, and diplomats, given that state theory is our best satisfactory explanation of these activities yet might turn out to be wrong? Philosophers call such reasoning "inference to the best explanation," (IBE) and much of the debate about realism turns on attitudes

---

[53] See Weldes (1989) for a critical review. It is interesting to note here that postmodernists agree with empiricists that we should eschew the search for unobservable deep structures, and focus instead on surface phenomena (e.g., Ashley, 1987: 407).

[54] Maxwell (1962), Musgrave (1985: 204–209).

toward it.[55] Realists argue that IBE is warranted, pointing out that even though as a form of induction it lacks the certainty we gain through deduction, it is at the heart of scientific method and is used routinely in everyday life. True to skeptical form, empiricists argue that because it is fallible IBE is not an adequate foundation for knowledge. Realists counter that the search for foundations is a chimera anyway, and that IBE is the surest road to knowledge we have. And on it goes.

Realism's commitment to inference to the best explanation assigns a special role to theorists, and one might say that ultimately it is their epistemic status – their authority to speak about what the world is like – which is at stake in the realist–anti-realist debate. In the realist view, the theorist baptizes an unobservable phenomenon by proposing a description of its properties and some hypotheses about how these relate to observable effects. Essentially, when dealing with unobservables the realist – in natural as much as social science – is combining a causal with a description theory of reference.[56] This baptizing often occurs through metaphors.[57] In good realist fashion, Waltz baptized the structure of the states system with a three-part definition (description), and a market metaphor for thinking about its effects. Constructivists baptize it a different way, but that does not mean the reality of the states system is somehow dependent on our theories. After all, both sides point to certain shared observations and argue that part of the explanation for these is the structure of relationships among states. We may disagree about how to describe it, but we can still be referring to the same thing, just as Ptolemy and Copernicus referred to the same sun. In the realist view, the states system exists independent of social scientists, and interaction with that reality should regulate their theorizing about it. Observation may be theory-laden, but it is not – or, as Montezuma's experience reminds us, should not be – theory-determined.

This suggests one final comment. Critics of realism, and of the theory of world politics presented in later chapters, may call it "essentialist." I accept this label as long as it is properly understood. Essentialism is sometimes equated with the idea that we can explain a phenomenon by appealing to an unanalyzed or occult essence. That

---

[55] Also known as "retroduction" or "abduction"; see Boyd (1984: 65–75), Ben-Menahem (1990), Lipton (1991), and Day and Kincaid (1994).
[56] Kroon (1985).   [57] Boyd (1979), McMullin (1984a), Cummiskey (1992).

idea is unscientific and no realist should endorse it. What scientific realists claim is that the behavior of things is influenced by self-organizing, mind-independent structures that constitute those things with certain intrinsic powers and dispositions. Discovering those structures is what science is all about, which is itself essentialist in this weak sense.[58] Implicit in this attitude is the belief that things *have* internal structures, which is debatable if they are unobservable, and perhaps doubly so in the case of social kinds. My point is that whether an object has an internal, self-organizing structure should be treated as an empirical question, not ruled out a priori by epistemological skepticism. Such skepticism can be just as dogmatic as appeals to occult essences. Few today would doubt that dogs, water, and even atoms have essential properties. More would doubt that states and states systems do, but I want the reader to be open to the possibility.[59]

2 The ultimate argument for realism

The most convincing argument for realism is what is known as the "Ultimate" or "Miracle" Argument. As Putnam puts it, "the positive argument for realism is that it is the only philosophy that doesn't make the success of science a miracle."[60]

The argument begins with the assumption that science has been a "success" in helping us manipulate the world. Since it is easy to get side-tracked here, it is important to emphasize what this claim of success is *not*. It is not a claim that human beings are better off today than in 1500 because of science. Science can be used for good or ill, and realists are not saying that on balance it has been the former. Nor is the assumption of success a claim that when science does good there are no negative externalities. New technologies may generate pollution, disease, or cultural disruption. Both issues are important but beside the point, and to raise them changes the subject. The claim is merely that because of science we can manipulate the environment in ways we could not before, *even when we wanted to*. By that limited criterion scientific knowledge is progressive. We can fly and the Romans could not. Why? That is the question.

---

[58] Leplin (1988).

[59] For defenses of moderate essentialism like the one endorsed here see O'Neill (1994), Sayer (1997), and Haslam (1998).

[60] Putnam (1975: 73). This argument is also made by Niiniluoto (1980), Boyd (1984), Musgrave (1988), Cummiskey (1992), Carrier (1993), and Brown (1994).

The realist answer is that we know things about the world that the Romans did not. More generally, science is successful because it gradually brings our theoretical understanding into conformity with the deep structure of the world out there. If mature theories did not correspond roughly to that structure, it would be a "miracle" they worked so well. This is an inference to the best explanation: given that being a miracle is not an explanation, and seeing no better explanations, realists argue that the best explanation for the success of science is that we are getting closer to the structure of reality.

Anti-realists have objected that it is no miracle that scientific theories enable us to control the world, since that is what we designed them to do, and so we do not need a meta-account of their success: science is its own best explanation.[61] On this view, the Ultimate Argument commits the fallacy of affirming the consequent, in which the conclusion is a hidden premise. In fact, this was a fair criticism of early versions of the Ultimate Argument that defined success broadly as the ability to manipulate the environment. But realists have responded by narrowing their definition of success. Success means the ability to predict things that were not objects of an original theory (novel facts), and to unite previously distinct bodies of knowledge.[62] There are many instances of such "strong" success in science,[63] and these would be miraculous if our theories did not correspond increasingly to the world.

The real difficulty for the Ultimate Argument is the problem of "reference failure." One virtue of the causal theory of reference is that it solves the problem faced by its competitors that we cannot refer successfully if we have the wrong theory (Ptolemy did not refer to the sun, and so on). On the other hand, realists have often neglected the opposite problem that a theory can be "successful" without referring to anything real or true. Successful reference is therefore not necessary for empirical success.[64] Larry Laudan has identified a number of theories in the history of science that were empirically successful for a time, but whose theoretical terms we believe today do not refer, like phlogiston theory or caloric theory.[65] If so, this suggests the following "pessimistic induction on the history of science":[66] given that many entities which we previously thought to exist we now believe do not,

[61] See Van Fraassen (1980), Laudan (1981), Fine (1984).
[62] Musgrave (1988: 232), Carrier (1991: 25–26), Brown (1994: 18–20).
[63] Carrier (1993: 404).   [64] Brown (1994: 20).   [65] Laudan (1981: 33).
[66] Kitcher (1993: 136); also see Hobbs (1994).

how can we be sure that those accepted today will not be similarly rejected in the future? And, given that, how can we be sure that changes of theory are progressive approximations to reality and not merely incommensurable changes in discourse? This is a serious challenge to realism; as Putnam puts it, "[i]t must obviously be a desideratum for the theory of reference that this meta-induction be blocked."[67]

There seems to be some disarray in the realist camp about how to deal with this problem. Philip Kitcher raises important doubts about Laudan's history, suggesting there is more continuity of reference over time than Laudan allows, thereby supporting a more optimistic induction over the history of science.[68] There are similar doubts about Kuhn's claim that scientific paradigms are incommensurable.[69] Nevertheless, the claim that science yields progressive approximations to reality depends on earlier theories having gotten *something* right, and realists disagree amongst themselves about what the object of this "retention requirement" should be.[70] Some say what must be retained is whole theories (like the subsumption of Newtonian by quantum mechanics), while others propose less demanding candidates like entities, natural kinds, theory constitutive metaphors, and explanatory structures.[71] These disagreements in part reflect different definitions of realism, and so a definitive realist retention requirement is not likely to be established soon.

The problem of reference failure might seem to leave anti-realists with the last word, but fortunately that is not so. Apart from keeping the faith that realists can eventually formulate a plausible retention requirement, there are two final rejoinders to the skeptical challenge.

First, there is still that persistent fact of the strong success of science, which anti-realists have yet to explain. Kuhn and Laudan are both puzzled by it,[72] the former claiming to have no explanation at all, the latter offering a pragmatist explanation that what matters is a theory's problem-solving ability, not its truth – but that begs the question of why some theories solve problems better than others. Van Fraassen

---

[67] Putnam (1978: 25).   [68] Kitcher (1993: 140–149).
[69] Miller (1991); on incommensurability in IR see Wight (1996).
[70] Carrier (1993: 393).
[71] See, respectively, Hacking (1983), Carrier (1993), Cummiskey (1992), and McMullin (1984a). For further treatments of scientific progress from a realist standpoint see Lakatos (1970), Niiniluoto (1980), and Kitcher (1993).
[72] Niiniluoto (1980: 447).

does better with the Darwinian argument that success is not miraculous because only successful theories survive the fierce competition to which all scientific theories are subjected.[73] But as Alan Musgrave points out, "this changes the subject. It is one thing to explain why only successful theories survive, and quite another thing to explain why some particular theory is successful."[74] The failure of anti-realists to explain success is important, since theories (here, the realist theory of science) are always judged against other theories, not facts. Until anti-realists come up with a viable alternative the realist explanation for strong success should be accepted.

Yet, there is a second "ultimate" response to skepticism, which is that non-realists are usually "*tacit* realists" in their own scientific practice,[75] and that this only makes sense if realism is true. Empiricist philosophers of science are explicit that scientists should go about their business as before, which means doing research as if they had access to unobservables – as if they were realists. More significantly, postmodernists implicitly do the same thing. Linda Alcoff argues convincingly that Foucault's work is based on an implicit common-sense realism,[76] and Campbell bases his study of US foreign policy on evidence that most IR scholars would agree bears on his problem. It is not clear why they would constrain their researches in this way if they had no access to reality. Why not choose arbitrary "evidence"? From a realist perspective it is perfectly clear why they would not do so: because the only way to generate reliable causal knowledge about the world is to allow one's theorizing about it to be disciplined by the empirical evidence it throws up. Anti-realists want their claims about how the world works to be taken just as seriously as realists do, but ironically the only way they can do that is if in their scientific practice they work "as if" they were realists. If in the end we are all realists in practice, it would seem that epistemological anxiety makes little difference to our study of the world.

3 The problem of social kinds

If the Ultimate Argument is convincing anywhere it will be in natural science, where mature theories exist that have enabled us to manipulate the world. It is less compelling in social science, which has

---

[73] Van Fraassen (1980: 39–40).   [74] Musgrave (1988: 242).
[75] Bunge (1993); also see Searle (1995: 183–189).   [76] Alcoff (1993: 110).

provided few "strong successes." There are some. Rational choice theory might be one, since one could claim that it would be a miracle the theory worked so well if the causal mechanisms to which it refers (rationality, preferences, and so on) did not exist.[77] In IR scholarship a similar situation may arise as we gain a better understanding of the "democratic peace." If it is true that democratic states solve their disputes non-violently, then it would be a miracle that a theory which predicts such a pattern did not tap into some of its causes. Balance of power theory might be another case. Nevertheless, most social scientists concede that their theories are relatively immature, and as such a key premise of the Ultimate Argument is not available to justify their practice.

Significant as it is, this is not the least of the problems facing the would-be social scientific realist. A more fundamental objection is that "social kinds" do not obviously satisfy the first premise of realism, that the world exists independent of human beings. Social kinds include all of the familiar objects of social scientific inquiry:

> physical objects which have a social function, like items of exchange and the trappings of devotion, social structures such as the family, the state and the working class, institutions such as banks, businesses and the cabinet, "offices" such as head of state, chairperson of the board, secretary of the club, together with more abstract kinds of things such as languages and other conventional systems like laws and customs. Particular instances of these things are exemplars of social kinds.[78]

Unlike natural kinds, these phenomena are constituted mostly by people's ideas, which seems to vitiate the subject–object distinction upon which the causal theory of reference depends. Realism about natural science is based on a materialist ontology, whereas the nature of social kinds seems to imply an idealist or nominalist one. The dependence of social kinds on ideas has led post-positivists to argue that we cannot study society in the mechanistic way in which we study nature, and should instead seek a hermeneutical understanding of actors' subjective interpretations and the social rules which constitute them.[79] This advice seems to have been heeded by many constructivist IR scholars, who tend to be post-positivist in their

---

[77] Though see Green and Shapiro (1994). Note that this implies a realist rather than instrumentalist interpretation of rational choice theory; cf. Satz and Ferejohn (1994).
[78] Currie (1988: 207); see also Haslam (1998).
[79] Taylor (1971); for a good overview see Hollis and Smith (1990: 68–91).

epistemological leanings. Moreover, as noted above many natural science realists unfortunately agree that realism is not appropriate to social science. This is if anything more damning than the post-positivist critique, because they reason in realist fashion from ontology (the nature of society) to epistemology (our theory of social science). In contrast to natural science, therefore, social science is a "hard case" for realism, a realist constructivism perhaps an oxymoron.

In this section I first explore in more detail the differences between natural and social kinds which give rise to these worries. I then argue that while these differences are real and indicate that social scientists must sometimes think in terms of the description and relational theories of reference, they do not fundamentally challenge a realist view of social science.

In a widely cited discussion, Roy Bhaskar identified three important ways in which social kinds differ from natural kinds.[80] To his list I will add a fourth.

1 Social kinds are more space–time specific than natural kinds because reference to certain places and eras is often part of their definition. The Industrial Revolution, for example, refers to a transformation in technological capabilities that occurred in nineteenth century Europe. This occurrence is not part of the contingent causal history of the Industrial Revolution, in the way that emerging five million years ago in Africa was of the history of homo sapiens (we could have emerged anywhere or anytime and still have been humans), but an essential or constitutive aspect of what that Revolution was. Thus, unlike natural kinds there can be no transhistorical theory of the Industrial Revolu-tion as such, since truths about it will be necessarily relative to a particular spatio-temporal context.

This is an important difference between natural and social kinds, but its significance often has been overstated. Critics say it precludes social "science" because they think science depends on truths being transhistorical. This may be true of an empiricist theory of science (perhaps), but not a realist one. On a realist view of explanation, with its emphasis on the description of causal mechanisms rather than deduction from universal laws (see below), theories do not have to be transhistorical to be scientific. We can explain how and why the

---

80 Bhaskar (1979: 48–49).

Industrial Revolution happened without generalizing beyond that case.

On the other hand, insofar as the Industrial Revolution is an instance of a broader social kind known as "technological revolutions," we may very well be able to make transhistorical claims about it. This bears on the controversy in IR about whether Political Realism or other theories of international politics can be generalized across time and space. I believe they can, *provided* the essential features of the relevant kinds are preserved. When and wherever states interact under anarchy – conditions which have been met in many times and places, but not all times and places, in history – systemic IR theory should be relevant. This is not to deny the significance of cultural variation in the meaning attached to states and anarchy, and indeed a central claim of this book is that "anarchy is what states make of it." But it is important not to confuse social kinds or "types," which can be described in terms of Boyd's idea of homeostatic clusters or fuzzy sets, with their particular exemplars or "tokens." The defining or essential properties of the state or anarchy are not historically variable; it is not the case that states in one period are what we would today call football teams – if so, they were simply not "states." The culture of international politics in ancient Greece may have been different than the culture of international politics today, but this does not mean there are no commonalities between the two worlds which distinguish them jointly from bowling leagues. That is an empirical question which can only be answered by scientific investigation of these social kinds, not a priori by philosophical fiat. As such, I do not see the potential time–space specificity of social kinds as a problem for realism about social science, and will not discuss it further here.[81] The remaining differences between natural and social kinds seem more serious.

2 Unlike natural kinds, the existence of social kinds depends on the interlocking beliefs, concepts, or theories held by actors. Drawing on the work of Foucault, for example, Ian Hacking – a realist about natural science – shows how the invention in the nineteenth century of the category of "homosexual" helped create or "make up" a certain kind of person and its associated social possibilities, which are not reducible to the material fact of engaging in same-sex behavior.[82] The

---

[81] See Greenwood (1991: 32–38).   [82] Hacking (1986).

same is true of witches, doctors, and states. Before the emergence of the shared ideas that constitute them (if not the actual words themselves), these social kinds did not exist. This seems to violate the core assumption of realism that the objects of science are mind/discourse-independent.

3 Unlike natural kinds, the existence of social kinds also depends on the human practices that carry them from one location to another. If people stop behaving as if there are witches (even if they still privately believe in them), then there are no witches. Social kinds are a function of belief *and* action.[83] This reinforces the previous point that social kinds are not independent of human beings.

4 Unlike natural kinds, many social kinds have both an internal *and* an external structure, which means that they cannot be studied solely in the reductionist fashion realists use to explain natural kinds. By external structure, I mean social kinds that are inherently relational – not in the sense of being caused by contingent interactions with other kinds (which also happens in nature), but in the sense of being *constituted* by social relations. To be a professor is, by definition, to stand in a certain relation to a student; to be a patron is, by definition, to stand in a certain relation to a client. The centrality of external (social) structures in constituting social kinds leads many to conclude that we can only know social kinds through the relational theory of reference. Social kinds seem to lack any essential, self-organizing core, making scientific study of them impossible.

Let us grant that these four differences between natural and social kinds exist. What is their implication for the possibility of a realist social science? Empiricists and post-positivists seem quite sure they preclude realism. Social kinds seem to lack the mind/discourse-independent, common internal structure that is the basis for realism about natural kinds.[84] There is no freestanding, prediscursive essence in virtue of which a witch is a witch, and thus no objective reality exerting a regulatory influence on our theorizing about witches. The baptism ceremony referred to above, that plays such a key role in the causal theory of reference about natural kinds, has an entirely different character in social life. Far from naming independently existing self-organizing objects, social baptisms *create* their objects. This is

---

[83] Currie (1988: 217).   [84] Little (1993).

what seems to collapse the distinction between subject and object. In the case of social kinds ontology seems to demand a nominalist or idealist epistemology, not a realist one.

How can we preserve a causal theory of reference when social kinds are made mostly of ideas? Although the problem is difficult, there are at least three responses available to the realist. Each calls attention to ways in which social kinds remain objective despite their basis in shared ideas.

One is to emphasize the role of material forces in constituting social kinds, which allows the social science realist to fall back on the arguments of natural science realists about how theory hooks on to reality. In the case of physical artifacts, like ICBMs or garages, the material base consists in the physical properties without which these things cannot exist: a thing cannot be an ICBM if it cannot fly long distances, nor a garage if it is not big enough to fit a car. (Note that this is not to say that the respective thing must be an "ICBM" or a "garage" for the people to whom it has meaning, but that is a different question.) In the case of social kinds that involve people more directly, like states or professors, the material base consists in the genetically constituted properties of homo sapiens. Like other animals, human beings are *natural* kinds with certain intrinsic material properties like large brains, opposable thumbs, and a genetic predisposition to socialize. Were it not for these material properties there could be no states or professors. Indeed, were it not for the materially grounded tendency of homo sapiens to designate things as "this" or "that" – to *refer* – there would be no social kinds at all.[85] In the last analysis a theory of social kinds must refer to natural kinds, including human bodies and their physical behavior, which are amenable to a causal theory of reference. Constructivism without nature goes too far.[86]

This argument points toward a research agenda that I take up in chapter 3, namely investigating the extent to which natural kinds determine social ones. This will vary from case to case, and can be judged in part by the extent to which material forces penalize and/or enable certain representations. In an overcrowded lifeboat the properties of natural kinds are highly constraining, such that if for social reasons the captain chooses to ignore them – and he may choose to do so – the boat will sink and people will die whether he likes it or not. At the other end of the spectrum, what counts as money is almost

---

[85] Harre (1986: 100–107).   [86] See Murphy (1995), New (1995).

wholly arbitrary. In other words, the extent to which material forces determine social kinds is a variable that can be examined empirically, and so the subject–object distinction varies when it comes to social kinds. The debate between materialists and idealists is about what values this variable takes on, the former saying generally high, the latter low. In testing any claims about the relative importance of material forces versus ideas, however, it is essential that the constituents of social kinds be properly separated. I argue in chapter 3 that materialists often "cheat," building implicit social/ideational stuff, like relations of production or egoistic identities, into their definition of material forces. A fair test depends on stripping the social from the material. Having done so, I think we will see that the role of the material base in international politics is relatively small, even if it remains essential for preserving a causal theory of reference.[87]

The foregoing argument nevertheless pushes us toward materialism, and as such provides little comfort to would-be realist constructivists. A second response is better in this respect, which is to focus on the role of self-organization in the constitution of social kinds.[88] Natural kinds are entirely self-organizing, in the sense that they are what they are in virtue solely of their internal structure. Human descriptions and/or social relationships to other natural kinds have nothing to do with what makes dogs dogs. The fact that natural kinds are self-organizing regulates our theories about them, as hypothesized by the causal theory of reference. It is in virtue of their self-organizing quality that they resist denials or misrepresentations of their existence. The same can be said to varying degrees about social kinds. Consider the distinction between the empirical and juridical sovereignty of the state.[89] The ability of a group to control and administer a territory (empirical sovereignty) historically has been the main consideration in its recognition by others as a state (juridical sovereignty). This is exactly what the causal theory of reference would predict. A state's ability to organize itself as a state creates resistance to those who would deny its existence, manifested when, for example, governments arrest illegal aliens or take military action against invasion. Over time such resistance should bring others' theories about that state into line with its reality – i.e., resistance should lead to "recognition" of its existence.

---

[87] See also Wendt (1995).
[88] On self-organization in social life see Luhmann (1990) and Leydesdorff (1993).
[89] Jackson and Rosberg (1982).

The fact that a state is constituted by shared ideas does not make this resistance any less objective or real than the more strictly speaking material resistance of natural kinds.

Note that the self-organization hypothesis does not preclude states *also* being constituted in part by relations to other states (by external rather than purely internal structures), as a holist would maintain, since recognition of juridical sovereignty may confer capacities or interests on a state that it would not have on its own. Luxemburg may be a self-organizing entity that resists denials of its existence, but it is clear that other states' recognition of its sovereignty enables it to survive. Nor does the self-organization hypothesis deny that social kinds like the state presuppose an on-going process of boundary-drawing, differentiating what is in and outside the state, as post-structuralists have emphasized.[90] The self-organization hypothesis is simply that this process of boundary-drawing receives much of its impetus from forces "inside" the space around which the boundary will be drawn. What makes, say, Germany "Germany" is primarily the agency and discourse of those who call themselves Germans, not the agency and discourse of outsiders. The Spanish state was a self-organized, objective fact for the Aztecs, whether their discourse acknowledged this or not. So, increasingly, is the Palestinian state for the Israelis.

Social kinds vary in the extent to which they depend on self-organization, however, and this bears on the propriety of a realist interpretation of them. Focusing specifically on kinds of people, Hacking makes the useful suggestion that we think about their constitution in terms of two "vectors:"[91]

> One is the vector of labelling from above, from a community of experts who create a "reality" that some people make their own. Different from this is the vector of the autonomous behavior of the person so labelled, which presses from below, *creating a reality every expert must face.* (emphasis added)

We might generalize this proposal by saying that social kinds lie on a spectrum of varying combinations of internal, self-organization and external, social construction, the relative weights of which determine whether we should be realists or anti-realists about them.

At the low end of the self-organization scale are artifacts like pencils, paperweights, or commodities, which are created by human

---

[90] Campbell (1992); also see Abbott (1995). [91] Hacking (1986: 234).

beings for certain purposes and as such have few intrinsic properties. A nominalist or description theory of reference is most appropriate here because these phenomena do not resist certain representations or regulate our theories on their own. In the middle are social kinds like "doctor" or, perhaps, "homosexual," which depend on external recognition and the taking of roles by an individual. And still higher, I will argue, are corporate actors like states, the powers and interests of which are in important part constituted by internal group dynamics, and which would most vigorously resist efforts to deny their existence. Even corporate actors are also constituted by external recognition and as such are not entirely self-organizing. But the farther one moves along this continuum, the more we can say an entity has an internal structure that causes it to act in the world in certain ways and to regulate our beliefs.

This relates to a final response to the anti-realist challenge. Even though social kinds are not mind/discourse-independent of the collectivity that constitutes them, they *are* usually independent of the minds and discourse of the *individuals* who want to explain them. These individuals could be professional social scientists, or anyone in their everyday capacity as "lay scientists"; the epistemological problems are the same. The international system confronts the IR theorist as an objective social fact that is independent of his or her beliefs, and resists an arbitrary interpretation of it. As lay scientists, foreign policy decision-makers experience a similar dualism of subject and object in their daily efforts to negotiate the world. Even though state actors are to some extent dependent on each other's recognition, they also confront each other as objective facts that simply cannot be wished away. Saddam Hussein acted as if Kuwait was a province of Iraq rather than a sovereign state. He failed because of resistance from the external world, which acted as a reality constraint on his efforts. Those who maintain social kinds never satisfy the subject–object distinction imply that professional or lay scientists can make the world anything they want. While it is true that individuals can represent the world any way they want to, that does not mean those representations will be correct or help them succeed. Individuals do not constitute social kinds, collectives do, and as such social kinds confront the individual as objective social facts.[92]

[92] For critiques of epistemological individualism see Manicas and Rosenberg (1985), Wilson (1995).

Still, I raised the ideas of external structure and boundary-drawing, which are distinct to social kinds, for an important reason. Usually social kinds confront members of the relevant collectives as seemingly natural facts – like a "state" or a "corporation." Berger and Luckmann characterize this situation as one where "reification" has taken place. By reification, they mean:

> the apprehension of the products of human activity *as if* they were something else than human products – such as facts of nature, results of cosmic laws, or manifestations of divine will. Reification implies that man is capable of forgetting his own authorship of the human world, and further, that the dialectic between man, the producer, and his products is lost to consciousness. The reified world is . . . experienced by man as a strange facticity, an opus alienum over which he has no control rather than as the opus proprium of his own productive activity.[93]

When social kinds are reified there is a clear distinction between subject and object. However, there are occasions when collectives become aware of the social kinds they are constituting and move to change them, in what might be called a moment of "reflexivity." For four decades, for example, the Soviet Union treated the Cold War as a given. Then in the 1980s it engaged in "New Thinking," an important outcome of which was the realization that aggressive Soviet foreign policies contributed to Western hostility which in turn forced the Soviets to engage in high levels of defense spending. By acting on that understanding to conciliate the West, the Gorbachev regime virtually single-handedly ended the Cold War. In effect, if a social kind can "know itself" then it may be able to recall its human authorship, transcend the subject–object distinction, and create new social kinds. Such reflexive potential is inherent to social life and is unknown in nature. Anthony Giddens has called it the "double hermeneutic": in both social and natural science observation of the world is affected by our theories, but social scientific theories alone have the potential to become part of their world as well.[94] Such transformations violate the assumptions of the causal theory of reference, since reality is being caused by theory rather than vice-versa. If societies were constantly doing this – in a sort of "permanent conceptual revolution" – we could not be realists about society.

In sum, the ontology of social life is consistent with scientific

---

[93] Berger and Luckmann (1966: 89).   [94] Giddens (1982: 11–14).

realism. To varying degrees, social kinds are materially grounded, self-organizing phenomena with intrinsic powers and dispositions that exist independent of the minds and/or discourse of those who would know them. These phenomena should regulate social scientific theorizing, even though they cannot determine it. In all but society's most reflexive moments, there is a distinction between subject and object. The distinction is blurred by the fact that all observation is theory-laden, but this does not mean it is theory-determined – or if it sometimes is, those who hold such self-contained theories are likely to fare poorly in the world. Academic and lay scientists alike have been aware of this philosophical "insight" all along, and as such it does not enable us to do anything we could not before. What it does is to provide epistemological cover against anti-realists who argue that social scientists cannot explain how society works. Realism shows that social science manifestly can explain social kinds. It does not deny the unique features of social science: ontologically, its objects do not exist independent of knowledgeable practices; epistemologically, reference to social kinds will often involve descriptive and relational elements; and methodologically, the hermeneutical recovery of self-understandings must be an essential aspect of explaining social action. But in the realist view social scientists can still hope to explain those realities, even though they are socially constructed.

4 On causation and constitution[95]

Having argued that the ideational structure of social life does not make it impossible to approach social kinds as scientists, the final question is how do we study them? How do we isolate the "difference that ideas make" in social life? Positivists typically see the business of all science as causal explanation. I am all for causal explanation; nothing in the nature of social kinds means they are uncaused. However, scientists also engage in a distinct kind of theorizing that I shall call constitutive. Part of the gulf that separates positivists and post-positivists in social science stems, I believe, from a mistaken view of these two types of theorizing. Positivists think natural scientists do not do constitutive theory and so privilege causal theory; post-positivists think social scientists should not do causal theory and so privilege constitutive theory. But in fact all scientists do both kinds of

---

[95] For further development of the ideas in this section see Wendt (1998).

theory; causal and constitutive theories simply ask different questions. Causal theories ask "why?" and to some extent "how?" Constitutive theories ask "how-possible?" and "what?" These questions transcend the natural–social science divide, and so do the corresponding forms of theorizing. Thus, answers to constitutive questions about the social world will have more in common with answers to constitutive questions about the natural world than they will with answers to causal questions about social life. This is true even though constitutive theorists might use different methods when thinking about the natural versus social world. In other words, I am arguing for a question-driven approach to social inquiry, in an attempt to transform the epistemological polemics of the Third Debate into more benign methodological differences. In this section I distinguish the two kinds of theorizing, and emphasize the importance of the constitutive.

This bears directly on some of the key questions in substantive IR theory. The states systemic project assumes that the structure of the international system matters to world politics. To fully explain how it matters we need to identify and separate out its causal and constitutive effects. One can see the significance of such a separation along both axes of figure 2, which I introduced in chapter 1 (p. 32). Along the x-axis (materialism vs. idealism), mainstream scholars tend to treat ideas as "variables" that interact with material forces to produce outcomes. They ask "how much variance in behavioral outcomes is explained by ideas as opposed to power and interest?" This is a causal question, and it captures an important aspect of the difference that ideas make. However, ideas also *constitute* social situations and the meaning of material forces. This is not a causal claim, and it is this that materialists ultimately reject. Along the y-axis (individualism vs. holism), mainstream scholars tend to treat the relationship between agency and structure as one of "interaction" between independently existing entities. They ask "to what extent do structures produce agents (or vice-versa)?" This too is a causal question, and it captures an important aspect of the difference that structures make. However, social structures also *constitute* actors with certain identities and interests. This is not a causal claim, and it is this that individualists ultimately reject. The distinctively constructivist hypotheses about the role of ideas and social structure in world politics are primarily about these constitutive effects.

Causal theorizing

In saying that "*X* causes *Y*" we assume that: (1) *X* and *Y* exist independent of each other, (2) *X* precedes *Y* temporally, and (3) but for *X*, *Y* would not have occurred. The first two conditions need to be highlighted here because they are *not* true of constitutive arguments, but they do not typically pose a problem for the causal researcher. Her real challenge is the third counterfactual condition, since "we can never hope to know a causal effect for certain."[96] As such there is always a problem of separating causation from correlation, necessary from accidental association. In the philosophy of science it is common to distinguish an empiricist and a realist approach to this problem.[97] As above, their differences turn on attitudes toward inference to the best explanation and epistemic risk.

I will talk about the empiricists first. The logical empiricist model of causal explanation, usually called the deductive–nomological or "D–N" model, is rooted in David Hume's seminal discussion of causality.[98] Hume argued that when we see putative causes followed by effects, i.e., when we have met conditions (1) and (2), all we can be certain about is that they stand in relations of constant conjunction. The actual mechanism by which *X* causes *Y* is not observable (and thus uncertain), and appeal to it is therefore epistemically illegitimate. Even if there is necessity in nature, we cannot know it. How then to satisfy the third, counterfactual condition for causality, which implies necessity? Since they are unwilling to posit unobservable causal mechanisms, which would require an inference to the best explanation, logical empiricists substitute *logical* for natural necessity. The relation between cause and effect in nature is reconstructed as a deductive relation between premise and conclusion in logic, with behavioral laws serving as premise and the events to be explained as conclusion. This preserves our intuition that what differentiates causation from correlation is necessity in the relation, without leaving us epistemically vulnerable to the charge of being metaphysical in our research.

As with the empiricist analysis of unobservables, the D–N model

---

[96] King, Keohane, and Verba (1994: 79).
[97] For overviews of the differences see Keat and Urry (1982), McMullin (1984b), and Strawson (1987).
[98] Hume (1748/1988); on the D–N model see Hempel and Oppenheim (1948) and Gunnell (1975).

was only intended as a reconstruction of scientific logic. It was not meant as a prescription for how to do science. Indeed, many explanations in natural science are not stated in D–N terms. Yet some social scientists have failed to heed this point and taken the D–N model as a description of what scientific explanations should look like. (Recall the quote from Bueno de Mesquita, p. 48 above.) This can negatively affect the practice of social science in various ways. In their effort to find the behavioral laws ostensibly needed for causal explanations, for example, social scientists may neglect forms of inquiry that might otherwise be valuable, like historical case studies, which do not contribute to this effort. Social scientists may also turn to false, "as if" assumptions as substitutes for the laws which we have not yet discovered. And because in a deductive relationship explanation and prediction are equivalent, social scientists may concentrate too heavily on the means of prediction rather than the end of explanation.

Among philosophers of science the claim that explanation and prediction are equivalent was the first element of the D–N model to fall. It turns out that there are many theories which we think explain things in the world but which cannot predict, like plate tectonics or evolution. The *a*symmetry of explanation and prediction is now conventional wisdom, even among empiricists,[99] although this does not vitiate the D–N model as *one* model of explanation.

A more serious objection to logical empiricism is that even if it was reasonable for Hume, given the science of his day, to reject talk of causal mechanisms and natural necessity as metaphysical, it is not reasonable today.[100] To be sure, our science of unobservables is fallible, and if we think that the only thing that counts as knowledge is the analytical certainties of logic and mathematics then the D-N approach makes sense. Yet, in view of our growing ability to manipulate the world, an inference to the best explanation suggests that we understand much more about its deep structure today than we did 250 years ago. Is it reasonable to deny that what scientists think they know about the causal mechanisms driving nuclear reactions is knowledge? From this historicized perspective (which is the perspective of the Ultimate Argument), the charge that realists engage in "metaphysical" appeals seems especially unwarranted. In fact the

---

[99] For example, van Fraassen (1980).
[100] See, for example, McMullin (1978: 142–143), Schlagel (1984), Kornblith (1993: 30), and Glennan (1996).

continued skepticism in light of scientific success seems more removed from reality.

Finally, subsumption under a law is not really explanation at all, in
the sense of answering *why* something occurred, but is simply a way
of saying *that* it is an instance of a regularity.[101] In what sense have
we explained peace between the US and Canada by subsuming it
under the generalization that "democracies don't fight each other"?
When what we really want to know is why democracies do not fight
each other, to answer that question in terms of still higher-order laws
merely pushes the question one step back. The general problem here
is failing to distinguish the grounds for expecting an event to occur
(being an instance of a regularity) with explaining why it occurs.[102]
Causation is a relation in nature not in logic. It is important to
document regularities where they exist, both to increase our capacity
to predict and to discern patterns of outcomes at the population
level. But in order to answer "why?" we need to show how a causal
process works, which depends on knowing mechanisms. This presupposes a willingness to tolerate the epistemic risks associated with
inference to the best explanation, but in taking those risks realists
think they are in good company: "[o]ver the past three centuries,
retroductive explanation [IBE] has gradually become accepted as the
basic form of explanation in most parts of the natural sciences."[103]
And although they do not describe themselves as realists or talk
about inference to the best explanation, in their study of social
scientific method Gary King, Robert Keohane, and Sidney Verba
concentrate in effect on ways to make inferences to the best explanation as sound as possible.[104]

Thicker constructivists might object that talk of causal "mechanisms" reflects an overly materialist discourse that misunderstands the
role of rules and self-understandings in social life, which they see as
constitutive rather than causal.[105] Certainly the term "mechanism" is
not ideal (though it is not clear how we could talk about causation
without it), and interpretivists are right that rules and self-understandings play a constitutive as well as causal role in social life.
However, it is also important to emphasize that there are many ways
in which society *is* caused in a mechanistic manner, and it should be

[101] McMullin (1984b: 214).   [102] Keat and Urry (1982: 27–32), Sayer (1984: 123).
[103] McMullin (1984b: 211).
[104] King, Keohane, and Verba (1994); also see Cook and Campbell (1986).
[105] For example, Fay (1986).

one task of social science to understand these relationships.[106] Social interaction is in part a causal process of mutual adjustment that often has unintended consequences. Socialization is in part a causal process of learning identities. Norms are causal insofar as they regulate behavior. Reasons are causes to the extent that they provide motivation and energy for action. And so on. All of these phenomena involve rules and self-understandings ("ideas"), but this does not preclude their having causal effects. Another way to defend application of "mechanism" to social life would be to distinguish two meanings of it, a narrow one that refers to the internal workings of actual machines like clocks, and a broad one that refers to systems that are merely *analogous* to machines, as in "market mechanism." The broad meaning does not impose any "a priori restrictions on the sort of allowable interactions which may take place between a mechanism's parts,"[107] and as such might help overcome unease about mechanistic metaphors in social science.

The realist model of causal explanation does not yield particular methodological prescriptions. It does not mean social scientists should avoid quantitative work, deductive theorizing, or increasing our predictive abilities. We should engage in such practices whenever the objects and domain of investigation warrant them. The primary significance of realism for causal theorizing is in cases where lawlike generalizations are not available, either because we are dealing with unique events or because the complexity or openness of the system defies generalization. In these cases the logical empiricist would have to give up on causal explanation; the realist would not. For the latter science is about the description of mechanisms anyway, not subsumption under regularities. The core of such description is "process-tracing," which in social science ultimately requires case studies and historical scholarship.[108] Some social scientists see realism as a philosophical justification for preferring case studies over other methods,[109] although case studies face the same problems of inference that confront other methods.[110] In my view the real lesson of realism in the realm of causal explanation is to encourage a pragmatic approach, with the methodological criterion being whatever helps us

---

[106] For discussions of causal mechanisms in social life see Stinchcombe (1991) and Hedstrom and Swedberg (1996).

[107] Glennan (1996: 51–52)

[108] See George (1979) and George and McKeown (1985).

[109] For example, Sayer (1984: 219–28).   [110] King, Keohane, and Verba (1994).

understand how the world works. Methods appropriate to answer one question may differ from those for another. Scientific realism corrects philosophies of science which say that all explanations must conform to a single model, but otherwise leaves science to scientists.

Constitutive theorizing

To the extent that causal explanations depend on describing causal mechanisms rather than subsuming events under laws, "[a]nswers to why-questions (that is, to requests for causal explanations) require answers to how- and what-questions."[111] Insofar as how- and what-questions are used to answer a why-question they are part of a causal explanation, but answering them can also be an end in itself. Some how-questions are straight-forwardly causal, like "how did World War II start?" This would be answered by a "genetic" explanation, a form of causal explanation that shows how a certain outcome came about.[112] However, other how-questions take the form of "*how-possible?*," like "how was World War II possible?," which is not a request for a causal explanation. And neither are "what-questions," like "what is sovereignty?" Rather than asking how or why a temporally prior X produced an independently existing Y, how-possible and what-questions are requests for explications of the structures that constitute X or Y in the first place.

Natural and social kinds can be constituted in two ways. One is by their *internal* structure. Water is constituted by the atomic structure H_2O; human beings are constituted by their genetic structures; doctors are constituted (in part) by the self-understandings that define the social kind known as "doctor"; states are constituted (in part) by organizational structures that give them a territorial monopoly on organized violence. In each case internal structures do not cause the properties associated with them, in the sense of being antecedent conditions for independently existing effects, but rather make those properties possible. When we account for the properties of natural and social kinds by reference to their internal structures we are engaged in "reductionism," which characterizes most of natural science and much of psychology.[113] In social science it finds expression

---

[111] Keat and Urry (1982: 31); cf. Foucault (1982).   [112] Cross (1991: 245).

[113] On reductionism in this sense see McMullin (1978) (cf. Waltz, 1979), and on its use in the natural and psychological sciences see Haugeland (1978) and Cummins (1983).

in the doctrine of atomism (a radical form of individualism), which tries to reduce society to the intrinsic properties of individuals (see chapter 4). One need not be an atomist, however, to acknowledge a role for the study of internal structures. All that is required is that an entity have an internal structure which helps account for its properties, which as I suggested above social kinds vary with respect to.

Kinds can also be constituted in a second, holist fashion by the *external* structures in which they are embedded. This might be true even of some natural kinds, but it is a difficult argument to make and I shall not do so here.[114] However, I argue in chapter 4 that there is a strong case for the proposition that social kinds often are constituted in important part by external, discursive structures. In some instances these structures place social kinds in relationships of conceptual necessity to other social kinds: masters are constituted by their relationship to slaves, professors by students, patrons by clients. In other instances external structures merely designate what social kinds are: "treaty violations" are constituted by a discourse that defines promises, "war" by a discourse that legitimates state violence, "terrorism" by a discourse that delegitimates non-state violence. In both instances the claim is not that external structures or discourses "cause" social kinds, in the sense of being antecedent conditions for a subsequent effect, but rather that what these kinds *are* is logically dependent on the specific external structure.

Within social theory there are various ways to characterize this dependency. Those with a Hegelian influence refer to discursive structures as "internal relations," relations to which the nature of the elements is internal.[115] Others, including two of the pioneers of the constructivist turn in IR, Kratochwil and Onuf, talk about it in terms of "speech act" theory, according to which speech acts do not describe independently existing phenomena, but define what they are.[116] My own thinking on this score has been most influenced by David Sylvan, who refers to "constitutive" relations.[117] But the point of these different terminologies is ultimately the same: that the properties of many social kinds do not exist apart from external conditions. This violates two assumptions of causal theorizing, namely that X and Y are independently existing and that one precedes the other in time.

---

[114] See Teller (1986).

[115] See Ollman (1971), Bhaskar (1979: 53–55) and Alker (1996: 184–206).

[116] Kratochwil (1989) and Onuf (1989).

[117] Majeski and Sylvan (1998); also see Smith (1995).

The "independent/dependent variable" talk that informs causal theorizing therefore makes no sense in constitutive theorizing.

Much of the work done in social science by interpretivists, critical theorists, and postmodernists deals primarily with constitutive questions, which creates misunderstanding when it is judged by the standards of causal questions. Given the role that ideas play in constituting social kinds, answering constitutive questions will require interpretive methods. This methodological difference from natural science is then thought to require an epistemological divorce from positivism. Positivists assume the only legitimate question that social scientists can ask is the causal question of "why?," while interpretivists think that the unique role of self-understandings in social life makes the epistemology and proper practice of social science fundamentally different from that of natural science.

In my view it is a mistake to treat the differences between causal and constitutive questions in zero-sum, epistemological terms. This is for three reasons. First, on a realist view of scientific explanation, answers to why-questions require answers to how- and what-questions, and so even positivists must engage in at least implicit constitutive analyses. Rational choice theory is a constitutive theory, insofar as it answers the question of "how is rational action constituted?"[118] Indeed, some of the most important theories in *natural* science are of this form: the double-helix model of DNA, the kinetic theory of heat.[119] Natural structures are just as amenable to constitutive theorizing as social ones. Second, and as I argued above, ideas and social structures can have causal effects, and as such the relevance of causal theorizing is not limited to natural science. Finally, constitutive theories must be judged against empirical evidence just like causal ones. Not all interpretations are equally valid, and so constitutive inquiry ultimately faces the same epistemological problem as causal inquiry: how to justify a claim about unobservables (whether constitutive rules or causal mechanisms) from what we can see? I agree with King, Keohane, and Verba, therefore, that there is no fundamental epistemological difference between Explanation and Understanding.

But there *are* significant analytical or methodological differences between causal and constitutive theorizing, which reflects the different kinds of questions that they answer. So even though I have framed

---

[118] See Rappaport (1995).   [119] Haugeland (1978: 216), Cummins (1983: 15).

the issue differently than Hollis and Smith, I agree with them that there are always "two stories to tell" in social inquiry.[120] These are not causal versus descriptive stories. King, Keohane, and Verba characterize constitutive theorizing as "descriptive inference," which they distinguish from "causal inference." Their treatment is accurate in an important way – constitutive theories have a large descriptive dimension – but it underplays the explanatory function of this type of theory. While they find the idea of non-causal explanation "confusing" (p. 75, footnote 1), at least some philosophers of science do not. In a discussion of the explanatory import of how-questions, Charles Cross endorses John Haugeland's definition of "morphological explanations," in which "an ability is explained through appeal to a specified structure and to specified abilities of whatever is so structured."[121] Cross cites the double-helix model of DNA, which is not a causal explanation. William Dray argued that the characteristic activity of historians is not explaining why an event occurred, but explaining *what* it was, which is done by classifying and synthesizing events under a concept, like revolution, hyper-inflation, or poverty trap.[122] Following Dray, Steven Rappaport has recently argued that many of the models developed by *economists* are "explanations-what" rather than "explanations-why."[123] And then there is Robert Cummins' useful distinction between "transition theories," which explain changes between events or states, and "property theories," which explain how things or processes are put together so as to have certain features.[124] Since causal relationships involve transitions from one state to another, property theories (which are static) cannot be causal theories, even if we can derive causal hypotheses from them. Like Rappaport, Cummins argues that property theories are often stated in the form of *models*, and like Cross he cites the double-helix, although his primary focus is the nature of explanation in psychology (which he says often takes the form of property theories). Coming from disparate sources, these arguments all suggest that theories which answer "what?" or "how-possible?" questions "explain" the world.

Whether or not one accepts that constitutive theories explain, however, let me press three concluding points. First, answering constitutive questions is an important end in itself, even if it is later

---

[120] See Wendt (1998).   [121] Cross (1991: 245), Haugeland (1978: 216).
[122] Dray (1959).   [123] Rappaport (1995).   [124] Cummins (1983).

tied in to a causal story. Partly this is because without good descriptions of how things are put together any explanations we propose will probably be wrong. In the case of natural kinds this may require nothing more profound than careful measurement of observable effects, but given that social kinds do not present themselves to the senses to the same degree, their description may require more conceptual analysis than many contemporary social scientists are accustomed to. In addition to providing a basis for causal explanations, moreover, constitutive theory is also valuable insofar as it shows that there are multiple ways to put a phenomenon together, some of which might be normatively preferable than others. Much critical IR scholarship is directed to precisely this end. Showing through historical or conceptual analysis that social kinds like sovereignty or the state can take different forms may open up desirable political possibilities that would otherwise be closed. For both reasons the bias of mainstream social science against "mere" description or history is unfortunate. Recognizing the distinctiveness and significance of constitutive questions will make for better all-round social science. If all observation is theory-laden, then constitutive theory gives us the lenses through which we see the world.

Second, constitutive theories are *theories*. They involve inferences from observable events to broader patterns, and inferences always involve a theoretical leap. This is true whether those inferences are purely inductive, generalizing from a sample of events, or abductive, positing underlying structures that account for those events. In neither case do data speak for themselves. In my view this also means that constitutive theories imply hypotheses about the world that can and should be tested. The holist claim that the causal powers of sovereign states are constituted in part by discursive structures that relate them to other states, for example, is a hypothesis about the nature of sovereign states that opposes the individualist hypothesis that the causal powers of sovereign states do not depend on other states. These hypotheses have different implications for the kinds of behavior we should observe in the world, and as such could be tested using publicly available evidence (though it may not be easy). Constitutive claims concern how social kinds are put together rather than the relation between independent and dependent variables, but they are no less "theoretical" for that.

Finally, and to summarize this section, to understand the difference that ideas and social structures make in international politics we need to recognize the existence of constitutive *effects*. Ideas or social structures have constitutive effects when they create phenomena – properties, powers, dispositions, meanings, etc. – that are conceptually or logically dependent on those ideas or structures, that exist only "in virtue of" them. The causal powers of the master do not exist apart from his relation to the slave; terrorism does not exist apart from a national security discourse that defines "terrorism." These effects satisfy the counterfactual requirement for causal explanations, but they are not causal because they violate the requirements of independent existence and temporal asymmetry. Ordinary language bears this out: we do not say that slaves "cause" masters, or that a security discourse "causes" terrorism. On the other hand, it is clear that the master–slave relation and security discourse are relevant to the construction of masters or terrorism, since without them there would not *be* masters or terrorism. Constitutive theories seek to "account for" these effects, even if not to "explain" them.

Toward a sociology of questions in international theory

Once we start thinking about explanations as answers to questions, it becomes clear that the distinction between causal and constitutive questions is not the only one that might be made. What seems like a simple request for a causal explanation can in fact be multiple questions calling for different answers. What was the "cause" of the Cold War? This depends on what is taken to be problematic: the fact that the conflict was cold rather than hot?; that it was with the Soviets rather than the English?; that it broke out when it did?; that it broke out at all? Philosophers of science who have explored this kind of problem argue that what counts as an explanation is relative to an interrogatory *context*.[125] The significance of this "explanatory relativity"[126] is clearest when dealing with the differences between why-, how-, and what-questions, but as the Cold War example shows, even within a single class of question the same phenomenon can be given different explanations depending on what exactly we are asking.[127]

I want to extract from the phenomenon of explanatory relativity three concluding points that might be of relevance to IR scholars.

---

[125] See van Fraassen (1980), Cross (1991).   [126] Garfinkel (1981).

[127] See Suganami (1990) for a good illustration in IR of how attention to the nature of questions can illuminate explanatory problems, in this case with respect to war.

First, the criteria for adequate knowledge depend on the question we have asked and the quality of evidence that can be brought to bear on it. All scientific theories must meet the minimum criterion of being in principle falsifiable on the basis of publicly available evidence, and social scientists should approach their knowledge claims with that in mind. Beyond this, however, we should be tolerant of the different standards of inference needed to do research in different areas. Causal theories in chemistry have to meet different standards than those in geology, and in geology different than sociology. Similarly, constitutive theories must be evaluated in different terms than causal ones. Constitutive theorists should attend more often than they have to the issue of what would count against their claims, but the nature of that evidence will vary with the claim in question.

Second, we should be sensitive to the politics of questions. Knowledge is always for some one or some purpose, and thus the form that questions take is a key factor in the uses to which their answers can be put. Especially important in this respect is what is taken to be problematic. We cannot problematize everything at once, but we should be aware that in not problematizing something we are temporarily naturalizing or reifying it, and the resulting knowledge may not be of much use in transforming it.[128] This is particularly significant given that typically it is not individual scientists who naturalize things but whole communities of them, who may be organized, often for decades, around certain uncontested assumptions.

Finally, we should encourage scholars to ask new questions. Problematizing the things that communities have naturalized is at least as important a function of science as finding the right answers. From this perspective the post-structural intervention in IR theory, beginning with Richard Ashley's work in the early 1980s, has been particularly important. One of my main goals in this chapter has been to challenge the epistemological skepticism that underlies post-structuralism, but the substantive theory that I develop in the following chapters is nevertheless indebted to it. Whatever else one might think about postmodernism, it is its nature to interrogate all aspects of social life as well as the status of those who claim to know them. Asking embarrassing questions embodies the reflexive, self-critical mindset of the Enlightenment at its best.

---

[128] Fay (1975); Cox (1986).

Conclusion

The discipline of International Relations today is polarized into incompatible epistemological standpoints, a positivist majority arguing that social science gives us privileged access to reality, a significant post-positivist minority arguing that it does not. This Third Debate will not be much of a "debate" if its protagonists are not speaking to each other, but that is where things largely stand. In this chapter I have tried to construct a via media between the two camps. Rather than an eclectic or split-the-difference approach, which given the different theories of reference involved cannot succeed, my strategy has been to try to change the terms of the discussion. I have suggested that since both sides are tacit realists in their substantive research, epistemological issues are relatively uninteresting. The debate should be about what the international world is made of – ontology – not how we can know it.

Epistemologically I have sided with positivists. Social science is an epistemically privileged discourse that gives us knowledge, albeit always fallible, about the world out there. Poetry, literature, and other humanistic disciplines tell us much about the human condition, but they are not designed to explain global war or Third World poverty, and as such if we want to solve those problems our best hope, slim as it may be, is social science. Post-positivists have reminded us that what we see out there is conditioned by how we see it, and also emphasized the importance of constitutive and interpretive processes in social life. However, these contributions do not mean that all theories are equally valid, that we do not have to justify them in light of empirical evidence, or that causal processes do not occur in society. A pluralistic approach to social science can absorb most of the post-positivist critique. Of course not all positivists are methodological pluralists, particularly those who think that scientific practice must conform to the logical empiricist reconstruction of scientific explanation. But those positivists who are question- rather than method-driven will probably have fewer quarrels with this chapter than will post-positivists.

This should be kept in perspective, however, since on ontology – which is to my mind the more important issue – I will side in subsequent chapters with post-positivists. Like them, I believe that social life is "ideas all the way down" (or almost anyway; chapter 3), and that deep, unobservable structures constitute agents and rules of interaction (chapter 4), both of which are at odds with mainstream IR theory. When it comes to what there is in the world post-positivists will probably have fewer quarrels with the rest of this book than positivists.

Scientific realism plays an essential role in finding this via media between positivist epistemology and post-positivist ontology. Despite their polemics against each other, empiricists and postmodernists are united by a shared epistemological anxiety about the relationship between theory and reality, the former doubting that we can know unobservable entities, the latter that we can know reality at all. The "difference that realism makes"[129] is to diffuse these anxieties by turning our attention to ontology. In one sense this changes nothing, since everyone can go about their business as before: empiricists looking for behavioral laws, rationalists building deductive theories, process tracers doing case studies, critical theorists thinking about deep social structures, postmoderns doing constitutive theory. But the point is that *everyone* gets to do what they do: from a realist stance epistemology cannot legislate scientific practice.

Realism does not entail any particular ontology, any particular methods, or any particular theory of society or, for that matter, of world politics. But insofar as it blocks a priori arguments against engaging in certain types of work, realism is a condition of possibility for the argument in the rest of this book. Beyond that realism is not relevant to the issues that divide IR theories. We should not expect philosophers of science to explain world politics.

---

[129] Shapiro and Wendt (1992).

3   "Ideas all the way down?": on the constitution of power and interest

In post-war scholarship the starting point for most theorizing about international politics has been power and national interest, with power understood ultimately as military capability and interest as an egoistic desire for power, security, or wealth. This is usually identified with a Realist approach to the subject. While conceding the importance of power and interest, in the early 1980s Neoliberals[1] began to argue that international institutions also play a significant role in international politics. Neorealists and Neoliberals disagree about their relative weight, but they would probably agree that together the three factors explain most of the variance in international outcomes. Moreover, although adherents of neither approach tend to call themselves "materialists," both Neorealists and Neoliberals routinely refer to power and interest, and sometimes even institutions, as "material" factors. Against this materialist consensus a number of IR scholars today are emphasizing a fourth factor, "ideas." This focus goes back at least to Snyder, Bruck, and Sapin,[2] who pioneered a tradition of cognitivist research on the role of belief systems and perceptions in foreign policy decision-making. But it has really taken off in the last decade with multiple lines of theorizing, both mainstream and critical, about identity, ideology, discourse, culture, and, simply, ideas. In other words, materialist assumptions are no longer unproblematic in IR theory, and materialist scholars are facing a resurgent idealism that puts the question of "what difference do ideas make?" clearly on the table.

There are two ways to approach this question, and thus two ways to

---

[1] Though they were only called this after the fact.
[2] Snyder, Bruck, and Sapin (1954).

frame the idealism–materialism debate. The dominant approach in mainstream political science is to treat ideas in causal terms as a (typically intervening) "variable" that explains some proportion of behavior beyond the effects of power, interest, and institutions alone. In an influential volume on ideas and foreign policy, for example, editors Judith Goldstein and Robert Keohane define the null hypothesis for the proposition that ideas matter as: "variation in policy across countries, or over time, is entirely accounted for by changes in factors *other than* ideas," by which they mean principally power and interest.[3] And in a recent symposium on the role of ideas in American politics, Karen Orren and Theda Skocpol unproblematically juxtapose ideas to institutions as rival causes, and Morris Fiorina does the same with ideas and interests.[4] In both collections power, interests, and even institutions are treated as idea-free baselines against which the role of ideas is judged.

This causal framing of the materialism–idealism debate gets at important effects. In one sense identity, ideology, and culture *are* distinct from power and interests, and *do* play a causal role in social life.[5] To explain world politics by reference to the hegemony of liberal ideology *is* different than doing so by reference to state interests. The superstructure *is* different than the base. As such, a causal approach is not "wrong." The problem rather is that it stacks the deck against idealists, largely conceding to materialists the study of war and conflict which seem particularly amenable to power and interest explanations. And theories that treat ideas as intervening or superstructural variables will always be vulnerable to the charge that they are derived from theories that emphasize the base variables of power and interest, merely mopping up unexplained variance.[6] In my view Neoliberals nevertheless have demonstrated amply the proposition that ideas and institutions are at least relatively autonomous determinants of international life,[7] which poses an important challenge to "vulgar" materialisms.

In this chapter I focus on a second way to frame the debate, which results in a deeper challenge to materialism. The causal approach

---

[3] Goldstein and Keohane (1993: 6).

[4] Orren (1995), Skocpol (1995), Fiorina (1995). Of the contributors to the symposium, only Rogers Smith (1995) raises questions about these dualisms, taking a line similar to the one I shall take below.

[5] Yee (1996).   [6] Krasner (1983a), Mearsheimer (1994/1995).

[7] See especially Keohane (1984) and Baldwin, ed. (1993).

favored by Neoliberals assumes that ideas matter only to the extent that they have effects beyond effects of power, interest, and institutions. This second, social constructivist approach inquires into the extent to which ideas *constitute* those ostensibly "material" causes in the first place. To the extent that material causes are *made* of ideas we will not get a full understanding of how ideas matter by treating them as variables distinct from other causes. On this view explanation by reference to power, interests, or institutions cannot be what defines "materialism" at all. Rather, what makes a theory materialist is that it accounts for the effects of power, interests, or institutions by reference to "brute" material forces – things which exist and have certain causal powers independent of ideas, like human nature, the physical environment, and, perhaps, technological artifacts. The constitutive debate between materialists and idealists is not about the relative contribution of ideas versus power and interest to social life. The debate is about the relative contribution of brute material forces to power and interest explanations. Materialists cannot claim power and interest as "their" variables; it all depends on how the latter are constituted.

Note that this interpretation of materialism conflicts with conventional usage, which owes much to Marxism.[8] Marxism defines the material base as the mode of production, and locates ideology, culture, and other ideational factors in a non-material superstructure. "Materialism" thereby becomes identified with explanations by reference to economic factors. This is easily extended to the military factors of concern to Realists – modes of destruction are as basic as modes of production. Either way, ideational factors are relegated a priori to non-economic, non-military considerations. Building on an argument of Douglas Porpora,[9] I am suggesting that this way of thinking about materialism and idealism is problematic. The problem is that Marxism defines the mode of production not only in terms of forces but also in terms of *relations* of production. Forces of production ("tools") are plausible candidates for being brute material forces. But relations of production are thoroughly ideational phenomena, namely institutions or rules – which are ultimately shared ideas – that constitute property and exchange relationships, who works for whom, class powers and

[8] See Little (1991: 114–135).
[9] Porpora (1993), who in turn draws on Rubinstein (1981). For different framings of the idealism–materialism issue see Mann (1979) and Adler and Borys (1993).

interests, and so on. The fact that relations of production are ideational means that capitalism is mostly a *cultural* form, not material, and as such Marxism's "material base" actually is shot through and through with ideas. Apart from the physical bodies of workers and capitalists, the only really material things about a capitalist economy are the forces of production. Indeed, since socialism uses identical forces of production, what constitutes one economy as capitalist and the other as socialist are in fact the relations of production. Rather than define materialism as a focus on the mode of production or destruction, therefore, it makes more sense to define it in terms of a particular hypothesis about these cultural forms. The materialist hypothesis is that the content of cultural forms largely can be explained by the characteristics of brute material forces, whether human nature (as in sociobiology) or technology (as in technological determinism).[10] Whatever cannot be explained in this way would then belong to an idealist account.

Restricting the meaning of materialism in this way is a key rhetorical move in this chapter, which is justified by the fact that the traditional framing of the debate stacks the deck against idealism. Part of what makes the traditional framing attractive is a tendency to conflate "objective" with "material." But the fact that relations of production and destruction consist of shared ideas does not change the fact that they confront actors as objective social facts with real, objective "material" effects. Inequality and exploitation still exist, even if they are constituted by ideas. Indeed, unlike the causal approach to the effect of ideas, which concedes power and interest to materialists but tries to show that they matter less than materialists think, the constitutive approach implies no such claim. At the end of this chapter power and interest will matter just as much as they did before. This raises the question of what is gained by redescribing them in ideational terms? Is this anything more than a philosophical point? Answering in the affirmative is the burden of my argument, but my claim is that the extent to which the "material base" is constituted by ideas is an important question that has been largely ignored in mainstream IR, and one that bears on the transformative potentials of the international system.

In sum, the goal of this chapter is to show that much of the apparent explanatory power of ostensibly "materialist" explanations is actually

---

[10] Bimber (1994) is very good on the latter.

constituted by suppressed constructivist assumptions about the content and distribution of ideas. The central thesis is that the meaning of power and the content of interests are largely a function of ideas. As such only after the ideational conditions of possibility for power and interest explanations have been exposed and stripped out can we assess the effects of materiality *as such*. In this chapter I focus on the constitution of power and interest only. Institutions are sometimes also seen as material (as in Orren and Skocpol's opposition of institutions to ideas noted above), but this makes little sense once we recognize that objectivity is not exhausted by materiality. Institutions are made of norms and rules, which are ideational phenomena – "shared mental models"[11] – and as such, despite being objective social facts, they are firmly on the idealist side of the equation. I defer analysis of institutions to chapter 4 instead.

The argument of the chapter proceeds in two main stages. In the first section I show that the explanatory power of Waltz's materialist theory of structure, the explicit elements of which are anarchy and the distribution of material capabilities, rests on implicit assumptions about the distribution of interests. In the second section I argue that these interests are in turn constituted largely by ideas. Here I play off rational choice theory, which treats ideas only as a means for realizing exogenous interests and thereby supports the presumption that interests are material. I agree that some ideas play such a role, but others constitute interests. In both sections I argue that brute material forces have some effects on the constitution of power and interest, and as such my thesis is not ideas *all* the way down (hence the question mark in the chapter title). My defense of this "rump" materialism is rooted in scientific realism's naturalistic approach to society, described in chapter 2. Rump materialism is an important concession to Political Realism, but as we will see it still leaves most of the action to non-Realists. The two sections together suggest that the most fundamental factor in international politics is the "distribution of ideas" in the system, the structure of which I take up in subsequent chapters.

The constitution of power by interest

The proposition that the nature of international politics is shaped by power relations invariably is listed as one of the defining character-

---

[11] Denzau and North (1994).

istics of Realism.[12] This cannot be a *uniquely* Realist claim, however, since then every student of international politics would be a Realist. Neoliberals think power is important, Marxists think power is important, postmodernists even think it is everywhere. The fact that almost everyone today agrees with this basic "Realist" contention might be taken as a measure of Realism's success in getting us to be realistic about the world, but that seems counter-productive. It debases the coinage of Realist theory to assimilate otherwise contradictory views under a single Realist rubric. Realism becomes meaningless or trivial. Better instead to differentiate theories according to *how power is constituted*. From this perspective, the distinctively Realist claim is the materialist hypothesis that the effects of power are constituted primarily by brute material forces. The rival idealist hypothesis is that power is constituted primarily by ideas and cultural contexts.

One of the important virtues of the dominant form of contemporary Realism, Neorealism, is that it is clear (if not entirely explicit) about its materialism. In conceptualizing international structure Waltz makes the distribution of material capabilities the key variable and specifically rejects more social conceptualizations of structure. This clarity distinguishes Neo- from Classical Realism and permits a clear comparison with idealist views. Waltz's emphasis on material capabilities is of course not unprecedented in Realism. Morton Kaplan was among the first to define system structure in terms of the "polarity" of the distribution of power, and Robert Gilpin has been an important exponent of the idea that international systems tend to be dominated by a materially hegemonic Great Power, the rise and fall of which drives systemic evolution.[13] But it is Waltz who has developed the most systematic conceptualization of international material structure, and is most identified with Neorealism. For that reason I focus on his theory below, although any theory which claims that the effects of power are constituted primarily by brute material forces will be vulnerable to the ensuing argument.

The discussion proceeds in three steps. I first present Waltz's *explicit* model of structure. Although my primary concern here is with the role of the distribution of material power under anarchy, with a view toward possible non-IR readers I take this opportunity to summarize other elements of his theory (with some commentary), which can be recalled in later chapters as they become relevant. I then argue that

---

[12] For example, Keohane (1986b: 165).   [13] Kaplan (1957), Gilpin (1981).

Waltz's explicit model can only explain what it purports to explain by relying on an *implicit* model of the "distribution of interests." Insofar as interests are themselves material this argument does not violate the spirit of Neorealism, and can be seen as a friendly amendment to the theory. On the other hand, to argue there is a distribution of interests also serves a subversive purpose, since later in the chapter I argue that interests are ideas. Finally, having shown that Waltz's hypotheses about material power depend on assumptions about interests/ideas, I remind the reader of my scientific realist premises by defending the rump materialist view that material capabilities do have *some* intrinsic causal powers. It is the relationship of these to interests (and shared ideas or culture) that determine the quality of international life.

Waltz's explicit model: anarchy and the distribution of power

In order to generate predictions a structural theory must make assumptions about the nature of structure, the motivations of agents, and the character of the process that connects them. This is true of all structural theories and Neorealism is no different.

Waltz conceptualizes the nature of structure along three dimensions.[14] *Ordering principles* refer to the principles by which the elements of structure are organized, and in particular whether they stand in relations of equality or super- and subordination. In domestic political systems units are organized hierarchically, with some entitled to command and others obliged to obey. In the contemporary international system the units (states) are sovereign equals, and the ordering principle is therefore anarchic. In the Neorealist view anarchy is a constant, having defined international politics for hundreds if not thousands of years. So even though it is thought to have certain consequences it does not explain variation in outcomes.

The character of the units refers to the functions performed by the system's elements. In domestic political systems units perform different functions; some deal with defense, others with welfare, still others with economic growth. In the international system, states all perform the same functions (internal order, external defense) and so are "like units." States vary in their capabilities and other attributes, but not functionally. Waltz says that units will be homogeneous as long as the system is anarchic (see below), and so this dimension of structure

---

[14] Waltz (1979: 79–101).

effectively drops out of his theory, although others have tried to reinstate it by arguing that anarchy is compatible with functional differentiation.[15]

Finally, *the distribution of capabilities* refers to the extent to which material power resources (especially economic and military) are concentrated in the system, with those states having significantly disproportionate shares known as poles. Since anarchy is a constant and functional differentiation has dropped out, it is this dimension which constitutes variation in international structure and thereby generates varying outcomes. Although the distribution of capabilities is an aggregate of unit-level attributes, it is a property of the system as a whole with effects that cannot be reduced to the unit-level.[16] Also noteworthy here is Waltz's argument that attributes of states which do not concern material capability, like ideology or bellicosity, as well as the quality of relations between states, like amity or enmity, should *not* be included in the definition of structure.[17] Drawing an analogy to markets, Waltz's argument is that just as what matters in assessing the structure of a market is only the number and size of firms, so in international politics what matters is only the number and power of states. It is this step in the argument which ultimately makes Waltz's theory of structure materialist.

Waltz concentrates his energy on elaborating this theory of structure and its implications, in part because he is critical of "reductionist" theories of international politics that emphasize domestic politics, the motivations of state agents, or the character of the interaction process among states. While he does not give unit-level variables a significant place in his theory, however, he too makes explicit assumptions about agents and process, without which his theory would not work.

An important goal of Waltz's argument is to show that international structure has certain effects even if states do not intend them. The actual intentions of states do not particularly concern him. His strategy here parallels that of neoclassical economists, who try to avoid making substantial assumptions about actors' psychology by explaining varying outcomes through reference to changing prices in the environment rather than changing preferences.[18] Like economists, however, Waltz has to make *some* assumptions about motivations,

---

[15] Ruggie (1983a), Buzan, Jones, and Little (1993).   [16] Waltz (1979: 97–98).
[17] Ibid.: 98–99.   [18] See especially Stigler and Becker (1977).

since without them his actors would be inert and there would be no movement in the system.[19] He makes two. One is that states are concerned first and foremost with security, since the pursuit of other goals only makes sense once survival is assured.[20] This opposes the view of many Classical Realists that states maximize power as an end in itself. The assumption of security-seeking says nothing about states' relationships toward each other as they think about their security, however, and as such is logically compatible with a collective rather than competitive security system. Waltz does not make the point himself, but he makes a second motivational assumption which rules that possibility out: that states are egoistic or "self-regarding."[21] Combine this assumption with anarchy, and "[s]tates [will] not enjoy even an imperfect guarantee of their own security unless they set out to provide it for themselves,"[22] which means the international system is by definition a "self-help" system.

Waltz's discussion of the process through which state agents and system structures relate is even more marginal in the text than his treatment of state motivations. In fact, the term "process" plays a largely pejorative role in Neorealist discourse because it seems to oppose "structural" theorizing. Waltz argues that structure relates to agents by affecting their behavior "indirectly," through two processes, competition and socialization.[23] However, the centrality of these processes to his theory raises doubts that international structure can be thought of in strict materialist terms, and Waltz must render considerably narrow conceptualizations of both, making them as mechanistic and unsocial as possible.

Competition selects outcomes according to their consequences. Actors whose behavior conforms with the incentives in a structure will prosper, whether or not they intend to do so, while others will not. Although Waltz's preferred analogy is to micro-economics, the selection metaphor also suggests an analogy to sociobiology, which aspires quite explicitly to a materialist analysis of social life.[24] The analogy is not perfect, since there is some ambiguity about whether the object of selection in Waltz's model is behavior or the actors

---

[19] On the necessity for any structural theory to make assumptions about motivation see Emmett (1976).
[20] Waltz (1979: 126).   [21] Ibid.: 91.   [22] Waltz (1959: 201).
[23] Waltz (1979: 74–77).
[24] On the relationship between economics and sociobiology see Hirshleifer (1978), and Witt (1985).

themselves.[25] Only the second is compatible with the meaning of selection in Darwinian theory. While Waltz does argue that competition helps produce like units, he concentrates mostly on selection of behavior. This is a problem for sociobiologists because behavioral tendencies can be selected through social learning, a "Lamarckian" or cultural mechanism at odds with the Darwinian's materialist emphasis on genetic inheritance.[26] I address these problems in chapter 7. What matters here is that the selection metaphor is more compatible with a materialist view of structure if it is limited to selection of units rather than selection of behavior.

This is even more true of socialization. At first glance the fact that Waltz discusses socialization at all is surprising. There is little that is "social" about his theory, least of all his conceptualization of what states are presumably being socialized *to*, namely "structure." Materialists in economics and sociobiology are not known for emphasizing socialization; its home is with idealists in sociology and social psychology. The anomaly disappears, however, when we consider the way in which Waltz treats the concept.

As with selection, socialization can have two distinct objects, behavior and attributes or properties. While acknowledging both possibilities,[27] Waltz focuses almost entirely on behavior. This is not surprising: it allows him to acknowledge the existence of norms and rules, which is necessary for any meaningful theory of socialization, but by treating them as patterns of behavior rather than as shared ideas he does not have to give up materialism.[28] Yet this behavioralism comes at a cost. Reducing norms and rules to patterned behavior makes it difficult to distinguish behavior that is norm-governed from behavior which is not, and this undermines the point of talking about norms, rules, and thus socialization in the first place. Dogs engage in patterned behavior, but we do not call it norm-governed nor its result a society. Why do so with the patterned behavior of states? Calling the production of behavioral conformity "socialization" says little if the structure that actors are being socialized *to* has no "social" content. Waltz does refer at least once to the international system as a "society,"[29] but if his failure to invoke Bull's

---

[25] McKeown (1986: 53).   [26] Boyd and Richerson (1985).

[27] Waltz (1979: 76).

[28] It also raises some interesting questions about the relationship between materialism and behavioral IR scholarship that I cannot explore here.

[29] Waltz (1986: 326).

distinction between system and society is any indication, he does not see this as significant for the nature of structure. Indeed, a key goal of Neorealist scholarship over the past two decades has been to show that social factors are *not* important in world politics, which may account for the fact that most Neorealists avoid talk of socialization altogether.[30]

This avoidance becomes even more understandable if we consider the possibility of a socialization process affecting the properties of states and not just their behavior. There are two types of attributes potentially at stake, material and ideational. To argue that socialization affects the former would be to argue that material structure is shaped by process, which Neorealism rejects. And to argue that it affects ideational attributes raises the question of what kind of structure those ideas would constitute in the aggregate if not a *social* structure, defined not merely as patterned behavior but as shared understandings. Neorealism also rejects this. On both scores, in other words, the possibility that socialization might change state properties would challenge a purely materialist view of structure. Waltz is forced to limit socialization to behavioral conditioning, but that gives him a second mechanism by which structure affects outcomes, without requiring him to conceptualize structure in social terms. This is not to deny that socialization may sometimes change only behavior, but if this is *all* it can do then the concept loses much of its significance.

Waltz's theory suggests at least four hypotheses, which subsequent Neorealist scholarship has clustered around. Perhaps the most important is that states will tend to balance each other's power.[31] In an anarchy there is no Leviathan that states can count on for security, nor can they count on each other unless it is in others' self-interest. In such a world the best way to ensure survival is to deter aggression by matching the capabilities of one's rivals, either by building up one's own power ("internal" balancing) or, if this is not enough, by recruiting allies ("external" balancing).

Another prediction is that states will tend to be concerned more with relative than absolute gains, and will therefore find it difficult to cooperate.[32] Even in domestic politics collective action is difficult in the absence of coercion or selective incentives because of the problem of free riding. However, in an anarchy actors must also worry that

[30] Cf. Ikenberry and Kupchan (1990). [31] Waltz (1979: 102–128).
[32] See especially Grieco (1988, 1990).

others will gain more from cooperation than they do, since those relative gains might be turned later on into military advantage. The fear of relative loss may make no cooperation preferable to some.

A third hypothesis is that states will tend to become "like units." There is some ambiguity in Waltz's discussion here, since he argues that international systems are created by the co-action of units that are *already* functionally equivalent and self-regarding, which would seem to suggest that their similarity cannot be effects of the system. However, it is not difficult to modify Waltz's presentation in light of a Darwinian perspective, such that in an anarchic environment, actors which lack a capacity for organized violence will tend to "die out" in the competition with actors which do have that capacity, i.e. states. (Whether such an argument can actually explain the evolution of the international system is another matter.)[33]

Finally, Waltz argues that bipolar systems have intrinsic advantages over multipolar ones.[34] In a bipolar world the important states are less likely to miscalculate their relative power position because there is less uncertainty about potential threats, and so are less likely to initiate wars by mistake. The poles will also be more self-sufficient, which reduces their vulnerability to the whims of others. And two poles will find it easier to cooperate in managing the world's common problems than will many. These advantages do not mean bipolarity will tend to replace multipolarity over time, since the distribution of power is driven largely by unit-level factors that have little to do with international structure,[35] but they do sound an important cautionary note about the celebration surrounding the end of the Cold War and collapse of the Soviet Union.[36]

Waltz's implicit model: the distribution of interests

On the surface it looks as if most of the explanatory work in Neorealism is done by anarchy and the distribution of power. Anarchies seem to be inherently competitive systems the logic of which states ignore at their peril, and the number and size of major powers seem to be the key factors for states when considering threats to their security. Yet if we look deeper it becomes apparent that much of the work is in fact being done by factors only implicit in the model.

---

[33] See Spruyt (1994) and chapter 7 below. [34] Waltz (1979: 161–210).
[35] See Gilpin (1981). [36] Mearsheimer (1990a, b).

There are two ways to develop such an argument. For now I focus on the distribution of interests in the system, a level of ideational structure that is dealt with by both Neoliberals and constructivists. Drawing on work carried out independently by Andrew Moravcsik, Randall Schweller, and Arthur Stein, as well as on my own previous efforts to conceptualize the role of the "structure of identity and interest" in international politics, I argue that Waltz's conclusions depend on the "distribution of interests" (the phrase is Stein's) in the system.[37] Note that this does not call Realism into question as long as those interests are in turn constituted by material forces. Later in this chapter I argue that interests are in fact ideas, which does problematize Realism.

The other way to make the argument would be to identify *cultural* formations at the systemic level – shared ideas making up norms, institutions, threat-systems, and so on – that constitute the meaning of the distribution of power, either by constituting states' perceptions of that distribution or by constituting their identities and interests. That shared ideas play such a role is of course a central thesis of this book, and throughout this chapter the reader should keep in mind that "'culture" lurks just behind "interest." In chapters 4 and 6 I discuss the role and effects of system-level cultural structures and relate them to the interest-constituting ideas discussed in this chapter.

The implicit role of the distribution of interests in Waltz's theory can be seen if we vary his two assumptions that states are egoists who are motivated primarily by security. Consider first the possibility that security is *not* states' top priority, which has been raised by Schweller. There is no dispute that states want to *survive*; this much is trivially true. By "security-seeking" Waltz means something more: that states want to preserve what they already have rather than try to get more, for example by conquering other states or changing the rules of the system. This does not follow from wanting to survive. After all, what if one can survive *and* conquer others? Or what if one believes the only way *to* survive is by doing so? Schweller argues that by assuming that states are security-seeking Waltz is tacitly assuming they are satisfied or "status quo" powers. For status quo states the accumulation of power is a means rather than an end, which will stop when security needs are met. An alternative assumption would be that states are "revisionists," out to grab territory, conquer each other, or change the rules of the system. For these states no amount of power is

---

[37] Moravcsik (1997), Schweller (1993, 1994), Stein (1990), and Wendt (1992).

too much, its accumulation is more an end in itself. This was an important theme for Classical Realists like Hans Morgenthau, who thought that human nature contained a will to power or "animus dominandi" that provided a constant well-spring for revisionism.[38] Waltz wants to get away from such a dubious psychology, but rather than leave psychology behind he simply substitutes a different one. Morgenthau's states are by nature aggressive and opportunistic, Waltz's defensive and cautious.[39]

Assumptions about motivation are necessary even in the most structural of theories, and so pointing out that Waltz makes them is not a criticism. The criticism is that he does not make clear that his conclusions about the effects of anarchy and the distribution of power *depend* on those assumptions. An anarchy of status quo powers will be a relatively stable world in which states generally respect each other's territorial property rights and are not looking for a fight. Live and let live will be the operative rule. Even weak states will thrive in such an environment because others do not want to conquer them, and as a result states will have a low overall "death rate."[40] Status quo states may still get into security dilemmas,[41] in which uncertainty about others' intentions causes arms races that sometimes lead to war, but this is the exception rather than the norm. In other words, states with status quo interests constitute one *kind* of anarchy. Compare this to an anarchy constituted by states with revisionist interests. In this world states will try to conquer each other, territorial property rights will not be recognized, and weak states will have a high death rate. Rather than balance, revisionists will "bandwagon" in aggressive coalitions that maximize their chances of changing the system.[42] Status quo states may deter them, but in general an anarchy of revisionist states will be much less stable than an anarchy of status quo states. As states in the two systems look out on the world, therefore, the *meaning* that anarchy and the distribution of capabilities have for them will be quite different.

Now vary Waltz's other motivational assumption, that states are egoists about their security. We all sometimes do things that have no instrumental benefit for ourselves: giving to charity, tipping a waiter

---

[38] Morgenthau (1946: 192).

[39] This difference underlies the contemporary debate between "offensive" and "defensive" Realists; see, for example, Zakaria (1998: 18–41).

[40] Waltz (1979: 137).　　[41] Herz (1950), Jervis (1978); cf. Schweller (1996).

[42] Schweller (1994).

in a foreign city, helping a stranger, voting in elections, even sacrificing our lives in war. These actions are usually situation-specific and as such do not imply that we are always or intrinsically altruistic. However, they do involve some degree of identification with the welfare of others, which cannot be explained by any non-tautological concept of self-interest.[43] What is needed is a way to think about collective identity. This might seem irrelevant to international politics, since states are hardly known for their altruism, although I argue later that states have much more collective identity than is usually thought. But in order to even raise the question, we need to first see that such a motivation is logically possible, and that it implies a different logic of anarchy.

Specifically, in an international system where states possess substantial collective identity, it is unlikely that they will feel their security depends on balancing each other's military power. As Stephen Walt argues, states balance against threats not power, and as long as states are confident that others identify with their security they will not see each other as military threats.[44] Admittedly such confidence is hard to come by, but it is possible. It seems doubtful that Canada is much worried these days about American threats to its security, or Britain about French threats. Instead of balancing, states that have achieved this level of mutual identification are more likely to secure themselves by observing the rule of law in settling their disputes, and by practicing collective security when threatened from outside, which is a kind of bandwagoning based on the principle of "all for one, one for all." This is not a self-help system in any interesting sense, since the self has become the collective.[45]

None of this is to deny that modern states are status quo egoists. Indeed, they might be mostly just that. Nor is it to argue that the logic of anarchy, and the distribution of interests that constitutes it, can be changed (though I later argue that it sometimes can). The claim is only that the effects of anarchy and material structure depend on what states *want*.[46] The logic of anarchy among revisionist states takes the form of a fight to the death; among status quo states, arms racing and some brawls; among collectivist states, perhaps heated but ultimately non-violent arguments about burden sharing. Game theory teaches us

---

[43] See Jencks (1990) and chapter 5, pp. 238–243.   [44] Walt (1987).

[45] Although this collectivism may be specific to military security, self-help might still rule in other issue-areas.

[46] Moravcsik (1997).

the same lesson: the configuration of preferences drives outcomes. The distribution of power matters, but *how* it matters, the *meaning* it has for actors, depends on what game they are playing. Bipolarity among friends is one thing, among enemies quite another. The one might be an "Assurance Game," the other "Deadlock."

It is important to note that this discussion of interests does not compromise the "systemic" nature of the argument. This is an argument about the distribution of interests in the system, not about the foreign policy preferences and choices of individual states. Different distributions of interests in populations[47] of states will generate different logics of anarchy. A collectivist in a system of revisionists is likely to do poorly, but so will a revisionist in one of collectivists. It is true that the distribution of interests is made up of unit-level properties, but so is the distribution of material capabilities. Both are systemic phenomena because their effects cannot be reduced to the unit-level. In sum, Waltz has done more than make an assumption about the motivations of individual states, who then interact with an independently existing material structure. He has made an assumption about the distribution of interests in the system as a whole, and in so doing he has added to his theory of structure two things which he says do not belong there: non-capability attributes (egoistic motivations), and the quality of relations among units (self-help). He has in other words made an implicit assumption about the *social* structure of international politics (leaving aside for now whether it has a material or ideational basis). This does not make his theory of structure wrong, just underspecified. Making the distribution of interests an explicit dimension of structure would take care of the problem.

Even if they might accept the distribution of interests as an important systemic phenomenon, however, Neorealists might argue that it can be derived from other elements of Waltz's model and so does not require independent analysis. The reason has to do with the problem of uncertainty about other states' intentions. People can never be 100 per cent certain about each other's intentions because they cannot read minds and minds can always change. This "Problem of Other Minds"[48] is particularly acute for states because of the relatively low level of institutionalization in the international system,

---

[47] "Population" is plural here because the international system may contain relatively autonomous sub-systems or "security complexes" (Buzan, 1991), with their own distributions of interests and logics of anarchy.

[48] Hollis and Smith (1990: 171–176).

which means that states have even less information to go on than actors do in domestic politics, and because of the danger of being wrong in their assessments, which could be fatal. In such a world it might be argued that prudent states will assume the worst about others' intentions, which means basing their interests on the possibilities inherent in the distribution of capabilities, rather than on the probabilities that others might be benign.[49] On this argument, in other words, what states want will be based on worst-case assumptions about the distribution of power. This already figures in Waltz's model and so the distribution of interests would drop out.

This argument has the form of a "self-fulfilling prophecy," and I will argue in chapter 4 that culture is a self-fulfilling prophecy.[50] Actors act on the basis of beliefs they have about their environment and others, which tends to reproduce those beliefs. The self-fulfilling prophecy idea can explain a great deal about the production and reproduction of social life.

However, the fact that cultures tend to be stable or sticky cannot do the work here of eliminating an independent structural role for the distribution of interests, because history also matters. If states really did know nothing about each other's minds, and if they really would get killed by a single mistaken inference, then it may be rational to assume the worst and focus only on the distribution of capabilities. Such conditions sometimes occur, as in "First Encounters" between alien peoples, and as a thought-experiment they are useful. But in real world international politics they are not the norm. Contemporary states have been interacting for dozens, even hundreds of years, during which they have accumulated considerable knowledge about each other's interests. They know something about each other's grievances and ambitions, and thus about whether they are status quo or revisionist states. They know something about each other's styles of dispute resolution. And they even know something about the conditions under which these conditions might change. None of this knowledge is perfect or complete, but neither is it wholly unreliable or irrelevant. Part of what makes it reliable is experience: over the course of their interactions states have made policies on the basis of inferences about each other's intentions (pessimistic or optimistic), which were then tested and revised against the reality of what those intentions really were. Through this process of interacting with reality,

---

[49] On the consequences of this assumption see Brooks (1997).   [50] See Kukla (1994).

states have learned a great deal about each other, and today can often assign reasonably confident probabilities to inferences about what others want. Would it be rational for states to forego this knowledge because it is merely probabilistic, and instead make judgements based solely on worst-case, possibilistic reasoning? Would it be rational today for Canada to assume the worst about American intentions? Or even France about German ones? Not in my view. States will always be prudent, and sometimes worst-case assumptions are warranted, but prudence does not mean they will (or should) throw experience to the wind. History matters. And since that history is based in part on what others' interests really are, the distribution of interests must have an independent role in constituting the meaning of anarchy and the distribution of power.

Toward a rump materialism I

The explanatory significance of the distribution of power depends on historically contingent distributions of state interests. If interests and culture plausibly can be treated as given and constant – and in relatively stable cultural structures like the Cold War this may be the case – then variation in the distribution of capabilities may explain a great deal. Still this does not reduce the importance of interests and culture in making those explanations possible in the first place. We might say, then, that Neorealism "fetishizes" material capabilities in the sense that it imbues them with meanings and powers that "can only correctly be attributed to human beings."[51] But to say this is not to deny the importance of the distribution of capabilities, since my argument has been that assumptions about interests (and, I will argue, systemic culture) have been implicit in Waltz's model all along. *Given* states with egoistic, status quo interests interacting in a "market-like" culture, Waltz's hypotheses about anarchy or bipolarity may hold. In this respect my argument is unlike Neoliberalism, which seeks to show that the distribution of power is less important than Neorealism claims because ideas and institutions explain much of the variance instead. I am not juxtaposing interest as a rival explanation to power, nor claiming that interests *cause* power to have certain effects. I am saying that power only explains what it explains insofar as it is given meaning by interest. The argument is constitutive, not causal.

[51] Dant (1996: 496).

Having criticized a vulgar or reductionist materialism, however, I now want to defend a "rump" materialism which opposes the more radical constructivist view that brute material forces have *no* independent effects on international politics. It may seem unnecessary to undertake such a defense, since it is difficult to find any IR scholar who explicitly endorses such a radical view. Yet, given the almost complete absence of discussion in most postmodern IR scholarship of material forces as independent constraints on state action it is difficult not to conclude that it is at least a connotation, if not a denotation, of this literature that international life is ideas *all* the way down. In my view it cannot be ideas all the way down because scientific realism shows that ideas are based on and are regulated by an independently existing physical reality. As John Searle puts it, brute facts have ontological priority over institutional facts.[52] Perhaps it is unfair to attribute to postmodernism a denial of this belief, even as only a connotation. The following discussion would then really be superfluous – although in that case there should also be relatively little disagreement with what follows. But given the ease with which a moderate constructivism can be tarred with the brush of implausible radical positions,[53] it seems useful to consider the point explicitly. Brute material forces have independent effects on international life in at least three ways.

1 The distribution of actors' material capabilities affects the possibility and likelihood of certain outcomes. Militarily weak states typically cannot conquer powerful ones, powerful states typically can conquer weak states, and a balance of military power makes any conquest difficult. This is the core insight of Neorealism. The fact that in the absence of a willingness to use those capabilities these effects would not be activated does not change the fact that, when activated by human purpose, the distribution of capabilities has independent effects on outcomes. If a weak state attempts to conquer a strong state it will encounter these effects.

2 The "composition" of material capabilities,[54] and in particular the character of the technology they embody, has similar constraining and enabling effects. The technological ability to interact over long dis-

---

[52] Searle (1995: 55–56).   [53] For example, Mearsheimer (1994/1995).
[54] The term is Deudney's (1993).

tances makes international systems possible in the first place.[55] Armies with tanks will usually defeat armies with spears. Muskets can penetrate chainmail but not shoot across oceans. The balance of offensive and defensive military technology in an era affects the incentives for aggressive war.[56] The possession of nuclear weapons with second-strike invulnerability makes nuclear war less likely.[57] And so on. It might be argued that technology is not a "brute" material capability, since it is created by purposeful agents and embodies the state of their technical knowledge (ideas) at that time. To be sure. But once in existence a technological artifact has intrinsic material capacities and it makes possible further technological developments. Whether those capacities are ever used or developments ever realized depends on what actors want and believe, but this does not change the fact that the character of existing technology makes a difference in social life. A stripped down technological determinism – i.e., one that does not include *relations* of production or destruction – is compatible with the kind of social constructivism I have in mind.[58]

3 And then there are geography and natural resources. The distribution of certain metals in a given area makes possible the technological development of primitive societies living there. Inhospitable living conditions discourage settlement. Weather patterns affect agriculture. In turn, human actions may have unintended consequences for the natural environment that feed back on society, with potentially devastating effect (global warming; ozone and resource depletion). Constructivism should not proceed "as if nature did not matter."[59]

Even when properly stripped of their social content, in other words, brute material forces – the true "material base" – can still have independent effects, defining "for all actors the outer limits of feasible activity and the relative costs of pursuing various options that require physical activity."[60] These effects interact with interests and culture to dispose social action and systems in certain directions and not others. The term "interaction" is significant here, since it means that at some level material forces are constituted independent of society, and affect society in a *causal* way. Material forces are not constituted solely by social meanings,[61] and social meanings are not immune to material

---

[55] Buzan and Little (1994).   [56] Jervis (1978).   [57] Waltz (1990).
[58] See especially Bimber (1994).   [59] Murphy (1995).   [60] Peterson (1997: 12).
[61] Freudenberg, Frickel, and Gramling (1995).

effects. On the other hand, it is only because of their interaction with ideas that material forces have the effects that they do; the material fact that Germany has more military power than Denmark imposes physical limits on Danish foreign policy toward Germany, but those limits will be irrelevant to their interaction if neither could contemplate war with the other. So the relationship between material forces and ideas works both ways, but we can only properly theorize this relationship if we recognize that at some level they are constituted as different kinds of independently existing stuff. This formulation of the materialism–idealism problem is ultimately Cartesian, insofar as it separates the world into two kinds of phenomena – in effect, mind and body – and may be criticized for that reason. But I do not see any other way to think about the problem if we are to be scientific realists about social life.

It might be objected that material constraints can be eliminated over time by human intervention, so that in the long run it *is* ideas all the way down. We can change the distribution of power by building military capabilities; we can change the composition of power by creating new technologies; and with these we can change geographical and resource constraints. This argument could extend all the way down to human nature, since humans someday may be able to change their nature through genetic engineering. From this perspective it looks like everything is endogenous to interest and culture, in which case even a "rump" materialism concedes too much theoretically, and in so doing disempowers us politically.

Our on-going and often successful effort to transcend the material constraints facing us is one of the distinctive features of the human condition, and it is clear that interests and culture give that effort impetus and direction. To that extent the effects of material forces are internal to society rather than externally given by nature. However, there are two senses in which I believe a rump materialism still holds. First, it is an open empirical question how much human beings will be able to transcend material constraints. We have certainly come a long way, and it may even be that we are becoming progressively less constrained over time by our material condition, but this does not guarantee that material constraints are infinitely malleable. Indeed, if the increasing negative externalities of technological evolution are any indication, we may be nearing significant absolute constraints now. Nature yields control only grudgingly, which an ideas "all" the way down perspective has difficulty comprehending. Second, even if in the fullness of time all material constraints are negotiable, in the meantime they are not. Whether we like it or not, the distribution and composition of material capabilities at any given moment help define the possibilities of our action. We can ignore those effects, like the Balinese marching into Dutch machine guns or the Polish cavalry charging German tanks, but we do so at our own risk. Radical constructivism reminds us to historicize what counts as a material constraint, but we should not neglect the synchronic question of how it constrains us in the here and now.

Even though a rump materialism may be too much for some, my main goal in this section has been to show that Neorealist attempts to explain international politics by reference to anarchy and material capabilities alone presuppose much more than this, and in particular the animating force of *purpose*. Ultimately it is our ambitions, fears, and hopes – the things we want material forces *for* – that drive social evolution, not material forces as such. Adding the distribution of interests to Waltz's theory is one way to capture this fact. Since an emphasis on interests is not inimical to Realism, this could be taken as a friendly amendment.

I now take the argument further. In the rest of this chapter I argue that when IR scholars explain state action by reference to interests, they are actually explaining it by reference to a certain kind of *idea*. If so, the concept of interest will be best explicated within an idealist ontology, and my amendment to Neorealism will prove to have been not so friendly after all.

The constitution of interests by ideas

If an emphasis on the role of power is usually seen as one of the defining features of Realism, then an emphasis on egoistic national interests would be the other. Realists of all stripes believe that states do what they do because it is in their national interest, and that the national interest is self-regarding with respect to security. As with power, however, these cannot be *uniquely* Realist claims, since then almost every IR scholar would be a Realist. No one denies that states act on the basis of perceived interests,[62] and few would deny that those interests are often egoistic. I certainly do not. To that extent I am

---

[62] Except perhaps post-structuralists, for whom the whole notion of intentional action is problematic.

113

a Realist, but interests should not be seen as an exclusively "Realist" variable. What matters is how interests are thought to be constituted.

As I see it, the uniquely Realist hypothesis about national interests is that they have a material rather than social basis, being rooted in some combination of human nature, anarchy, and/or brute material capabilities. The argument in the preceding section was largely agnostic about this question. It acknowledged that material forces constrain and enable social forms at the margin, but its primary claim was that the distribution of interests helps constitute the meaning of power. Nevertheless, it is widely thought in IR that power and interest are both "material," and therefore that the only way to challenge theories which emphasize them, like Realism, is to show that factors like ideas, norms, or institutions explain a lot of behavior. This has been the intuition behind Neoliberalism, which frames the explanatory problem as power and interest versus institutions, versus norms, versus ideas. This framing has been fruitful, since there is much in international politics that power and interest cannot explain. On the other hand, this view implicitly suggests that power and interest are not themselves constituted by ideas. And since Realists have already claimed power and interest as "their" variables, this limits a priori the role of ideas – and thus non-Realist theories – to the superstructure, and thereby privileges Realist arguments about the base.

Neoliberalism focuses on the ways in which ideas can have causal effects independent of other causes like power and interest. However, ideas also have constitutive effects, on power and interest themselves. Here I discuss how ideas constitute interests. If in some sense interests *are* ideas, then the causal, "ideas-versus-interests" model will be incomplete. This does not mean that all ideas are interests. Most are not. Nor does it mean that interests no longer have an independent explanatory role. They explain just as much as they did before, and exist independently of ideas that do not constitute them, as required by causal explanations. The claim is only that among the different kinds of ideas are some that constitute interests, and that the explanatory power of these ideas therefore cannot be compared to interests as competing causal variables.

To say interests are ideas brings us again to the definition of materialism. I argued above that meaningful power is constituted in important part through the distribution of interests. Here I argue that only a small part of what constitutes interests is actually material. The material force constituting interests is human nature. The rest is ideational: schemas and deliberations that are in turn constituted by shared ideas or culture. As in my discussion of power-explanations, in other words, my goal here is not to show that interests do not matter, but to show how little of them a properly specified materialism can explain, and to claim the rest for idealism.

Rational choice theory is the conventional framework in mainstream IR for thinking about the relationship between ideas and interests. For that reason I shall organize my discussion with reference to it. The core of rationalist explanations is the view that preferences and expectations generate behavior. This is known in philosophical literature as the equation, "desire plus belief equals action." It is not hard to see how this equation might encourage the interests "versus" ideas thinking that I'm arguing is problematic, and as such play into the materialist bias in IR theory. Rationalism treats desire (or preference or interest) and belief (or expectations or ideas) as distinct variables, which suggests that desires do not depend on beliefs and are therefore material. This connotation is further enabled by the fact that rationalists do not usually ask where interests come from. It is in this way that methodology can become tacit ontology. By the same token, however, strictly speaking the theory is agnostic about that question. Interests might be material or ideational; it simply does not say. Moreover, rationalism has a strong subjectivist aspect, which has led some people to emphasize its affinities to interpretive social science and thus, implicitly, an idealist ontology.[63] These considerations suggest rational choice theory might be compatible with an idealist view of interests. Thus, in what follows I shall not be arguing "against" rational choice theory (nor, it might be noted, will I bring up some familiar, long-standing criticisms, such as about the theory's realism); on the contrary – I see it as part of my own understanding of agency (see chapter 7). But it is only part of the story and as such must be assimilated into a constructivist framework. In what follows I first discuss the standard rationalist view of the relationship between interests and ideas, and then propose an alternative.

---

[63] See Ferejohn (1991), Esser (1993); cf. Srubar (1993).

The rationalist model of man[64]

Rationalism has both a macro- and micro-dimension. The macro-dimension is concerned with explaining broad patterns of behavior and aggregate outcomes rather than the behavior of individual agents. Often the patterns and outcomes arise via unintended consequences of behavior. What matters here are the structural constraints on choice rather than individual psychology, since the same aggregate outcome may be realizable under various psychological conditions.[65] While this might suggest that rational choice theory does not depend on assumptions about agents, in fact it does. Even if a macro-outcome is compatible with a variety of desires and beliefs, rationalist explanations presuppose that agents act at least "as if" they are maximizing certain desires and beliefs (see below). The macro level is important and it relates to arguments about the role of culture in constituting interests that I develop in chapter 4, but since my concern in this chapter is only with the nature of interests, I shall limit my discussion here to its micro-aspect, focusing on the logic of desire/belief explanation and the assumptions about human agency which it makes.

To explain action as a product of desire and belief is to offer an "intentional" explanation.[66] This is the kind of explanation most of us would intuitively give if asked to explain why we went to the grocery store: we had a desire for food and a belief that that desire could be satisfied there. This combination of desire and belief was the "reason" we went to the store, and in the intentionalist view reasons are causes of behavior.[67] In effect, the intentional theory of action is a dressed up version of the folk psychology implicit in our everyday explanations of behavior.[68] In the social sciences it has received its most systematic use in economics, however, and is now often seen as the core of an "economic" approach to human behavior, from where it has been

---

[64] That it may be a model of *man* is an important issue that I shall pass over here. For a feminist critique of rationalism see England and Kilbourne (1990).

[65] Satz and Ferejohn (1994).

[66] See Elster (1983a: 69–88) and Dennett (1987). The terms "desire" and "belief" are conventional in the philosophical literature, but no particular importance attaches to them. The former I take to be equivalent to the social scientist's "interest," "taste," or "preference," while the latter is equivalent to "expectations," "information," or "knowledge."

[67] Davidson (1963).   [68] Bilmes (1986: 187).

colonizing other social sciences.[69] Alexander Rosenberg offers a good summary:

> Economics is an intentional science. It holds that economic behavior is determined by tastes and beliefs, that is, by the desire to maximize preferences, subject to the constraint of expectations about available alternatives. Differences between the choices made by individual agents who face the same alternatives are due either to differences in preferences, to differences in expectations, or to both. Similarly, changes in the choices of an individual agent over time are due to changes in one or both of these causal determinants of his behavior.[70]

It is important to note that this explanatory logic says nothing about the *content* of desires and beliefs. This can be seen by distinguishing "thin" and "thick" versions of rational choice theory.[71]

The thin theory consists of propositions about the nature of desire and belief and their relationship – in short, intentional explanation as such. In the intentional theory of action the concept of desire refers to a motivation that moves the body in the direction of the object of desire. Desire is always *for* something, and as such plays an active explanatory role in the sense that it is the force or energy which moves the body. This force is activated only if an actor also believes the object of desire can be attained by acting, and so desire by itself is not sufficient to explain action, but given appropriate beliefs the energy for activity comes from desire. Belief plays a more passive explanatory role in the thin theory. Whereas desire is for things, belief is *about* them.[72] Two kinds of beliefs are important: beliefs about states of the external world, and beliefs about the efficacy of different means to satisfy desires in that world. It does not matter whether these beliefs are accurate, only that actors take them to be true. A key assumption of the traditional rationalist model is that beliefs have no motivational force of their own; they merely describe the world. This creates within the model an explanatory bias in favor of desire/interest, which is deeply rooted in the intellectual history of rationalism, going back to Hobbes and Hume.[73] Beliefs play an important enabling role in

---

[69] In fact, the "economic" approach to behavior also makes assumptions about the content of desire and belief that go beyond the logic of intentional explanation per se; in Ferejohn's (1991) terms below, it involves a "thick" rather than merely "thin" theory of rational choice. On "economic imperialism" see Hirshleifer (1985) and Radnitsky and Bernholz, eds. (1986).

[70] Rosenberg (1985: 50); cf. Elster (1983b: 2–25).

[71] Ferejohn (1991: 282).   [72] Schueler (1995: 125).   [73] Hollis (1987: 63).

behavior by activating and facilitating the realization of desires, but the active, primary explanatory work is done by desire.

Thick versions of rational choice theory add to this skeleton assumptions about the content of desires and beliefs. One of the most common thick theories is that actors are egoists with complete information about their environment, but thick rationalist theories could alternatively assume altruism and incomplete information. There is no one thick theory of rational choice, and so we need more than the thin theory. Many disagreements in IR scholarship are rooted in different thick theories of human nature and/or the national interest.[74] Classical Realists offer varying permutations of fear, power, glory, and wealth as candidates. The debate in Neorealism about whether states are status quo or revisionist is in part about whether they are motivated more by fear or power. The debate between Neorealists and Neoliberals about the extent to which states seek relative or absolute gains is in part about whether states are more interested in security or wealth. The question of whether states are capable of collective security depends on whether they are necessarily selfish or capable of having collective interests. And so on. These are important disagreements, but all sides seem to accept the key rationalist premise that desire (the national interest) causes states to act in certain ways.

The intentional equation is also a common baseline in recent IR work on beliefs. One stream of scholarship has focused on the belief systems and perceptions of decision-makers.[75] This work presents a challenge to thick rationalist theories that assume complete information, but it does not threaten the thin theory.[76] And there is also recent rationalist work on the role of ideas in foreign policy.[77] Goldstein and Keohane actually contrast this work to the "rationalist" concern with interests,[78] but it should be clear from the foregoing discussion that beliefs play an essential role in rationalist theory. In the past rationalist scholars may have neglected belief in favor of desire (usually by assuming that actors have complete information), which encouraged the view that rational choice theory is a materialist theory. Goldstein and Keohane have issued an important reminder that it need not be seen this way. But in itself a focus on ideas poses no inherent threat to rational choice theory's explanatory logic. Most of

---

[74] See Smith (1983).   [75] For example, Jervis (1976), Little and Smith, eds. (1988).
[76] Cf. Lebow and Stein (1989), Wagner (1992).
[77] For example, Goldstein (1993), Goldstein and Keohane, eds. (1993).
[78] Goldstein and Keohane (1993: 4).

the recent mainstream IR scholarship on ideas is clearly based on an intentional theory of action: treating desire and belief as if they were distinct, with the latter relating to the former in instrumental rather than constitutive terms.

Of course, to some extent desire and belief *are* distinct phenomena. Desire is "for," belief "about." The one is motivation, the other cognition. An interesting way to think about the difference is that they have different "directions of fit" with the world.[79] Desire aims to fit the world to the mind, belief aims to fit the mind to the world. However, this difference does not rule out the possibility that desire may itself be a kind of belief – a belief not about the world, but a belief *that something is desirable*.[80] I explore below the possibility that cognitive factors constitute desire.

This raises the crucial question of "what is desire (interest)?" The received view, going back at least to Hume, is that desire is constitutionally unrelated to belief. Desire is a matter of passion, not cognition; and while beliefs activate and channel desires, they cannot be desires. Hume's view is "dualistic" in that it explains action by reference to two unrelated mechanisms. This view has two important theoretical consequences. First, if desires are not a function of belief, then it is natural to treat them in materialist fashion as material, and to treat ideas in rationalist fashion as a means for realizing exogenously given interests. Second, the Humean view also makes life difficult for the constructivist, because her point is that culture (a shared idea) constitutes interests. If interests and ideas are entirely different kinds of stuff, then it is not clear how they can mix and transmogrify one (mind) into another (body). Constructivism needs to overcome the Humean dualism of desire and belief. It can do so with an alternative, *cognitive* theory of desire.[81] Simply put, we want what we want because of how we think about it. As we shall see, this need not vitiate intentional explanation, but it does suggest that there is more to the relationship between desire and belief than rationalism acknowledges.

Beyond the rationalist model

The Humean view that desire and belief are constitutionally unrelated is deeply embedded in rationalist discourse. It appeals to important intuitions in our everyday understandings of behavior,

---

[79] Smith (1987), Platts (1991).   [80] Howe (1994b: 179).   [81] Howe (1994a).

and the structure of intentional explanation (desire *plus* belief) tacitly connotes it. On the other hand, there is a growing body of scholarship in philosophy, cognitive psychology, anthropology, and even economics which argues that desire is not separate from belief but constituted by it. This literature too appeals to important intuitions in everyday life. I discuss two different but related versions of this thesis, cognitive and deliberative. Judging from citations their advocates seem unaware of each other, and one seems to pose a deeper challenge to the traditional theory of intentional action than the other. But rather than assess their relationship, at this stage it seems more useful simply to present the two accounts and show how each links ideas to interests.

An important premise of the argument I make here is that we should care about how preferences are constituted. The premise comes from scientific realism and many rational choice scholars might disagree with it. For them, as for the empiricist anti-realists I discussed in chapter 2, "as if" assumptions about preferences are sufficient for theorizing. A sophisticated version of this argument is advanced by Debra Satz and John Ferejohn and it merits a response.[82]

Satz and Ferejohn argue that rationalist explanations do not need to show that agents "really" are motivated by desires and beliefs, just that they act "as if" they are. If this is right, then the issue of what desires are made of is without substantive import, beside the point. Satz and Ferejohn are expressing a consensus among contemporary economists on an old debate about whether their discipline needs robust psychological assumptions about "utility." In the nineteenth century most economists thought it did. Systematized by Stanley Jevons, this view can be traced back to Bentham, who argued that utility was constituted by experiences,[83] and before that to Hobbes and Hume, who argued that "passions" were the source of desire. Beginning with seminal work by Paul Samuelson in the 1930s, however, economists have today largely abandoned this "internalist" view ("internal" because it referred to states of consciousness), because of its intractability, unrealistic psychology, and, importantly, appeal to unobservable causes.[84] Like behaviorists in psychology, rational choice theorists now take an "externalist" view, which treats desire in behavioral or operational terms *as* choice (revealed prefer-

---

[82] Satz and Ferejohn (1994).
[83] Haslett (1990: 68–69), Kahneman and Varey (1991: 127–129).   [84] Cohen (1995).

ences) rather than as an unobservable cause *of* choice.[85] This is legitimate, Satz and Ferejohn argue, because in rationalist theory what explains outcomes are the structural constraints in a system, which will often have the same effects regardless of individual motivations (back to the macro-level aspect of rational choice above). The result is an instrumentalist reading of rationalism, in which no assumptions are made about the ontological status of desire and belief.[86] In a sense we are back to the epistemological anxiety discussed in chapter 2, which leads to a focus on what we can see and measure.

In a response to Satz and Ferejohn, Daniel Hausman defends the necessity of an internalist view of action,[87] on the grounds that even if the structure of a choice situation is highly constraining (as in a hotel fire), our explanation of the outcome (the occupants flee) depends on the accuracy of our assumptions about desires and beliefs. In the hotel fire example these assumptions are trivial (most people want to live and know that fire can kill them), and as such little will be gained by devoting much energy to refining them. But it remains the case that "the correctness of the explanation depends on their truth."[88] An adequate externalist story depends on an adequate internalist one.[89] Otherwise it is a mystery why the occupants flee, and we should want to know why. One reason is practical: structural theories that make false motivational assumptions may sometimes successfully predict outcomes, but if we ignore their falsity we will not know when they might fail us or how to revise them most efficiently.[90] From this standpoint, encouraging social scientists to ignore the truth of their assumptions is "bad methodological advice." Another reason we should care about motivation is philosophical: unlike the instrumentalism espoused by Satz and Ferejohn, in which the goal of science should be merely to "save the appearances," Hausman is a scientific realist who thinks that science should try to describe the causal mechanisms that generate appearances, and so we "must care whether the psychological claims employed in rational-choice explanations are true. Scientific realists about rational-choice theory must be internalists."[91] Social scientists do not always need to worry about

---

[85] Sugden (1991: 757–761); on the relationship of rational choice to behaviorism see Homans (1990) and Rosenberg (1995).

[86] See Friedman (1953) and chapter 2, pp. 60–62.   [87] Hausman (1995).

[88] Ibid.: 101.   [89] Hollis and Sugden (1993: 26–32).   [90] Hausman (1995: 99).

[91] Ibid.: 98.

the truth of their assumptions, but the question of how desire is constituted is not something that should be side-stepped completely.

The cognitive basis of desire

The first argument against a materialist view of interest is that interests are themselves cognitions or ideas. We find this thesis in two distinct bodies of scholarship, one in cultural anthropology, the other in philosophy.

Drawing on cognitive psychology, anthropologist Roy D'Andrade argues that motivations, desires, or interests should be seen as "schemas" (or "scripts," "frames," or "representations"), which are knowledge structures that "make possible the identification of objects and events."[92] Many schemas are simply beliefs about the world that have no connection to desires. Other schemas are *goals* or desires that energize action. D'Andrade (p. 35) gives the example of a motivation for "achievement." Achievement implies a social standard about what counts as a legitimate aspiration – and as such is a cultural rather than material fact. Individuals who have a desire to achieve have internalized this standard as a cognitive schema. Similarly, in capitalist societies some people have a desire to get rich on the stock market. This is a schema which includes beliefs about the external world (how the market works, where it is going, etc.), and also constitutes its holder with a particular motivation that drives her behavior in that world. Symbolic interactionists would argue that many of these goal-schemas or interests are constituted by identities, which are schemas about the Self.[93] The identity or self-schema of professor, for example, constitutes an interest in teaching and publishing. Like other schemas, motivational schemas are organized hierarchically within the Self and so not all equally "salient,"[94] which is important in trying to explain what someone will do in a particular situation.

The important point is that none of these schemas is given by human nature. D'Andrade is careful to acknowledge that motivation is *partly* rooted in biological drives and as such is truly material.[95] Sometimes, as in the example of fleeing the hotel fire, these are more important in explaining action than culturally constituted schemas.

---

[92] D'Andrade (1992: 28).

[93] For example, Morgan and Schwalbe (1990), Stryker (1991).

[94] Stryker (1980: 60–62).   [95] D'Andrade (1992: 31).

But biological drives explain few of the almost infinite goals human beings seem to be capable of pursuing. Most of these are learned through socialization. Those who would explain how desire is constituted, therefore, would do well to focus more on culture and its relationship to cognition than on biology.[96]

Much the same conclusion is reached without much reference to cognitive psychology by R.B.K. Howe, who uses recent philosophical discussions to articulate a cognitive theory of desire.[97] Like D'Andrade Howe acknowledges a role for biological drives in the constitution of desire. Needs for food, water, reproduction and so on matter, and these are material. Yet Howe argues that even very primitive desires are mostly "directionless,"[98] and depend on beliefs about what is desirable to give them content. Beliefs define and direct material needs. It is the *perception* of value in an object that constitutes the motive to pursue it, not some intrinsic biological imperative. Such perceptions are learned, partly through interaction with nature (fire hurts; dirt tastes bad), in which case they have a materialist explanation, but mostly they are learned through socialization to culture. Desires always involve a mixture of biological drives and beliefs, with the importance of beliefs varying along a continuum from low (a desire for water when thirsty) to high (a desire to do the right thing).[99] These desire-constituting beliefs or cognitions have a different "direction of fit" with the world than the beliefs-"about" which figure on the belief side of the desire plus belief equation. To highlight their distinctiveness philosophers have dubbed them "desiderative beliefs." "Goal-schema" would do just as well.

The arguments of D'Andrade, Howe, and others concerned with the relationship between desire and belief refer mostly to individuals rather than groups.[100] I argue in chapter 5 that certain groups, including states, also have desires. This is an assumption of all state-centric IR theory, and one virtue of the cognitive approach to interests is that it is easier to defend this assumption than it is to defend it with a materialist approach, since states are not biological beings. Assuming for the moment that states have desires, let me illustrate the argument in this section with reference to the three state interests that

---

[96] For a good overview see DiMaggio (1997).
[97] Howe (1994a, b). See also Humberstone (1987), Smith (1987), Platts (1991), and Schueler (1995).
[98] Howe (1994a: 4).   [99] Howe (1994b: 182–183).   [100] Though see Clark (1994).

figured in the earlier discussion of the distribution of power: status quo, revisionist, and collectivist.

A status quo state is one that has no interest in conquering other states, redrawing boundaries, or changing the rules of the international system. It may attack another state to preempt a threat, but it has no intrinsic desire to infringe on other states' rights. How is this interest constituted? Undoubtedly part of the answer lies in basic material human needs for security and stability, but since all states are presumably subject to these needs and not all have status quo interests, this does not tell us enough. The cognitive theory of desire directs our attention to the schemas or representations through which status quo states define their interests.[101] They may be hypothesized to have schemas as "satisfied" with their international position, as "law-abiding," as "members of a society of states," the rules of which are seen as "legitimate," and so on. These beliefs are not merely about an external world: they also constitute a certain identity and its relationship to that world, which in turn motivates action in certain directions. Status quo states have the interests they do, in other words, in virtue of their perceptions of the international order and their place within it as desirable, not because of brute material facts.

Revisionist states, in turn, have the desire to conquer others, seize part of their territory, and/or change the rules of the game. Human nature helps constitute these desires too, most likely in the form of self-esteem needs, but again this explains little. More significant will be self-schemas like "victim" or "master race," representations of Others as "infidels" or "evil empires," of the system as "illegitimate" or "threatening," war as "glorious" or "manly," and so on. These schemas are a function of culturally constituted cognitions, not biology.

Collectivist states have the desire to help those they identify with even when their own security is not directly threatened. Realist cynicism notwithstanding, biology surely plays a role here as well, since humans are social animals whose brains are hard-wired for "team play,"[102] but this cannot explain why some states identify and some do not. The presence of certain schemas can: "we-ness," "friend," "special relationship," "doing the right thing," "regional policeman," and so on. In foreign policy discourse these "moral" schemas are often juxtaposed to "interests," as in the debate about US

[101] Cf. Weldes (1996, 1999).   [102] Wilson and Sober (1994: 601).

124

intervention in the Bosnian civil war. One way to interpret President Clinton's speech to the American people justifying intervention is that it tried to define US "interests" in terms of the *belief* that Americans are the kind of people who do the right thing.

In chapters 4 and 6 I will argue that these interest-constituting ideas are in turn constituted by the *shared* ideas or culture of the international system. Here I am arguing that ideas at that macro level get into the heads of states and become interests at this other, more micro level of international structure.

The cognitive theory of desire violates the spirit but not the letter of the intentional theory of action. The traditional interpretation of intentionalism, following Hume, ruled out the hypothesis that beliefs could motivate, but nothing in the theory's propositional structure (the thin theory of rational choice) requires such an interpretation. It is perfectly consistent with the idea that beliefs and desires are distinct to hold that certain beliefs are about the external world and other beliefs constitute desires, and that the two play different explanatory roles. Desires are no less desires for being constituted by beliefs. As such, nothing said so far is inherently incompatible with rational choice theory, as long as rationalists concede that ideas play a larger role in explaining social action than is captured by the desire "plus" belief model. The resulting opening has been exploited by some rationalists in economics, who have modeled preferences as constituted by beliefs,[103] and others in IR, who have argued that state interests are affected by expectations about the environment.[104] Precisely because it is agnostic about what preferences are and where they come from, rational choice theory can be adapted to either an idealist or a materialist ontology.

The deliberative basis of desire

Cognitivism challenges the materialist view of desire, but it does not call into question the key assumption of the intentional theory, that desire and belief alone explain action. Desire still does all the motivational work, even if it has been reconceptualized as a kind of belief. An alternate argument for what explains action brings in reason or deliberation. Martin Hollis and G.F. Schueler, drawing from Kant,

---

[103] For example, Cohen and Axelrod (1984), Geanakoplos, Pearce, and Stacchetti (1989).
[104] Niou and Ordeshook (1994), Powell (1994), Clark (1998).

argue that Reason or deliberation should be considered a third factor in the model: desire plus belief plus reason equals action.[105]

The rationale for looking to a third factor stems from rational choice theory's paradoxically impoverished conception of "rational choice." Rationality is normally defined in instrumental terms as nothing more than having *consistent* desires and beliefs, and choice involves nothing more profound than their automatic enactment in behavior that maximizes expected utility. Rationalists rarely ask whether preferences are rational in the sense of justifiable, and often specifically abjure such assessments. "Rationality of action is always relative to the current desires of the agent,"[106] whatever their content. In this light humans differ from other animals only in the greater complexity of their desires and beliefs, not in their rationality. And indeed, experiments have shown that humans, rats, and pigeons are equally rational as defined by rational choice theory.[107] What is missing from this conception of rationality is any sense of deliberation, which goes back to the Humean model of man. In that model deliberation involves nothing more complicated than weighing up one's desires on a "grocer's scale,"[108] or doing a "vector analysis"[109] of their relative strength. There is no sense in the Humean model of Reason as a distinct faculty of mind that decides what desires to have, which to act upon, or even whether to act at all. The perhaps surprising result, therefore, is that rational choice theory is highly *deterministic*.[110] This is seen in the many metaphors which its critics have coined to describe it. Schueler calls it the "blind forces" model of intentionality, in which agents (now rather mixing metaphors) are pushed and pulled by desire "rather in the way currents of air act on a falling leaf"; Hollis prefers the electronic imagery of agents as "throughputs" for desires and beliefs; Margaret Gilbert offers the mechanical metaphor of desire causing choice in "hydraulic" fashion; Harry Frankfurt calls people who do not reflect on their desires "wantons"; Amartya Sen calls them "rational fools."[111] For rhetorical punch none tops Hume, who argued that Reason "alone can never be a motive to any action of the will," and "is, and ought only to be the slave of the passions."[112] But

---

[105] Hollis (1987), Schueler (1995); also see Morse (1997). [106] Hollis (1987: 74).
[107] Satz and Ferejohn (1994: 77 n. 19). [108] Hollis (1987: 68).
[109] Schueler (1995: 169). [110] See Latsis (1972).
[111] See, respectively, Schueler (1995: 171), Hollis (1987: 68), Gilbert (1989: 419), Frankfurt (1971), and Sen (1977).
[112] Hume (1740/1978: 413, 415), quoted from Hollis (1987: 68) and Sugden (1991: 753).

all point to the fact that his model of man lacks the free, deliberating agent which one intuitively associates with "rational choice."

Indeed, whereas rational choice seems to be nothing more than a formalization of folk psychology – and on one level it is – on a closer read it is also somewhat out of sync with our common sense understandings of how and why people act. For example, the assumption that human beings do not reflect upon and choose their desires is hard to square with our intuitions about responsibility. If we are merely throughputs for desires and beliefs that we cannot control (since we are nothing *but* them), then how can we be held responsible for our actions?[113] The reason we do not blame animals for their behavior is because we assume they lack the capacity for deliberation about their desires which would enable them to act differently than they do.[114] Yet as we saw above in rational choice theory humans and animals are equally rational.

Another problematic intuition is that people often engage in practices of delayed gratification, "self-binding," and "character planning" which involve acting on behalf of desires they do not yet have.[115] Rationalists may try to explain such behavior by introducing discounted future desires into the present, but this still raises the possibility of Reason shaping desire, which contradicts the Humean view.[116]

Finally, the desire/belief model ignores the sense in ordinary language that people can act against or in spite of their desires, that we can do something even though we "wanted" to do something else. Human beings are often deeply torn about whether to act on their desires, and sometimes restrain themselves because of Reason or morality. "External" rather than "internal" reasons sometimes prevail.[117] Rationalists may try to explain such behavior as resolving a conflict between lower desires (e.g., be selfish) and higher desires (e.g., do the right thing), such that whatever an agent decides to do must have been what she really "wanted" to do: either lower or higher desires simply won out. But Schueler argues such an explanation conflates two senses of desire: "proper desires," which are in the head and can be acted against, and "pro attitudes," which are the

---

Hume's views on Reason were more complex and subtle than these famous passages suggest. For a good introduction see da Fonseca (1991: 81–116).

[113] For literature on "moral autonomy" see Christman (1988).

[114] Though see Evans (1987).   [115] See Elster (1979, 1983b).

[116] Hollis (1987: 85–86).   [117] Ibid.: 74–94.

actual choices agents make. The distinction matters because pro attitudes are known through choices, not before, and as such cannot enter into an agent's own calculus about what to do.[118] Reducing all deliberation to a weighing of conflicting desires, in other words, is a non-falsifiable proposition that cannot explain behavior. The desires that can truly explain behavior are proper desires, and in order to know how proper desires affect choices we need to bring in deliberation.

These intuitions all call into question the two-factor model of intentional action, but like the cognitivist argument, they can be made consistent with rational choice theory, if we detach it from its Humean moorings and view it as only a partial theory of action. In fact these intuitions suggest the fruitfulness of distinguishing two versions of intentional explanation, which Schueler calls the "blind forces" and "reflective" models.[119] The former, corresponding to the traditional Humean view, treats human agency as "impulsive" and lacking meaningful deliberation. The latter, corresponding to a Kantian view, treats Reason as a third factor that deliberates about and helps choose interests.[120] While the blind forces model characterized rational choice scholarship for some time, rationalist social theory today is developing and strengthening its notions of deliberation and self-governance.[121] Schueler sees an "enormous difference" between the two models (p. 186), but argues that the best description of a choice process in a given context, blind versus reflective, is always an empirical question. Moreover, since deliberation is a learned capacity, the balance between them for a given agent may change over time.

The addition of Reason to rational choice theory seems particularly apposite for IR scholarship. The philosophical literature on deliberative rationality concentrates on individuals. A strong case exists even in that context against the traditional, two-factor model of intentionality. But an emphasis on the role of deliberation in constituting interests seems even more appropriate for decision-making in groups. Often one of the most difficult tasks facing foreign policy decision-makers is figuring out what their interests *are*. This process does not typically consist of weighing competing interests on a "grocer's scale" of intensity, or even of aggregating the exogenously given preferences

[118] Schueler (1995: 156–161).
[119] Ibid.: 174–196; also see Hollis (1987) and Alker (1996: 207–237).
[120] Cf. Hirschman (1977, especially at 111–112).
[121] See Sen (1977), Elster (1983b), Schelling (1984), Schmidtz (1995), and Morse (1997).

of different individuals. It typically consists in a complex and highly contested process of discussion, persuasion, and framing of issues. In short, what goes on is collective deliberation about what their interests in a given situation should be. These deliberations do not take place in a vacuum, either domestic or international, but neither are they strictly determined by domestic or systemic structures. There are relatively few "hotel fires" in international politics. And sometimes deliberation can generate dramatic "preference reversals" even while structural conditions remain constant.[122]

Such was arguably the case with Soviet New Thinking under Gorbachev. Those wedded to the blind forces model of intentional action will say that the Soviet leadership *had* to change its policies because of its declining relative power position. Certainly the economic and military pressures on the Soviet state were a crucial impetus for change. However, a structural pressure theory alone cannot explain the form the Soviet response took (ending the Cold War rather than intensifying repression) or its timing (the material decline had been going on for some time). And it also ignores the role that the leadership's realization that its own policies were part of the problem played in conditioning that response. Structural conditions did not force self-awareness on the Soviets. Soviet behavior changed because they redefined their interests as a result of having looked at their existing desires and beliefs self-critically. The reflective model of intentional explanation captures this process more naturally than the blind forces model.

This example also points to ways in which the cognitive and deliberative arguments may overlap. The principles informing Soviet "Reason" were not wholly independent of beliefs about the identity of the Soviet state, the feasibility of certain actions, and even about right and wrong. Deliberation about national interests takes place against the background of a shared national security discourse, in other words, which may substantially affect its content.[123] This blurring of Reason and belief is also evident in the philosophical literature. Howe, who does not make the Kantian argument that Reason is a distinct factor in intentional explanations, treats morality as a belief or schema. Schueler, who does make the Kantian argument, places moral

---

[122] For a thought-provoking discussion of the implications of preference reversals for our conventional understandings of "preference," which includes the one above, see Slovic (1995).

[123] Campbell (1992), Weldes (1996, 1999).

considerations under the heading of Reason. My own inclinations lie with Schueler because the cognitive theory alone, with its continued reliance on just desire and belief to explain action, does not escape the determinism of rational choice theory. But the relationship between the two idealist critiques of materialist theories of desire is complicated and need not concern us here.

Toward a rump materialism II

The overlap between the cognitive and deliberative critiques suggests a general proposition about the relationship between interests and ideas: "interests are beliefs about how to meet needs."[124] Since this depends on a distinction between interests and needs,[125] let me first say a few words about the latter and then return to interests. As in my concluding remarks about power, having now taken the idealist line that interests are constituted mostly by ideas, in this section I turn around and defend the rump materialist view that they nevertheless must ultimately hook on to a material ground, human nature.

Needs refer to the functional reproduction requirements of a particular kind of agent, what some would call "objective interests."[126] Two types of needs may be discerned: identity needs and material needs. Identity needs are as variable as the identities they sustain, which is to say practically infinite. To reproduce the identity of a state a group needs to sustain a monopoly on the legitimate use of violence in their territory. To reproduce the identity of a professor an individual needs to teach. In both cases these needs reflect the internal and external structures that constitute these actors as social kinds. There is no guarantee identity needs will be translated into appropriate beliefs about how to meet them, which is to say into (subjective) *interests*, but if they are not translated then the agents they constitute will not survive. Identity needs are ultimately a matter of individual and social cognitions rather than biology. They are still real and objective, but given that they are not material to focus on them here would do little to clarify the role of materialism. So let me turn to the material needs stemming from human nature and show just what exactly is a material basis for desire.

Scientific realism assumes that human beings are self-organizing

---

[124] Rosenberg (1992: 167).   [125] See Doyal and Gough (1984).
[126] McCullagh (1991).

natural kinds with material reproduction requirements. All animals have such requirements. Material needs are no guarantee that individuals will try to meet them (people do commit suicide), but it seems likely that were humans not predisposed to meet their needs we would never have survived evolution. The content of this predisposition is "human nature." Radical constructivists might deny the existence, or at least social significance, of biological needs. But despite its well-intentioned resistance to biological determinism, there is an anthropic exceptionalism or human chauvinism in the radical view that is hard to justify from the standpoint of evolutionary theory. It is impossible to explain social action without making at least implicit assumptions about human nature, since, without it, it is hard to explain why our bodies move at all, let alone their direction or resistance to societal pressures.[127] If this is right, then even postmodernists have a theory of human nature. I shall not examine competing views of human nature here, but if all sociologies presuppose one there is not much point dodging the issue either.

Let me therefore stipulate the following rump materialist "theory" of human nature. Unlike the open-ended list of identity needs, it posits just five material needs. These are needs of individuals, not groups. Groups also have needs, but since they do not have bodies these will be identity needs which cannot be reduced to the material needs of their members, even though they help meet the latter (see chapter 5). Material needs may generate contradictory imperatives and thus practices, but they vary in importance and people will generally – though not always – try to meet their more fundamental needs first. In roughly descending order of importance:[128]

1 *Physical security*: human beings need food, water, and sleep to sustain their bodies, and protection from threats to their physical integrity. Fear of death comes under this heading.
2 *Ontological security*: human beings need relatively stable expectations about the natural and especially social world around them. Along with the need for physical security, this pushes human beings in a conservative, homeostatic direction, and to seek out recognition of their standing from society.

---

[127] Carveth (1982: 202).
[128] This list combines elements from Giddens (1984), Turner (1988), Johnson (1990), Maslow (see Davies, 1991), and Honneth (1996).

3 *Sociation*: human beings are social animals who need contact with each other. Needs for love and group membership are met through sociation.

4 *Self-esteem*: human beings need to feel good about themselves. This is achieved primarily through social relationships, and as such its content can vary hugely, including "needs" for honor, glory, achievement, recognition (again), power, group membership (again), and so on.

5 *Transcendence*: human beings need to grow, develop, and improve their life condition. This is a source of creativity and innovation, and of efforts to remake their material circumstances.

In the last analysis the energy that human beings expend in their lives stems from efforts to meet these material needs, and people will define their interests in ways that facilitate doing so in the material and cultural environments in which they find themselves. When needs are met people experience the emotion of satisfaction. When needs are not met we experience anxiety, fear, or frustration, which depending on the circumstances will motivate us to redouble our efforts, to change our interests, or to engage in aggression. Thus, in contrast to Classical Realists who would posit fear, insecurity, or aggression as essential parts of human nature, I am suggesting these feelings are effects of unmet needs and therefore contingent. The effort to prevent the fear and anxiety associated with unmet needs is part of human nature, but fear and anxiety themselves are socially constructed.

Regardless of the truth of this particular "theory" of human nature, rump materialism is an ontological argument that we need some such theory to explain human behavior. Ironically, Neorealists seem as uncomfortable with this suggestion as radical constructivists, preferring to ground their theory on the "structural" materialism of power rather than the "reductionist" materialism of human nature. Human nature cannot be avoided, however, and the assumptions we make about it will condition our theorizing about world politics. Like power, interests are not ideas *all* the way down. This is a significant idealist concession to materialism, but the two are not contradictory. Biological realism is compatible with social construction.[129] The ques-

---

[129] Sabini and Schulkin (1994), Mead (1934).

132

tion is *to what extent* does biology constitute interests? Perhaps thinking that it cannot or need not be answered, systemic IR scholars have largely avoided this question in recent decades, but with the emergence of sociobiology there is now the potential for a renewed and fruitful discussion. Sociobiologists would say biology matters quite a lot in the constitution of interests,[130] as would perhaps most Classical Realists. Even Neorealists, when necessary to sustain their pessimism about anarchy, will fall back on the view that human nature is inherently selfish or power-seeking.[131] In contrast, even though the kind of constructivism I favor is thin, in my view biology matters relatively little. Human nature does not tell us whether people are good or bad, aggressive or pacific, power-seeking or power-conferring, even selfish or altruistic. These are all socially contingent, not materially essential. Much more than other animals, human behavior is underdetermined by our nature, a fact attested to by the remarkable variety of cultural forms we have created. In developing this hypothesis we should not forget that human beings are animals whose material needs are a key constituting element of their interests, but in the end their interests are mostly a function of their ideas, not their genes.

Let me conclude with three virtues of an idealist approach to the study of interests in IR. First, and most important, it suggests a program of empirical research for studying the content of real world state interests. Most traditions of IR theory rely on intentional explanations of action, and as such need a model of state interests. In practice mainstream IR scholars typically assume a model. This is perfectly legitimate for certain purposes, but it is nevertheless striking just how little empirical research has been done investigating what kinds of interests state actors actually have.[132] Perhaps this is because everyone "knows" that states are egoists who want power (and wealth?, or security?), or because the influence of rationalism on the field has discouraged the empirical study of preferences, but it might also reflect the fact that materialist social theory offers little guidance about how exactly to find and study interests, especially in a corporate person like the state. By hypothesizing that interests are constituted by ideas, idealism suggests that schema theory and attention to

---

[130] Witt (1991), Maryanski and Turner (1992).

[131] For example, Fischer (1992: 465).

[132] Krasner (1978) was for long an important exception. Today also see Zurn (1997) and Kimura and Welch (1998).

deliberation processes – suitably adjusted for the fact that states have collective rather than individual cognitions – might prove to be fruitful approaches to this problem.[133]

Second, and by extension, an idealist approach to interests also suggests ways to operationalize the relationship between cognition (agency) and culture (structure). In social (and IR) theory it has become commonplace to describe action as culturally or discursively structured, but rarely is a mechanism supplied through which this effect might actually work.[134] Somehow it is thought to be enough to point to the existence of cultural norms and corresponding behavior, without showing how norms get inside actors' heads to motivate actions. The materialist theory of interests may help explain this neglect, since it makes it difficult to see how an ideational phenomenon like culture could affect a material phenomenon like interests. Recognizing that interests are constituted by ideas removes the problem of mixing two kinds of "stuff." In IR this points toward a potentially fruitful dialogue between cognitive theories of foreign policy and cultural theories of structure, perhaps organized around the concept of foreign policy "role" (see chapters 4 and 6).

Finally, this approach suggests new possibilities for foreign policy and systemic change. In raising this issue it should be emphasized that saying that interests are made of ideas does not mean they easily can be changed in any given context. Idealism is not utopianism, and it is often harder to change someone's mind than their behavior. As such, ironically enough materialists may sometimes have a rosier view of the future than idealists, as in Waltz's view that controlled nuclear proliferation can cause system stability.[135] However, to the extent that interests are constituted by beliefs we can have more hope of changing them than we could if they simply reflected human nature (short of genetic engineering). It may be difficult for an actor to change its interests if the beliefs that constitute them are part of a culture that simultaneously constitutes the interests of other actors. This helps explain why cultures tend to reproduce themselves once created. But the fact remains that if interests are made of ideas, then discursive processes of deliberation, learning, and negotiation are

---

[133] See, for example, D'Andrade and Strauss, eds. (1992), Schneider and Angelmar (1993), and Weldes (1999).

[134] D'Andrade (1992: 41).   [135] Waltz (1990).

potential vehicles of foreign policy and even structural change that would be neglected by a materialist approach.

Conclusion

The argument of this chapter has been that the meaning of the distribution of power in international politics is constituted in important part by the distribution of interests, and that the content of interests are in turn constituted in important part by ideas. The constitutive as opposed to causal nature of this claim bears emphasis. The claim is *not* that ideas are more important than power and interest, or that they are autonomous from power and interest. Power and interest are just as important and determining as before. The claim is rather that power and interest have the effects they do in virtue of the ideas that make them up. Power and interest explanations *presuppose* ideas, and to that extent are not rivals to ideational explanations at all. My claim is therefore different than the Neoliberal argument that a substantial proportion of state action can be explained by ideas and institutions rather than power and interest. That treats ideas in causal terms which, while important, is not enough. The issue of "how" ideas matter is not limited to their causal effects.[136] They also matter insofar as they constitute the "material base" in the first place, that is, insofar as it is "ideas all the way down."

An argument that power and interest are just as important as before, but constituted more by ideas than material forces, inevitably raises the question, "so what?" If the balance of variables has not changed, what difference does this make to our understanding of international politics? Part II of this book is one answer to this question. But let me answer for now in programmatic terms by proposing a rule of thumb for idealists: when confronted by ostensibly "material" explanations, always inquire into the discursive conditions which make them work. When Neorealists offer multipolarity as an explanation for war, inquire into the discursive conditions that constitute the poles as enemies rather than friends. When Liberals offer economic interdependence as an explanation for peace, inquire into the discursive conditions that constitute states with identities that care about free trade and economic growth. When Marxists offer

---

[136] Cf. Goldstein and Keohane (1993: 6).

capitalism as an explanation for state forms, inquire into the discursive conditions that constitute capitalist relations of production. And so on. Enmity, interdependence, and capitalism are to a large extent cultural forms, and to that extent materialist explanations that presuppose those forms will be vulnerable to the kind of idealist critique featured in this chapter.

This is not to say that we should never treat cultural contexts as given, within which materialist explanations may be compelling, but in doing so we should recognize that the latter acquire their causal powers only in virtue of the contexts of meaning which make them what they are. Nor, on the other hand, is this to say that material forces like human nature, technology, or geography play no role in state action whatsoever. However, the materialist explanations offered above go well beyond such factors, in effect "cheating" on the materialism–idealism test by building implicit cultural elements into their claims. Only after we have stripped the discursive conditions of possibility from those claims will we know what material forces can really do.[137]

This argument tries to change the terms of the materialism–idealism debate in social theory by reducing "materialism" from its traditional, expansive definition focusing on the mode of production (or destruction), to a stricter, rump definition focusing on materiality per se.[138] This is not definitional sleight of hand, but an attempt to get at issues that are obscured in the traditional base–superstructure model. The key here is recognizing that materiality is not the same thing as objectivity. Cultural phenomena are just as objective, just as constraining, just as *real* as power and interest. Idealist social theory is not about denying the existence of the real world. The point is that the real world consists of a lot more than material forces *as such*. Unlike a potentially more radical constructivist position I do not deny the existence and independent causal powers of those forces, but I do think they are less important and interesting than the contexts of meaning that human beings construct around them.

Finally, this reframing of the issue casts new light on the Neorealist–Neoliberal debate. In my view, Neoliberals are caught in a Realist

---

[137] For a productive attempt to articulate a stricter materialist view of international politics see Brooks (2000).

[138] Bimber (1994) makes an analogous effort to differentiate meanings of technological determinism, some of which he argues are not technological determinism at all, but socio-cultural arguments about how technology gets used.

trap. It is the same trap that structural Marxists like Louis Althusser and Nicos Poulantzas were caught in when they tried to show, against orthodox Marxists, that the superstructure was "relatively autonomous" from its base.[139] Structural Marxists conceded primary explanatory importance to the mode of production (material base), but tried to show that institutional and ideological superstructures were important intervening variables. This theory ultimately failed, however, because of the inability to make coherent the argument that the superstructure was "relatively autonomous" while the material base remained still "determinant in the last instance."[140] (Interestingly, with the failure of structural Marxism many erstwhile adherents became post-structuralists, a move not unlike what happened in the 1980s in IR.) As in the case of structural Marxists, Neoliberals have done important work showing that by itself the material base (here, power and interest) cannot explain international outcomes by itself, but by conceding the base to Neorealists they have nevertheless exposed themselves to the same problem. This trap underlies Mearsheimer's argument that Neoliberals are tacit Realists; structural Marxists, after all, were still Marxists.[141] From Mearsheimer's perspective and mine, in other words, Neoliberals face a hard choice: either acknowledge the ultimately Realist character of their theory (because it buys into the base–superstructure interpretation of materialism) and deal with the problems of sustaining an independent theoretical position using a "relative autonomy" thesis, or refuse the Realist trap by problematizing the "materialist" nature of power and interest explanations from the start. Either way, in the end there can only be two possibilities, materialist and idealist, because there are only two kinds of stuff in the world, material and ideational.

Throughout this chapter I have used the language of ideas and the term idealism to make the case against materialist approaches to structure. This permitted economy of expression, but it might have suggested that I advocate a subjectivist approach to social theory in which all that matters is how individual agents perceive the world, or a voluntarist one in which agents are thought to be free to choose any ideas they wish. I advocate neither. How agents perceive the world is important in explaining their actions, and they always have an

---

[139] Althusser (1970), Poulantzas (1975).   [140] See Hall (1977) and Hirst (1977).
[141] Mearsheimer (1994/1995). The fact that regime theory, the forerunner of what became known as Neoliberalism, originally emerged from a Realist perspective is evidence for this line of reasoning. On the limits of Realism see Krasner (1983b).

element of choice in defining their identities and interests. However, in addition to idealism, a key feature of constructivism is holism or structuralism, the view that social structures have effects that cannot be reduced to agents and their interactions. Among these effects is the shaping of identities and interests, which are conditioned by discursive formations – by the *distribution* of ideas in the system – as well as by material forces, and as such are not formed in a vacuum. I have so far largely ignored the effects of this distribution, as well as the senses in which it might be structured. It is to these issues that I now turn.

4 Structure, agency, and culture

In chapter 3 I used the language of ideas to argue against a materialist approach to the study of structure. As I see it, however, social constructivism is not just about idealism, it is also about structuralism or holism. Structures have effects not reducible to agents. With that in mind this chapter looks at the structure of ideas in the system and asks: What does it mean to say that there is an ideational structure in a system? And what effects can such a structure have?

The structure of any social system will contain three elements: material conditions, interests, and ideas. Although related these elements are also in some sense distinct and play different roles in explanation. The significance of material conditions is constituted in part by interests, but they are not the same thing. Oil does not have the same kind of causal powers as an interest in the status quo. Similarly, interests are constituted in part by ideas, but they are not the same thing. The ideas constituting an interest in revisionism do not have the same kind of causal powers as the belief that other states obey international law. These distinctions mean that it may be useful for analytical purposes to treat the distributions of the three elements as separate "structures" (material structure, structure of interests, ideational structure). If we do so, however, it is important to remember that they are always articulated and equally necessary to explain social outcomes. Without ideas there are no interests, without interests there are no meaningful material conditions, without material conditions there is no reality at all. In the end for any given social system there is just structure, in the singular. The task of structural theorizing ultimately must be to show how the elements of a system fit together into some kind of whole.

Even if social structures always contain all three elements, it is nevertheless the case that idealists and materialists disagree importantly about their relative weight. As shown in chapter 3, interests are the central battleground. Materialists privilege material conditions, and try to show that they largely determine interests. Idealists privilege ideas, and try to show that *they* largely determine interests. Given that all three elements must figure at least tacitly in any structural theory, both sides can give some ground to the other, materialists conceding that ideas have some autonomous role and idealists that material conditions do. But their centers of gravity are fundamentally different. Since Neorealism offers a well-developed theory of the material structure of international politics, in this chapter I focus on the ways in which distributions of ideas may be structured and, more specifically, on how this ideational structure relates to interests. I do so as an analytical strategy only however, not to assert that ideas matter apart from material conditions. In subsequent chapters I try to put them back together.

A key premise of idealist social theory is that people act toward objects, including each other, on the basis of the meanings those objects have for them.[1] People have many ideas in their head, however, and only those they take to be true bear on these meanings; I may right now have the idea that I am the President, but I do not think this idea is true and so I do not act on it. From the impossibly broad category of "ideas" we can therefore narrow our focus at least somewhat to "knowledge," using this term in the sociological sense of any belief an actor *takes* to be true.[2] The American and Soviet belief in 1950 that they were enemies was knowledge in this sense, as is my expectation that the stock market will continue to rise. The ideational aspect of social structure might now be seen as a "distribution of knowledge."[3] The distribution of knowledge is a broader phenomenon than the distribution of interests, including both the ideational component of interests and general beliefs and expectations. In the language of chapter 3, the distribution of knowledge includes not only Belief but a good portion of Desire.

Knowledge can be either private or shared. Private knowledge consists of beliefs that individual actors hold that others do not. In the case of states this kind of knowledge will often stem from domestic or

[1] Blumer (1969: 2).
[2] As opposed to the philosophical sense of "justified true belief." See Berger and Luckmann (1966: 1–18).
[3] Barnes (1988); also see Hutchins (1991) on "socially distributed cognition."

ideological considerations. It can be a key determinant of how states frame international situations and define their national interests, and so is a major concern in the study of foreign policy. Its relevance goes beyond explaining the foreign policy behavior of individual states, however, because when states start interacting with each other their privately held beliefs immediately become a "distribution" of knowledge that may have emergent effects. When the Spanish met the Aztecs in 1519, each side began the encounter with private, domestically rooted beliefs about Self and Other that constituted their interests and definition of the situation, beliefs taken on each side to be true even though they lacked any basis in relevant experience. Upon interaction these beliefs became a social structure of knowledge that generated outcomes neither side expected. Even if states' private beliefs are completely exogenous to the international system, in other words, when aggregated across interacting states they become an emergent, systemic phenomenon in the same way that aggregate material capabilities are a systemic phenomenon. For Weber, this constitutes a minimally *"social"* structure as long as the actors within it engage in meaningful action that "takes account of the behavior of others and is thereby oriented in its course."[4]

Yet a social structure whose ideational aspect consisted only of privately held knowledge would nevertheless be very "thin." Thus, while the argument in this chapter bears on distributions of privately held knowledge, its primary focus is on a subset of social structure, socially *shared* knowledge or *"culture."*[5] Socially shared knowledge is knowledge that is both common and connected between individuals. Before 1519, an Aztec might have "shared" a belief in slavery with a Spaniard, but those beliefs were no more connected than the fact that both individuals may have had blue eyes, and as such were not social. When I say "shared" I will mean socially shared. Shared knowledge can be conflictual or cooperative; like game theory, cultural analysis is analytically indifferent toward the content of social relationships. Being enemies can be as much a cultural fact as being friends. Culture takes many specific forms, including norms, rules, institutions, ideologies, organizations, threat-systems, and so on, but the discussion below concentrates on what they have in common as cultural forms.

---

[4] Weber (1978: 88). Note that this is a thinner definition of a "social" system than Bull's (1977: 13) definition of "society," which presupposes *shared* knowledge and, indeed, common interests. Bull's "society" is a subset of what I call "culture" below.

[5] D'Andrade (1984: 88–90)

Finally, this perspective implies that culture is not a sector or sphere of society distinct from the economy or polity, but present wherever shared knowledge is found. If economy and polity are institutionally distinct spheres in a society, as in capitalism, therefore, that is because culture constitutes them as such.[6]

In IR, the differences between materialists and idealists about whether culture matters at all tend to obscure the equally real differences among those who concede the importance of ideas, about what it means to say that there is a cultural structure to international politics. In contemporary IR scholarship there are two main approaches to this issue, constructivist and rationalist.[7] Constructivists in IR have only recently begun to use the term "culture,"[8] but a concern with shared knowledge in the form of discourse, norms, and ideology has been at the heart of their work from the start. Culture may seem even more remote from rational choice theory, which is often associated with a materialism that privileges interests over beliefs. Yet, rationalist work on international regimes is also very much concerned with shared knowledge, and game theorists have generalized this to an explicit focus on culture defined as "common knowledge."[9] This creates the possibility for a fruitful dialogue between constructivists and rationalists, but it also raises some hard questions for constructivists in light of rational choice theory's strong conceptual apparatus and privileged status in the discipline. Do constructivists have anything to say about culture beyond what rationalists can tell us? In what sense does the game-theoretic analysis of common knowledge *not* exhaust the nature of culture? Identifying the value-added of constructivist over rationalist first principles in the study of culture is a core concern of this chapter.

IR's debate between constructivists and rationalists about culture mirrors a broader controversy within social theory between holist and individualist approaches to the question of how agents relate to the structures (ideational or material) in which they are embedded. It is in terms of this larger "agent–structure problem" that I shall address the problem of culture. Individualists and holists agree that agents and

---

[6] Wood (1981), Walzer (1984); cf. Buzan, Jones, and Little (1993).
[7] See Keohane (1988a).
[8] See Katzenstein, ed. (1996), Lapid and Kratochwil, eds. (1996), Weldes, *et al.*, eds. (1999).
[9] For expressions of this development in political science see Denzau and North (1994), Morrow (1994), Weingast (1995), Schofield (1996), and Bates, de Figueiredo, and Weingast (1998).

structures are somehow interdependent, and as such both are engaged in "systemic" theorizing, but they disagree on exactly how. Individualists say structure can be reduced to the properties and interactions of agents; holists say that structure has irreducible emergent properties. It is impossible to do social science without taking an at least implicit position on this issue, and this in turn will condition the content of substantive IR theory.

The position I take is synthetic, combining elements primarily from structuration theory[10] and symbolic interactionism.[11] To develop this position I make three distinctions: between two "levels" and two "effects" of structure on two "things." The two levels are micro and macro, where micro-structures refer to structures of interaction and macro-structures refer to what I'll call structures of multiply realizable outcomes. Applied to culture, this leads to a distinction between "common" and "collective" knowledge. The two effects are causal and constitutive, as I discussed in chapter 2. The two things are behavior and properties, where properties refers to agents' identities and interests (chapter 1).

All three distinctions concern how reality is structured, and to that extent the ontological debate about structures and agents ultimately is an empirical debate,[12] with rationalist and constructivist social theorists simply interested in different aspects of how reality is structured. To be more concrete, we can map the argument in matrix form (see figure 3).

My purpose in creating this figure is not to set up a literature review of social theory resolutions to the agent–structure debate, which I shall not undertake to do, but rather to suggest different ways researchers ask questions about structure. Often social theorists assume that the phenomena they are interested in are the only phenomena present in the system. This is not the case: both levels, both effects, on both things, are usually present in the same system. Much of the confusion in social scientific scholarship about the nature of "structure" and "structural" theory could be sorted out if we recognized the distinctiveness and potential plurality of these various "faces" of structure. Rational choice scholarship tends to be interested

[10] I have drawn especially on Giddens (1979, 1984), Bhaskar (1979, 1986), and Sewell (1992).
[11] Mead (1934), Berger and Luckmann (1966), Stryker (1980), Howard and Callero, eds. (1991).
[12] Kincaid (1993).

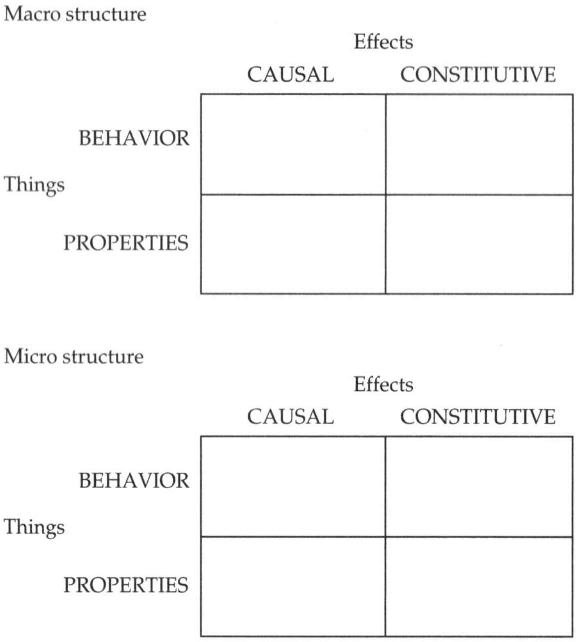

Macro structure

Effects

	CAUSAL	CONSTITUTIVE
BEHAVIOR		
PROPERTIES		

Things

Micro structure

Effects

	CAUSAL	CONSTITUTIVE
BEHAVIOR		
PROPERTIES		

Things

Figure 3 The faces of structure

in micro-level structures, and within that the causal effects of structure on behavior. Constructivists tend to be interested in macro-level structures, and within that the constitutive effects of structure on identity and interests (properties). In IR, constructivists have also analyzed the causal effects of structure on identity and interests, which tend to be neglected by individualists, but the primary value-added of a constructivist approach to culture lies in the analysis of constitutive effects at the micro- and especially the macro-levels.

The chapter first distinguishes between micro- and macro-level structures. To make meaningful the distinction and underscore the need for it to the IR reader, I develop it with reference to Waltz, pointing out some problems with his understanding of structure. Quite apart from his materialism (chapter 3), a problem is that he does not see that there are two levels of structure. I show the need for and articulate such a distinction and then apply it within the broad idea of culture to distinguish between common and collective knowledge. In the second section I then turn to the causal and constitutive effects of each level, paying particular attention to common knowledge to highlight the distinct contribution of a holist perspective. I conclude the chapter, and part I overall, with an argument that culture can be seen as a self-fulfilling prophecy. This argument highlights the importance of the social process, and ultimately process is the resolution of the agent–structure debate. Culture is a self-fulfilling prophecy, but process is also where we find the potential for structural change.

Two levels of structure

Waltz divides theories of world politics into two levels of analysis: the level of states and the level of the international system.[13] Theories pitched on the level of the former, which he calls "reductionist" or "unit-level," explain outcomes by reference to the attributes or interaction of the system's parts. "Systemic" or "structural" theories explain outcomes by reference to the structure of the system. In his view the business of third image IR is with structural theorizing alone.

This conceptualization of the nature and relationship between unit/agent-level and structural theorizing has become the standard in the field. Yet there has also been some unease about its dichotomous character, and in particular about treating theories that focus on interaction as unit-level. The problem is reflected in Waltz's own discussion. He initially defines reductionist theories as those "that concentrate causes at the individual or national level," which suggests that what makes a theory reductionist is an exclusive focus on the attributes or properties of states.[14] So far so good. In the next paragraph, however, without comment he adds "and interaction" to the definition. This is a very different matter, since interaction may have emergent effects that are not predicted by properties alone. Whereas property theories explain in a strictly "inside-out" fashion, interaction theories include features of the external context and thus have an "outside-in" aspect. The distinctiveness and significance of the interaction level is an important theme of Keohane and Nye's study of interdependence.[15] And it is also highlighted by Buzan, Jones, and Little,[16] who in a generally sympathetic discussion criticize Waltz for collapsing interaction and attribute theories into an "undifferentiated mass" of unit-level theorizing, and who then move to

---

[13] Waltz (1979).   [14] Ibid.: 18.
[15] Keohane and Nye (1989); see the "Afterward" pp. 260–264.
[16] Buzan, Jones, and Little (1993: 49–50).

salvage interaction (or "process") as a distinct causal mechanism. Interestingly, however, they fail to follow through on their argument, and in the end agree with Waltz that we should not call contexts of interaction "structures" because this would "fatally blur the distinction between unit and structural levels," nor even make them a distinct level of analysis.[17] Instead, they call them "process formations," and locate theories about interaction *at the unit level* (albeit as a kind of unit-level theory distinct from attribute theory).

I think Waltz is right to emphasize the relative autonomy of what he calls the structural level, but his strategy for doing so, which is reproduced by Buzan, Jones, and Little, is problematic and actually undermines the systemic project in two ways. The strategy's premise seems to be that there can only be one level of structure in the international system, anarchy, and that its autonomy depends on existing and having effects apart from the properties and interactions of states. If that were true it certainly would establish the autonomy of system structure, but as I suggested in chapter 3 and will show in more detail in chapter 6, it cannot be the case. The effects of anarchy are contingent on the desires and beliefs states have and the policies they pursue. There simply *is* no "logic of anarchy." As we shall see, however, this does not mean that anarchy's effects can be *reduced* to agents and their interactions, which would vitiate structural theorizing in Waltz's sense. What it means is that agents and interaction are essential to the causal powers of structure; to think otherwise is like thinking the mind exists or has effects apart from the brain. One problem with Waltz's formulation of the unit-level/structural distinction, therefore, is that it "reifies" structure in the sense of separating it from the agents and practices by which it is produced and reproduced,[18] which makes it difficult to assess the extent to which the effects of structure are sensitive to variation in the properties or interactions of units. The other problem is that by assigning the study of interaction to the unit-level, a topic that has an inherently outside-in aspect is removed from the definition of the systemic project.

Buzan, Jones, and Little's effort to differentiate attributes and inter-

---

[17] They later introduce an "interaction" level between the unit and structural levels, but by this they mean a system's physical capacity for interaction rather than interaction as such. I understand the interaction level in the way they understand process formations.

[18] Maynard and Wilson (1980).

action should be taken to its logical conclusion, which is to treat interaction as a distinct level of analysis between the unit and structural levels, and locate it firmly within the purview of systemic theorizing. Moreover, this interaction level has, and should therefore be recognized as having, "structure." The nature and effects of interaction structures are different than the structures Waltz is talking about, but theories of inter-state interaction share with Waltz's view of structural theory a concern with the logic of the international system. As such they have an equal claim on that level to the designation "structural." In order to avoid confusion with Waltz's view, structures of interaction may be called "micro"-structures because they depict the world from agents' point of view. The structures Waltz is talking about are "macro"-structures, because they depict the world from the standpoint of the system. Note that the terms "micro" and "macro" imply nothing about the size of actors or the proximity of their interaction.[19] The interaction of states across the ocean is micro-structured in the same sense as the interaction of individuals across the room. Nor does "micro" from the state-systemic perspective refer to the internal structures of states, of units. States have structures of their own, but I am concerned with the structure of the states *system*, not of states. There are as many micro-structures in the states system as there are interaction complexes among states.

In what follows I first define the two systemic levels of analysis (distinguishing both from unit-level analysis) and show how they parallel positions in the individualism–holism debate. Since this analysis is indifferent to whether structure is material or cultural, I then separate out culture and use the micro–macro distinction to discuss two of its "faces," common and collective knowledge.

Micro-structure

We saw above that Waltz includes interaction in his definition of reductionism. In contrast, by "unit-level" or "reductionist" I shall mean theories that explain outcomes by reference *only* to the attributes, *not* interactions, of individual states. In social theory this kind of position is considered "atomist" (which is considered distinct from "individualist").[20] Examples in IR of reductionism of this sort would be theories that explained international politics solely by reference to

---

[19] Archer (1995: 8–9).   [20] Bhargava (1992: 40–42).

internal, domestic factors like bureacratic politics. By explaining outcomes solely in an inside-out fashion such theories assume tacitly that states are autistic.

In contrast to unit-level theories, interaction-level micro-structural theories explain outcomes by reference to the relationships between a system's parts. One can theorize about the effects of interaction even when the parts are not intentional agents, as when warm and cold air currents interact to produce a storm. But since states are the relevant parts of the international system and they are intentional actors, let me limit the discussion to that context. Intentional actors interact when they "take each other into account" in making their choices. This can take two basic forms. In some cases, exemplified by consumers in a market, agents treat each other as a parameter of the environment over which they have no control, and so they "interact" only through the unintended consequences of their actions. In other cases, exemplified by bargaining, the outcome for each depends on the choices of the others, and so the actors act strategically, trying to second-guess each other in order to maximize their own pay-off. Here interaction is built into the choice problem itself. In rationalist discourse the former is characteristic of micro-economic theorizing, the latter of game theory.

Both kinds of interaction are structured by the configuration of desires, beliefs, strategies, and capabilities across the various parties. The structure of a market, for example, is constituted by what individuals jointly demand and supply, which is summarized in a good's price. The structure of a Prisoner's Dilemma game, in turn, is constituted by players having two strategies (cooperate and defect), a preference ordering over outcomes $(DC > CC > DD > CD)$, and an environment in which they are unable to establish credible commitments. Its outcome (that the parties will defect) is sub-optimal and unintended (hence the "dilemma"), but is forced on rational agents by the *structure* of their situation. The actors' attributes alone cannot explain this result; what matters is how they interact, the outcome of which is emergent from rather than reducible to the unit-level. Thus, explaining international politics by reference to interaction says nothing about, and indeed even competes with, explaining by reference to domestic politics. The two kinds of theories invoke causes on different levels of analysis and generate correspondingly different conclusions. One treats states as autistic, the other as social; one works in an inside-out manner, the other outside-in; one is psychological in spirit, the other social psychological. Calling both reductionist, as Waltz does, obscures these differences.

Attributes nevertheless play a crucial role in interaction-level explanations and this may be what leads Waltz to call them reductionist. Change what actors demand and supply and you change the structure of a market. Change the desires and beliefs constituting Prisoner's Dilemma and you can get Chicken, with a very different logic and outcome. Yet a key concept in Waltz's own theory of structure, the distribution of capabilities, is equally dependent on unit-level properties. Like a game constituted by desires and beliefs, different distributions of power are aggregates of state capabilities, and each distribution has a distinctive logic (though all conditioned, in Waltz's view, by an overriding logic of anarchy). As Waltz points out, however, what might be predicted by individual states' capabilities may not occur when capabilities are aggregated into a distribution.[21] And so it is with the distribution of interests, and the structures of interaction they help constitute. Our prisoners could reduce their jail time if they could cooperate, but the logic of their situation prevents it. To that extent even though attributes help constitute the nature of interaction, interaction is a determinant of the actors' fates above and beyond their attributes.

Apart from the fact that both appeal to unit-level attributes, there is one more similarity between unit- and interaction-level theories that may lead Waltz to treat them as both reductionist: both explain the behavior of particular agents. This contrasts with "Waltzian" or what I call macro-level structures, which explain broad tendencies in the system as a whole. As Waltz puts it, the one kind of theory explains foreign policy, the other explains international politics. Now, it is not clear how a theory of international politics could explain a systemic tendency like balancing without being able to explain foreign policy behavior *at all*, but as we shall see there is a sense in which Waltz is right. However, even though unit- and interaction-level theories both explain foreign policy, the explanatory reach of the latter goes further. Interaction-level theories explain not just an individual's choices but the overall outcomes of interaction, which have an inherently systemic dimension. The logic of Prisoner's Dilemma tells us about the likely choices of each prisoner; it also explains why each receives a suboptimal outcome, which attributes alone cannot explain. To that

[21] Waltz (1979: 97–99).

extent, unit- and interaction-level theories have different objects of explanation. So, we shall see, do interaction- and macro-level theories. There are three levels of analysis relevant to theorizing about world politics, not just two.

The analysis of interaction structure, and with it the intentional theory of action, is often associated with methodological individualism (and especially with rational choice theory), the view that social explanations must be reducible to the properties and/or interactions of independently existing agents. Interaction-level explanation is highly desirable from such a standpoint. Unlike unit-level (or atomist) explanations, individualist explanations allow for attributes *and interaction*, which makes them a useful tool for analyzing many of the unintended, emergent outcomes of social life. Holists can claim a distinctive insight into interaction insofar as they can show that agents are mutually constituted, but the macro explanations favored by some holists leave out the interaction level altogether. That is, just like Waltz some holists deny this level of structure. This is problematic because macro-level structures are only produced and reproduced by practices and interaction structures at the micro level. Macro structures need micro-structural foundations, and those foundations should be part of systemic theorizing.

Macro-structure

Interaction is not the only level of analysis on which the international system is structured. Waltz points to at least two tendencies in international politics that he argues cannot be explained solely by reference to the properties and/or interactions of state actors: to balance power and to become "like units."[22] Regardless of the content of states' intentions or the history of their interaction, according to Waltz they will tend either to balance each other's power and become isomorphic or be eliminated from the system. He takes the root cause of these tendencies to be the logic of anarchy, which works its effects indirectly through two proximate causes, competition and socialization. To illustrate how macro-structure has effects in Waltz's framework, I will tell his story about anarchy from the standpoint of competition. This is because the evolutionary story about natural

---

[22] Waltz (1979: 74–77).

selection is unproblematically a materialist story, and so fits nicely into his materialist understanding of structure.

According to Waltz, anarchies are necessarily "self-help" systems because they lack centralized means of enforcing agreements and because states are self-interested actors who, in lieu of centralized authority, cannot count on each other in time of need. These two factors put each state in the position of having to protect its own security and be highly risk averse. Threats must be assessed in a specific way: since the costs of being wrong about other states' intentions can be fatal, states must assume the worst about each other's motives and focus their estimates on capabilities, on the harm that others *could* do. If another state builds new capabilities, then so should you (by either building up your own power or recruiting allies). Similarly, if other states develop innovative ways of fighting or mobilizing resources, then so should you. These incentives do not guarantee that states will respond properly, since decision-makers may misperceive threats or be prevented by domestic factors from dealing with them adequately. Waltz is not trying to explain foreign policy. But in an anarchy, actors who fail to "keep up with the Jones's" will tend to die out (get conquered), leaving the field to those who do. It is this *selection effect* that produces the tendencies toward balancing and like units, not the fact that states intend to balance or imitate. Indeed, states may have had no such intention, but if the unintended consequences of their policies is to balance then they will prosper, while states who may fully intend to balance but cannot will fall by the wayside.

This may or may not be a satisfactory explanation for balancing and institutional isomorphism among modern states.[23] What matters for my purposes here is the form of the explanation, and in particular that the posited causal mechanism operates at the level of the *population* of states, not the level of individual or interacting states. Although it depends on a "tyranny of small decisions," Waltz is arguing that anarchy "programs"[24] outcomes in certain directions, and to that extent its effects are not reducible to the attributes or interactions of particular actors. This Darwinian logic has interesting affinities with Foucault's view of power as something that produces agents but does not belong to them.[25] In both cases a pattern of effects is explained not

---

[23] For doubts see Wendt (1992) and Spruyt (1994).   [24] Jackson and Pettit (1993).
[25] See Atterton (1994), Foucault (1980: 94–95).

so much by choices or even intentionality as by the properties of the system as a whole. Waltz calls explanations of this form "structural." This makes sense, but if we accept the argument that interaction too has a structure and that its effects are different than these, we now have two levels of structure. Having suggested that we call the latter "micro"-structural explanations because they treat structure from agents' point of view, it seems appropriate to call Waltz's kind of theory "macro"-structural because it treats structure from the standpoint of the system and does not seek to explain the behavior of individual actors. As with micro-structure, "macro" here does not refer to the size of the actors or scale of the system. Macro-structure is found in households as well as the international system.

The causal mechanism in macro-structural explanations need not take the form of natural selection. Social learning – socialization rather than competition – might have equally sui generis effects at the population level (chapter 7). Nevertheless, natural selection is instructive here because many philosophers have seen it exemplifying a fundamental problem for individualist explanatory strategies, namely "multiple realizability."[26] Whether it is the relationship of particles to atoms, atoms to molecules, brain states to mental states, speech to language, or individual to social facts, there are often many combinations of lower-level properties or interactions that will realize the same macro-level state. No particular states' actions create the tendency toward balancing and institutional isomorphism. No particular, unchanging distribution of territory or citizens "is" the United States. No particular words are essential to English. World War II would still have been that if Germany had not attacked Greece. And so on. In each case certain unit- or interaction-level states of affairs are *sufficient* for the existence of a macro-state, but not *necessary*. Macro-states are "over-determined." As Boyd puts it, macro-level facts often display "compositional and configurational plasticity,"[27] in which case macro-level regularities will be discontinuous with micro-level ones.[28]

Methodological individualism has difficulty with multiple realizability because it is committed to "micro-foundationalism." Perhaps due to the growing stature of rational choice theory, in recent years it has become widely agreed that social explanations should have

---

[26] Among philosophers on multiple realizability see, for example, Kincaid (1986, 1988) and Henderson (1994); in IR the phenomenon and its implications for theory are discussed, without the philosophical baggage, by Most and Starr (1984).

[27] Quoted by Currie (1984: 352).   [28] Pettit (1993: 112).

micro-foundations. This concept has been understood in two different ways, but multiple realizability poses problems for both.[29] The upshot is that while individualist attention to micro-foundations is valuable, it can lead to a failure to see or explain important things that are not reducible to the micro-level.

One, more radical, understanding of the micro-foundations requirement is that all macro-theory must be "reducible" to micro-theories, where this means that the propositions of the macro-theory are to be translated, without loss of explanatory content, via deductive "bridge principles" into propositions cast at the micro-level.[30] In the social sciences efforts at inter-theoretic reduction have been confined mostly to economics,[31] but the principle is entirely general: sociology is to be reduced to social psychology, social psychology to psychology, psychology to biology, biology to chemistry, and chemistry to physics. The effort in economics has so far failed, however, and it is now widely conceded that in most cases inter-theoretic reduction is impossible because the required bridge principles do not exist.[32] One cannot reduce a macro-theory if it can be realized in multiple ways at the micro-level. This may be just as well for individualists, since an often overlooked implication of inter-theoretic reductionism is that it grants no special status to individuals. Individuals have to be reduced to sub-atomic particles along with everything else, since to treat them as an ontologically primitive starting point for theory is itself a form of holism and therefore illegitimate.[33] Few individualists today make inter-theoretic reduction their goal.

Instead, most who now advocate micro-foundationalism are merely asking us to identify the micro-level *mechanisms* by which macro-structures achieve their effects. This requirement seems to have two motivations. One is to avoid functionalist explanations, which are widely viewed as faulty in the absence of identifiable causal mechanisms.[34] The other is a belief that causality operates locally in space and time, which means that getting ever more fine-grained understandings of causal mechanisms is a measure of scientific progress. On this view, therefore, macro-level explanations are not "complete" until

---

[29] For criticisms of micro-foundationalism see Garfinkel (1981: 49–74) and Kincaid (1996: 142–190).

[30] Nagel (1961: 336–397), Mellor (1982).   [31] See Nelson (1984).

[32] Friedman (1982), Kincaid (1986), Bhargava (1992).

[33] Jackson and Pettit (1992: 8–9).

[34] Levine, Sober, and Wright (1987), Little (1991: 195–199).

they show how structural effects are the intended or unintended consequences of the properties and interactions of individuals.[35]

Holists generally agree that we should try to identify micro-level mechanisms. Scientists should seek out causes wherever they may be found. But macro-theory is important as an end in itself because of multiple realizability. An excessive emphasis on the micro-level is problematic for two broad reasons.

The first is that when the same outcome can be multiply realized, when many different micro-level combinations could result in the same macro-state, then micro-level information may supply irrelevant detail.[36] The best explanation for why the window broke is that John threw a rock at it, not an analysis of the particular combination of subatomic particles that broke it, since many other combinations would have had the same effect. The best explanation for why a recession occurred might invoke macro-level factors that caused aggregate demand to fall, which could have had various micro-level instantiations.[37]

The second problem is that some causal mechanisms exist only on a macro-level, even though they depend on instantiations at the micro-level for their operation. Natural selection is one such case,[38] temperature may be another,[39] and "collective memory" a third (see below). By directing us exclusively "downward," therefore, the micro-foundational strategy may generate *disparate* explanations for events that in fact have a *common* macro-level cause.[40] Events may appear unrelated at the micro-level and yet be caused in a macro sense by the same mechanism. Micro-foundationalism may be useful for explaining why one world happens rather than another, but it neglects how that world might "run on patterns found in a variety of possible worlds."[41] The irony is that an explanatory strategy designed to deepen our understanding of how the world works may actually lead to a loss of information. This is not to say that we should no longer try to understand how macro-structural causes work at the micro-level, but an understanding of the micro does not replace an understanding of the macro.[42] Frank Jackson and Philip Pettit conclude that "there is no reason to think that finding smaller and smaller levels of causal grain

[35] Little (1991: 197).   [36] Kincaid (1988: 254).   [37] Sensat (1988: 201).
[38] See Wilson and Sober (1994: 599) on its potentially hierarchical nature.
[39] Kincaid (1993: 235).   [40] Kincaid (1988: 265).
[41] Jackson and Pettit (1992: 15).
[42] Henderson (1994); see also Meyer (1977), Wilson (1989).

means getting better and better explanations," and advocate instead a pragmatic or "ecumenical" approach to explanation that relates the type of mechanisms being sought to the question being asked.[43]

These problems suggest that those interested in understanding the structure of a system would do well to adopt a pluralistic, multi-method strategy. At the micro-level, in addition to game theory the tools of network theory seem particularly appropriate, since they are designed to show how relationships among particular actors shape behavior.[44] For macro-level analysis a different set of structural tools is called for. Rather than focusing on interaction, here we might turn, following macro-economists, to quantitative methods that capture broad patterns in a system, or, following discourse theorists, to linguistic methods that show how observed patterns of speech are possible.[45]

The implications of multiple realizability for individualism depend on whom you ask; some think it damages individualism decisively, others do not.[46] One way to reconcile these views is to distinguish ontological from explanatory individualism.[47] The essence of individualism is an ontological requirement that individuals are independently existing. This requirement is violated if it can be shown, as I try to do below, that structures constitute agents, but the phenomenon of multiple realizability does not imply such constitution, and as such in itself does not undermine the hard core of individualist social theory. What multiple realizability *does* damage, fatally in my view, is the requirement of explanatory individualism that the effects of structures be reducible (whether in the strong or weak sense above) to the properties and interactions of individuals. There is much in social life that can be explained by properties and interactions, but the existence of relatively autonomous macro-level regularities means there is also much that cannot.

The concept of "supervenience" provides a useful way to summarize this relationship between macro- and micro-structures, i.e., the fact that macro-structures are both not reducible to and yet somehow

---

[43] Jackson and Pettit (1992). Also see Stinchcombe (1991).

[44] Wellman and Berkowitz, eds. (1988). For different interpretations of the relationship of network theory to individualism and holism see Haines (1988) and Mathien (1988).

[45] On the analytics of the former, more Durkheimian approach see Turner (1983, 1984). On the latter see Sylvan and Glassner (1985), and Fairclough (1992).

[46] Cf. Ruben (1985: 95–104), Levine, Sober, and Wright (1987).

[47] Bhargava (1992: 19–52).

dependent for their existence on micro-structures. Supervenience has been developed especially by philosophers of mind, who face a problem similar to that facing social scientists: they have a strong intuition at the level of ontology that mental (macro-) states exist only in virtue of brain (micro-) states, but brain science suggests that the same mental state can be realized by a variety of brain states, which vitiates any 1:1 reduction at the level of explanation. The concept of supervenience is meant to square this circle. It describes a non-causal, non-reductive relationship of ontological dependency of one class of facts on another (mental on physical, social on individual, etc.).[48] It comes in various forms, but, in each form, one class of facts (macro) is said to "supervene" on another class of facts (micro) when sameness with respect to micro-states entails sameness with respect to macro-states.[49] The mind supervenes on the brain, for example, because two people in identical brain states will be in identical mind states. Similarly, social structures supervene on agents because there can be no difference between those structures without a difference among the agents who constitute them. Note that these relationships are constitutive, not causal; the supervenience claim is not that minds and social structures are caused by brains and agents, but that in one sense they *are* these things. Yet because the supervenience relation is non-reductive, with multiple micro-states realizing the same macro-state, the door is open to relatively autonomous macro-level explanations.

The number of ways in which a given macro-level structure can be realized by its elements is an empirical question. Some macro-structures may have quite narrow unit- and interaction-level requirements, others may not. This bears on the question of structural change at the macro-level: the tighter the sub-system control, the more sensitive the macro-structure will be to changes at lower levels. In this light, different systemic IR theories usefully might be seen as offering different answers to the question of how multiply realizable tendencies like balancing and power politics are under anarchy. Neorealists seem to be arguing that these outcomes are almost infinitely realizable; no matter what states are like or what policies they pursue, the structure of anarchy generates certain tendencies. Liberals argue that realpolitik outcomes will not be realized if states are democratic. In chapter 6

---

[48] See Horgan (1993) for a good overview of the philosophical literature, and Currie (1984) on implications for social science.
[49] Currie (1984: 347).

I argue that there are at least three cultures of anarchy, each with its own logic and tendencies. As we shall see, these differences come down in part to differences about the content and effects of international structure, but they all presuppose two distinct levels.

Culture as common and collective knowledge

The suggestion that the structure of any social system, including the international system, may be organized into two distinct levels says nothing about what that structure is made of. It might consist mostly of material conditions, mostly of ideas, or a balance of both; the micro/macro distinction is agnostic and applicable to each. The dominant theory of macro-structure in IR today, Neorealism, is materialist, and although Waltz eschews the analysis of micro-structure, his materialism could easily be applied to it: treat national interests (desire) as a function of human nature, and show how the distribution of material capabilities affect state choices.[50] Since micro-structural explanations of social life at least tacitly assume an intentional theory of action, this would require downplaying the idealist half of that theory, namely belief, either by showing that beliefs can be explained by material conditions or that the latter are so constraining that it does not really matter what actors believe. Having done so, however, we would have a two-level structural materialist theory of the international system.

In chapter 3 I indicated some limits of such an approach. On the one hand, material conditions do play an independent role in society, making certain actions possible or impossible, costly or cheap, whether or not actors perceive them as such. Actors who ignore these effects are likely to pay a price. The meaning of a hotel fire for those trapped inside depends on their beliefs, but those whose beliefs prevent them from trying to escape (because it is "God's will," for example) will die. There are few "hotel fires" in social or even international life, however, and as such material conditions per se typically explain relatively little, even though they are an essential part of the structure of social systems.

A first step away from a strictly materialist view of structure, therefore, would be to show that people act on the basis of private meanings that are at least relatively autonomous from material

---

[50] For an application of Neorealism to foreign policy see Elman (1996).

conditions. Long a staple of cognitivist theories of foreign policy, some scholars coming recently out of Realism have turned to forms of this argument as well.[51] This move creates something of a dilemma for Realists, since the more they emphasize beliefs the more explanatory power they are likely to gain, but the more they make what is ultimately a degenerating problem shift for a materialist ontology. However, it is important to note that even if states act on the basis of the meanings they attach to material forces, if those meanings are not shared then the structure of the international system will not have a *cultural* dimension. Private knowledge may affect foreign policy, and when aggregated across actors adds an interaction layer to international structure that affects outcomes, but even a "distribution" of private knowledge does not constitute culture *at the system level*, which may preserve the hard core of Realism as a "materialist" theory of international politics.

Sometimes international politics has no culture. It is an empirical question whether actors share any ideas, and sometimes they do not. When the Spaniards encountered the Aztecs in 1519, their interaction was highly structured by their beliefs about each other, beliefs that were rooted in pre-Encounter experiences and thus not shared.[52] The structure of their interaction was "social" (because, in Weber's terms, each side took the other "into account") but it was not "cultural." Today, however, states know a lot about each other, and important parts of this knowledge are shared – not all, to be sure, but important parts nonetheless. States and scholars alike treat these shared beliefs as the background, taken-for-granted assumptions that any competent player or student of contemporary world politics must understand: what a "state" is, what "sovereignty" implies, what "international law" requires, what "regimes" are, how a "balance of power" works, how to engage in "diplomacy," what constitutes "war," what an "ultimatum" is, and so on. Compared to the situation facing Cortez and Montezuma, this represents a substantial accretion of culture at the systemic level, without an understanding of which neither statesmen nor Neorealists would be able to explain why modern states and states systems behave as they do.

In the rest of this section I apply the distinction between micro- and

---

[51] Walt (1987), Wohlforth (1994/5), Mercer (1995).
[52] Although this did not stop Columbus from acting *as if* such knowledge was shared, as seen in his claim that he was "not contradicted" by the natives when he proclaimed ownership of the New World for Spain; see Greenblatt (1991: 58–59).

macro-levels of structure to the analysis of culture, with a view toward beginning to clarify the value-added of a constructivist relative to rationalist approach. I argue that the game-theoretic concept of common knowledge provides a useful model of how culture is structured at the micro-level. What constructivism adds to this model is an emphasis on its constitutive aspect. I then suggest we think about structure at the *macro* level in terms of Durkheim's idea of "collective" representations or knowledge. Like the macro-/micro-relation more generally, collective knowledge supervenes on but is not reducible to common knowledge, and as such has a reality that is *sui generis*.

The interest of game theorists in common knowledge constitutes an important "idealist" turn in a theory often associated with materialism. Unlike the recent interest of some Realists in the role of beliefs, there is no danger here of a degenerative problem shift since belief was always an essential element in the intentional theory of action. As such, attention to common knowledge does not point to any shift in the basic structure of rationalist theory; rather, it represents a renewal of attention to a factor that rationalists typically have neglected in favor of interests (hence the association with materialism). The change is due in important part to the "Folk Theorem," which shows that in repeated games actors can often sustain equilibria which they could not in a one-shot game, but that in most of these games there are *multiple* equilibria, the choice of which cannot be explained by the structure of preferences and private knowledge alone. If game theory is to explain the relative stability of real-world action, therefore, it needs to explain how people overcome this indeterminacy and coordinate their expectations around particular outcomes. Common knowledge is the answer.[53]

Common knowledge concerns actors' beliefs about each other's rationality, strategies, preferences, and beliefs, as well as about states of the external world. These beliefs need not be true, just believed to be true. Knowledge of a proposition P is "common" to a group G if the members of G all believe that P, believe that the members of G believe that P, believe that the members of G believe that the members

---

[53] Lewis (1969) is the principal contemporary philosophical source for this idea, although it goes back first to Schelling's (1960) work on tacit communication and salience, and before that to Hume's analysis of convention. For philosophical implications see Bach (1975) and Ruben (1985: 105–117); for game-theoretic approaches see Kreps (1990) and Geanakoplos (1992).

of *G* believe that *P*, and so on.[54] There is some debate about whether this layered series of beliefs must be infinite,[55] but all sides agree that commonness is not established simply by everyone believing that *P*, since unless each actor believes that *others* believe that *P*, this will not help them coordinate their actions. Common knowledge requires "interlocking" beliefs,[56] not just everyone having the same beliefs. This interlocking quality gives common knowledge, and the cultural forms it constitutes, an at once subjective and intersubjective character. Common knowledge is subjective in the sense that the beliefs that make it up are in actors' heads, and figure in intentional explanations. Yet because those beliefs must be accurate beliefs about others' beliefs, it is also an *inter*subjective phenomenon which confronts actors as an objective social fact that cannot be individually wished away. Neither a unit-level structure because of its intersubjective nature, nor a macro-level structure because of its subjective one, common knowledge is firmly an interaction-level phenomenon.

Specific cultural forms like norms, rules, institutions, conventions, ideologies, customs, and laws are all made of common knowledge.[57] Thus, while most Neoliberals in IR do not use the concept of common knowledge as such, their analyses of international regimes presuppose it.[58] The distinctive contribution of Neoliberalism, in other words, lies in an idealist argument, although in saying this it is worth reiterating that shared ideas are just as objective, just as constraining, just as *real* in their effects as material forces. Nevertheless, given the tendency in IR scholarship to equate cultural factors with cooperation, it is important to emphasize that the relevance of common knowledge is not limited to cooperative relationships. Shared beliefs can constitute a Hobbesian war of all against all or a Kantian perpetual peace.[59] Like game theory more generally, common knowledge is analytically neutral between conflict and cooperation, and so in principle as applicable to Realist as Neoliberal concerns.

I believe the concept of common knowledge is equivalent to that of "intersubjective understandings" favored by constructivists.[60] Both refer to the beliefs held by individual agents about each other

---

[54] Lewis (1969: 52–60).   [55] Geanakoplos (1992: 73–78).

[56] Bhargava (1992: 147).

[57] For discussion of these concepts and their differences see Lewis (1969), Bach (1975), Bhargava (1992: 143–156), and Denzau and North (1994).

[58] See especially Weingast (1995).   [59] Gilbert (1989: 43); see chapter 6 below.

[60] Also see Morrow (1994: 390).

("inter"-"subjectivity"), and both explain in intentional fashion, entering into social explanation through the belief side of the desire plus belief equation. The convergence can be seen in Kratochwil's use of David Lewis' and Thomas Schelling's rationalist work on convention,[61] and, going the other direction, in arguments that Alfred Schutz's phenomenological theory of action is compatible with expected utility theory.[62] This does not mean the uses to which the two traditions put the concept are identical, since constructivists tend to emphasize the constitutive effects of common knowledge while rationalists tend to emphasize its causal effects (see figure 3 and below). But the empirical phenomenon to which each is pointing, shared beliefs that orient action, is the same.

By way of summary and setting up a contrast with collective knowledge, let me emphasize two points. First, the relationship of common knowledge to actors' beliefs is one of reducibility, not supervenience. Common knowledge is *nothing but* beliefs in heads, *nothing but* "shared mental models."[63] This means that with each change in belief, or each change in membership, the cultural forms constituted by common knowledge become literally different. If culture is exhausted by this "summative" view of belief,[64] in other words, the apparent historical continuity of things like "Canada" or "the norm of non-intervention" is really nothing more than a metaphor. Unless culture is multiply realizable by individuals' ideas, strictly speaking it cannot ever be the same thing twice. Second, common knowledge explains outcomes via the intentional theory of action. Culture matters insofar as it affects the calculations of actors, no more, no less. To that extent not only is the ontology of common knowledge compatible with individualism, but so is its explanatory logic.

I do not dispute either of these points. On one level culture *is* beliefs in heads, and *does* explain in intentional fashion. But it is also something more, which following Durkheim I shall call "collective" representations or knowledge.[65] These are knowledge structures held by groups which generate macro-level patterns in individual behavior

[61] Kratochwil (1989: 72–81).
[62] Esser (1993), Schutz (1962). For critical reaction see Srubar (1993).
[63] Denzau and North (1994).   [64] Gilbert (1987).
[65] Durkheim (1898/1953); Gilbert (1994). For discussion in IR see Larkins (1994) and Barkdull (1995). A substantial literature has also developed in social psychology on "social" representations, which has roots in Durkheim's concept (e.g. Farr and Moscovici, eds., 1984; Breakwell and Canter, eds., 1993).

over time. Examples include capitalism, the Westphalian system, apartheid, the Afrika Korps, the free trade regime, and, as I argue in the next chapter, states. It is true that whether shared knowledge is common or collective may depend on your level of analysis: France is collective knowledge to all citizens who have been, are, and will be French, and its existence is common knowledge among its particular members at any given time. But the point is that collective knowledge is different and has different effects than common knowledge.

The relationship between collective knowledge and the beliefs of individuals is one of supervenience and thus multiple realizability.[66] This means, on the one hand, that a collective representation cannot exist or have effects apart from a "sub-stratum" of individuals' beliefs.[67] Structures of collective knowledge depend on actors believing *something* that induces them to engage in practices that reproduce those structures; to suggest otherwise would be to reify culture, to separate it from the knowledgeable practices through which it is produced and reproduced.[68] On the other hand, the effects of collective knowledge are not *reducible* to individuals' beliefs. Beliefs about capitalism might be wrong or incomplete, yet the actions they generate could still tend to reproduce the collective representation known as "capitalism." Similarly, since at least 1867 a collective representation known as "Canada" has existed which, despite a 100 per cent turnover in membership, helps explain aggregate continuities in its citizens' behavior – obeying Canadian laws, fighting Canadian wars, honoring the Canadian flag – even if they had no intention of being "good Canadians." Indeed, as Margaret Gilbert points out, we can ascribe beliefs to a group that are not held personally by *any* of its members, as long as members accept the legitimacy of the group's decision and the obligation to act

---

[66] To my knowledge no one has explicitly rendered Durkheim's idea in terms of the concept of supervenience, but Durkheim (1898/1953) compared the relationship of collective to individual representations to that between the mind and the brain, the latter being the paradigm case of a supervenience relationship in the modern literature. The similarities between Durkheim's discussion and supervenience are evident in Pettit (1993: 117–163), Gilbert (1994), and Nemedi (1995).

[67] Nemedi (1995: 48).

[68] There is growing interest among social psychologists in bridging the gap between individual and collective representations (e.g., Augoustinos and Innes, 1990; Morgan and Schwalbe, 1990; Howard, 1994). This is an important effort, but to the extent that the relationship is one of supervenience we should not expect a full integration, as seems to be the hope.

in accordance with its results.[69] In the interest of consensus, for example, a divided political party might adopt as part of its platform – as its group belief – a compromise that none of its members holds personally, and which in turn helps explain certain macro-level patterns in their behavior.

Group beliefs are often inscribed in "collective memory," the myths, narratives, and traditions that constitute who a group is and how it relates to others.[70] These narratives are not merely the shared beliefs held by individuals at any given moment (though they depend on those beliefs), but inherently historical phenomena which are kept alive through the generations by an on-going process of socialization and ritual enactment. It is in virtue of such memories that groups acquire continuity and identity through time. As long as individuals see themselves as having an allegiance and commitment to the group, collective memories will be available as a resource for mobilizing collective action even if they are not believed, in a phenomenological sense, by individuals, and in that way they can help explain patterns in aggregate behavior.

Consider the debate about the causes of the recent Bosnian Civil War. Critics of the "primordial ethnic hatred" theory rightly point to the fact that prior to the outbreak of war in 1992 few Serbs believed that Croats and Muslims were fanatics out to deprive them of their rights. They explain the war and "ethnic cleansing" instead in terms of the opportunistic policies of a Serbian leadership bent on resisting economic reform. As a proximate cause this may be right, but a key resource that made those policies possible was a collective memory that throughout their history Serbs had been periodically victimized, first by Ottoman Turks and then by Croatian and German fascists. The existence of this cognitive resource helps explain the relative ease with which the Serbian leadership was able to mobilize its people to respond so aggressively to Croatian and Muslim actions at the start of the conflict, as well as the larger, aggregate tendency for such seemingly irrational conflict to recur over time. This sounds an important cautionary note about the possibilities for social change: once collective memories have been created it may be hard to shake their long-term effects, even if a majority of individuals have "forgotten" them at any given moment.

---

[69] Gilbert (1987: 190–192).
[70] See Connerton (1989), Fentress and Wickham (1992), Halbwachs (1992), and Olick and Robbins (1998).

In sum, culture is more than a summation of the shared ideas that individuals have in their heads, but a "communally sustained" and thus inherently public phenomenon.[71] To the extent that this is the case cultural forms will be multiply realizable. Even though particular beliefs may be *sufficient* to realize a cultural form in a given setting, they may not be *necessary*. In contrast to common knowledge, structures of collective knowledge and the patterns of behavior to which they give rise do not by definition change simply because their elements have changed, even though – by supervenience – a change at the macro-level does imply one at the micro-level. In these respects Durkheim's concept of collective representation has much in common with Foucault's "discourse." Both concepts refer to individuals only incidentally; neither reduces knowledge to "what's in the head," and so neither is exhausted by self-understandings.[72] And both refer to macro-level regularities that are discontinuous with micro-level ones; neither explains the behavior of particular actors or relies on the intentional theory of action.

Some Durkheimians or Foucauldians might go farther, and dismiss altogether the study of individuals' mental states, and with them common knowledge, as either illicit or spurious. If this "de-centered" view of subjectivity is intended as an empirical claim that the beliefs in people's heads do not help explain their actions, then (I argue later) it is false. In addition, this view reifies culture, making it impossible to explain its production in anything but functionalist terms. Collective knowledge structures depend for their existence and effects on microfoundations at the unit- and interaction-level; without agents and process there is no structure. The important idea with respect to collective knowledge is its *explanatory* autonomy, since it is perfectly conceivable for common and collective knowledge to exist side by side, the one explaining particular actions (Waltz's "foreign policies"), the other systemic tendencies (his "international politics"). It is one thing for constructivists to argue that macro-level cultural forms have been relatively neglected in an IR scholarship dominated by rationalists,[73] quite another to deny the significance of micro-level forms altogether. In my view constructivists need to take the fact of common

---

[71] Taylor (1971: 60).

[72] For suggestive discussions of how one studies collective knowledge or discourse empirically see Sylvan and Glassner (1985), Bilmes (1986), Fairclough (1992), and Breakwell and Canter, eds. (1993).

[73] Laffey and Weldes (1997).

knowledge seriously, not least because they may have insights into its effects that elude rationalists.

Two effects of structure

What difference does structure make? In chapter 2 I argued that structures can have two kinds of effects, causal and constitutive. The one describes a change in the state of Y as a result of a change in the state of an independently existing X. The other describes how the properties of an X make a Y what it is. The structure of the master–slave relationship *causes* slaves to rebel when the master becomes too abusive. It *constitutes* them as slaves, and their protests as rebellion, by defining them as the property of the master in the first place. These differences are reflected in the terms appropriate to characterizing the relationship between agency and structure. The former is a relationship of "interaction" or "co-determination," the latter of "conceptual dependence" or "mutual constitution." Although sometimes used interchangeably, these are not the same thing. Mainstream IR scholars almost always use the language of causal interaction to describe the agent–structure relationship.[74] In this section I argue that this is correct as far as it goes, but there is more to the story.

In social theory it is sometimes assumed that causal and constitutive effects must be generated by different structures and corresponding social processes, for example, "regulative" and "constitutive" norms respectively.[75] But that seems like a problematic assumption. It may be that some norms and processes have primarily one effect, but others – probably most – have both. The same norms that constitute the identity of the slave also regulate his behavior in a causal fashion. Following Giddens and Onuf, therefore, I assume that norms are norms but that they vary in their balance of causal and constitutive effects.[76] After determining empirically that a particular norm has only causal effects we might decide to call it "regulative," but this should be taken to describe a pattern of effects, not a "kind" of norm.

The causal and constitutive effects of culture on agents can be exerted on just their behavior, on their properties (identities and interests), or on both. Starting from a premise that identities and

---

[74] For example, Waltz (1979: 99); Buzan, Jones, and Little (1993).
[75] See especially Searle (1969, 1995); cf. Rawls (1955).
[76] Giddens (1979: 66–67), Onuf (1989: 51–52); also see Tannenwald (1999).

interests are exogenously given, rationalists have focused on causal effects on behavior. Wanting to show that agents themselves are socially constructed, constructivists have concentrated on causal and constitutive effects on identities and interests (see figure 3). Since rationalists are associated with individualism and constructivists with holism, it is therefore often thought that the debate between the two ontologies is about whether or not agents are "socially constructed." In my view this is only partly true. Even though for reasons addressed below individualism tends to discourage the study of identity-formation, individualism as a whole, including rational choice theory, does not rule out the possibility that culture socially constructs agents (in a causal sense). Given that rational choice theory is the dominant expression of individualism today, this means that contemporary individualism contains unused space for thinking about the social construction of agents, which existing constructivist theories like symbolic interactionism might help it realize. Thus far, however, rationalist scholarship has largely neglected the study of causal effects of structures on agents' properties. The real debate between individualists and holists is not about whether culture constructs agents, but about the character of this construction process, and in particular whether it is limited to causal effects or also includes constitutive ones. I shall argue that individualism precludes the latter a priori because the notion of constitutive effects implies that individuals are not independently existing. To the extent that constructivism can show that culture not only causes but also constitutes agents, therefore, its value-added over rationalism is *two*fold. It helps us look at causal effects on the properties of agents and it helps us think about constitutive effects on behavior and properties.

The discussion takes up first the causal and then the constitutive effects of culture. I pay particular attention to effects on identities and interests, since this is where the contribution of constructivism mostly lies, but I consider effects on behavior as well. The overall argument is applicable to both levels of culture, micro and macro, but given their differences would take a different form in each. I make my argument with respect to common knowledge only, for two reasons. First, by staying on the same turf as rationalists who analyze ideational structure, I can specify how rationalism's individualist center of gravity leads its practitioners to miss important things. In addition, staying at the level of common knowledge makes this a difficult argument (a "hard case") for a holist to make, since the argument addresses subjective mental states of individuals. The holist center of gravity is at the level of the big picture and how structures get in the heads of agents is not the thrust of their approach. I conclude by discussing an apparent contradiction in the claim that culture has both causal and constitutive effects. This leads to a distinction between individuality *per se* and the *terms* of individuality, and since individualism privileges one and holism the other, paves the way toward a synthetic view.

Causal effects

Causal relationships can exist only between independently existing entities. In order for culture to have causal effects on or "interact" with agents, therefore, there must be some sense in which agents and their properties do not depend conceptually or logically on culture for their existence. Since culture is carried by agents, this effectively becomes the claim that agents do not depend *on each other* for their existence. They must be "freestanding." This requirement is not met merely by the fact that culture is an aggregate phenomenon that impinges on agents in an external fashion, since I show below that this is compatible with the mental states of agents being constituted by culture. The freestanding claim can only be met if at some level agents are *self-organizing* entities; if this were not the case, if agents were constituted by culture "all the way down," then culture could not have causal effects on them. The view that agents are self-organizing entities who exist independent of culture, and thus of each other, is the kernel of truth in individualism, and must serve as a reality constraint on holistic inclinations.

The game-theoretic analysis of common knowledge reflects this worldview. Game theorists have become interested in common knowledge because it helps solve games in which the structure of preferences and capabilities alone ("material" structure) generate multiple equilibria, which are probably most games in real life. Common knowledge solves these games by defining "salient outcomes" or "focal points" around which actors' expectations can converge, reducing transaction costs and uncertainty and thereby enabling actors to coordinate their strategies around a single equilibrium. The canonical example is Schelling's story of two people who, given a problem of having to meet on a certain day in New York City but being unable to communicate and not being told when or where, draw upon their shared understandings to settle on noon at the information booth in Grand Central Station.[77]

Two features of Schelling's story stand out for my purposes here. First, it highlights the effects of common knowledge on behavior, not on identities and interests. Schelling notes that the fact that his subjects had these particular shared understandings may have been due to the fact that his experiment was done in New Haven, Connecticut – which is to say that his subjects had "New Yorker" identities, broadly defined.[78] However, his point in the example is that their common knowledge affected their behavior, not their identities. Second, the effects on behavior that Schelling highlights are causal rather than constitutive. He does not emphasize the ways in which shared understandings made the meeting meaningful for the individuals involved. It might have been a business meeting, a lovers' rendezvous, or a drug deal – in each case the effect of common knowledge on behavior would have been more than merely causal: it would have also defined what kind of behavior they were engaged in, what they were *doing*, in the first place. This is not to discount the importance or distinctiveness of the causal or "regulative" effect. My point is only that this effect does not exhaust the difference that shared ideas might make. They might also constitute the meaning of behavior, and even construct identities and interests.

Schelling's story exemplifies how rationalist IR scholars tend to approach the effects of common knowledge.[79] It captures a great deal. It helps explain how agents coordinate their actions under complexity and uncertainty. In so doing it helps explain the relative predictability and stability of social life. And it can even help explain cultural change. In repeated games, behavior feeds back on shared expectations, causally confirming or transforming them in a dynamic of social learning. Robert Axelrod's[80] model of the "evolution of cooperation" examines just such a process of creating new knowledge through experience over time. Like Schelling, however, Axelrod concentrates on behavior, not identities and interests, and as such is concerned with "simple" rather than "complex" learning.[81] Moreover, within this behavioral focus he too is concerned with causal rather than constitutive effects. By showing these limitations of Axelrod and

---

[77] Schelling (1960: 55–56).   [78] Ibid.: 55 fn 1.
[79] See, for example, Goldstein and Keohane, eds. (1993), Weingast (1995).
[80] Axelrod (1984).   [81] Nye (1987).

Schelling I am not arguing that interaction over time always changes identities and interests (it may not). Nor am I denying that common knowledge has causal effects (it certainly does). But rationalist scholarship tends to neglect the other possibilities.

While this neglect is characteristic of individualist approaches to social explanation, it is only in part essential to them. Critics and proponents alike sometimes treat individualism as if it required agents to be Leibnizian monads, preexisting and totally unformed by society. This connotation is partly rooted in the individualist view that "rock-bottom" explanations can appeal only to individuals and their interactions, which is itself partly rooted in a desire to avoid any kind of societal determinism that would compromise individual freedom. But there is nothing in the denotation of an individualist ontology that precludes the social construction of agents, as long as a key requirement is met: the process by which agents are constructed must be explicable solely by reference to the properties and interactions of independently existing individuals. *Individuals must be constitutionally independent.* This in turn has an important implication: in any would-be individualist theory of how agents are constructed, individuals, and thus culture (which is carried by them), can play *only* a causal, not constitutive, role. Causal relationships imply independent existence, meeting the individualist requirement, constitutive relationships do not. This is a significant a priori constraint on how we can theorize about the social construction of identities and interests, which I problematize below, but what I want to emphasize here is that it does not rule "social construction" theorizing out altogether. In principle, individualism can accommodate a story about how culture constructs agents, as long as that story is causal.

This is all to the good for individualists. Rationalists tend not to be very interested in explaining interests, preferring to see how far they can get by focusing on behavior while holding interests constant.[82] Still less are they interested in issues of identity. But on both counts a dogmatic position rejecting the study of identity- and interest-formation altogether makes little sense. It may be that we can gain much insight into social life by taking interests as given, but this does not deny the fact that interests are socially constructed. To assume a priori that interests are never socially constructed is to assume that people are *born* with or make up entirely on their own all their interests,

---

[82] See especially Stigler and Becker (1977).

whether in getting tenure, making war, or marrying their high school sweetheart. Clearly this is not the case. A rationalist neglect of identity seems equally misplaced. To have an identity is simply to have certain ideas about who one is in a given situation, and as such the concept of identity fits squarely into the belief side of the desire plus belief equation. These beliefs in turn help constitute interests (see chapter 3). Politicians have an interest in getting re-elected because they see themselves as "politicians"; professors have an interest in getting tenure because they see themselves as "professors." As such, rationalists cannot avoid building tacit assumptions about identities into their assumptions about preferences, even if they do not call them identities. Interests and identities come from somewhere, and that obviously includes society.

The process by which identities and interests get formed is called "socialization." Socialization is in part a process of learning to conform one's behavior to societal expectations (Nye's "simple" learning), and as such it is possible to study it without studying identity- and interest-formation ("complex" learning), as in Waltz and Axelrod. Dynamic forms of rational choice theory may be quite useful for analyzing these behavioral effects. However, socialization is also a process of identity- and interest-formation, which in the long run individualists can hardly afford to ignore: if this aspect of socialization were inconsistent with individualism, then holism would be almost trivially true.[83] Fortunately, rationalists are increasingly taking an interest in both preference[84] and identity-formation,[85] which means that it is increasingly important for holists to pay attention as well.

Rationalist models of identity- and interest-formation may prove fruitful, but in developing them rationalists would do well to consider the work of symbolic interactionists, which to date they generally have not – who have been thinking about this issue at least since George Herbert Mead's *Mind, Self, and Society,* published posthumously in 1934.[86] Like game theorists, symbolic interactionists are interested in interaction, but unlike them they have made the con-

---

[83] Pettit (1993: 170).

[84] Elster (1983b), Cohen and Axelrod (1984), Raub (1990), Becker (1996), Clark (1998).

[85] Hardin (1995b), Laitin (1998).

[86] See especially Berger and Luckmann (1966), Hewitt (1976, 1989), McCall and Simmons (1978) and Howard and Callero, eds. (1991). For a suggestive attempt in IR to bring rationalist and constructivist models of interaction together see Barnett (1998).

struction effects of interaction on identities and interests a central theoretical concern. Interactionist hypotheses about identity – and interest – formation address both of what I am calling causal and constitutive effects. Their hypothesis about causal effects, which I believe is consistent with individualism, is that actors learn identities and interests as a result of how significant others treat them ("reflected appraisals"). Actors learn to be enemies, for example, by being treated by others in ways that do not recognize their right to life and liberty. The interactionist hypothesis about constitutive effects, which I will argue does violate individualism, sees identities as roles that are internally related to the role-identities of other actors ("altercasting" and "role taking"). I discuss the causal hypothesis in chapter 7, and the constitutive one now.

Constitutive effects

The difference that culture makes is in part a causal difference, and social theories associated with methodological individualism, like rational choice theory, have much to tell us about its effects and thus the agent–structure relationship. In this section, however, I argue that culture can also have constitutive effects. This argument challenges the core individualist assumption that agents exist independent of one another, and supports the holist view that agency has an inherently relational dimension.[87] Although holism is often associated with macro-theorizing, constitutive effects exist at both the micro- and macro-levels, and in what follows I focus on the micro. As I see it, although individualists have to stretch to analyze macro-structures, what ultimately distinguishes holism is not a focus on the macro-level, but on constitutive more than causal effects. If such effects are present, then there is at least some sense in which the relationship between agency and structure is not one of "interaction" but of "mutual constitution" instead.

The idea that social structure constitutes agents goes back at least to Rousseau and Hegel, both of whom argued that thought was intrinsically dependent on language. More recently it was captured by Maurice Mandelbaum at the outset of the contemporary individualism–holism debate in the philosophy of social science in his example

---

[87] For what looks to be a powerful development of this idea that I was not able to address here see Emirbayer (1997).

of cashing a check at a bank.[88] In order to perform this action teller and patron must both understand what a check is and what their roles are, and this shared knowledge must be backed up by the institutional context of a bank and banking system. Individualists will try to reduce all of this to the beliefs of independently existing agents, but Mandelbaum argued that any such effort will presuppose irreducible "societal facts." After four decades the claim that some individual predicates imply irreducible social ones remains a key philosophical objection to individualism. It is a central premise of a variety of social scientific traditions, including cultural psychology and cognitive anthropology,[89] cognitive sociology,[90] post-structuralism,[91] Wittgensteinian social psychology,[92] symbolic interactionism,[93] structuration theory,[94] and ethnomethodology.[95] There are many differences among these traditions, but all assume that in some important sense agents are constituted by their relationships to each other. Rather than review these literatures or privilege one, let me try to characterize that common thread. I have found it most clearly expressed in recent debates in the philosophy of mind and language about the nature of intentionality.[96]

In IR scholarship it is routine to refer to states as "intentional" entities, meaning that they act in a purposive fashion on the basis of desires and beliefs about the world. Desires and beliefs are mental phenomena, which differ from physical phenomena in at least one crucial way: in some sense they contain within them the objects to which they refer. As John Searle puts it, "[i]ntentionality is that property of many mental states and events by which they are directed at or about or of objects and states of affairs in the world."[97] All sides agree that intentionality has this quality of relating agents to the external world. The debate is about how the "content" of actors' ideas about this world is constituted. Is it strictly in their heads, or does it presuppose the world? In short, where are desires and beliefs "located"?

The individualist answer is that they exist solely in the heads of individuals. Mental contents are "about" the world but do not

---

[88] Mandelbaum (1955).   [89] Shweder (1991), D'Andrade (1995), DiMaggio (1997).
[90] Howard (1994), Zerubavel (1997).   [91] Foucault (1979).   [92] Jost (1995).
[93] Mead (1934).   [94] Giddens (1984), Bhaskar (1986).   [95] Coulter (1989).
[96] Recent debates in philosophy about "socializing" epistemology reflect similar concerns; see, for example, Manicas and Rosenberg (1985) and Schmitt, ed. (1994).
[97] Searle (1983: 1).

172

presuppose it. This position, known today in the philosophy of mind as "internalism," in modern times goes back to René ("I think therefore I am") Descartes and the classical empiricist epistemologies of Locke, Berkeley, and Hume.[98] The intuitions behind internalism on the surface appear to be decisive. First, individuals seem to have privileged access to their own thoughts in the sense that they do not need to check with others to know what they are thinking. When it comes to knowing our minds each of us has "first-person authority."[99] Second, what matters in explaining our behavior seems to be our own thoughts, not someone else's. To explain why Jones robbed the bank we need to get inside *his* head, at *his* desires and beliefs, not the heads of those who "made him do it." Finally, science tells us that mental states depend on brain states, and since brains are self-organizing physical phenomena that do not presuppose each other, this seems to clinch the individualist picture. On the internalist view, therefore, in order to explain intentional action we need look no farther than the mental states of individuals. Psychology is ultimately a solipsistic affair, and sociology is ultimately reducible to the inter-psychological relations among independent mental worlds. Note that this does not preclude interaction among individuals having a *causal* impact on mental states, for example through socialization. Internalism claims only that the content of an actor's mental state does not logically presuppose other people, and therefore culture. After all, as Descartes argued, we can imagine having our thoughts even if the world did not exist.[100] In sum, according to individualism/internalism, "[t]hought is logically prior to society,"[101] and society is reducible to an aggregate of interlocking but independently existing "idiolects."

The intuitions behind internalism are powerful, and thus it may surprise social scientists that most philosophers of mind today are externalists.[102] Externalism is the view that the content of at least some mental states is constituted by factors external to the mind.[103] To the extent that this is true, whenever social scientists explain behavior by reference to desires and beliefs they will inevitably be smuggling characteristics of an irreducible environment into their explanations.

---

[98] On the relationship of individualism to the Cartesian theory of mind, see Markova (1982) and Wilson (1995).

[99] Bernecker (1996).   [100] Bilgrami (1992: 1–3).   [101] Gilbert (1989: 58).

[102] Bernecker (1996: 121).

[103] Horowitz (1996: 29). For varying forms of externalism see Biro (1992), Antony (1993), Peacocke (1993), Bernecker (1996), de Jong (1997), and Kusch (1997).

On this view, far from being logically prior to society, thought is intrinsically *dependent* upon it, and as such it will be impossible to reduce society to an aggregate of independently existing idiolects. Whereas internalism leads to an individualist ontology, externalism leads to a holist one.

Although it supports holism, which historically has Continental roots, the externalism that currently dominates the philosophy of mind and language is rooted in the Anglo-American analytical philosophical tradition. Its popularity stems in part from the influence of two thought experiments. One is Putnam's[104] story about our friends on Twin Earth, whom we met in chapter 2; the other is a structurally similar story that Tyler Burge tells about arthritis.[105] The aim of both is to show that two people in identical mental states can differ in intentionality, which must therefore be accounted for by their environments.

Recall Putnam's story: two worlds exactly alike, people and languages identical in every way, the term "water" equally applied to a potable clear liquid, except that on one planet the (unknown) chemical structure of this substance is H_2O and on the other it is XYZ. The subjective meanings held by $Oscar_1$ and $Oscar_2$ on the two planets are the same – they have the same ideas in their heads – yet they pick out different natural kinds. Putnam concludes that the meaning of water "ain't in the head," but lies in a relationship to the external world.

Putnam's story is an argument that mental contents are constituted by nature. Burge's story extends this to society, and as such is more relevant to this chapter's focus on culture. An individual (I will call him Max) has various correct beliefs about arthritis – that he has it in his ankle, that his father had it, that it is painful, and so on – as well as the *in*correct belief that it can afflict the thigh. Concerned about recent pains, Max tells his doctor that he fears his arthritis has spread to his thigh. His doctor says that is impossible because arthritis is an inflammation of the joints. Surprised but relieved, Max changes his belief. Now imagine a counterfactual ("Twin") world in which Max is in every way identical – same beliefs, same physical history – but in this community the term "arthritis" *is* applied to pains in the thigh. Hence, upon complaint, Max's doctor treats him for "arthritis." Burge

[104] Putnam (1975).
[105] Burge (1979: 77–79). On the similarities and differences between these "Twin Stories" see Bilgrami (1992: 22–24).

concludes that the content or meaning of Max's belief is different than in the first case, even though his mental state is the same. The difference is due to his social context.

Externalist philosophers have drawn three implications from these stories.[106] The first is that thoughts are constituted at least in part by external context rather than solely in the heads of individuals, since how thoughts get carved up or "individuated" depends on what "conceptual grid" is used.[107] Context determines what meanings we can properly attribute to an agent, and if that context is cultural, as in Burge's story, then thought presupposes society. Note that this is a constitutive claim.[108] It is not that mental contents are caused by contact with the outside world (though that is certainly also the case), but that they *presuppose* the world in the sense that they "are dependent upon the usages of words in a society and cannot be individuated in a context-independent way."[109] Thinking depends *logically* on social relations,[110] not just causally. As Richard Shweder puts it, human beings "think through culture."[111] And since the structure of shared beliefs is ultimately a linguistic phenomenon, this means that language does not merely mediate thinking, it makes thinking possible.[112]

Second, the Twin stories suggest that a term's meaning and thus truth conditions are "owned" by the community, not by individuals. Two further pieces of evidence support this proposition. (1) In many cases we depend on the "testimony" of others, past and present, for access to the objects about which we speak. I have not been to the court of Henry VIII, but I can use that concept meaningfully because I rely on the testimony of others who have. (2) If we are unsure about the meaning or appropriateness of a mental state, we may take advantage of the "division of linguistic labor"[113] in society by deferring to experts to explicate our own beliefs.[114] Jones may think he saw a Bigfoot, but after talking to the experts may defer to their judgment that he could have seen no such thing. This willingness to communi-

---

[106] See Bhargava (1992: 194).   [107] Ibid.: 223; Antony (1993: 260).
[108] As Currie (1984: 354), Burge (1986: 16, 1989: 177), Bilgrami (1992: 23), Peacocke (1993: 226), and Pettit (1993: 170) all point out.
[109] Bhargava (1992: 200).   [110] Pettit (1993: 169).   [111] Shweder (1991).
[112] Searle (1995: 59–78). In IR Kratochwil (1989) and Onuf (1989) are particularly clear on this, which forms the basis for their use of speech act theory, itself rooted in important part in the work of Searle.
[113] Putnam (1975: 227–229), Bhargava (1992: 182–189).   [114] Burge (1989: 184).

cate *"by reference to standards partly set by a wider environment"*[115] is a significant challenge to internalism. Individualists will try to reduce authority over meaning to the rational choices of independent agents, but it seems more natural to say that ultimately authority lies with the community.

Finally, meanings depend on the practices, skills, and tests that connect the community to the objects represented in discourse. This is because the only way for the community to know the meaning of say, "tiger," is to engage in public activities that determine what counts as such. "This test does not exist in anyone's head,"[116] even if it depends on actors having something in their heads. The argument here is fairly intuitive for natural kinds since, given the theory-ladenness of all observation, what counts as a tiger will depend in part on the public measurement procedures by which that determination is made. Yet, what counts as a lawyer or a state is equally not reducible to what is in people's minds, but out there in public *practices*.[117] Putnam and Burge do not draw on Wittgenstein, but they end up in a similar position, since he too argued that meaning exists only in the practices or "use" of language communities.

Having tried to characterize the philosopher's case for the constitutive effects of culture, let me offer a social scientist's one. Consider the effects on behavior and identity of material inequality in two international systems, one in which material dominance is recognized by subordinate states as constituting certain rights and responsibilities on the part of dominant states, and one in which it is not.

Take the behavioral effects first. Assume the dominant states in the two systems engage in the same dominance behaviors: giving military aid to weak states, forbidding them to ally with other Great Powers, intervening in their domestic politics, and so on. Assume, moreover, that they have the same beliefs that what they are doing is their right by virtue of might, and that both hegemons are ignorant of what other states think. The content of those beliefs will nevertheless be different because of the different intersubjective contexts. In one system their meaning will be constituted as "interference," in the other as "assistance," in one as "legitimate," in the other as "illegitimate." This is not a causal difference. Certainly in the two cases different beliefs create different incentives, which will affect foreign

---

[115] Burge (1986: 25), his emphasis.   [116] Bhargava (1992: 193).
[117] Taylor (1971: 57).

policy behavior in a causal fashion. But the difference between the two systems also concerns what *counts* as "intervention" as opposed to "invasion," as "right" as opposed to "aggression," as "responsibility" as opposed to "paternalism." Put more abstractly, the two systems have different *truth conditions* for statements about dominant states' intentionality, despite identical beliefs in their "heads." What makes the statement that the US "intervened" in Haiti in 1995 true, and that it "aggressed against" Haiti false is not a difference in behavior or even in US beliefs, but in the (system-level) cultural context in which it took place. In the contemporary international system it is the community of states which owns the meaning of "intervention" (although it may be contested). A world in which no such shared belief existed would sustain different counterfactuals about US intentionality. This is the key insight of an externalist approach to mental contents.[118]

Now consider the constitutive effects of culture on identities and interests. Assume that in both systems materially dominant powers fulfill a similar function of stabilizing the system, and that they also understand that to be their responsibility, that they have the identical subjective mental states of a "hegemon." The content of those identities will still be different. In the system where the dominant state is legitimate, it will be empowered by the community of states to perform the functions of, and thus literally *be*, a "hegemon." In the other system, where the dominant state's intentions have a strictly internal basis, other states will attribute to it the identity of "bully" or "imperialist," and cooperate with its policies only when bludgeoned or bribed. A state literally cannot *be* a hegemon in such circumstances, any more than a person can be a master without a slave, or a wife without a husband. This does not prevent someone from *thinking* they are a master, wife, or hegemon, but in the absence of a relevant Other they are deluding themselves. The same self-perception has a different content depending on whether or not it has an *external* basis in shared understandings. As with behavior, in other words, the truth conditions for identity claims are communal rather than individual. It is the "generalized other"[119] that decides whether the US is a hegemon, not the US by itself, and in that sense the cultural constitution of identity (or subjectivity) is a form of power, as post-structuralists have

---

[118] Peacocke (1993: 204–205).   [119] Mead (1934).

emphasized.[120] The US may eventually be able to socialize other states to accept its self-ascribed hegemonic identity, but until it does it will be only a materially dominant state.

Toward a synthetic view

In the story so far I have emphasized holist objections to individualism, but I do not want to leave intentionality or agency behind. By way of looking for a via media, to conclude my discussion of the effects of culture I turn around and defend the individualist intuition that mental states have an independent explanatory status (a "rump" individualism), and therefore that culture has causal effects on agents.

The individualist hypothesis is in effect that all identities are personal identities, all interests personal interests, all behaviors meaningful because of personal beliefs. Nothing in or about the actor or his behavior logically or conceptually presupposes other actors or culture. The holist hypothesis is that culture constitutes role identities and their corresponding interests and practices. Regardless of the thoughts in one's head, one cannot be a certain kind of agent, or engage in certain practices, unless these are recognized by others. If holists are right then it will be impossible to reduce society to independently existing idiolects, as required by the individualist view that thought is logically prior to society. Individualist approaches to social inquiry may still be useful for some questions, but will be inherently incomplete insofar as they presuppose irreducible societal facts. If the holist is right, in other words, we will have to revise our conventional view of intentional agency, which is rooted in individualism, if not jettison it altogether.

There are at least two radical holisms that would do just that. Poststructuralists seek to deconstruct the individual by showing that it has no essence prior to society. Intentionality is merely an effect of discourse, not a cause in its own right. This "decentering" of the Cartesian subject is rooted in Saussure's linguistic structuralism, in which meaning stems from relations of difference between words rather than reference to the world, in this case the consciousness of individuals (see chapter 2). Even if discourse only has these effects in virtue of the actions of people (supervenience), which post-structuralists need not deny, in their view those effects cannot be explained by

---

[120] Foucault (1979, 1982), Dews (1984).

reference to a pre-social individuality, since intentionality is shot through with discourse "all the way down."

Post-Wittgensteinian philosophers of action reach a similar anti-individualist conclusion. In his later work Wittgenstein was highly critical of "mentalism," a "disease of thinking" which holds that subjective mental states are causes of behavior, as assumed by the intentional theory of action.[121] Rather than referring to mental states, Wittgenstein argued that motives and intentionality actually refer to the public criteria by which we make behavior intelligible, by which we make *ascriptions* of motive.[122] A murder trial is a typical example: lacking direct access to the mind of the defendant, the jury relies instead on social rules of thumb to infer his motives from the situation. Did he have a history of conflict with the victim? Did he resist arrest? Is there evidence linking him to the crime scene? In effect, the jury is capitalizing on Burge's point that the contents of an individual's thoughts reflect his context. Wittgensteinians go one step farther, however, by arguing that in the end the defendant's motives cannot be distinguished from the rules of thumb through which the jury tries to know them, and as such there is no reason to treat the former as internal springs of action in the first place.[123] If this seems counter-intuitive, this is only because in daily life we "condense" the public criteria by which we ascribe intentions into putative mental acts, which thereby seem to acquire a hidden existence and mysterious causal force.[124] Once seen for what they are, social scientists can eschew intentions as causes of action and focus instead on the structures of shared knowledge which give them content.[125]

These arguments directly challenge the fundamental individualist intuition that mental states should have a privileged status in social explanation. They also have an important corollary: the relationship between agents and culture cannot be causal. If agents are constituted by culture all the way down, then there is no sense in which they are independent of it, which is necessary for them to stand in a causal

---

[121] See Bloor (1983) and Rubinstein (1986) for overviews of Wittgenstein on this issue; for a sense of how a Wittgensteinian might criticize the argument I make below see Coulter's (1992) response to Bilmes (1986).

[122] Blum and McHugh (1971).   [123] Sharrock and Watson (1984), Coulter (1989).

[124] Bloor (1983: 19).

[125] Rubinstein (1977: 229). As Harold Garfinkel puts it, "there is no reason (for sociologists) to look under the skull since nothing of interest is to be found there but brains" (quoted in Coulter, 1983, frontispiece).

relationship. If radical holism is right, in other words, agents and culture cannot *interact*, since "inter"action presupposes distinct entities.[126] In Giddens' terms, the relationship between agent and structure would be all "duality" and no "dualism," two sides of the same coin rather than distinct phenomena interacting over time.

I want to retain a moderate holism about culture, which means I need to resolve the apparent contradiction in asserting that agents are both independent of culture and dependent on it. How can agents and structure be both "mutually constituted" *and* "co-determined,"[127] how can we have both duality *and* dualism? In short, how is a synthesis of holism and individualism possible?

Two converging lines of argument point to the problem with radical holism, one emphasizing the intrinsic powers of agents, the other the limits of structural explanations. The first is that no matter how much the meaning of an individual's thought is socially constituted, all that matters for explaining his behavior is how matters seem *to him*.[128] In Burge's story, it may be that the content ascribed to the thoughts of the two Maxs, and the treatment they received from their doctors, depended on how their communities constituted the meaning of "arthritis." But what caused them to go to the doctor in the first place was their own thoughts (pain; a belief it was caused by arthritis), into which they had privileged access. These may have been mistaken from a social point of view, but this does not mean they did not cause the action. The second argument turns this around and asks, what is the mechanism by which culture moves a person's body, if not through the mind or Self? If an actor is *unaware* of shared knowledge, or does not care about it, how can it explain his actions?[129] An isolated culture meeting an anthropologist for the first time might "explain" her failure to follow its norms as the work of demons, but of course that way of constituting her intentions in fact has nothing to do with explaining *her* behavior, even if it does explain *its* behavior toward her. Similarly, in Burge's story Max has different beliefs than his society, which suggests that the cause of his actions can be discovered

---

[126] A perceived failure to secure the possibility of causal interaction between agency and structure has been a persistent criticism of Giddens' theory of "structuration." See Archer (1982, 1995) and Taylor (1989).

[127] Where the latter denotes a causal as opposed to constitutive relationship.

[128] This argument is developed in more detail by Loar (1985) and Biro (1992), and I think is implicit in Bhargava's (1992) approach to the issue.

[129] See Porpora (1983: 132–133), Bilgrami (1992: 4), and D'Andrade (1992).

independent of it. Even in the event of perfect correspondence between subjective and shared knowledge, the truth of an externalist explanation of action that appeals to culture depends on the truth of an implicit internalist one that appeals to subjective motives.[130] People are not like rocks. Rocks move only when pushed by an outside force. People move all by themselves, and culture cannot explain that behavior unless it somehow gets in their heads. A purely constitutive analysis of intentionality is inherently static, giving us no sense of how agents and structures interact through time.

These criticisms do not preclude a moderate holism. Their point is not that culture does not help constitute the meaning of an agent's desires and beliefs, but that agents have a role to play in social explanation which cannot be reduced to culture. Radical holists conflate acting *with* a reason with acting *for* a reason,[131] but this does not mean that society is merely an aggregate of independently existing idiolects. Such a mixed position seems to be the response of many philosophers to the Burge/Putnam stories: most agree that externalism/holism captures important truths, which vitiates a strict internalism/individualism, but they also recognize that it has important limits. In an effort to transcend the dichotomy many now distinguish between two kinds of mental content.[132] "Narrow" content refers to the meanings in an actor's head which motivate her actions, while "broad" or "wide" content refers to the shared meanings which make her thoughts intelligible to others. The two play different roles in social explanation.

The same point might be made more usefully here in a social scientific idiom by distinguishing between individuality *per se* and the social *terms* of individuality. The former refers to those properties of an agent's constitution that are self-organizing and thus not intrinsically dependent on a social context. Some of these properties are material: individuals live in genetically constituted bodies that do not presuppose other bodies, and have minds in virtue of independent brains. Others are cognitive: agents exist partly in virtue of their own thoughts, which they can continue to have even if they are marooned on a desert island. Both kinds of properties are essential to intentional agency, and, even if they are caused by society, they exist independent of them. They give the Self an "auto-genetic" quality,[133] and are the

---

[130] Bruce and Wallis (1983).   [131] Bhargava (1992: 137).
[132] For example, Biro (1992); cf. Walsh (1998).   [133] Schwalbe (1991).

basis for what Mead called the "I," an agent's sense of itself as a distinct locus of thought, choice, and activity.[134] Without this self-constituting substrate, culture would have no raw material to exert its constitutive effects upon, nor could agents resist those effects. The intuitions that sustain individualism are rooted in this aspect of individuality.

The *terms* of individuality refer to those properties of an agent's constitution that are intrinsically dependent on culture, on the generalized Other. Hegemons and priests only exist as such when they are culturally recognized. While this recognition is partly external, out there in the understandings of Others, it is also internal, in what Mead called the "Me": the meanings an actor attributes to itself while taking the perspective of Others, while seeing itself as a social *object*. This willingness to define the Self by reference to how Others see it is a key link in the chain by which culture constitutes agents, since unless actors appropriate culture as their own it cannot get into their heads and move them, but through this very willingness the terms of their individuality become an intrinsically cultural phenomenon. The intuitions that sustain holism are rooted in this inherently social aspect of individuality.

One can see both aspects of individuality at work in the concept of state "sovereignty" (see chapter 6). Being sovereign is, on the one hand, nothing more than having exclusive authority over a territory, which a state can have all by itself. A state controlling a lost island or a world government would still both be sovereign, and to that extent sovereignty is an intrinsic, self-organizing property of their individuality. It is in virtue of this feature of sovereignty that states can causally interact with each other, and thus with a structure of sovereign states, because it means they are independently existing. Unlike many systems of sovereign states, however, in the particular culture of the Westphalian states system sovereignty is also a *right* constituted by mutual recognition, which confers on each state certain freedoms (for example, from intervention) and capacities (equal standing before international law) that only the most powerful states might be able to enjoy based on intrinsic properties alone. This feature of state agency does not "interact" with the structure of mutual recognition, as if the two existed apart from each other; it is not a "dependent variable" which is explained by a separate "independent

---

[134] Mead (1934), Lewis (1979).

variable." It is logically dependent on that structure, and as such concerns the terms of state individuality rather than its individuality per se.

One way to capture this distinction methodologically would be to extend Martin Hollis' suggestive distinction between conventional games and Wittgensteinian language games into a distinction between two kinds of "game theory."[135] Conventional or von Neumann–Morgenstern game theory takes an individualist view. It assumes that the structure of a game is an aggregate of independently existing actors, which in turn has causal or regulative effects on them. This gets at the role of narrow mental content, of individuality per se, in interaction. Wittgensteinian "game theory" takes a holist view, treating the structure of a game as shared knowledge that constitutes agents with certain identities and interests. This gets at the explanatory role of wide content, of the social terms of individuality, in interaction. The two game theories can be pursued separately since they have different objects of explanation: the former, what choices actors make in a given game, the latter, who they are and what game they are playing in the first place. And they imply correspondingly different "structural" methodologies: the causal methods of network theory on the one hand,[136] the constitutive methods of discourse-theoretic or grammatical models on the other.[137] The two kinds of game theory also tacitly implicate each other, however, since conventional game theory presupposes a holist view insofar as it builds intrinsically social attributes into its specification of players, while Wittgensteinian game theory presupposes an individualist view because it is only in virtue of the causal interaction of independently existing agents that their social properties get produced and reproduced over time. This does not mean that conventional game theorists need to become Wittgensteinians, or vice-versa, but it does suggest some possibilities for conversation.

The distinction between individuality per se and its social terms allows us to see how the relationship between agents and structure can be at once independent and dependent, causal and constitutive; we can have both dualism and duality. The distinction resolves the apparent paradox by showing that two kinds of properties are

---

[135] Hollis (1994).

[136] For example, Wellman and Berkowitz, eds. (1988), Porpora (1989).

[137] For example, Sylvan and Glassner (1983, 1985), Coulter (1989), Emirbayer (1997).

involved in constituting agents, self-organizing properties and social properties. Moderate forms of individualism and holism are not incompatible, because they are calling attention to these different constituting properties of individuality, in effect asking different questions. The problem arises with radical forms of each ontology, when someone says that intentional agency is *nothing but* self-organization, or *nothing but* an effect of discourse. It is *both*, and recognizing this is essential to a proper understanding of each. The challenge for social scientists is to disentangle what is intrinsically social about agents from what is not, and to maintain that distinction in our subsequent theorizing about the "structure" of social systems.

Culture as a self-fulfilling prophecy

The approach to culture laid out above is intended to give equal weight to agency and structure. They are *mutually* constitutive and *co-determined*. My narrative has nevertheless concentrated on structure for two reasons. A sociology of knowledge consideration is that with the emergence of rational choice and game theory as important analytical tools in IR we now have a fairly well-developed framework for thinking about agency and interaction. Not complete, since rationalism tends to neglect the role of interaction in constructing agents, but by comparison our thinking about structure is relatively impoverished. This is so despite the centrality of the concept in systemic IR. Waltz's materialist conceptualization is a valuable beginning, but it is only that, an opening to further thinking about the issue. A second reason, noted by Waltz, is that structural theorizing is likely to yield a high rate of explanatory return. Even if we lack detailed knowledge about actors and their intentions, we should be able to explain, and even predict, patterns of their behavior if we know the structure of rules in which they are embedded. Structure confronts actors as an objective social fact that constrains and enables action in systematic ways, and as such should generate distinct patterns. This may strike contemporary IR readers as swimming against the tide, since one of the most common complaints about "structural" (i.e., Neorealist) IR theory is that it does not seem to explain very much. But a premise of this book is that the problem with Neorealism is its materialism, not its structuralism. An approach which recognizes that structure is constituted not only by material conditions but by shared ideas should do better.

Because of this chapter's bias toward structure, however, the following point cannot be emphasized too strongly: *structure exists, has effects, and evolves only because of agents and their practices.* All structure, micro and macro, is instantiated only in process. As Herbert Blumer puts it with respect to cultural structure:

> [a] gratuitous acceptance of the concepts of norms, values, social rules and the like should not blind the social scientist to the fact that any one of them is subtended by a process of social interaction – a process that is necessary not only for their change but equally well for their retention in a fixed form. It is the social process in group life that creates and upholds the rules, not the rules that create and uphold group life.[138]

I would modify the language of the last sentence, which suggests an either–or view of a relationship that should be seen as both-and, but otherwise his point is crucial, and applies at least partly to material structures as well. The distribution of capabilities only has the effects on international politics that it does because of the desiring and believing state agents who give it meaning.

The dependence of structure on agency and the social process is both constitutive and causal. On the one hand, the distribution of knowledge in a social system at any given moment exists only in virtue of actors' desires and beliefs. This is clearest in the case of common knowledge, which depends quite directly on ideas "in the head," but it is also true of collective knowledge, which supervenes on desires and beliefs even if it cannot be reduced to them. If culture exists only in virtue of desires and beliefs, it has effects, in turn, only in virtue of agents' behavior. The ability of Prisoner's Dilemma to generate a certain outcome, or of a competitive structure to select certain actors for survival, presupposes actions that *carry* those effects. This prompts many social scientists to argue that, for example, norms are only "norms" if they are manifested in behavior; I prefer to say that norms are shared beliefs which may or may not manifest in behavior depending on their strength, but norms can only have effects if they are so manifested.

On the other hand, social structures also depend on agents and practices in a causal sense. Constitutive analysis is inherently static. It tells us what structures are made of and how they can have certain effects, but not about the processes by which they move through time,

---

[138] Blumer (1969: 19).

in short, about *history*. This is clearest in the case of structural change, which is caused by actions that undermine existing structures and generate new ones. But as Blumer's quote emphasizes, structural *re*production too is caused by a continuous process of interaction that has reproduction as its intended or unintended consequence. From this perspective, in other words, culture looks like a "tool-kit" that knowledgeable agents use to try to meet their needs,[139] and which in so doing has causal and constitutive effects on culture.

In both a causal and constitutive sense, therefore, structure is an on-going effect of process, at the same time that process is an effect of structure. This does not mean we always have to (or even can) theorize about both at once. Structural theorizing and process theorizing answer different questions and as such we may want to "bracket" one while doing the other.[140] In this chapter process took a back seat to structures and agents, and in chapter 7 I do the reverse, but in making these moves we should not lose sight of their inter-dependence. In particular, we should not treat structure and process as different levels of analysis, as Waltz and Buzan, Jones, and Little do, since that implies that structure exists or has effects apart from process ("reification"), and that process is not itself structured. There are two levels of analysis (micro and macro), yes, but *both* are structured, and *both* instantiated by process. There are no structures without agents, and no agents (except in a biological sense) without structures. Social processes are always structured, and social structures are always in process.

The fact that agents are constructed by society and that structure is continually in process might seem to suggest that society is infinitely changeable and even highly unstable, especially in comparison to Waltz's more deterministic argument. Yet if anything the opposite is true, because the dialectical relationship between structure and agency suggests the following hypothesis: *culture is a self-fulfilling prophecy*.[141] Given cause to interact in some situation, actors need to define the situation before they can choose a course of action. These definitions will be based on at least two considerations: their own identities and interests, which reflect beliefs about who they are in such situations; and what they think others will do, which reflect

---

[139] Swidler (1986).   [140] Giddens (1979: 81).

[141] Krishna (1971). Krishna makes the point using the concept of "society" rather than "culture." For an analysis of different kinds of self-fulfilling prophecies see Kukla (1994); my discussion concerns what Kukla calls "Type III" prophecies.

beliefs about their identities and interests. When these various beliefs are not shared, when there is no cultural definition of the situation, then actors are likely to be surprised by each other's behavior, and the outcomes of their interaction will call their beliefs into question. If I am driving my car in a culture in which, unbeknownst to me, "Red" means "Go" and "Green" means "Stop," then at an intersection another driver and I will anticipate each other's actions incorrectly and probably get into an accident. Our expectations or "prophecies" about the situation will have been falsified, which may in turn challenge our cultural beliefs about traffic lights. If on the other hand we have shared understandings, then I will stop on Red and he will proceed safely through Green. Our "prophecies" will have been "fulfilled," which will reinforce our cultural beliefs about traffic lights.[142] The same logic operates in all culturally constituted situations. In the classroom teacher and student have shared beliefs about who they are and how they should behave, which motivate them to act in ways that reproduce those understandings. Once the cultural formation known as the "Cold War" was in place, the US and Soviets had a shared belief that they were enemies which helped constitute their identities and interests in any given situation, which they in turn acted upon in ways that confirmed to the Other that they were a threat, reproducing the Cold War. In each case socially shared knowledge plays a key role in making interaction relatively predictable over time, generating homeostatic tendencies that stabilize social order. Culture, in short, tends to reproduce itself, and indeed must do so if it is to be culture at all.

That human beings everywhere live in such relatively homeostatic worlds is almost certainly no accident. Culture meets basic human needs for sociation and ontological security (chapter 3, pp. 131–132), and by reducing transaction costs it helps solve the otherwise enormous practical problems of getting anything done. Most of the time we take the performance of these functions for granted, and in part that is the point, since it is the ability to treat culture as given that enables us to go about our business. Often it is only when someone violates our shared expectations, "breaching" the social order, that we realize how important they are in constituting who we are and what we do. In this respect cultures are different than social systems based on private knowledge alone, like First Encounter situations. In the

---

[142] The example is adapted from Kukla (1994: 21).

latter actors are relatively free to change their beliefs because there are no commitments to Others that reinforce particular ways of thinking, whereas in cultures actors depend on Others to act in certain ways so that they can realize their own interests. In contrast to the voluntarism and social plasticity that is sometimes associated with idealism, therefore, the argument here emphasizes how social systems can get "locked in" to certain patterns by the logic of shared knowledge, adding a source of social inertia or glue that would not exist in a system without culture. The Self in the "prophecy" is the community not the individual, and as such social change must be a joint affair.

But while it creates a lot of stability, adding culture to structure does not leave us back in Neorealist determinism. Culture can only be a self-fulfilling prophecy on the backs and in the heads of the agents who carry it. It is actors' beliefs that make up shared knowledge, and their practices which confirm or falsify that knowledge over time. Culture is constantly in motion, even as it reproduces itself. It is what people make of it, even as it constrains what they can do at any given moment. It is an on-going *accomplishment*.[143] Despite having a conservative bias, therefore, culture is always characterized by more or less contestation among its carriers, which is a constant resource for structural change. This contestation has at least five overlapping sources. One is internal contradictions between different logics within a culture. Cultures consist of many different norms, rules, and institutions, and the practices they induce will often be contradictory.[144] A second is the fact that agents are never perfectly socialized, such that they only have shared beliefs. Every one of us has private beliefs that motivate us to pursue personal projects that can change our environments. The unintended consequences of shared beliefs are a third source of conflict. A tragedy of the commons can be rooted in a shared understanding of something as a commons, but produce an outcome that eventually causes a change of that belief. Exogenous shocks are a fourth factor. A revolution, cultural imperialism, or an invasion by conquistadores can all transform cultural order. And finally there is creativity, the invention of new ideas from within a culture. This is just the start of an inquiry into structural change, to which I return in chapter 7. My point here is simply that nothing in the hypothesis that culture is a self-fulfilling prophecy precludes contestation and change. It points only to a tendency, not an inevitable outcome. Holism does

---

[143] Ashley (1988).   [144] For an application to IR see Bukovansky (1999a, b).

not imply determinism, any more than language implies speech.[145] Reified social facts can become problematized and can change. Agents are not cultural dopes or automatons, even when they reproduce their culture, and in chapter 7 we will see just how transformative they can be.

Conclusion

The concept of structure in international politics means different things to different people. For Neorealists it refers to anarchy and the distribution of material capabilities. In chapter 3 I argued that in order for this conceptualization to explain anything we have to make at least implicit assumptions about the distribution of interests in the system, but this need not conflict with Neorealism's materialist world-view if we treat interests as constituted by human nature. Given the idealist approach of this book, it is worth emphasizing that I agree with Realists that there are strictly material elements in the structure of social systems. The actors who make up social systems are animals with biologically constituted capacities, needs, and dispositions not at all unlike their cousins lower down the food chain. These animals have various tools ("capabilities") at their disposal, material objects with intrinsic powers, which enable them to do certain things. In emphasizing the ideational aspect of international structure, therefore, we should not forget that it supervenes on this material base, the analysis of which is a key contribution of Realism.

While an essential starting point for structural theorizing, however, material conditions by themselves explain relatively little. In chapter 3 I argued that interests are constituted largely by ideas, which means that social systems are also structured by distributions of knowledge. This opens the door to an idealist analysis of structure, but does not in itself imply *cultural* structure. Sometimes, as in First Encounters, actors interact in the absence of shared understandings, in which case the distribution of knowledge in the system will consist entirely of private beliefs. In this chapter I bracketed structures of private knowledge in order to concentrate on shared knowledge, where the value-added of a constructivist as opposed to rationalist idealism will mostly be found. Cultural structures are complex in both their nature and effects, and so in an effort at clarification I set out a typology

---

[145] See Pettit (1993).

based on three distinctions: (1) between two levels on which they are organized, micro and macro, manifested as common and collective knowledge respectively; (2) between their causal and constitutive effects; and (3) between their effects on behavior and on identities and interests. Analysis of these different modalities requires different kinds of structural methods, and as such the approach to culturalism taken in this chapter is inherently pluralist. In analyzing any of them, however, it is essential to show how cultural forms articulate with and give meaning to material forces, and how the latter in turn constrain the former. It may make sense for analytical purposes to distinguish between "material" structure and "ideational" structure, but in the end a social system has just one structure, composed of both material and ideational elements.

I suspect that few IR scholars, even the most hardened Neorealists, would deny that contemporary states share a great many beliefs about the rules of the international game, who its players are, what their interests are, what rational behavior is, and so on. Few would deny, in other words, that the structure of the contemporary international system contains a lot of culture. This culture is deeply embedded in how both statesmen and scholars understand the nature of international politics today, literally making those politics possible in their modern form, which suggests that IR might benefit from the insights of anthropologists alongside those of political economists.[146] What IR scholars will disagree about, fiercely, is how significant this cultural superstructure is in governing state behavior, relative to the base of rump material conditions. In short, they will disagree about how much international culture "matters." That disagreement is part of the backdrop against which I develop the substantive argument of part II.

[146] See Weldes, *et al.*, eds. (1999).

Part II International politics

5 The state and the problem of corporate agency

In part I I described a constructivist ontology of social life. Against materialism constructivism hypothesizes that the structures of human association are primarily cultural rather than material phenomena, and against rationalism that these structures not only regulate behavior but construct identities and interests. In this ontology material forces still matter and people are still intentional actors, but the meaning of the former and the content of the latter depend largely on the shared ideas in which they are embedded, and as such culture is a condition of possibility for power and interest explanations. Analysis should therefore begin with culture and then move to power and interest, rather than only invoke culture to clean up what they leave unexplained.

Constructivism is not a theory of international politics. Like rational choice theory it is substantively open-ended and applicable to any social form – capitalism, families, states, etc. – so to say anything concrete we have to specify which actors (units of analysis) and structures (levels) we are interested in. The discipline of International Relations imposes some broad limits on these choices, and within IR this book is concerned with states and the states system. States are key actors in the regulation of organized violence, which is one of the basic problems of international politics, and the structure of the states system is relatively autonomous from other structures of the modern international system, like the world economy, which enables us to study it at least partly on its own terms. As with any designation of actors and structures this will affect the resulting story;[1] the one I tell in the next three chapters would be very different were it about

[1] Frey (1985).

193

multinational corporations and the world economy. While we might not fully understand world politics until we understand the states system, however, this does not mean that world politics and the states system are equivalent, or even that states are more important than other international actors, whatever that might mean. Lots of things come under the heading of "IR." The states system is just one.

Political Realism has dominated thinking about the states system for so long that IR scholars sometimes assume states systemic theorizing is by definition Realist. This cannot be right, at least not if "Realism" is to be an interesting category. Taking the states system as our point of departure is a description of the world, like saying we are interested in the solar system. It is not in itself an explanation. Just as there can be competing theories of the solar system (Ptolemaic, Copernican), there can be competing theories of the states system. Realism is one such theory, and as I showed in part I it builds on a materialist and individualist ontology. Having laid the foundations of an idealist, holist ontology for IR, in part II I sketch another. This theory has many "Idealist" features, but I will not adopt that label. This book is an attempt to shed light on the states system by thinking through the logic and implications of constructivist social theory, and as such a constructivist theory of the states system best describes what it is about. Since constructivist social theory emphasizes the co-determination of agents and structures through process, my presentation of this approach is organized around the three elements of the agent–structure problem: chapter 5 addresses state actors, 6 the structure of the states system, and 7 their interaction through the process of international politics.

There cannot be a states system without states any more than there can be a (human) society without people. The units make their respective systems possible. Moreover, it is clear that at least in the case of society, the fact that these units are purposive actors makes a difference. Society would be a very different place were people not intentional creatures, even if there is much in society that is unintended. I shall argue that states are also purposive actors with a sense of Self – "states are people too" – and that this affects the nature of the international system. Note that this does not reduce a theory of international politics to a theory of foreign policy or state choices. As I argued in chapter 4, social life at any level cannot be explained solely through the lens of intentional action because macro-outcomes may be multiply realized at the micro-level, and because social structures may constitute agents. However, human behavior is driven in important part by intentions, and as such even the most relentless macro-theory will depend upon at least implicit assumptions about their nature and distribution.[2] In chapter 3 we saw that this is true of Waltz's theory, which assumes that states are actors with egoistic, status quo interests. His theory of international politics is based on a particular theory of the state, in other words, even if it is not reducible to that theory.[3] This is not a criticism, since systemic IR theorists cannot avoid having a theory of the state anymore than sociologists can of people. Their only choice is whether to make it explicit.

State theory literature is concerned with many important issues: the state's autonomy from society, its class composition, institutional capacity, legitimating discourse, and so on.[4] Of these I shall be concerned here with only one, the constitution of states as "unitary actors," which is the starting point for theorizing about the international system. Let me also note that the modifier "unitary" seems to be the object of much of the ire that is directed at the state-as-actor assumption, but since it is not clear how something can be an "actor" at all if it is not "unitary," I will treat it as redundant.

The issue of how states get constituted as the "people" of international society has been neglected in the state theory literature. This literature is oriented toward domestic politics where the agency of the state may be less apparent than its internal differentiation. But state agency also has been neglected in IR, an essay first published in 1959 by Arnold Wolfers being virtually the last word on the subject.[5] Paradoxically, this neglect may be due in part to the very centrality of the state-as-actor assumption to systemic theory, which could hardly begin without it. Yet it is not just academics who anthropomorphize the state, but all of us. In our daily lives citizens and policymakers alike routinely treat states as if they were people, talking about them as if they had the same kinds of intentional properties that we attribute to each other. We think the United States has "security interests" in the Persian Gulf, that it "believed" those were threatened by Iraq's "conquest" of Kuwait, that as a result it "attacked" Iraq, that its actions were "rational" and "legitimate," and so on. International law recognizes this anthropomorphic talk as referring to state "per-

---

[2] Emmet (1976).   [3] Buzan, Jones, and Little (1993: 116–121).
[4] For introductions to this literature see Carnoy (1984), Jessop (1990), and Poggi (1990).
[5] Though see Achen (1989) and Cederman (1997).

sonality" (just as corporations are recognized as actors in domestic law);[6] and indeed it is so deeply embedded in our common sense that it is difficult to imagine how international politics might be conceptualized or conducted without it. As Carr[7] points out, it would be impossible to make sense of day-to-day IR without attributions of corporate actorhood. It is through such talk, in other words, that the realities of the international system are constituted.

This may be reason to leave well enough alone and not worry about the constitution of state actors. After all, even if sociology depends on an implicit theory of people, sociologists do not need to become biologists or psychologists to do sociology. In recent years, however, scholars have problematized the assumption that even people are (unitary) actors,[8] and still more so the state-as-actor assumption, which has come under so much theoretical pressure from so many directions that denunciations of it are now de rigueur. Some critics simply emphasize the explanatory importance of domestic factors in international politics. Liberals, for example, argue that in order to explain state action we need to study the interest groups of which the state is an expression.[9] Students of foreign policy decision-making argue similarly for opening up the "black box" of the state and focusing on the bureaucracies and individuals within.[10] Other critics take aim more explicitly at the state itself. Individualists argue that the state is reducible to individuals and their interactions, with executives functioning as gatekeepers in a social choice process.[11] Postmodernists argue that agents are always effects of discourse anyway and so should be "decentered" rather than made a starting point for theory.[12] Empiricists argue that we have no epistemic warrant to give ontological status to unobservables like state actors. Even Realists seem skeptical, with Stephen Krasner[13] reducing the US state to top decision-makers in the White House and State Department, and Robert Gilpin[14] conceding that "the state does not really exist."

What unites these otherwise disparate views is the proposition that state actorhood is just a "useful fiction" or "metaphor" for what is "really" something else. The state is not *really* an actor at all, but merely a "theoretical construct."[15] Philosophers would call this a "nomin-

---

[6] See Coleman (1982).   [7] Carr (1939: 147–149).

[8] For example, Henriques, *et al.* (1984), Elster, ed. (1986).   [9] Moravcsik (1997).

[10] Allison (1971).   [11] Bueno de Mesquita (1981: 12–18).   [12] Ashley (1987).

[13] Krasner (1978: 11).   [14] Gilpin (1986: 318).

[15] Ferguson and Mansbach (1991: 370), Powell (1991: 1316).

alist," "instrumentalist," or "skeptical" view of the state because it assumes that the concept of state actor does not refer to a real entity (see chapter 2). According to nominalism the opposing, (scientific) "realist" view engages in "reification."[16] Although rarely made explicit, an important implication of nominalism would seem to be that once we know what states "really" are – admittedly some way off – it should be possible in principle to dispense with the fictions and metaphors and still explain international politics *without loss of meaning or explanatory power.* This is similar to the view of materialists in the philosophy of mind who think that folk psychology eventually can be reduced without loss to neuro-science.

In this chapter I argue that states are real actors to which we can legitimately attribute anthropomorphic qualities like desires, beliefs, and intentionality. Toward that end I pursue three more specific objectives in four sections.

The first is to give our model of the state a "body" by showing that it is an actor which cannot be reduced to its parts. This task is complicated by the fact that states are conceptually related to societies, and state theorists think about this relationship in different ways. In the first section I take up this problem, arriving at a synthetic definition that has as its core a Weberian view of the state as an organizational actor, but which partakes of the Pluralist and Marxist view that its character is constituted in important part by the structure of state–society relations. When states interact they do so as parts of state–society complexes which affect their behavior, much like the interaction between capitalists is affected by the fact that they employ workers, but this does not mean states can be reduced to societies – any more than capitalists can be reduced to workers. In the second section I narrow the focus to states per se, using the philosophical literature on corporate agency to show how their internal structure constitutes them as real, unitary actors. Applying the discussion of the agent–structure problem from chapter 4, I emphasize the key role that concrete individuals (who as agents form "governments") play in instantiating states, but show that this does not vitiate a realist view of state agency.

The second objective is to give our model of the state "life" by identifying its intrinsic motivational dispositions or "national inter- ests." Since the concept of interest is related to that of identity and

[16] Cederman (1997).

there are different kinds of both, this discussion begins, in the third section, with a typology of identities and interests. I distinguish four kinds of identity (corporate, type, role, and collective), and two of interest (objective and subjective). Each identity has associated needs or objective interests, and actors' understandings of these in turn constitute the subjective interests that motivate their action. The last section applies this framework to the concept of national interest. I define the national interest as the objective interests of state–society complexes, consisting of four needs: physical survival, autonomy, economic well-being, and collective self-esteem. I argue in conclusion that states' interpretations of these needs tend to be biased in a self-interested direction, which predisposes them to competitive, "Realist" politics, but that this does *not* mean that states are inherently self-interested.

This talk of states' nature brings me to my last objective, which I develop throughout the chapter but state explicitly only in the conclusion: I want to show that states are ontologically prior to the states system. The state is pre-social relative to other states in the same way that the human body is pre-social. Both are constituted by self-organizing internal structures, the one social, the other biological. In effect, what emerges in this chapter is a theory that is "essentialist" in certain key respects, which supports the key intuition that motivates individualist approaches to the states system. Since this book takes a constructivist approach to the states system this will require some explaining. Against anti-essentialists to the "left," like postmodernists, I argue that we can theorize about processes of social construction *at the level of the states system* only if such processes have exogenously given, relatively stable platforms. But against thicker essentialists to the "right," like Neorealists and Neoliberals, I defend a minimalist vision of these platforms, arguing that many of the qualities often thought to be inherent to states, like power-seeking and egoism, are actually contingent, constructed by the international system. To do systemic theory in IR one has to give some ground to an essentialist view of the state, but this still leaves a lot of room for constructivist theories of international politics.

The essential state

In order to show how states are constituted as unitary actors we first need to be clear on what we mean by the state. This would be difficult enough if we were dealing only with states, since the fact that states are not observable provides ample room for disagreements that are relatively unconstrained by evidence. Thus there are at least three significantly different conceptualizations – Weberian, Pluralist, and Marxist. But the task is made even more difficult by the fact that it seems impossible to define the state apart from "society." States and societies seem to be conceptually interdependent in the same way that masters and slaves are, or teachers and students; the nature of each is a function of its relation to the other. Weberian, Pluralist, and Marxist theories think about this relationship in different ways, differences that affect more than just their conceptualizations of the state. Pluralists and Marxists hesitate to define the state as an "actor" at all. In other words, it is not that state theorists disagree about whether the state is defined by X, Y, and Z or just X and Y, as if they were all talking about the same underlying phenomenon, but that they disagree about what the putative object is to which the term "state" is supposed to refer in the first place. To that extent their definitions of the state seem incommensurable, not just different; one might say that the state is an "essentially contested concept." Undaunted, in this section I first offer brief, stylized representations of the three theories with a view toward identifying a common referent object, and then discuss in more detail five properties which define the essential state.

The state as referent object

Weberians define the state as an organization possessing sovereignty and a territorial monopoly on the legitimate use of organized violence.[17] Two features of this definition stand out for my purposes here. The first is that the state is seen as an *organizational actor*. The Weberian view is the most anthropomorphic of the three – states have interests, make decisions, act in the world – and for that reason it is particularly well suited to systemic IR. The second is that this actor is seen as ontologically independent of society.[18] Weberians emphasize the functions that the state performs for society (internal order and external defense), but for Weber the state's nature is not conceptually dependent on society. For example, a state may happen to exist in a

---

[17] On Weber's definition of the state see (1978: 54), and for contemporary Weberians, Poggi (1990: 19), Tilly (1990: 1), and Mann (1993: 44–91).

[18] Poggi (1990: 20–21).

capitalist system but to Weberians this makes it nothing more than a "state-in-capitalism," not an inherently "capitalist state."

Pluralists are a mirror-image of Weberians. Whereas Weberians highlight the state's agency and differentiation from society, Pluralists attempt to reduce the state to interest groups and individuals in society. Classical Pluralists even denied the existence of "the state" altogether, saying it was nothing more than "government," the concrete individuals who head the state at any particular time (see below).[19] For Pluralists, the referent object of the term "state" differs from that of Weberians, if it is an object at all. In IR this society-centric approach is particularly useful for exploring the extent to which foreign policy behavior is affected by domestic politics; it has also become the basis for an emerging "Structural Liberal" theory of international politics.[20]

Marxist state theory can be seen as a framework for integrating these two perspectives. If the referent object of "state" for Weberians is an organizational actor, and for Pluralists is really just society, then for Marxists the referent is the *structure* that binds the two in a relationship of mutual constitution.[21] The state is "the enduring structure of governance and rule in society."[22] To say that this structure mutually constitutes state actors and society is to say that each is what it is only in virtue of its relation to the other. On this view, for example, a capitalist state is a structure of political authority (not an actor) that constitutes a society with private ownership of the means of production, and simultaneously constitutes a state actor that is authorized and required to protect that institution. In a sense, Marxists agree with both Weberians and Pluralists, since for Marxists state actors are "relatively autonomous" from society and yet not ontologically independent of it. But Marxists go beyond the others in emphasizing that neither state actor nor society can exist apart from the structure of political authority that constitutes them, any more than master and slave can exist apart from the structure of slavery.

---

[19] The Classical Pluralist position is represented by Bentley (1908) and Truman (1951), and more contemporary Pluralisms by Almond (1988).

[20] Moravcsik (1997).

[21] I am equating Marxism here with the "structural" or "neo-"Marxist tradition of Althusser (1970), Poulantzas (1975), and Jessop (1982); for other Marxist theories of the state see Carnoy (1984).

[22] Benjamin and Duvall (1985: 25).

All three of these state theories – one might call them organizational, reductive, and structural respectively – get at phenomena commonly denoted by the term "state." Each has a different referent object, only one of which (the Weberian state) is an "actor" at all. This is a book on systemic international politics, which assumes states are actors and so seems to privilege a Weberian approach. But when states interact they do so with their societies conceptually "in tow," and this calls for supplementing our conceptualization of the state with insights from a Marxist or Pluralist analysis. From this standpoint, in other words, the referent object of "the state" should be conceptualized as an organizational actor that is internally related to the society it governs by a structure of political authority, which in effect rolls all three views up into one.

Defining the state

States take many forms – democratic, monarchical, communist, and so on – that reflect the structure of state–society relations. However, here I am interested only in what all states in all times and places have in common, in the "essential state" or "state-as-such." This is not to suggest that variations in the state do not matter to international politics. They clearly affect foreign policy, and in my view the logic of states systems as well. But in this chapter I am guided by the narrower concern of grounding systemic IR theory in a theory of how states are constituted as its moving parts. Since all states are actors this calls for a minimalist view of the state, stripped of its contingent forms. The purpose is not to help us analyze real historical states but rather to provide the necessary platform or "body" to begin doing systemic theory.

Anti-essentialists might argue that even a stripped down view of the state will be inappropriate because as social constructions states cannot have *any* transhistorical, cross-cultural essence.[23] I think states do have a common core, and must if we are to make sense. If states have nothing in common, then what distinguishes them from any other social kind? If the members of the Swedish state reorganize themselves as a bowling team but still call themselves a state, does that mean states can now take the form of bowling teams, or that

---

[23] For some postmodern interpretations of the state from which this conclusion might be drawn see Mitchell (1991), Campbell (1992), and Bartelson (1995).

Sweden is no longer a state? Can a state, in short, be *anything*? To my mind there seem to be significant constraints on what we can plausibly call a state, which I take to be their essential properties. On the other hand, the fact that states must have certain properties does not necessarily mean that these can be precisely specified, since social and even natural kinds have borderline cases. It might be useful, therefore, to think of the state as a fuzzy set, no element of which is essential but which tend to cohere in homeostatic clusters (chapter 2, pp. 59–60). The state does not seem particularly "fuzzy" as social kinds go, but it too has borderline cases,[24] which indicate that our emphasis should be on the cluster of properties, not individual ones.

The discussion in the preceding section suggests that the essential state has five properties: (1) an institutional-legal order, (2) an organization claiming a monopoly on the legitimate use of organized violence, (3) an organization with sovereignty, (4) a society, and (5) territory. (1) is the Marxist's state-as-structure, (2) and (3) the Weberian's state-as-actor, and (4) the Pluralist's state-as-society. (5) is common to all three. These properties form a homeostatic cluster, which provides a rationale for the familiar "billiard ball" model of states in systemic IR. Strictly speaking, however, only (2) and (3) refer to the state as an actor, and since in this chapter I am trying to clarify that notion it is important that my terminology be more precise. Thus, I will use the term "state" to denote the Weberian's organizational actor, "state structure" to denote the Marxists' structure of political authority, and Cox's[25] "state–society complex" to refer to all five properties at once. I now take up these properties in more detail.

An institutional-legal order

The state understood as a structure of political authority is constituted by the norms, rules, and principles "by which conflict is handled, society is ruled, and social relations are governed."[26] This structure distributes ownership and control of three material bases of power to state and societal actors: the means of production, the means of destruction, and the means of (biological) reproduction.[27] Different forms of state structure are constituted by how this distribution is organized. Capitalist state structures divide forms of power between

---

[24] Crawford (1979: 52–71).   [25] Cox (1987).
[26] Benjamin and Duvall (1985: 25–26).
[27] If the last seems an unlikely candidate for state control, consider the current Chinese policy of one child per family.

capital, state, and family; totalitarian state structures consolidate them in state elites; and so on. Regardless of the particular distribution of political authority, however, state structures are power structures that both regulate the behavior of preexisting subjects, and constitute who those subjects are and what they are empowered to do.

State structures are usually institutionalized in law and official regulations. This stabilizes expectations among the governed about each other's behavior, and since shared expectations are necessary for all but the most elementary forms of social interaction, state structures help make modern society possible. Institutionalization also stabilizes expectations about the use of force within society by state actors, who are empowered by law to use violence to enforce the rules. Security from the arbitrary use of force by officials is crucial if people are to go about their daily lives, and state structures achieve this end by formalizing how and why state actors can coerce society. Broadly speaking, then, law is essential to state–society complexes. Any structure meriting the designation "state" will have a legal order.[28]

Institutional-legal orders constitute state–society complexes and as such include both state and societal actors within their reference. These complexes will be capable of varying degrees of agency depending on the character of the state structure. "Strong" state structures enable state actors to mobilize significant resources from society, and at the limit enable state and society to act routinely as a single agent. Systemic IR theorists implicitly assume that states are strong when they treat state–society complexes as billiard balls under the complete control of a state actor. In reality most state structures are considerably weaker than this, incapable of sustaining a perfect fusion of state and societal agency for any length of time. Thus, despite its limited potential for agency, the Marxist definition of the state as an institutional-legal order is best not seen as referring to an *actor* at all. It does not have identities, interests, or intentionality.

If we want to conceptualize state agency we need a Weberian view of the state. The connection to the Marxist view is that structures of political authority constitute state actors as organizations distinct from their societies, empowered with the right and duty to use force to secure those structures. This translates into two key functions: the maintenance of internal order, which involves reproducing the domestic conditions of society's existence; and the provision of external

---

[28] D'Entreves (1967).

defense, which protects the integrity of those conditions from other states. In order to fulfill these functions state actors are empowered by state structures with a monopoly on the legitimate use of organized violence and sovereignty, which constitute the second and third features of the essential state.

Monopoly on the legitimate use of organized violence

States are specialists in the legitimate use of organized violence.[29] In Charles Tilly's[30] evocative terms, states are "protection rackets." In some societies state actors also control the means of production or even reproduction, but control over the means of destruction is the ultimate and distinctive basis of state power, and only this is essential to stateness.

"Organized violence" refers to the coordinated use of deadly force by a group. There are many kinds of violence that do not fit this description. Some refer to non-deadly force; states may engage in this as well, but so do private citizens (abusive spouses, bullies). Others refer to violence that is not really force, like the "structural" violence to which disadvantaged groups may be subject by structures of economic, racial, or other kinds of oppression. Still others refer to violence by individuals which is not generally done by groups (murder, rape), or which is done by groups but not organized (riots, mob violence). All of these forms of violence are important and can be found in varying degrees in world politics. In saying that we need to recognize the special role of organized violence in constituting the state, therefore, I do not mean to suggest that IR scholars should ignore other kinds of violence. But it is an essential and distinctive feature of state agency that states are capable of organized violence. Even states that have disbanded their armies, like Costa Rica, retain a capacity for it in their police. An organization incapable of organized violence would be hard pressed to qualify as a state.

The concept of a "monopoly" of violence is more problematic. Most modern states divide their coercive potential into two organizations, a police force for internal security and an army for external, and then further divide these into various functionally and territorially distinct organizations (local, provincial, and national police; army, navy, air force). What is it about this plethora of organizations that constitutes them jointly as a "monopoly"?

---

[29] Poggi (1990: 21).   [30] Tilly (1985).

The conventional answer is that their command and control is centralized in the head of state. Ultimately in the state there is a single locus of authority to make decisions concerning the relationship between its various coercive arms. However, the fact that this authority may reside in a single individual is in some sense beside the point: his or her authority is in any case a function of the institutional-legal order, and if the same result could be achieved in a more decentralized fashion then for all practical purposes we would still have a monopoly of force. What matters in constituting monopoly is the *effect* of centralization, not centralization itself. This effect must be twofold. First, the coercive agencies of the state must be *non-rivals* in the sense that they do not settle their disputes (for example, over budgets or jurisdiction) by force. In IR this is known as a "security community"[31] which Deutsch argues can be either "pluralistic" (decentralized) or "amalgamated" (centralized) as in the modern state. Second, coercive agencies must be *unified* in the sense that each perceives a threat to others as a threat to itself, so that all defend against it together. In IR this is known as "collective security," in which actors define their individual security in terms of the collective, on the principle of "all for one, one for all." This requirement goes beyond non-rivalry, since non-rivals might be indifferent to each other's fate; unified actors are not.

Centralized states achieve non-rivalry and unity by subsuming coercive agencies under a single point with the authority to command obedience, but the same effect could be achieved by institutional mechanisms that relied on a decentralized consensus, as in a cartel. For example, when it comes to military security, a well-functioning collective security system like NATO does not seem essentially different than the security system of a territorial state like Brazil. In both cases functional and territorial responsibilities regarding the use of force are delegated to non-rival agencies with considerable autonomy in their domain, and a physical threat to one will be seen as a threat to all. From the standpoint of outside aggressors both systems will be *de facto* "monopolies" of force. This suggests the possibility of decentralized or "international" state structures that do not have a single head but are still capable of institutionalized collective action.[32]

---

[31] Deutsch, *et. al.* (1957).

[32] On the concept of an international state see, Cox (1987), Picciotto (1991), Wendt (1994), Caporaso (1996), and Shaw (1997).

The most conceptually troublesome requirement here is that a monopoly of organized violence be "legitimate." The state must have not just the ability to maintain the monopoly, but a *right* to do so which members of society accept even in the absence of coercion or self-interest.[33] This is a problem because a state's right is almost always being contested by someone somehow somewhere, and as such legitimacy is in the eyes of the beholder. What about drug cartels that exercise monopolies of force in the territories they control over people who willingly support them? Or totalitarian states where people cannot express their true feelings? Is tacit consent sufficient for legitimacy? What about non-violent resistance to the state, like tax evasion or refusal to say a pledge of allegiance? Is legitimacy a matter of majority opinion? And so on.

These are hard questions that I cannot answer here. They can be side-stepped for IR purposes, however, by privileging the state's *claim* to a monopoly on the legitimate use of organized violence, and treating that claim as a right until it is clear that popular opposition has made it impossible to sustain. The problem with this move, of course, is that the state's capacity for violence enables it to defend its "legitimacy" by force if necessary, which means that in some cases there may be a big gap between claim and reality. Moreover, it is precisely this kind of analytical privileging that helps states reproduce their claim, which illustrates how the epistemic aspects of the states systemic project support its political aspect. Given an interest in how states *systems* work, however, what matters is the efficacy of the state's monopoly, not its legitimacy.

Sovereignty

State structures also constitute state actors with sovereignty, which is in turn traditionally divided into "internal" and "external" sovereignty.[34]

Internal sovereignty means that the state is the supreme locus of political authority in society. After all is said and done, it is states, rather than the Church, corporations, or private citizens who have the right to make final, binding political decisions – indeed, to decide what is (officially) "political" in the first place.[35] The fact that this is a "right" is crucial. Sovereignty is not about *de facto* freedom of action

---

[33] Hurd (1999).   [34] For example, Fowler and Bunck (1996).
[35] Thomson (1995).

relative to society, or "state autonomy,"[36] but about being recognized by society as having certain powers, as having *authority*. These powers may be limited, as in the night-watchman state, or extensive, as in the totalitarian, but as rights they are legal rather than political facts, de jure rather than de facto.[37] Democratic states are no less sovereign than fascist states, despite the greater domestic constraints they face.

The emergence of the doctrine of popular sovereignty in the eighteenth century complicates this simple conclusion. Popular sovereignty removes ultimate authority to the people, such that if they perceive a state as illegitimate they have the right to revolt, which would seem to undermine the whole idea of "state" sovereignty.[38] Even so, however, a democratic state will still have de facto sovereignty insofar as it remains a distinct organization delegated to make decisions and enforce the law on society's behalf. The people may have ultimate authority over this organization, but short of a collapse of state legitimacy the state will be sovereign in all but name.

This relates to the vexed question of whether sovereignty can be divided. Bodin and Hobbes argued that sovereignty must be concentrated in a single person, but contemporary opinion generally holds that it can be disaggregated[39] – by functions (executive, legislative, judicial), levels (local, provincial, national, perhaps international), or issue areas (economic, military, welfare). The view that sovereignty can be "unbundled" enables us to grasp the fact that heads of state today do not have unlimited authority, but as Bodin and Hobbes foresaw, it does create the problem of how to conceptualize the state's unity. Where is the state's sovereignty if it is not concentrated in a single person?[40]

One answer is to recognize that, even as a property of state actors, sovereignty is really a property of a structure. The Weberian conceptualization of the state as an actor itself refers to a structure – not the structure denoted by the Marxist definition of the state-as-structure, which includes society, but the *organizational* structure that constitutes the state as a corporate agent (see below). This "physiological" structure relates the various individuals and bureaucracies which make up a state actor to each other, assigning functional, territorial, or issue-area sovereignties within a framework of rules and procedures

---

[36] Nordlinger (1981).   [37] Dickinson (1927).   [38] See Antholis (1993).

[39] D'Entreves (1973: 316).

[40] For a good discussion of the difficulties of specifying the locus of sovereignty see Bartelson (1995: 12–52).

for settling jurisdictional conflicts and ensuring their harmonious operation. The argument here is similar to that made above about the state's monopoly of force: what gives a state sovereignty in the face of its internal division is an organizational structure of *non-rival, unified authority* that enables its parts to work together as a unit or "team." In this light we can see why it is difficult to find sovereignty in the modern state, since structures do not have a single location. The sovereignty of a state actor only becomes apparent when we look at the structure through which its parts become a corporate whole.

In contrast to these difficulties, the concept of external sovereignty is relatively straight-forward, denoting merely the absence of any external authority higher than the state, like other states, international law, or a supranational Church – in short, "constitutional independence."[41] As with internal sovereignty it is important to emphasize that the issue here is not one of autonomy. Rising international interdependence means that states increasingly are subject to powerful external constraints on their action. This creates a gap between their *right* to do what they want and their ability to *exercise* that right, but it does not mean that outsiders have "authority" over states. Authority requires legitimacy, not mere influence or power.

Nevertheless, there is an important difference between external sovereignty that is recognized by other states and external sovereignty that is not. When the Aztec and Spanish states encountered each other in 1519 they both were constitutionally independent, but at least Spain did not recognize (in the sense of "accept") this, and as such considered the Aztecs fair game for conquest. One of the important contributions of constructivist IR scholarship has been to emphasize the role of mutual recognition of external sovereignty in mitigating the effects of international anarchy,[42] and this forms a key part of the argument in chapter 6. However, what I want to emphasize here is that a state can have external sovereignty even if it is *not* recognized by other states. In Hobbesian international systems states may *claim* external sovereignty, but others do not recognize it as a *right*; external sovereignty is de facto or "empirical" only.[43] In Lockean international systems, however, states do recognize each other's sovereignty as a right. External sovereignty is here "juridical," not merely empirical.

---

[41] James (1986).
[42] See, for example, Ruggie (1983a, 1993), Strang (1991), Wendt (1992), and Biersteker and Weber, eds. (1996).
[43] Jackson and Rosberg (1982).

This has significant implications for foreign policy: states that recognize each other's sovereignty tend not to conquer each other, not because they cannot, but because recognition implies a willingness to live and let live.

In contrast to some constructivists,[44] then, in my view sovereignty does not presuppose a society of states. Sovereignty is intrinsic to the state, not contingent. Empirical statehood can exist without juridical statehood. Recognition confers upon states certain powers in a society of states, but freedom from external authority *per se* does not presuppose it. This is an important source of the essentialist character of my argument, and I come back to it below.

Society

State actors are constituted by state structures with political authority over societies, and as such conceptually presuppose their societies. State actors are differentiated from their societies, but internally related to them: no society, no state. Thus, even though in this book I am concerned with relationships between state actors, and for that reason use the term "state" in the Weberian sense to denote an organization, we cannot understand the behavior of these actors without considering their internal relation to society. The content of this relation will depend on the form taken by state structures. Fascist, communist, and democratic structures create very different relationships between state and societal actors, even if in this section we are interested only in what is inherent to all state–society relationships.

What, then, is "society"? This question obviously cannot be answered here, but let me offer some intuitions that could in principle be developed into an argument. It seems useful to proceed by separating these intuitions into constitutive and causal issues.

The constitutive issue concerns the conceptual requirements for being a society. There seem to be at least two. One is that people have shared knowledge that induces them to follow most of the rules of their society most of the time. Although stateless societies exist, complex societies all have states, and as such many of these rules will normally be codified in law. The other requirement of society is that it have boundaries. These might be fuzzy, as in the case of frontier regions that are only loosely subject to state authority. But as long as there is more than one state there will be more than one society, since

---

[44] For example, Giddens (1985: 255–293).

each state has its own rules which the members of its society are expected to follow. To say that states and societies are internally related in a state–society complex means that not only is the state constituted by its relationship to society, but so is society constituted by the state.

The causal question concerns where societies come from. Common sense suggests two types of causes, bottom–up and top–down. On the one hand, there are important aspects of social life that seem prior to the state. Human beings are group animals, so much so that a case can be made that the most elementary unit in the "state of nature" was the group rather than the individual.[45] Group identities (from tribe to clan to nation, among others) are based first and foremost on things like language, culture, religion, and ethnicity. These things sometimes are effects of state policy, but some groups existed long before there were states, and some have endured despite states. To that extent these groups can be thought of as self-organizing social facts welling up from the "bottom" of the human experience.[46] Self-organizing group identities are still "constructions" (what else could they be?), but relative to states and states systems, these constructions are often external or exogenous.

Let me emphasize that in suggesting that societies may have self-organizing qualities I do not mean to suggest that this is always or even largely the case. The emergence of states, in which coercive resources become monopolized by political-military elites, creates enormous potential for constructing societies from the top–down. Indeed, since a law-abiding society is a more efficient basis for a state than an unruly, resentful subject population, this will often be a key goal of state policy. Education policy tries to teach children to become loyal citizens; language policy tries to build solidarity by erasing communal differences; foreign policy tries to convince people they face a common danger from external Others.[47] These policies all are backed up, if necessary, by organized violence. Given the power at states' disposal, however, one cannot help but be impressed with the extent to which their efforts to construct societies (let alone nations) can founder on the rocks of preexisting group identities. A potential key factor in constructing societies, therefore, is the extent to which

---

[45] Alford (1994).   [46] See Smith (1989).
[47] Campbell (1992); also see Walker (1993: 125–140).

the boundaries and policies of the state coincide with the boundaries and needs of the preexisting groups subject to its rule.

Territory

In addition to societies, states are also internally related to territory. No territory, no state. States are not literally the same thing as territories, but in an important sense Michael Mann is right that "the state is . . . a place."[48] The term "territory" itself suggests the connection, joining the Latin *terra* ("earth" or "land") to *torium* ("belonging to" or "surrounding," presumably the state).[49] In this respect the authority of states is unlike the authority of churches or firms, neither of which is intrinsically territorial in character. State authority is.

An important implication of this is that an inquiry concerned with relations *among* states must take territory as in some sense given, in the same way that sociology must take as given the fact that people have spatial extension. This is not to say that we should never problematize territory "all the way down," but in doing so we should recognize that such a move changes the subject. Rather than a sociology of the states system we would be engaged in a "biology" of the state. On the other hand, the fact that territoriality is in some sense exogenous to states systemic theory does not mean it is in every sense exogenous. An important contribution of critical IR scholarship in the last decade has been to show that there are important aspects of territoriality which should not be treated as given by students of international politics.[50] This has both constitutive and causal aspects.

At least two points have emerged on the constitutive side. First, even though territory must have boundaries of some kind if it is to be anything more than simply land (which would make a state's internal relation to territory trivial, since people do not live in the water), the breadth and depth of this boundary may vary. In the modern world we are used to thinking of territorial boundaries as vanishing thin lines on a map, so that the state's spatial extension is precisely delimited. A state is complete up to its boundary, and then disappears equally completely as we cross it. Yet historically there have been many organizations with a monopoly of organized violence over some land, but the precise boundaries of which were contested,

---

[48] Mann (1984: 187).

[49] Gottmann (1973: 16). For discussion of some interesting ambiguities in this etymology see Baldwin (1992: 209–10).

[50] Ruggie (1993), Walker (1993), Agnew (1994).

overlapping, or simply faded away into nothing. This was the case in the frontier zones of ancient empires, in the heteronomous authority structures of medieval Europe, and is arguably reemerging today with the rise of a "neo-medieval" international system.[51] The question of whether medieval structures of political authority were "states" is difficult for reasons beyond their ambiguous territoriality,[52] but ancient empires seem very much like modern states except for the occasional imprecision of their boundaries. Some might say they were not "states" for exactly this reason, but this ignores the fact that all empires had geographical cores over which their monopoly of force was complete; does this mean they were states in some areas and not others? In my view the assumption that precise borders are inherent to states mistakes a contingent feature of the state for an essential one. A more fruitful approach would be to recognize that in principle states can have "fuzzy" boundaries, even if in practice they do not. This preserves our intuition that states must have some kind of boundary without prejudging the form it must take.

A second constitutive point is that even if the location of territorial boundaries is clear and constant, their social *meaning* can vary.[53] Realists tend to assume that territorial boundaries must also be boundaries of identity and interest, such that where a state's authority stops so must its conception of Self and interest. Yet this is not even true of people, who are more constrained by their bodies than states. Despite having basic needs that our physical constitution predisposes us to meet as individuals, most of us identify cognitively in varying degrees with some Others, and sometimes even sacrifice our lives for them. Below I agree with Realists that states too have basic needs that predispose them to conflate cognitive boundaries with territorial ones, and so to be self-interested. If this exhausted the possibilities for state identity then territorial boundaries would always have a "Hobbesian" meaning: walls of exclusion to be policed and defended at all costs. But as I suggest below and argue at length in subsequent chapters, states' territorial nature does not preclude expanding their sense of Self to include other states, and thus defining their interests in more collective terms. In that case territorial boundaries would take on a

---

[51] See, respectively, Kratochwil (1986), Ruggie (1983a), Bull (1977: 264–276).

[52] On the feudal state see Poggi (1990: 16–35).

[53] See especially Walker (1993) and Agnew (1994). The variable meaning of space is an importent theme of the literature in radical geography; see Gregory and Urry, eds. (1985).

"Lockean" or even "Kantian" meaning: still differentiating states, but embedding them within a larger "cognitive region"[54] that works together toward common ends.

If the constitutive questions about territorial boundaries concern where they are located and how they are meaningful, then the causal questions concern how and why they acquire the locations and meanings that they do. As with the causes of society here too we can distinguish between bottom–up and top–down causes. Thus, on the one hand, territories stem in part from self-organizing groups seeking to settle in relatively stable places,[55] which induces them to push out on the world around them. If there are no other groups in the area then boundaries will be determined by the interaction of a group's size and technology with the natural environment. Groups lacking navigational technology, for example, will find their borders constrained by oceans, whereas sea-faring groups will not. Even in the more usual situation where other groups are present, boundaries of a particular group will be determined in part by factors welling up from self-organizing processes that are exogenous to the states system. On the other hand, war and diplomacy between groups are clearly also important causes of territorial boundaries, and to that extent the process will have a systemic or top–down dimension. As Tilly puts it, not only do states make war but "war makes states,"[56] and a key aspect of that process is defining their boundaries. To that extent states are effects of boundary construction as much as they are its causes.[57] Moreover, systemic interaction is important not only in the initial determination of boundaries but in sustaining them over time. If boundaries are stable, this will either be because states have enough power to prevent others from changing them unilaterally, or because they recognize each other's borders as legitimate. Both involve ongoing causal interactions, and to that extent the construction of state boundaries is never a finished affair, even if it becomes unproblematic in some cases.

In sum, the essential state is an organizational actor embedded in an institutional-legal order that constitutes it with sovereignty and a monopoly on the legitimate use of organized violence over a society in a territory. The class of states may be somewhat "fuzzy" in practice, but it excludes lots of things from ever being states: dogs, trees,

---

[54] Adler (1997a).   [55] Sack (1986: 19); cf. Abbott (1995: 873).   [56] Tilly (1985).
[57] Abbott (1995).

football teams, universities, and so on. On the other hand, it is important to emphasize how stripped down this model is, which can be seen if we briefly consider what it does *not* attribute to the essential state. Being a state does not imply any particular political system, any particular mode of production, recognition by other states, nationalism, or undivided sovereignty. I argue below that it even does not imply self-interest. All of these involve contingent forms of state, not the essential state. Critics might reply that this definition is *so* stripped down that it is of little use for analyzing states in the real world, which necessarily take on various and complex forms. To be sure, but that was not my intention: it was to identify what is common to all discussions of how states are constructed by the states system.

A minimalist definition also has another virtue: it helps us see that the state is not an inherently modern phenomenon, and thus, once we have identified its motivational dispositions, as I purport to do below, it should be possible to develop transhistorical generalizations about its behavior.[58] The attempt to identify such generalizations has long been a staple of Realism, and animates several recent studies of international politics.[59] Critics may argue that these efforts are anachronistic because the term "state" has only been used since the thirteenth century,[60] which might be thought to imply that there were no states before then. To my mind this illustrates the problem with nominalist thinking. In the realist view, if there were organizations with sovereignty and a territorial monopoly on organized violence before the thirteenth century then there were states. And there clearly were: Greek city-states, Alexander the Great's empire, the Roman Empire, and so on. Social kinds are constituted by how they are organized, not by what they are called. This is not to say that there are no important dangers in making transhistorical claims, such as projecting contingent features of the modern state backward, and ignoring important differences in the systemic contexts in which states operate. This latter danger is especially likely if, as in Realism, structure is not conceptualized in cultural terms. These problems suggest that any valid transhistorical generalizations about the essential state will be very thin, but such generalizations are not ruled out altogether.

[58] Much the same point could be made about transcultural generalizations.
[59] See Watson (1992), Buzan and Little (1994), and Kaufman (1997); cf. Reus-Smit (1999).
[60] Harding (1994).

"States are people too"

In the previous section I defined the state as an actor, but did not show that such talk refers to a real corporate being to which we can properly attribute human qualities like identities, interests, and intentionality. I have not yet shown, in other words, that the state has a "Self," as suggested, for example, by the Realist assumption that states are "self"-interested. The question of whether we can anthropomorphize corporate actors goes back at least to medieval debates about the Church. It concerned Hobbes, figured prominently in nineteenth and early twentieth century debates about the nature of the state and the corporation, and continues to interest scholars in a variety of disciplines today.[61] All sides seem to agree that corporate agency is actually a kind of *structure*: a structure of shared knowledge or discourse that enables individuals to engage in institutionalized collective action. (Not to be confused with the broader structures in which corporate agents might in turn be embedded, like structures of state–society relations.) But there is deep disagreement between nominalists and realists about the ontological status of this structure. Nominalists, who seem lately to hold the upper hand in IR scholarship, believe that corporate agency is just a useful fiction or metaphor to describe what is "really" the actions of individuals. Scientific realists believe it refers to a real, emergent phenomenon which cannot be reduced to individuals. In what follows I defend the realist view, explore the internal structure of corporate agency that makes it possible, and conclude with some thoughts on the limits to anthropomorphic talk about corporate agents. In my discussion I focus on states, but the argument is applicable to other forms of corporate agency as well.

On the ontological status of the state[62]

One reason that centuries of debate have not solved the problem of corporate agency is that nominalists and realists each face difficulties.

---

[61] See, for example, Dewey (1926), Copp (1980), Coleman (1982), French (1984), Douglas (1986), Gilbert (1987), Tuomela (1989), Vincent (1989), Searle (1990), Sandelands and St. Clair (1993), and Clark (1994). Runciman (1997) looks to be a superb study of corporate personality that came out too late to address in this discussion.

[62] The heading is taken Ringmar (1996).

The problem for realists is that corporate agents are unobservable. What we see are only individuals and their behavior. Individuals may say they belong to the same organization, and engage in collective action to prove it, but we never actually see the state. What we see is at most *government*, the aggregate of concrete individuals who instantiate a state at a given moment. State action depends on the actions of those individuals, since social structures only exist in virtue of the practices which instantiate them. The challenge for realists is to show that state action is anything more than the sum of these individual governmental actions.

The problem for nominalists stems from the fact that despite this dependence of states on individuals, we routinely explain their behavior as the "behavior" of corporate agents, and these explanations *work* in the sense that they enable us to make reliable predictions about individuals. If on June 21, 1941 we had attributed to "the German state" the intention to invade the Soviet Union the next day, we would have correctly predicted the behavior of millions of individuals on the 22nd. Without that attribution it would have been difficult, even impossible, to predict and make sense of what was going on. The challenge for nominalists is to explain why this is the case. If the concept of state agency is merely a useful fiction, *why* is it so useful as to seem almost indispensable?

The realist has a ready answer: because it refers to a real but unobservable structure. Drawing on the Ultimate Argument for the reality of unobservables discussed in chapter 2, the realist could argue that it would be a "miracle" if a concept that predicted observable behavior so well did not refer to something real. Like quarks, capitalism, and preferences, we know that states are real because their structure generates a pattern of observable effects, as anyone who denies their reality will quickly find out. If John refuses to pay taxes on the grounds that the US state is merely a fiction, then he is likely to experience consequences just as real as he does when he stubs his toe on a table. The reasoning here is abductive: positing a structure that is capable of intentional action is "an inference to the best explanation" for the patterns of behavior that we observe (chapter 2, pp. 62–63). In the realist view, any system, whether biological or corporate, whose behavior can be predicted in this way counts as an intentional agent.[63]

It may be that the concept of state agency refers to a real but

[63] See Campbell (1958: 22–23), Dennett (1987: 15), Clark (1994: 408).

unobservable structure, but what if this structure is reducible to the properties and interactions of the individuals who make it up? By invoking realist philosophy of science we may solve the nominalist's problem of explaining why attributions of state agency work so well, but what about the realist's problem of showing that the state is anything more than the government? The answer is that the structure of states helps explain the properties of governments, which can be seen by invoking the two arguments against individualism made in chapter 4.

The first is that most social structures (here, states) have a collective dimension that causes macro-level regularities among their elements (governments) over space and time. Social systems are structured on two levels, micro and macro. The former refers to the desires and beliefs of existing individuals. If this were the only level on which states were structured then they would be reducible to governments. Yet, we normally think of states as persisting through time despite generational turnover,[64] in part because their properties seem quite stable: boundaries, symbols, national interests, foreign policies, and so on. Such continuities help give temporal continuity to the succession of governments, enabling us to call every national government in Washington, DC for 200 years a "US" government. And even at any given moment we normally think of states as being more than just their current members. Had Bob Dole won the 1996 election, even though the US government would have changed the US state would have remained the same. These temporal and existential continuities are explained by structures of *collective* knowledge to which individuals are socialized,[65] and which they, through their actions, in turn reproduce. Individuals are the "leading edge" of state action, so to speak, but insofar as macro-level regularities are multiply realized by their behavior, we have a situation in which state action cannot be reduced to action by governments.

The other argument against the individualist attempt to reduce states to governments is that we cannot make sense of the actions of governments apart from the structures of states that constitute them as meaningful. Structures can have two kinds of effects, causal and constitutive.

The former assume that cause and effect are independently existing, and so if corporate structures had *only* causal effects it might be

---

[64] Carr (1939/1964: 150); cf. Sandelands and St. Clair (1993).
[65] Gilbert (1989: 274–288).

possible to reduce them to individuals, since nothing about the latter would presuppose the former. A state would be reducible to individuals' shared belief that "we are a [state]."[66] However, this ignores the constitutive effects of structures. Individualism depends on aggregating independently existing parts into a whole. Holists think this presupposes the truth of holism, since assuming that we can know a whole from its parts begs the question of how we can know ourselves as parts if not by prior knowledge of the whole.[67] What gives meaning to an individual's belief that he or she is a member of the "US government," for example, is not only their own beliefs but the structure of shared beliefs in which they participate. This structure is both a micro- and macro-level phenomenon: Bill Clinton's belief that he is the President, for example, only has the content that it does as long as other members of his administration (and society) recognize this, and the common knowledge of his administration is in turn constituted as the "US government" by the structure of collective knowledge which defines the US *state*. A group of individuals only becomes a government, in other words, in virtue of the state which it instantiates.

The structure of state agency

The foregoing discussion suggests that state actors are real and not reducible to the individuals who instantiate them. This is true of most social structures, not just states. Most social structures are not corporate agents and as such are not capable of intentional action. In order to become an agent a structure must have three particular features: an "Idea" of corporate agency and a decision structure that both institutionalizes and authorizes collective action.[68]

The first requirement is that individuals' shared knowledge reproduces an Idea of the state as a corporate "person" or "group Self." There is a Hegelian quality to this claim, although as I argued above it is compatible with a realist view of the state.[69] As

---

[66] Bar-Tal (1990: 36), Tuomela (1989).

[67] Sandelands and St. Clair (1993: 433–434); also see Douglas (1986: 67), Searle (1990), and Sugden (1993).

[68] Cf. Buzan (1991: 65–66).

[69] Palan and Blair (1993); cf. Abrams (1988). Given my realist interpretation of the state a less ambivalent forerunner of my argument might be the nineteenth century German jurist Otto von Gierke's "reality theory of the state" (see French, 1984: 36–37, and Vincent, 1989: 706–708).

Weber put it, "one of the important aspects of the 'existence' of a modern state . . . consists in the fact that the action of various individuals is oriented to the belief that it exists or should exist."[70] Elements of this belief will include a representation of the state's members as a "we" or "plural subject,"[71] a discourse about the principles of political legitimacy upon which their collective identity is based,[72] perhaps written down in a Constitution or "Mission Statement,"[73] and collective memories that connect them to the state's members in the past. All of this commonly takes a narrative form,[74] which means that the empirical study of state identities and their evolution over time will include a substantial element of discursive and intellectual history.[75] It should also be noted that these narratives are structures of collective rather than common knowledge, and so saying, with Weber, that individuals' actions must be "oriented" toward the corporate Idea does *not* mean that everyone in the group must have this idea in their heads. Common knowledge is neither necessary for corporate actors, which can believe things that their members do not, nor sufficient, since individuals can have common knowledge and not constitute a corporate actor.[76] What matters is that individuals accept the obligation to act jointly on behalf of collective beliefs, whether or not they subscribe to them personally. Acting on this commitment is how states acquire their causal powers and get reproduced over time. The concept of state agency is not simply a useful fiction for scholars, in other words, but how the members of states themselves constitute its *reality*.

In addition to an Idea of the state as a corporate person, state actors must also have an "internal decision structure"[77] that institutionalizes and authorizes collective action by their members. Since these two requirements are distinct let me address them separately.

To say that collective action is institutionalized is to say that individuals take it for granted that they will cooperate. The expectation of cooperation is sufficiently deep that their collective action problem is solved. Corporate structures achieve this through centralization and internalization. Centralization involves hierarchical

---

[70] Weber (1978).   [71] Gilbert (1989).   [72] Bukovansky (1997).

[73] See Swales and Rogers (1995).   [74] Ringmar (1996), Barnett (1998).

[75] See especially Bukovansky (1999b).

[76] Gilbert (1987); on the collective character of organizational knowledge see also Schneider and Angelmar (1993).

[77] French (1984).

decision-making that discriminates in favor of some individuals over others.[78] Top officials ("principals") are given a disproportionate role in determining corporate policies, and control over selective incentives to induce subordinates ("agents") to cooperate.[79] Rationalists tend to emphasize centralization as a solution to the collective action problem because in their view people only cooperate when it is in their self-interest. However, this is unlikely to succeed unless a second condition is also met: that individuals have *internalized* corporate norms in how they define their identities and interests. When norms are not internalized people have an instrumental attitude toward them; they may go along with the group, but only because they have calculated that it is useful for them as individuals at that moment to do so.[80] In this situation individuals will constantly question the rationality of their cooperation, constantly look for ways to free ride, and so on, and as such corporate cultures will survive only as long as they are efficient. This is a recipe for institutional frailty, not taken-for-grantedness. Internalization means that corporate culture is considerably thicker than this.[81] In most organizations people cooperate not merely because of what is in it for themselves, but out of a sense of loyalty to and identification with corporate norms. Principal–agent problems might still exist, but overall it will be much easier to institutionalize collective action under these conditions than if actors have a purely self-interested attitude toward corporate structures (see chapter 7).

The institutionalization of collective action gives corporate agency the unity and persistence that it needs, but by itself does not fully convey the sense that the entity which is doing the acting is a corporate agent rather than merely a set of individual agents who happen to work together on a regular basis. The "authorizing" effect of internal decision structures is thus a final constituent of corporate agency: a structure must be organized such that the actions of its members can be attributed to or redescribed as the actions of a corporate body.[82] The key to this are rules that specify relations of authority, dependency, and accountability among a group's members that transfer the responsibility for individual actions to the collective,

---

[78] See Achen (1989).   [79] Olson (1965), Moe (1984).   [80] Hardin (1995a, b).
[81] For a good overview of the implications of this point see Dobbin (1994).
[82] French (1984: 46–47). This requirement is often seen as impotant for distinguishing the action of "mobs" or "crowds" from that of corporations; see, for example, Copp (1980), Gilbert (1989), and Tuomela (1989).

so that individuals act as representatives or on behalf of the latter.[83] This is not an "as if" claim. Authorization means that individuals' actions are constituted *as* the actions of a collective. For example, we do not hold the soldier who kills an enemy in war responsible for his actions because he is authorized to kill by his state. Of course, how one draws this boundary between individual and corporate responsibility is a complicated issue and at the heart of debates about war crimes. It is questionable whether individual responsibility ever is fully given over to the state. Still, corporate agency cannot be reduced completely to the actions of its elements because the latter are not merely "actions of its elements" in the first place.

In sum, concrete individuals play an essential role in state action, instantiating and carrying it forward in time, but state action is no more reducible to those individuals than their action is reducible to neurons in the brain. Both kinds of agency exist only in virtue of structured relationships among their elements, but the effect of those structures is to constitute irreducible capacities for intentionality. These capacities are real, not fictions. This is not to say we should never decompose the state into its elements, any more than the fact that the mind cannot be reduced to the brain means we should not do brain science. A reductionist analysis will shed much light on the constitution of state agency. Insofar as the state is ontologically emergent, however, anthropomorphizing it is not merely an analytical convenience, but essential to predicting and explaining its behavior, just as folk psychology is essential to explaining human behavior.

Why anthropomorphizing the state is still problematic

There are nevertheless at least three important differences between individual and corporate agents which point to the limits of anthropomorphizing the state.[84] Acknowledging these limits moves us considerable distance toward the critics of the unitary actor model, but does not entail their conclusions.

The first difference is that corporate agents are less unitary than individual ones. Although people can have multiple identities, and often engage in contradictory or irrational behavior, biology gives their bodies more coherence, and constrains their action to a greater

---

[83] On corporate responsibility see French (1984).
[84] The following discussion is indebted to Geser (1992).

extent, than is the case for the discursively constituted state. Because they are made up of many individuals (and organizations), each with their own intentional capacities, states can do more things at once than people can, often without "the right hand" knowing what "the left hand" is doing. From an observer's (or another state's) point of view, in other words, there may be more "noise," perhaps much more, in the "signal" of state agency. Interestingly, this may be less of a problem in state agency than for other corporate bodies – which scholars seem more willing to call actors – since even if a state has multiple personalities domestically they may manage to work together when dealing with outsiders. Nevertheless, there is at least a difference in degree between the unitariness of individual and corporate agents, which makes attributions of intentionality to the latter problematic.

Second, and in some sense conversely, it may actually be easier to assess the intentions and therefore predict the behavior of states than it is of individuals. Political Realists have often extrapolated from the difficulties of reading the human mind (the "Problem of Other Minds")[85] to a supposed difficulty in knowing the intentions of states, and on that basis justified worst-case assumptions about the threat posed by those intentions. This inference may be unwarranted. It is hard to read individual minds because we cannot see inside them. Lacking telepathic powers, we have to fall back on context and behavior to infer what others are thinking. In contrast, the structure of corporate "minds" is typically written down in organizational charts that specify the functions and goals of their constituent elements, and their "thoughts" can often be heard or seen in the public debates and statements of decision-makers. To be sure, any claim that states are more transparent than individuals must be tempered by several considerations: the difficulty of knowing which of the many statements of officials represents the "official" line (the signal to noise ratio problem), the relatively thinner social context in which states operate (which provides fewer external cues to intentions), and the fact that states may want to maintain secrecy about their decision-making processes for security reasons. Yet, very few states today are complete black boxes to each other (North Korea is one of the few whose "mind" seems as hard to read as the human mind), not least because states are internally related to societies over which they rarely have

---

[85] Hollis and Smith (1990: 171–176).

actors distinct entities.[90] My argument in this chapter that states are actors with certain essential properties concerns this kind of identity.[91] An actor can have only one such identity. It always has a material base, the body in the case of people, many bodies and territory for states. But what really distinguishes the personal or corporate identity of intentional actors from that of beagles and bicycles is a consciousness and memory of Self as a separate locus of thought and activity. People are distinct entities in virtue of biology, but without consciousness and memory – a sense of "I" – they are not agents, maybe not even "human." This is still more true of states, which do not even have "bodies" if their members have no joint narrative of themselves as a corporate actor, and to that extent corporate identity presupposes individuals with a collective identity (see below). The state is a "group Self" capable of group-level cognition.[92] These Ideas of Self have an "auto-genetic" quality,[93] and as such personal and corporate identities are constitutionally exogenous to Otherness.

To be sure, as postmodernists have emphasized, constituting an actor as a physically distinct being depends on creating and maintaining boundaries between Self and Other, and to that extent even personal and corporate identities presuppose "difference."[94] But this important point becomes trivial if it leads to a totalizing holism in which everything is internally related to everything else. If a constitutive process is self-organizing then there is no particular Other to which the Self is related. Having a body means you are different than someone else's body, but that does not mean his body constitutes yours in any interesting way.

Personal/corporate identity is a site or platform for other identities. The term "type" identity, which I borrow from Jim Fearon,[95] refers to a social category or "label applied to persons who share (or are thought to share) some characteristic or characteristics, in appearance, behavioral traits, attitudes, values, skills (e.g. language), knowledge, opinions, experience, historical commonalities (like region or place of birth), and so on."[96] In addition to speaker of a certain language or native of a certain place, Fearon lists teenager, party affiliation, and heterosexual as examples. An actor can have multiple type identities

---

[90] For discussions of personal identity see especially Hewitt (1989) and Greenwood (1994).
[91] Campbell (1958: 17) calls this "entitativity."
[92] Kohut (1985: 206–207), Wilson and Sober (1994: 602).   [93] Schwalbe (1991).
[94] Cf. Abbott (1995).   [95] Fearon (1997).   [96] Ibid.: 14.

at once. Not just any shared characteristic counts as a type identity, however, like having dry skin or being named Max, but only those that have social content or meaning. This content is given by more or less formal membership rules that define what counts as a type identity and orients the behavior of Others toward it. These rules vary culturally and historically. There have always been people who had sex with other members of the same sex, for example, but they only became "homosexuals," with its attendant social consequences, in the nineteenth century.[97] The role of membership rules in transforming individual characteristics into social types means that Others are involved in their constitution. As such, type identities have an inherently cultural dimension which poses problems for methodological individualism. Unlike role and collective identities, however, the characteristics that underlie type identities are at base *intrinsic* to actors. The qualities that make Max a teenager exist whether or not Others are present to recognize them as meaningful, and to that extent he can be a teenager all by himself.

This simultaneously self-organizing and social quality can be seen especially clearly in the states system, where type identities correspond to "regime types" or "forms of state,"[98] like capitalist states, fascist states, monarchical states, and so on. On the one hand, forms of state are constituted by internal principles of political legitimacy[99] that organize state–society relations with respect to ownership and control of the means of production and destruction. These principles may be caused by interaction with other states (Japan became a democracy after 1945 because it was occupied by the United States), but in a constitutive sense they are exogenous to the states system because they do not depend on other states for their existence. A state can be democratic all by itself. On the other hand, not all shared characteristics become type identities. Two states may have identical parliamentary systems, for example, but in the contemporary states system this category is not meaningful. Yet, states with presidential and parliamentary systems, which a student of comparative politics would see as quite different, are constituted in that system with the *same* type identity as democratic. Moreover, the meaning of the identity "democratic state" is changing as states begin to internalize the belief that democratic states do not make war on each other. If democratic peace theorists are right this regularity has always

---

[97] Hacking (1986).   [98] Cox (1987).   [99] Bukovansky (1997).

existed,[100] but only recently has it become part of the meaning of the democratic type.

Role identities take the dependency on culture and thus Others one step further. Whereas the characteristics that give rise to type identities are pre-social, role identities are not based on intrinsic properties and as such exist *only* in relation to Others. There is no preexisting property in virtue of which a student becomes a student or a master a master; one can have these identities only by occupying a position in a social structure and following behavioral norms toward Others possessing relevant *counter*-identities. One cannot enact role identities by oneself. The sharing of expectations on which role identities depend is facilitated by the fact that many roles are institutionalized in social structures that pre-date particular interactions. Professor and student are positions in a stock of collective knowledge. When we internalize this knowledge its structure becomes mirrored in the structure of what Mead called the "Me," the Self as it sees itself through the Other's eyes.[101] In effect, we are able to enact role identities because we carry Others around with us in our heads. This is not to say that enacting role identities is a purely mechanical affair, since most roles allow a measure of freedom or interpretation, but only within certain parameters. When those parameters are breached, or absent to start with, then role identities are contested. When Columbus first encountered the "Indians" he positioned them as savages needing to be saved by Christianity; they resisted this representation; in the end coercion stabilized their respective roles.

The concept of role identity has been applied to states by "foreign policy role theorists."[102] Interestingly, however, despite the fact that the concept of role seems to imply one of social structure, there has been little contact between this literature and structural IR.[103] Since Holsti's seminal article, role theorists have tended to assume that the social structure of international politics is too "ill-defined, flexible, or weak"[104] to generate significant role expectations, and so states' foreign policy roles are entirely a function of policy-makers' beliefs and domestic politics, rather than their relations to Others. In effect, the agentic, role-*taking* side of the equation has been emphasized at

---

[100] Russett (1993).   [101] See Mead (1934), Burke (1980), Stryker (1980).

[102] Holsti (1970), Walker, ed. (1987).

[103] See Walker, ed. (1987). For recent efforts to build a bridge between role theory and a more social systemic theory see Walker (1992) and Barnett (1993).

[104] Holsti (1970: 243).

the expense of the structural, role-*constituting* side, which strips the concept of role of much of its interest. Neorealists seem to agree. The index of *Theory of International Politics* contains no entry for "role," and Waltz discounts its closest approximation, "functional differentiation," on the grounds that it is reducible to the distribution of power. Buzan, Jones, and Little[105] reinstate functional differentiation as an important issue for systemic theory, but specifically argue against extending it to role differentiation on the grounds that roles are unit-level phenomena which do not concern the "deep structure" of the system.

The fact that the international system is poorly institutionalized does raise questions about the applicability of the concept of role identity for systemic IR. Nevertheless, there are three reasons for thinking that foreign policy roles may be a more structural phenomenon than is often assumed. One is a tendency in the literature to take certain international institutions and their associated role identities for granted. The most important example of this is sovereign equality. Neorealists and foreign policy role theorists alike assume that states are sovereign, but treat this only as a corporate identity, as nothing more than an inherent feature of being a state. As I argue in chapter 6, the fact that the sovereignty of the modern state is recognized by other states means that it is now also a *role* identity with substantial rights and behavioral norms. A second problem is a presumption that the concept of role implies normative integration and cooperation, which are hard to come by in the "state of war" of international politics.[106] This assumption is unwarranted and tacitly privileges a materialist understanding of structure over a cultural one. Shared ideas can be conflictual or cooperative, which means that "enemy" can be as much a role identity as "friend." Finally, as the enemy example indicates, what really matters in defining roles is not institutionalization but the degree of interdependence or "intimacy" between Self and Other.[107] When intimacy is high, as in the Arab–Israeli conflict, role identities might not be just a matter of choice that can be easily discarded, but positions forced on actors by the representations of significant Others. In this situation even if a state wants to abandon a role it may be unable to do so because the Other resists out of a desire to maintain *its* identity. These considerations suggest that the divorce between role

[105] Buzan, Jones, and Little (1993: 46).   [106] Holsti (1970: 243).
[107] See Blumstein (1991).

theory and systemic IR has been premature. By adopting a more social conceptualization of the international system the structural aspects of states' role identities may come more clearly into view.

Collective identity[108] takes the relationship between Self and Other to its logical conclusion, identification. Identification is a cognitive process in which the Self–Other distinction becomes blurred and at the limit transcended altogether. Self is "categorized" *as* Other.[109] Identification is usually issue-specific and rarely total (though may come close in love and patriotism), but always involves extending the boundaries of the Self to include the Other. This process makes use of but goes beyond role and type identities. It builds on role identities in that it too relies on the mechanism of incorporating the Other into the Self in the form of a socially constituted "Me." But whereas role identities do so in order that Self and Other can play *different* roles, collective identity does so in order to merge them into a single identity.[110] And it builds on type identities because collective identity involves shared characteristics, but not all type identities are collective because not all involve identification. One can be a "French-speaker" without identifying with the French (the example of France's failed effort to form a collective identity with Algeria comes to mind). Collective identity, in short, is a distinct combination of role and type identities, one with the causal power to induce actors to define the welfare of the Other as part of that of the Self, to be "altruistic."[111] Altruistic actors may still be rational, but the basis on which they calculate their interests is the group or "team."[112] This enables them to overcome collective action problems that can stymie egoists, a conclusion which has received substantial experimental support.[113]

I address collective identity more systematically in chapter 7, so let me just say a word here about its relevance to international politics, where the conventional Realist wisdom has something of a split personality. On the one hand, Realists have always emphasized that it is naive and potentially even dangerous to think that states could ever form collective identities. States are by nature fundamentally self-interested, and the sooner we accept this the sooner we will have a

---

[108] This is also known as "social" identity in the social identity theory literature; see Mercer (1995).
[109] Turner, *et al.* (1987).   [110] See Lancaster and Foddy (1988).
[111] Jencks (1990), Monroe (1996: 6–7); cf. Teske (1997).   [112] Sugden (1993).
[113] See, for example, Caporael, *et al.* (1989), Dawes, *et al.* (1990), and Kramer, *et al.* (1995).

realistic approach to foreign policy and international order. On the other hand, the very possibility of the state – and thus of an "international" politics – assumes that individuals identify with an Idea of the state, and as such its *corporate* identity will depend on powerful and enduring notions of *collective* identity among individuals.[114] In other words, it is only in virtue of the most thoroughly social individual identity (collective identity) that the anti-social corporate identity of the "Realist" state is possible in the first place. Of course, just because individuals are capable of forming collective identities is no guarantee that states can form them, and as we shall see there are good reasons for thinking that the one actually inhibits the other. This is an important challenge to any non-Realist theory of international politics, which I take up below in discussing the national interest and in chapter 7. For now I simply ask the reader to keep an open mind to the possibility.

I have identified four kinds of identity, of which all but the first can take multiple forms simultaneously within the same actor. We all have many, many identities, and this is no less true of states. Each is a script or schema, constituted to varying degrees by cultural forms, about who we are and what we should do in a certain context. If they all pressed upon us equally at every moment we surely should be confused, but fortunately most identities are activated selectively depending on the situations in which we find ourselves.[115] When a student gives me his paper to grade I know it is time to be a professor, and the fact that I am also a US citizen does not figure in our interaction. Even so, many situations call up several identities that may point in different directions, leaving us unsure how to act.

There is no way to predict a priori how internal identity conflicts will be resolved. However, it might be useful to consider the following general hypothesis: (1) in any situation the solution to identity conflicts within an actor will reflect the relative "salience" or hierarchy of identity commitments in the Self,[116] and (2) that hierarchy will tend to reflect the order in which I presented the four kinds of identity above. The Self is a structure of knowledge, "the totality of an individual's thoughts and feelings having reference to himself as an object."[117] Identities are arrayed hierarchically in this structure by an

---

[114] See Bloom (1990).   [115] Alexander and Wiley (1981).

[116] See McCall and Simmons (1978), Stryker (1980), and Burke and Reitzes (1991).

[117] Rosenberg (1981: 7), Pratkanis and Greenwald (1985).

actor's degree of commitment to them; some are fundamental to our self-concept, others more superficial. When conflicts arise the requirements of the former tend to win out. Self-organization has evolutionary advantages for individuals, and for states its priority reflects the relative importance of domestic politics in shaping their character. On the other hand, this is clearly a very crude generalization that is often violated. People frequently give up their lives (personal identity) for their country (collective), which turns this supposed hierarchy upside down, and states sometimes subordinate domestic to international concerns. Much depends on the extent to which an identity is threatened; a non-salient identity which is highly threatened may dominate a more salient one that is not. But as a first approximation to a general, long-term tendency the proposition may have merit.

All four kinds of identity imply but are not reducible to interests. Identities refer to who or what actors *are*. They designate social kinds or states of being. Interests refer to what actors *want*. They designate motivations that help explain behavior. (I say "help" because behavior also depends on beliefs about how to realize interests in a given context.) Interests presuppose identities because an actor cannot know what it wants until it knows who it is, and since identities have varying degrees of cultural content so will interests.[118] Identities may themselves be chosen in light of interests, as some rationalists have argued, but those interests themselves presuppose still deeper identities. However, identities by themselves do not explain action, since being is not the same thing as wanting, and we cannot "read off" the latter from the former. This suggests that the efforts of partisans of each concept to ignore or trump the other are misguided. Without interests identities have no motivational force, without identities interests have no direction. Identities belong to the belief side of the intentional equation (desire + belief = action) I discussed in chapter 3, while interests belong to the desire side. As such there will always be at least implicit assumptions about identity in "interest explanations" and vice-versa. They play complementary explanatory roles, and so rather than define them as rivals we should explore how they work in tandem.

The social theory literature distinguishes two kinds of interests, objective and subjective. Objective interests are needs or functional imperatives which must be fulfilled if an identity is to be repro-

---

[118] Wildavsky (1994).

duced.[119] All four kinds of identity have such reproduction requirements: the US cannot be a state without its monopoly on organized
violence (corporate), a capitalist state without enforcing private property rights (type), a hegemon without its clients (role), and a member
of the West without its solidarity with other Western states (collective).
Such needs are "objective" in the sense that they exist even if the US
government is not aware of them, and if they are not met then the
identities they support will not survive. When actors internalize such
identities they acquire two dispositions – to understand their requirements, and to act on those understandings – which ensures an on-
going effort to reproduce them. But these dispositions explain action
only indirectly, because the fact that actors want to know their identity
needs does not mean they will always correctly perceive them. People
are sometimes wrong or deceived about their needs and as such may
act contrary to them.[120]

The concept of *subjective* interests refers to those beliefs that actors
actually have about how to meet their identity needs, and it is these
which are the proximate motivation for behavior. This is equivalent to
what rationalists mean by "preferences" or "tastes," and philosophers
by "desire," and to avoid confusion we might want to use one of
those terms instead and reserve "interest" for "objective" interests.
Either way, however, it is important to recognize two points. The first
is that preferences are motives, not behaviors. As Robert Powell[121]
puts it, subjective interests are "preferences over outcomes," not
"preferences over strategies." The distinction matters because in
intentional explanations, behavior is caused not only by what an actor
wants (Desire) but also by what he thinks it possible to attain (Belief),
and as such we cannot infer preferences from behavior. Second,
desires are not distinct from beliefs but themselves a species of belief,
namely "desiderative" beliefs or interpretations about how to meet
needs (chapter 3, pp. 122–128). This need not violate the $D + B = A$
formula, but it does indicate that "B" needs to be disaggregated into
different kinds of beliefs. Some beliefs constitute who we are (identities and their associated needs), others the goals we think will help
us realize those needs (subjective interests or desires), and still other
beliefs relate those goals to the external environment (the rationalist

---

[119] This needs-based view of objective interests draws on Wiggins (1985) and McCullagh (1991); also see Benton (1981) and Connolly (1983).
[120] Connolly (1983).   [121] Powell (1994).

understanding of "Belief"). None of these determines any of the others directly, even if they are not altogether unrelated either.

Given that a persistent failure to understand and act on identity needs will lead to the loss of those identities, one of the key problems that actors face is trying to align their subjective and objective interests. Sometimes this is not difficult. If someone is trapped in a hotel fire they will usually determine quite quickly that the way to reproduce their personal identity is to acquire a desire to get out. But in many situations the implications of identity needs are more complex or even contradictory. To successfully reproduce her identity, a beginning professor must typically have two interests: to publish and to teach. How should she weigh them? That will depend on both personal and contextual factors, but the possibility of mistakes – not just in behavior but in how she defines her interests in the first place – is very real. If she is disposed to understand her interests, however, she will proceed as a lay scientist, using a combination of Reason and Experiment to continually test whether her beliefs about her interests are helping her enact the identity of "professor." This might not become clear for several years, during which time she may face structural uncertainty about whether her subjective and objective interests are properly aligned – and this is an example where the implications of an identity are relatively well defined. Corporate actors may have an even more difficult time because the implications of their identities for interests are often more open-ended, and in part for that reason subject to considerable political contestation about which interpretation of interests is best.[122] Or at least so it seems in thinking about national interests.

The national interest

States are actors whose behavior is motivated by a variety of interests rooted in corporate, type, role, and collective identities. Since most of these identities vary culturally and historically it is impossible to say much about the content of state interests in the abstract. However, I have argued that states share essential properties in virtue of their corporate identity as states, and I now want to suggest that these generate universal "national interests" about which it is possible to generalize. As a function of corporate identity these interests are

[122] See Weldes (1996) and Kimura and Welch (1998).

intrinsic to states; relative to the international system they are not social constructions. Since one of my goals in this book is to show that many state interests *are* constructions of the international system, the notion of pre-social interests sits uneasily with my overall argument. I argue that the content even of these pre-social interests is affected by states' type, role, and collective identities, which to varying degrees are constructed by the international system, but these constructions are still constrained by the nature of corporate stateness. The state is not a tabula rasa on which any interest can be written. In this section I first discuss these basic interests, but then argue that they do not entail that states are inherently self-interested. States are not Realists by nature.

The concept of national interest refers to the reproduction requirements or security of state–society complexes. An important feature of this definition is that it refers to *objective* interests. This is not the way that most IR scholars think about interests. Systemic theorists have mostly adopted an economic discourse in which interest is understood in subjective terms as preferences, and although more oriented toward psychology, students of foreign policy decision-making and of national roles also focus on "conceptions" of interest. This approach makes sense when our goal is to explain behavior, of which subjective states are a proximate cause. I too want to explain behavior, and so will also speak of interests in these terms. Students of the "national" interest, however, emphasize that it exists *independent* of perceptions.[123] No one to my knowledge has used the concept of objective interests to make this point, but the connection is clear. This objectivist approach tends to reflect a different goal: to answer the normative question of what states should do rather than the scientific one of explaining what they actually do. However, for both approaches objective national interests are not merely normative guidelines for action, but causal powers that predispose states to act in certain ways. It is in part because states have certain security needs (objective interests) that they define their subjective interests as they do. The relationship between objective and subjective interests is under-determined, but in the long run a persistent failure to bring subjective interests into line with objective ones will lead to an actor's demise. It is this causal impact of objective interests that is of concern here.

---

[123] See, for example, George and Keohane (1980), Kratochwil (1982), and Clinton (1986: 497–505).

George and Keohane[124] identify three national interests – physical survival, autonomy, and economic well-being – which they describe informally as "life, liberty, and property." I will add a fourth, "collective self-esteem." The form these interests take will vary with states' other identities, but the underlying needs are common to all states and must somehow be addressed if states are to reproduce themselves.

Physical survival refers in the last analysis to the individuals who make up a state–society complex, but since no individual is essential to the identity of a collective, what we are really talking about here is the survival of the complex. Individuals can be sacrificed to that end, as in war, and even parts of the collective. France did not "die" when it lost Alsace-Lorraine in 1871, and in the eighteenth century ceding territory to other states as compensation was common. This practice has been made nearly unthinkable today by a growing identification of survival with the preservation of existing territory, although states still sometimes decide that it is in the national interest to allow peripheral territories to secede, as did the Soviet and Czechoslovak states. But this merely indicates that what counts as survival varies historically, not that it is not a national interest. Russia was the core of the Soviet state while Bohemia was of the Czechoslovak, and both in effect survived by ceding their peripheries – a fact acknowledged by the international community when it recognized Russia and the Czech Republic as "successor" states.

Waltz[125] assumes that survival is the only national interest of states. While there is analytical value in seeing how far such a thin model will take us, empirically a case can be made that states have at least three other objective interests.

Autonomy refers to the ability of a state–society complex to exercise control over its allocation of resources and choice of government. In order to reproduce its identity it is not enough for a state–society complex to merely survive, it must also retain its "liberty." This follows from the fact of state sovereignty. Indeed, a case can be made that *all* organizations, not just states, have an interest in autonomy, since without it they will be constrained in their ability to meet internal demands or respond to contingencies in the environment.[126] On the other hand, autonomy is always a matter of degree and can be

[124] George and Keohane (1980).   [125] Waltz (1979).
[126] Pfeffer and Salancik (1978), Oliver (1991: 945–947).

traded away when the benefits of dependence outweigh the costs.[127] As with survival, what counts as securing autonomy will vary from case to case.

Economic well-being refers to the maintenance of the mode of production in a society and, by extension, the state's resource base. Most IR scholars would probably argue that this implies an interest in economic *growth*, and that is in fact how well-being is defined in most states today. However, it may be a mistake to assume that growth is an essential interest of states. Growth is essential in those modes of production that need it for their reproduction, like capitalism. Whether because of the logic of the market or the need to legitimate the economic order by increasing material benefits to the population as a whole, in capitalist systems growth is the criterion of well-being. Yet throughout most of human history this was not the case. Slave and feudal modes of production were not inherently growth oriented, nor are the subsistence economies that dominate parts of the contemporary Fourth World. Does this mean that states in these systems were not acting in their national interest? It seems more reasonable to conclude that the interest in economic well-being only becomes a need for growth in particular state *forms*, and as such is a function of historically contingent type identities rather than of states' corporate identity. This does not make growth any less essential to the modern (capitalist) state's national interest, and so for most practical purposes we can substitute "growth" for "well-being" above. But in a world that rapidly may be nearing its ecological carrying capacity precisely because of the growth imperative, there may yet come a day when the national interest requires a different articulation of well-being.

Collective self-esteem refers to a group's need to feel good about itself, for respect or status. Self-esteem is a basic human need of individuals, and one of the things that individuals seek in group membership. As expressions of this desire groups acquire the need as well.[128] Like other national interests it can be expressed in different ways. A key factor is whether collective self-images are positive or negative, which will depend in part on relationships to significant Others, since it is by taking the perspective of the Other that the Self sees itself. Negative self-images tend to emerge from perceived disregard or humiliation by other states, and as such may occur frequently in highly competitive international environments (the Germans after World War I? the

---

[127] George and Keohane (1980), Oliver (1991).   [128] Kaplowitz (1984).

Russians today?). Since groups cannot long tolerate such images if they are to meet the self-esteem needs of their members, they will compensate by self-assertion and/or devaluation and aggression toward the Other.[129] Positive self-images, in contrast, tend to emerge from mutual respect and cooperation. Recognition of sovereignty by other states seems particularly important here, since it means that at least formally a state has an equal status in the eyes of Others.[130] Recognition reduces the need to secure the Self by devaluing or destroying the Other, which is a key requirement of a Lockean culture of anarchy (chapter 6). Thus, whereas in a Hobbesian world self-esteem needs tend to take the form of needs for "glory" and "power" at others' expense, in a Lockean one they are more likely to do so as "virtue" and "being a good citizen." What this suggests, in other words, is that the institution of sovereignty may help pacify states not only by reassuring them against the physical threat of conquest (the traditional explanation), but also against the *psychic* threat of not having standing.

These four interests are needs that must be met if state–society complexes are to be secure, and as such they set objective limits on what states can do in their foreign policies. They may on occasion have contradictory implications that require prioritization, but in the long run all four must be satisfied. States that do not will tend to die out. While in this respect national interests are a selection mechanism, their real significance lies in the fact that they dispose states to try to understand them, to interpret their implications for how subjective security interests should be defined. When the international environment is highly constraining these implications may be quite clear. If enemy troops are shooting their way across your border the survival interest says fight back (though even here one might debate whether it is better to be "Red than dead"). But most of the time states do not find themselves in hotel fires, in which case a variety of beliefs about how to meet security needs may be compatible with the national interest. Often these beliefs will be contested, as in the debate in the US between isolationists and internationalists, although in many cases certain representations are simply never considered because of political inertia, ideological hegemony, or lack of imagination,[131] which

---

[129] Kaplowitz (1990).   [130] See Honneth (1996).
[131] For discussion of such counter-factual possibilities in the case of the Cuban Missile Crisis see Weldes (1996, 1999).

may help account for the relative stability of interpretations of the national interest over time.[132] The fact that national interests can be interpreted in different ways suggests that social scientists would do well to approach them inductively rather than deductively.[133] Yet in doing so we should not assume that states are unconstrained or unmoved by national interests. States need to do certain things to secure their identities, and it is in their nature to try to discover what these things are and act accordingly. They may have room for interpretive license, but that does not mean they are free to construct their interests any way they like.

This points to an important conclusion: states are homeostatic structures that are relatively enduring over time. Like other cultural forms states are self-fulfilling prophecies (chapter 4); once up and running they acquire interests in reproducing themselves that create resistance to disappearing of their own accord. This creates substantial path-dependency and "stickiness" in international politics. Construct-ivists are sometimes thought to be saying that because reality is socially constructed it must be easy to change. It is true that one reason for emphasizing processes of social construction is to highlight possibilities for change that might otherwise not be seen, but it is no implication of the argument here that change is easy. Indeed, I am impressed with how resilient the state is. No matter how much transnational actors grow in importance, no matter how much state autonomy is undermined by international regimes or economic inter-dependence, states keep trying – and apart from a few "failed states" mostly successfully – to reproduce themselves. Continued success may depend ultimately on profound adaptations in their form (like internationalization), but their structure gives them a powerful homeostatic disposition which makes it unlikely they will wither away.

Are states "Realists"? A note on self-interest

The proposition that national interests give states a self-fulfilling "nature" prompts a concluding question: is this nature "Realist"? This might mean different things to different kinds of Realists: for some it

---

[132] On the importance of stability of interpretations for a national interest to exist see Krasner (1978: 44).
[133] Kimura and Welch (1998).

might mean that states seek power, for others that states seek security, and for still others that states seek security and wealth.[134] All Realists would probably agree, however, that states are inherently *self-interested* or egoistic. Waltz says that international systems are created by states who are intrinsically "self-regarding"; Sondermann treats the national interest as a synonym for "national egoism"; and, while noting the possibility of other interests, George and Keohane[135] also assume that self-interest is the core of the national interest. So let us define the question as: "are states self-interested?"

In one sense, sometimes, even most of the time, the answer is clearly yes. The violent history of international politics hardly could suggest otherwise. However, the question is not whether states are self-interested *sometimes*, or even *most* of the time, but whether they are by *nature*. A metaphysical question perhaps, but all theories of international politics contain answers to it that affect their choice of methods and substantive conclusions. If states are self-interested by nature, then we can take self-interest as given and use rationalist theory to analyze its behavioral implications. If they are "Realists" only contingently, by nurture, however, then investigating the processes by which state interests are formed becomes a high priority.

The concept of self-interest is notoriously slippery and so the first step is to be clear on exactly what we mean. A major source of confusion is that it is often used as though it were equivalent to saying that an actor did X because X was "in its interest." This implies that self-interest is whatever the Self is interested in, which strips the concept of any explanatory power. If the discussion of interests above is correct then all behavior is "interest*ed*" in the sense that it is expected to have some perceived benefit for the Self; people rarely do things which they think will have a negative impact on their net utility. But the proposition that people act on perceived interests does not explain anything in particular because it says nothing about their *content*. The murderer who kills an innocent child and the hero who dies to save his friends may have an equal "interest" in what they do, but a conception of self-interest that cannot discriminate between these cases is tautological and of no theoretical interest. For the concept of self-interest to do any explanatory work it must be defined

---

[134] Morgenthau (1948/1973), Waltz (1979), Gilpin (1981).
[135] Waltz (1979: 91), Sondermann (1977: 123), George and Keohane (1980).

as a *kind* of interest, which means rooting it in a conception of identity. We cannot understand self-interest, in short, without understanding the Self,[136] and especially its relationship to the Other.

Self-interest is a belief about how to meet one's needs – a subjective interest – that is characterized by a purely *instrumental* attitude toward the Other: the Other is an object to be picked up, used, and/or discarded for reasons having solely to do with an actor's individual gratification.[137] This belief is normally issue- and Other-specific rather than global. When it is present, however, it implies the absence of identification with the Other, of collective identity. The distinction between Self and Other is total, such that the latter has no intrinsic value for the former. An important implication of this definition is that one cannot be self-interested by oneself. Self-interest is not an intrinsic property of actors, like having blue eyes or brown hair, but a contingent belief about how to meet needs that gets activated in relation to specific situations and Others, and as such it is culturally constituted.[138]

Since it is easy to over-interpret this claim I should note two things I do *not* intend by it. First, self-interest does not mean being oblivious to the Other's interests. Taking the Other's interests into account, being "social" in Weber's sense, is essential to anticipating his behavior and thus in an interdependent world to gratifying the Self. Self-interest does not mean autism; but "taking into account" is not "identifying with." Second, self-interest does not mean refusing to cooperate with or help Others. Self-interest is about motivation, not behavior. As long as cooperation is purely instrumental – a state helps another state only because its own security is also threatened, for example – then it is egoistic. On the other hand, if a state helps another because it identifies with it, such that even when its own security is not threatened it still perceives a threat to the Self, then it is acting from collective interest. Motivation is notoriously difficult to measure, a problem compounded when actors have mixed motives, but this is a problem for self- and collective interest explanations alike. How do we know that a self-interest explanation of cooperation is true if we do not know whether an actor was in fact self-interested? On a scientific realist view of explanation, which eschews "as if" thinking in favor of describing causal mechanisms, there is no alternative to trying to identify motivations empirically. Defining self-interest in

---

[136] Morse (1997: 180).   [137] See especially Jencks (1990).   [138] Wildavsky (1994).

terms of a particular belief about the relationship of Self to Other is an essential first step.

Armed with this definition, does the national interest mean that states are "Realists"? On the surface there are good reasons to think yes. States have intrinsic, objective interests which they are disposed to try to understand and meet. This will at least "bias" them toward egoistic interpretations of their interests, since they cannot be sure Others will look out for their interests, and in a world of scarce resources meeting the needs of the Self will often conflict with those of the Other. Human beings probably never would have survived evolution without such a self-interested bias, and the same is probably true of states. Moreover, unlike human beings, whose personal identity is in part a function of biological processes over which they have no control, the corporate identity of states only exists as long as their individual members maintain a *cognitive* differentiation between the (group) Self and Other. A substantial body of scholarship in social psychology, known as "social identity theory," has shown experimentally that the process of making such cognitive differentiations is routinely accompanied by discrimination against the members of out-groups in favor of the in-group.[139] This tendency is clearly manifested in the case of states, who depend politically on domestic constituencies that clamor relentlessly for their own interests to be met before those of foreigners. As postmodernists might put it, group "difference" seems to tend naturally toward "Othering." In a thoughtful critique of my "Anarchy is what states make of it," in which I made a tabula rasa assumption about state interests, Jonathan Mercer[140] uses social identity theory to argue that states are by nature self-interested, and anarchic systems therefore inherently self-help, Realist worlds.

I accept much of this critique. Perhaps even more so than individuals, states are predisposed to define their objective interests in self-interested terms. All other things being equal, the international system contains a bias toward "Realist" thinking. The question, however, is not whether there are pressures on states to be self-interested – there are – but whether states are capable ever of transcending those pressures and expanding the boundaries of the Self to include Others. This they might do initially for self-interested

---

[139] See, for example, Tajfel, ed. (1982), Turner, *et al.* (1987), and Abrams and Hogg, eds. (1990).
[140] Mercer (1995).

reasons, but if over time the identification becomes internalized, such that a group of states learns to think of itself as a "We," then its members will no longer be self-interested relative to each other with respect to the issues that define the group. The question, in short, is whether the members of states can ever learn additional "social" (what I am calling "collective") identities above and beyond the state, creating "concentric circles" of group identification.[141] The Realist hypothesis that states are motivated solely by self-interest rules out this possibility (Mercer's discussion, for example, is striking in its neglect of learning by groups), as does the rationalist premise that egoistic interests should be treated as given. These are strong claims. They rule out the possibility that states would ever help each other when their own security is not directly threatened, or would ever internalize international norms – norms simply being practices upheld by *many* Others (Mead's "generalized" Other). If Realists are right, in other words, states will never learn to follow norms out of a sense of obligation or legitimacy, and instead will do so only to the extent that there is "something in it for them."

Despite their biological bias toward self-interest, individuals routinely have overcome such thinking and formed collective identities. This is what social identity theory is all about: the determinants of group identification. Human beings are social animals, and probably would never have formed societies were they always self-interested. In chapter 7 I argue that states too can learn to identify with each other. Social identity theory does not rule this out,[142] and indeed even emphasizes the plasticity of group identities.[143] Mercer himself acknowledges that at least in the European Union some states have managed to form a collective identity, and I shall argue in chapter 6 that states' collective identity goes much deeper than this. The vast majority of states today see themselves as part of a "society of states" whose norms they adhere to not because of on-going self-interested calculations that it is good for them as individual states, but because they have internalized and identify with them. This is not to deny that states are self-interested in much of what they do *within* the boundaries of that society. But with respect to many of the fundamental

---

[141] Lasswell (1972), Linklater (1990).   [142] See Gaertner, *et al*. (1993).

[143] Hogg, *et al*. (1995). As such, in my view Mercer draws exactly the wrong conclusion from social identity theory.

questions of their co-existence states have already achieved a level of collective interest that goes well beyond "Realism."

Conclusion

This chapter had three objectives. The first was to justify the practice of treating states as real, unitary actors to which we can attribute intentionality. This practice is essential to both the explanatory and political aspects of the states systemic project, but proponents have neglected its justification, tending instead to take state agency as an unproblematic given. Skeptical critics have called this into question. Using a constructivist framework, I first combined Weberian and Marxist insights by defining the state as an organizational actor possessing sovereignty and a territorial monopoly on organized violence, whose form is constituted in relation to the society it governs by a structure of political authority. I then justified ascriptions of agency by showing how states are constituted by internal structures that combine a collective Idea of the state with rules that institutiona- lize and authorize collective action by their members, and by arguing that these structures are real because they have real effects.

The second objective was to identify the core interests of these corporate bodies. I first proposed a tentative typology of identities and interests, dividing the former into corporate, type, role, and collective identities. Each of these has certain reproduction require- ments, or objective interests, that condition beliefs about how to meet them, or subjective interests. I then applied this framework to the concept of national interest, defining it as the objective interests of state–society complexes in survival, autonomy, economic well-being, and collective self-esteem. States' interpretations of these needs are biased toward self-interest, but on any non-trivial definition self- interest cannot be essential to the state. Interests are a variable because the boundaries of the Self are a variable. This claim departs from the conventional depiction of the state in systemic theory, and it plays a key role in subsequent chapters. But in most respects what this chapter has done is simply provide ontological foundations for what most systemic scholars take as their starting point: unitary actors with intrinsic motivational dispositions.

The chapter also confirms some mainstream intuitions in its final argument, the pieces of which I now pull together for the first time. In justifying the essentialist proposition that states are self-organizing, homeostatic actors with intrinsic identities and interests, I implicitly have defended the individualist view that states (individuals) are ontologically prior to the states system (society). In their intrinsic properties states are constitutionally exogenous to the states system, and as such agent and structure in international politics are *not* mutually constitutive "all the way down." On the contrary, as Waltz[144] says, states systems emerge from the interaction of preexisting units. This has an important implication: it is necessary to treat states as, at some level, *given* for purposes of systemic IR theory. Since constructivist IR scholarship was born out of a rejection of this individualist view, let me be clear about what is being said. The claim is *not* that we should never problematize states "all the way down." There are important dangers, both theoretical and political, to leaving the internal constitution of states unexamined,[145] and some of the most interesting work in IR today, both postmodern and Liberal, takes up that challenge.[146] My claim is that *systemic* theorists cannot do so because systems of states presuppose states, and so *if* we want to analyze the structure of those systems we cannot "de-center" their elements all the way down. Thus, just as Richard Ashley and other critical theorists rightly criticized individualists for failing to problematize the state at all because it silenced certain questions, to do so all the way down would do the same thing to other, systemic, questions. We cannot study everything at once, and as such it is important to distinguish criticisms of how a given subject is being handled from calls to change the subject.

Since this chapter supports some important mainstream sensibilities, it should be emphasized that none of this means that states are not "socially constructed," both internally and externally. Internally, the fact that states are self-organizing is consistent with constructivism because states are not natural kinds, and as such what else could they be but social constructions? This highlights an important difference between states and people: whereas the individuality of the human body is constituted by internal *material* structures about which constructivism tells us little, the individuality of the state is constituted by internal *social* structures about which it should tell us a lot. In exploring those structures, however, we should recognize that there are different *levels* of social construction, such that what is social

---

[144] Waltz (1979: 91).   [145] Cf. Dobbin (1994: 140).
[146] Campbell (1992), Moravcsik (1997).

relative to one may be pre-social relative to another. Self-organization means that the essential state does not presuppose other states (a state can be a state all by itself), but its internal structure is still thoroughly social.

This limits the strength of the constructivist hypothesis that can be entertained at the *system* level, but it still leaves plenty of room for processes of social construction at that level, of both the causal and constitutive variety. Causally, the fact that states' bodies are constituted by internal structures in no way precludes them forming identities and interests by interacting with each other (chapter 7), anymore than the fact that people are constituted by nature precludes them acquiring identities and interests through socialization. Both involve causal processes of social construction operating on exogenously given platforms, which mainstream systemic theorists have largely ignored. And, constitutively, the fact that some aspects of state identity are exogenous to the states system does not mean that every aspect is. Just as most of the interesting properties of people are constituted by their social relationships, in chapter 6 I show that much of what is interesting about states in the international system is constituted by their social relations with each other. The fact that my model of the essential state is "stripped down" plays a key role in this argument, since it leaves open for social constitution at the international level many properties that Neorealists and Neoliberals assume are inherent to states: egoism, the meaning of power, the terms of sovereignty, perhaps even the nature of rationality.

Individualists would have us believe that nothing about the state is constructed by the international system, while holists would have us believe that everything is. The truth is somewhere in between. Individualism captures a key insight, that states are not constituted by each other all the way down, but that is just the beginning of the story.

6   Three cultures of anarchy

In chapter 5 I argued that states are intentional, corporate actors whose identities and interests are in important part determined by domestic politics rather than the international system. Within domestic politics states are still socially constructed, of course, but this is a different level of construction; relative to the international system states are self-organizing facts. This means that if we are interested in the question of how the states *system* works, rather than in how its elements are constructed, we will have to take the existence of states as given, just as sociologists have to take the existence of people as given to study how society works. Systemic theory cannot problematize the state all the way down,[1] in short, since that would change the subject from a theory of the states system to a theory of the state. The fact that state identities and interests are at least partly exogenous to the system, in turn, satisfies the first principle of individualist approaches to systemic theory, like Neorealism and Neoliberalism. However, these theories usually make the much broader assumption that *all* state identities and interests are exogenous, which does not follow. The fact that state agents are not constructed by system structures all the way down does not mean they are not constructed by them to a significant extent. The per se individuality of states may be given outside the system, but the meanings or *terms* of that individuality are given within. Having accepted a key individualist constraint on systemic theorizing, in this chapter I show that a holist approach can still tell us a lot about the structure of international politics which would elude a pure individualism.

I assume at the outset that this structure is an anarchy, defined as

[1] Cf. Ashley (1984), Campbell (1992).

the absence of centralized authority. Disparities of power between Great and Small Powers raise doubts about this assumption on the centralization side, and states' acceptance of international norms raise more on the authority side. These questions highlight the limits of the "anarchy problematique" in IR scholarship,[2] but I shall set them aside for this chapter. Anarchy poses a distinctive and important problem of order for international politics, to which a constructivist approach suggests some new solutions.

Debates about the nature of the international system are in important part about the causal powers of anarchic structures. Under this heading I address two questions in this chapter, what might be called the variation question and the construction question.[3]

The first is whether anarchy is compatible with more than one kind of structure and therefore "logic." It is important here to distinguish between micro- and macro-level structures (chapter 4, pp. 145–157), between what Waltz calls the domains of "foreign policy" and "international politics." Everyone agrees that micro- or interaction-level anarchic structures vary. Some are peaceful, others warlike. The US and Russia interact under anarchy, and so did the US and the Soviet Union. Few would deny that their structures of interaction differ. The real question is whether the fact of anarchy creates a tendency for all such interactions to realize a single logic at the macro-level. In the Neorealist view they do: anarchies are inherently self-help systems that tend to produce military competition, balances of power, and war. Against this I argue that anarchy can have at least three kinds of structure at the macro-level, based on what kind of roles – enemy, rival, and friend – dominate the system. Adapting language from Martin Wight and the English School, I will call these structures Hobbesian, Lockean, and Kantian,[4] although in doing so I claim no close adherence to their views; the labels are intended merely as metaphors or stylized representations. I argue that only the Hobbesian structure is a truly self-help system, and as such there is no such thing as a "logic of anarchy."[5]

The other question is whether the international system constructs states. Do anarchic structures affect state identities and interests, or merely their behavior (see chapter 1)? Rationalist models assume that

---

[2] Ashley (1988); see also Alker (1996: 355–393).
[3] On the importance of distinguishing these issues see Lamborn (1997).
[4] See Wight (1991).   [5] Buzan, Jones, and Little (1993).

only the behavior of states is affected by system structure, not their identities and interests. Against this I argue the holist hypothesis that the structure of international politics also has construction effects on states. I focus on causal effects in chapter 7; here I address mostly constitutive ones. If such effects exist this would have important – and given that constructivism is often associated with ease of social change, perhaps unexpected – implications for the possibility of change in international politics: actors whose interests are constituted by a structure will have a stake in it which will make it more stable than would otherwise be the case. Showing that identities and interests are socially constructed may reveal new possibilities for change, but those constructions can also be powerful sources of inertia if they are institutionalized.

Apart from its implications for change, the answer to the construction question also bears on the variation question, since if anarchic structures have no construction effects then it is more likely that anarchy does not have a single logic. Game theory teaches us that the outcomes of interaction stem from configurations of desires and beliefs, which can vary from "Harmony" all the way to "Deadlock."[6] If the content of these games is not constrained by anarchic structures then any claims about the logic(s) of anarchy will depend on producing behavioral convergence despite potentially infinite variation in desires and beliefs. There may be such convergence, but it is hard to show. In this light it is not surprising that Waltz hypothesizes that anarchy tends to produce "like units" (a construction hypothesis), though for good measure he also assumes that states are by nature self-regarding and security seeking. These moves eliminate much of the possible variation in interests that could undermine the idea of a single logic of anarchy. By the same token, it is not surprising that Liberals, among the key opponents of Realism, take the individualist view that state interests are determined by societal factors, and therefore highly variable, with the states system relegated to a domain of strategic interaction with no construction effects.[7] This would force Realists to make the case for a single logic on the basis of behavioral effects alone, which the variety of domestic forms ensures will be difficult.

The choice between Realism and Liberalism is often seen as one

---

[6] For a good discussion of varieties of games see Snyder and Diesing (1977).
[7] See especially Moravcsik (1997).

between "top–down" vs. "bottom–up" theorizing, between the view that international politics contains a single logic which depends in no way on its elements, and the view that the logic of anarchy is reducible entirely to its elements. In effect, we can either study structure or study agents; either anarchic structure has one logic or none at all. I defend a third possibility: (1) anarchic structures do construct their elements, but (2) these structures vary at the macro-level and can therefore have multiple logics. Anarchy *as such* is an empty vessel and has no intrinsic logic; anarchies only acquire logics as a function of the structure of what we put inside them. This accommodates Liberalism's emphasis on domestic politics, but within a structural approach to the international system.

The key to this argument is conceptualizing structure in social rather than material terms. When IR scholars today use the word structure they almost always mean Waltz's materialist definition as a distribution of capabilities. Bipolar and multipolar distributions have different dynamics at the level of foreign policy, but they do not construct states differently or generate different logics of anarchy at the macro-level. Defining structure in social terms admits those possibilities, and without any real loss of parsimony, since I believe that Waltz's theory itself presupposes a social structure, a Lockean one (see below and chapter 3). To say that a structure is "social" is to say, following Weber, that actors take each other "into account" in choosing their actions. This process is based on actors' *ideas* about the nature and roles of Self and Other, and as such social structures are "distributions of ideas" or "stocks of knowledge."[8] Some of these ideas are shared, others are private. Shared ideas make up the subset of social structure known as "culture" (on these definitions see chapter 4, pp. 140–142). In principle Hobbesian, Lockean, and Kantian structures might be constituted entirely by private ideas, but in practice they are usually constituted by shared ones. In this chapter I address the nature and effects of shared ideas only. In what follows, therefore, the structure of the international system is its "culture"[9] even though in reality social structure is more than that. Following

---

[8] The notion of societies as "stocks" of knowledge is developed by Berger and Luckmann (1966) and Turner (1988).

[9] On culture at the level of the international system see Pasic (1996), Meyer, *et al.* (1997), and Bukovansky (1999b). The concept of culture is more commonly used with reference to unit-level factors; see Johnston (1995), Katzenstein, ed. (1996), and Weldes, *et al.*, eds. (1999).

Mlada Bukovansky, I call this its "political" culture.[10] Its political culture is the most fundamental fact about the structure of an international system, giving meaning to power and content to interests, and thus the thing we most need to know to explain a "small number of big and important things."[11]

Showing that anarchic structures are cultures does not show that they construct states. To see this it is useful to consider three reasons why actors may observe cultural norms: because they are forced to, because it is in their self-interest, and because they perceive the norms as legitimate.[12] These explanations correspond roughly to Neorealist, Neoliberal, and Idealist [constructivist?] theories of "the difference that norms make" in international life,[13] and perhaps for that reason they are often seen as mutually exclusive. However, I believe it is more useful to see them as reflecting three different "degrees" to which a norm can be *internalized*, and thus as generating three different pathways by which the same structure can be produced – "force," "price," and "legitimacy." It is an empirical question which pathway occurs in a given case. It is only with the third degree of internalization that actors are really "constructed" by culture; up to that point culture is affecting just their behavior or beliefs about the environment, not who they are or what they want. There has been relatively little work in IR on the internalization of norms[14] and so I address all three degrees below, but since the third is the distinctively constructivist hypothesis it is there that I will concentrate.

The next section defends two assumptions of the subsequent discussion. I then examine the structure of Hobbesian, Lockean, and Kantian cultures in turn, showing how the degree to which they are internalized affects the difference that they make. As a structural analysis I say little in this chapter about questions of system process (see chapter 7). Thus, even though I show that the structure of anarchy varies with relationships between states, I do not argue here that "anarchy is what states make of it." In conclusion I address the

---

[10] Bukovansky (1999b); cf. Almond and Verba (1963).   [11] Waltz (1986: 329).

[12] See Spiro (1987: 163–164), D'Andrade (1995: 227–228), and Hurd (1999); cf. Henkin (1979: 49–50).

[13] Cf. Hasenclever, *et. al.* (1997). I received this volume too late to incorporate into my treatment here, but their analysis makes an excellent starting point for further discussion.

[14] For exceptions see Ikenberry and Kupchan (1990), Muller (1993), Cortell and Davis (1996); cf. Wendt and Barnett (1993).

question of progress over time, suggesting that although there is no guarantee that international time will move forward toward a Kantian culture, at least it is unlikely to move backward.

Structure and roles under anarchy

The approach to structural theorizing used in this chapter is discussed in chapter 4 and will not be reiterated here. However, it has two implications for international theory that challenge deeply held assumptions in IR scholarship, and so to prevent misunderstanding some elaboration seems appropriate. The first implication is that there is no relationship between the extent of shared ideas or culture in a system and the extent of cooperation. Most IR scholarship assumes that there is such a relationship. I believe there is not. Culture may constitute conflict or cooperation. The second implication is that the concept of "role" should be a key concept in structural theorizing about the international system. Most IR scholarship assumes that roles are unit-level properties with no place in structural theory. I believe this misunderstands the nature of roles, which are properties of structures, not agents. The culture of an international system is based on a structure of roles. To defend these claims I begin with the Neorealist definition of structure and its basis in a particular view of the problem of order.

There are two problems of order in social life.[15] One is getting people to work together toward mutually beneficial ends like reducing violence or increasing trade, and for this reason it is sometimes known as the "cooperation problem."[16] This is what political theorists going back to Hobbes have usually meant by the problem of order, and it justifiably has been central to IR scholars and foreign policymakers alike, given the difficulties of cooperation under anarchy and potential costs of failure. There is another problem of order, however, what might be called the "sociological" as opposed to "political" problem, which is creating stable patterns of behavior, whether cooperative *or* conflictual. Regularities are plentiful in nature, where they are determined primarily by material forces. These matter in society as well, but social regularities are determined primarily by shared ideas that enable us to predict each other's behavior.

---

[15] See Elster (1989: 1–2) and Wrong (1994: 10–12).
[16] For example, Axelrod (1984), Oye, ed. (1986).

Following Hobbes, scholars in the Realist tradition have tended to argue that shared ideas can only be created by centralized authority. Since in anarchy there is no such authority states must assume the worst about each other's intentions, that others will violate norms as soon as it is in their interest to do so, which forces even peace-loving states to play power politics. Any shared ideas that emerge will be fragile and fleeting, subject to potentially violent change with changes in the distribution of power. The only shared idea that can be stable under such conditions is that "war may at any moment occur,"[17] but for Realists this is simple prudence, not culture. In the Realist view, therefore, if anarchy displays any order in the second, sociological sense it will be because of material forces, not shared ideas, not unlike order in nature.

These Hobbesian considerations seem to underlie Waltz's materialist definition of structure. Waltz defines structure along three dimensions: the principle according to which units are ordered, the differentiation of units and their functions, and the distribution of capabilities. In international politics the ordering principle is anarchy, for Waltz a constant, and unlike domestic politics the units are functionally undifferentiated, so this dimension drops out. This leaves the distribution of capabilities as the only variable dimension of international structure. Patterns of amity and enmity and international institutions, both of which are based on shared ideas, are seen as unit-level phenomena, presumably because in anarchy there can be no such ideas at the macro-level. Waltz does not seem to have set out specifically to be a "materialist," but purging shared ideas from his definition of structure makes his theory reminiscent of the more "Fundamentalist," technological determinist forms of Marxism, which try to derive relations of production from the forces.[18]

Hedley Bull has called part of this reasoning into question.[19] Bull pointed out that Realists are making a "domestic analogy" which assumes that shared ideas at the international level must have the same foundation – centralized authority – that they have at the domestic. If that were true then because it is an anarchy, the international system could be at most a "system" (parts interacting as a whole), not a "society" (common interests and rules). Bull argued that the analogy does not hold, that at least limited forms of inter-state cooperation based on shared ideas – respecting property, keeping

[17] Waltz (1959: 232). [18] See Cohen (1978). [19] Bull (1977: 46–51).

promises, and limiting violence – are possible, and as such there can be an "anarchical society" of the kind envisioned by Grotius or Locke. Neoliberals have extended this insight to the study of a whole range of cooperation in international regimes. Although neither Bull nor Neoliberals conclude that we should define the structure of the international system in social or cultural terms, this seems to be a natural implication of saying that the system is a "society."

In contrast to Waltz, then, a reading of Bull suggests that the structure of anarchy can vary, resulting in distinct logics and tendencies. My argument in this chapter builds directly on Bull's.[20] Yet Bull seems to agree with Waltz on one crucial point and this is where we differ: for Bull the movement from system to society (and perhaps on to community) is a function of a growth in shared knowledge. Like Realists, Bull associates highly conflictual anarchies ("systems") with a state of *nature*, in which no shared ideas exist, and more cooperative anarchies ("societies") with the presence of shared ideas. Realists and Grotians may disagree about the prospects for the emergence of shared ideas under anarchy, but they agree that shared ideas are associated with cooperation. In effect, both sides are reducing the sociological problem of order to the political: assuming that shared ideas depend on working together toward a common end. That suggests that in the absence of cooperation whatever order exists in the international system must be due to material rather than cultural factors. On that view, the relevance of an idealist approach goes up and a materialist one goes down, as the system moves from conflict toward cooperation. This seems to lead to a natural conclusion, drawn most explicitly by Buzan, Jones, and Little, that offers the best of both theories: treat shared ideas as a distinct "sector" of the international system (the "societal" sector), where cooperation rules and an idealist analysis may be appropriate, and leave the more conflictual, economic, political, and strategic sectors to materialists.

This framing of the issue shortchanges idealists and materialists both, the former because shared ideas may constitute conflict, the latter because material forces may induce cooperation. The mistake here is thinking that "culture" (shared knowledge) is the same thing as "society" (cooperation). Shared knowledge and its various manifestations – norms, rules, etc. – are analytically neutral with respect to cooperation and conflict. As Nina Tannenwald says about norms,

---

[20] For other similarities see Dunne (1995).

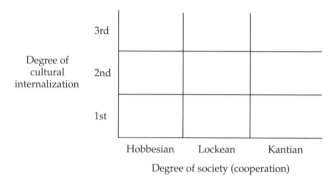

Figure 4   The multiple realization of international culture

norms may be "good" or "bad"; they may tell states that it is heinous to make war, or that it is glorious.[21] In a recent critique of Bull, Alan James[22] makes much the same argument about rules, which he points out are necessary for all but the most elementary forms of interaction. Conversely, there is nothing about the absence of shared knowledge, a world of only material forces, that necessarily implies a war of all against all. The difference between Hobbesian and Grotian worlds is not about the presence of shared ideas. Shared ideas can solve the sociological problem of order even if they do not solve the political one. The significance of this should become clear by considering figure 4,[23] which summarizes the framework of this chapter.

When it is not busy trying to reduce anarchy to a single logic, as in Neorealism, IR scholarship tends to move along the diagonal from bottom left to top right, implicitly reducing the role of shared ideas to cooperation. This assumes that logics of anarchy are a function of how deeply culture is internalized. I argue this is a mistake. Hobbesian logics can be generated by deeply shared ideas, and Kantian logics by only weakly shared ones. Each logic of anarchy is *multiply realizable*: the same effect can be reached through different causes.[24] Which pathway realizes a given anarchy is an empirical question. All nine cells of figure 4 should be in play in international theory, not just those along the diagonal.

---

[21] Tannenwald (1996: 48); for examples of good and bad norms see Elster (1989: 97–151).
[22] James (1993).
[23] I leave out of this picture the possibility that an anarchy might be based on no shared knowledge at all.
[24] On multiple realizability see chapter 4 and Most and Starr (1984).

254

This has two important implications. The first is that the amount of conflict in a system does not bear on the relative utility of idealist and materialist theories. Conflict is no more evidence for materialism than cooperation is for idealism; it all depends on how conflict and cooperation are constituted. As someone concerned to advance a constructivist analysis of phenomena that many scholars treat as a Realist monopoly, I am most interested in the upper-left cells of figure 4, but there are equally interesting neglected possibilities for Realists in the bottom right. The second implication concerns structural change. Realist pessimism notwithstanding, it is easier to escape a Hobbesian world whose culture matters relatively little, and notwithstanding Idealist optimism, harder to create a Kantian one based on deeply shared beliefs. It is Realists who should think that cultural change is easy, not constructivists, because the more deeply shared ideas are internalized – the more they "matter" – the stickier the structure they constitute will be.

This suggests a rethinking of Waltz's definition of structure. In order to make clear that structure contains both material and ideational elements let me begin by building on Dan Deudney to make an analogy between modes of production and "modes of *destruction*."[25] On the material side of the latter are "forces of destruction": technological artifacts like spears, tanks, and ICBMs that have the ability to kill people and destroy property. These vary quantitatively, which is captured by Waltz's "distribution of capabilities," and qualitatively, which is reflected in the changing balance between offensive versus defensive weapons technologies and in Deudney's[26] "composition" of power. The strength of Realism lies in assessing the social possibilities of these artifacts.

As I argued in chapter 3, however, the *probability* that any given possibility will be realized depends on ideas and the interests they constitute. Five hundred British nuclear weapons are less threatening to the US than five North Korean ones because of the shared understandings that underpin them. What gives meaning to the forces of destruction are the *"relations* of destruction" in which they are embedded: the shared ideas, whether cooperative or conflictual, that structure violence between states. These ideas constitute the roles or terms of individuality through which states interact. The concept of

[25] Deudney (1999); also see Mouzelis (1989) on "modes of political domination."
[26] Deudney (1993).

"terms of individuality," which I borrow from constructivists in social psychology,[27] plays the same function in this model as "principles of differentiation" does in Waltz's. Both concern the ways in which agents are constituted by structures. Waltz drops these principles from his theory, and with them all possibility of giving it a social dimension, because he assumes that differentiation must be functional. But functional differentiation in social life is in important part based on role differentiation, and roles may be asymmetric *or* symmetric. The role of "enemy," for example, constitutes identities even though enemies are functionally equivalent. The generality of Waltz's intuition becomes clear in Ruggie's work on sovereignty, which combines Waltz's language of differentiation with the language of terms of individuality to show how the meaning of sovereignty – a form of subjectivity in which differentiation is spatial rather than functional – varies historically.[28] Until he dropped principles of differentiation, in other words, Waltz had an at least implicitly cultural theory of structure.

Apart from making explicit and extending that theory to role differentiation, however, I am also reversing his materialist hypothesis about the relationship between ideas and material forces. The analogy to Marxism is again helpful here. In contrast to Waltz's "Fundamentalist" assumption which reduces relations to forces of destruction, and also in contrast to Neoliberalism's Structural Marxist assumption that ideas are a superstructure "relatively autonomous" from but determined in the last instance by the material base (see chapter 3, pp. 136–137), in my view no necessary relationship between forces and relations of destruction – between nature and culture – can be specified a priori. In some cases material conditions are decisive, in others it will be ideas. It is my expectation that empirically we will find that ideas usually are far more important. There sometimes may be an international equivalent of a "hotel fire" that effectively eliminates a meaningful role for ideas, but in most cases it will be ideas that give meaning to material conditions rather than the other way around. Rather than follow Neorealists in focusing first on material structure, therefore, I believe that if we want to say a small number of big and important things about world politics we would do better to focus first on states' ideas and the interests they constitute, and only then worry about who has how many guns.

[27] See, for example, Turner and Oakes (1986: 239), Sampson (1988), and Shotter (1990).
[28] Ruggie (1993).

Shared understandings about violence vary from the general ("kill or be killed") to the specific (use white flags to surrender). While each may be studied individually, my proposal, adapted from Bull and Wight, is that they tend to cluster into three cultures with distinct logics and tendencies, Hobbesian, Lockean, and Kantian.[29] I shall treat these cultures as ideal types, although I believe all three have been instantiated at different times and places in international history. I do not claim that they exhaust the possible forms of anarchy, only that they are particularly salient. They may be found in regional sub-systems of the international system – Buzan's "security complexes"[30] – or in the system as a whole. Finally, although they may be affected by cultures at the domestic and/or transnational level, the cultures of interest here are states system-centric. This means that even if states' domestic cultures have little in common, as in Huntington's "clash of civilizations,"[31] the states *system* could still have one culture that affected the behavior of its elements.

A key aspect of any cultural form is its role structure, the configur-ation of subject positions that shared ideas make available to its holders.[32] Subject positions are constituted by representations of Self and Other as particular kinds of agents related in particular ways, which in turn constitute the logics and reproduction requirements of distinct cultural systems (schools, churches, polities, and so on).[33] The reproduction of these systems only occurs when roles are filled by real people, but since different people can fill the same position over time and realize it in different ways, roles cannot be reduced to individuals. Roles are attributes of structures, not agents. In principle these could be micro-structures, but I shall focus on roles as properties of macro-structures, as *collective* representations. Although in most cultures roles are functionally differentiated, anarchy makes it difficult to sustain role asymmetry until the problem of violence is mitigated,[34] and so I propose that at the core of each kind of anarchy is just one

---

[29] I have adapted these labels from Wight (e.g., 1991), although he used them to refer to *theories* (Realist, Rationalist, and Revolutionist, or, sometimes, Machiavellian, Grotian, and Kantian), while I will be using them to refer to real world *structures*, much as Bull (1977) used the terms "system" and "society."

[30] Buzan (1991).   [31] Huntington (1993).

[32] The treatment of the concept of role below draws especially on symbolic interactionist ideas; see McCall and Simmons (1978), Stryker and Statham (1985), and Callero (1986).

[33] On the concept of subject position see Doty (1996) and Weldes (1999).

[34] Waltz (1979: 95–97); also see Elias (1982: 235).

subject position: in Hobbesian cultures it is "enemy," in Lockean "rival," and Kantian "friend." Each involves a distinct posture or orientation of the Self toward the Other with respect to the use of violence, which can be realized in multiple ways at the micro-level. The posture of enemies is one of threatening adversaries who observe no limits in their violence toward each other; that of rivals is one of competitors who will use violence to advance their interests but refrain from killing each other; and that of friends is one of allies who do not use violence to settle their disputes and work as a team against security threats.

The proposition that structures can be analyzed in terms of roles is hardly radical. Sociologists routinely think this way about structure, and it was no less a Realist than Carl Schmitt who argued that the friend–enemy distinction was the fundamental structure of the political.[35] Yet modern, structurally oriented Realists explicitly reject the incorporation of roles into structural theorizing on the grounds that roles are unit-level phenomena.[36] In doing so they receive support from an unlikely, "reductionist" quarter, foreign policy role theorists, who argue that the social structure of the international system does not contain thick enough shared expectations to support roles.[37] Discouraged by both sides from thinking structurally, when IR scholars talk about roles they are almost always referring to the domestically constituted beliefs of individuals or elites, i.e., unit-level properties.

The skeptics have a point. If foreign policy roles are defined as the beliefs of decision-makers or state elites then they cannot be structural phenomena in the *macro* sense, which is the only sense of structure that Neorealists recognize. The distribution of those beliefs is structural at what I have called the *micro-* or interaction-level sense, and in that capacity they constitute key ingredients in the international process, but that is precisely why Neorealists think roles are not "structural." As I indicated above, however, this is not how roles should be understood. Roles are structural positions, not actor beliefs. To be sure, in order for actors to enact and reproduce subject positions they have to incorporate them into their identities and interests, and

---

[35] Schmitt (1932/1976); for good introductions to this aspect of Schmitt's work see Schwab (1987) and Sartori (1989).
[36] For example, Buzan, Jones, and Little (1993: 46), Waltz (1979: passim); cf. Schroeder (1994: 124–9).
[37] Holsti (1970: 243).

in that way roles constitute unit-level properties, but role-*identities* are not the same thing as roles. Role-identities are subjective self-understandings; roles are the objective, collectively constituted positions that give meaning to those understandings. The former come and go as individuals take on or discard beliefs; the latter persist as long as someone fills them. Bill Clinton currently occupies the role of US President, and has taken on identities and interests that enable him to play the part, but whereas his identities and interests will presumably change when he leaves office, the position will live on. Similarly, in the nineteenth century, Great Britain played the role of "balancer" in Great Power politics,[38] but that was a property of the social structure of the Concert of Europe, not of Great Britain. Had no state filled that role the structure might not have survived.

The structure and tendencies of anarchic systems will depend on which of our three roles – enemy, rival, and friend – dominate those systems, and states will be under corresponding pressure to internalize that role in their identities and interests. As for Holsti's argument that shared ideas at the international level are not thick enough to support roles: if he is making the empirical claim that cultures of anarchy are never internalized deep enough to construct state interests, then he may be right (though I will argue otherwise). Like others operating along the diagonal line in figure 4, however, I suspect he is actually making a tacit assumption that shared ideas must be cooperative, which would mean that since there is not much cooperation in international politics there is no structural basis for roles. Once we recognize that culture does not imply cooperation we can see that roles belong in structural theories of world politics even if states have nothing more in common than the knowledge that they are enemies.

The Hobbesian culture

Although there is no necessary connection between a Hobbesian anarchy and Realism, it is a natural link to assume because this anarchy is a "hard case" for constructivism. Its high death rate makes it difficult for shared ideas to form, and if they do form it is still difficult to see why states would have the stake in them that is implied by the constructivist proposition that internalized ideas constitute identities and interests. Because it is a hard case and the first application of my

---

[38] Gulick (1955).

framework, I will pay more attention to this culture than to the others. The discussion is organized into three sections. The first section addresses the nature of enmity as a position for the Other and its implications for the posture of the Self. I then examine the logic and tendencies that result when this role dominates a system, the "war of all against all." My description of this condition is familiar; what is less traditional is my claim that the state of war is constituted by shared ideas, not by anarchy or human nature. The last section explores the three degrees to which this culture can be internalized.

Enmity

Enemies lie at one end of a spectrum of role relationships governing the use of violence between Self and Other, distinct in kind from rivals and friends. All three positions constitute social structures, insofar as they are based on representations of the Other in terms of which the posture of the Self is defined. As R.S. Perinbanayagam puts it, "[t]he other is the social-psychological form of that abstraction that sociologists and anthropologists call social structure."[39] By understanding how Self and Other are represented, therefore, we can explain (and predict) a great deal of what goes on in a social system. I look first at the representations of the Other in this position and then at its implications for the Self.

Enemies are constituted by representations of the Other as an actor who (1) does not recognize the right of the Self to exist as an autonomous being, and therefore (2) will not willingly limit its violence toward the Self. Taking its cue from Schmitt,[40] this is a narrower definition than one normally finds in IR, where "enemy" is often used to describe any violent antagonist, as in "Britain and Argentina were enemies during the Falklands War." Since my definition is based on a distinction that in turn distinguishes Hobbesian and Lockean cultures, it is important to be clear. The distinction concerns the perceived scope of the Other's intentions, in particular whether he is thought to be trying to kill or enslave the Self or merely trying to

---

[39] Perinbanayagam (1985: 135–136).
[40] Schmitt (1932/1976). As Schwab (1987) points out in a commentary on Schmitt, the notion that the Other will engage in unlimited violence is more accurately applied to the term "foe" than "enemy," but this meaning of the former has largely died out. On enemy images in IR see Wolfers (1962: 25–35), Finlay, *et al.* (1967), Volkan (1988), Rieber, ed. (1991), and Herrmann and Fischerkeller (1995).

beat or steal from him. Enmity and rivalry both imply that the Other does not fully recognize the Self and therefore may act in a "revisionist" fashion toward it, but the object of recognition and revisionism is different. An enemy does not recognize the right of the Self to exist as a free subject at all, and therefore seeks to "revise" the latter's life or liberty (call this "deep" revisionism). A rival, in contrast, is thought to recognize the Self's right to life and liberty, and therefore seeks to revise only its behavior or property ("shallow" revisionism). Both impute to the Other aggressive intent, but the enemy's intentions are unlimited in nature, the rival's are limited.[41] This relates to the level of violence expected from the Other. Violence between enemies has no internal limits; whatever limits exist will be due solely to inadequate capabilities (a balance of power or exhaustion) or the presence of an external constraint (Leviathan). This is the kind of violence found in a state of nature. Violence between rivals, in contrast, is *self-limiting*, constrained by recognition of each other's right to exist. This is the kind of violence characteristic of "civilization," the essence of which Norbert Elias argues is self-restraint.[42]

Enemy images have a long pedigree, and some states continue to position each other in such terms today. The Greeks represented the Persians as "barbarians"; the Crusaders perceived the Turks as "infidels"; medieval Europeans feared their defeat at Liegnitz at the hands of the Mongols heralded Armageddon; later Europeans treated the peoples of the Americas as savages; conservatives thought civilization was threatened by the French Revolution; and, in our own century, we have the Armenian genocide, the Holocaust, the early Cold War, Northern Ireland, Pol Pot, Palestinian and Israeli fundamentalists, the Bosnian Civil War, Hutus and Tutsis – all based on representations of the Other as intent on destroying or enslaving the Self.

It is important to emphasize that this concept implies nothing about whether enemy images are justified. Some enemies are "real," in that the Other really does existentially threaten the Self, as the Nazis did the Jews, and others are "chimeras," as the Jews were to the Nazis.[43] This difference may affect the dynamics of enmity and whether it can be overcome, but it does not affect the reality of Hobbesian cultures.

---

[41] Herrmann and Fischerkeller (1995: 426). This seems to parallel the distinction between offensive and defensive Realism.
[42] Elias (1982).   [43] Smith (1996).

Real or imagined, if actors think enemies are real then they are real in their consequences.[44]

Representing the Other as an enemy tends to have at least four implications for a state's foreign policy posture and behavior, which in turn generate a particular logic of interaction.

First, states will tend to respond to enemies by acting like deep revisionists themselves, i.e., they will try to destroy or conquer them. This does not necessarily mean their *interests* will be revisionist; a state might actually have status quo interests, but the threat of the enemy forces it to *behave* "as if" it were a deep revisionist, on the principle of "kill or be killed." Second, decision-making will tend to heavily discount the future and be oriented toward the worst-case. (Negative) possibilities rather than probabilities will dominate, which reduces the likelihood of reciprocating any cooperative moves made by the enemy. One might say that prospect theory rather than expected-utility theory will be the basis of "rational" behavior.[45] Third, relative military capabilities will be seen as crucial.[46] Since the enemy's revisionist intentions are "known," the state can use the enemy's capabilities to predict his behavior, on the assumption that he will attack as soon as he can win. Power becomes the key to survival, and as such even status quo states will vigorously arm themselves on the principle of "if you want peace, prepare for war." Enmity, in short, gives capabilities a particular *meaning*, which derives neither from their intrinsic properties nor from anarchy as such, but from the structure of the role relationship. Finally, if it comes to actual war, states will fight on the enemy's (perceived) terms. This means observing no limits on their own violence, since that would create a competitive disadvantage, unless it is clear that self-limitation is safe. And if war has not yet broken out but clearly will soon, states must also be prepared to preempt, especially if offensive technology is dominant, lest the enemy get a fatal advantage from a first strike.

What states facing a enemy must do, in sum, is engage in no-holds-barred power politics. It has become common practice in recent IR scholarship to refer to such behavior as "Realist." If Realism is taken to be merely a description of power politics then this practice is harmless, but taken as an *explanation* it invites confusion, since it

---

[44] Thomas and Thomas (1928: 572).
[45] On the significance of this distinction see Brooks (1997) and Levy (1997).
[46] See Grieco (1988).

suggests that the existence of power politics is somehow evidence for Realist theory. This cannot be the case, at least on any non-tautological definition of Realism; conflict is no more evidence for Realism than cooperation is for non-Realism. It all depends on what explains it. The account developed here explains power politics by reference to perceptions of Self and Other, and as such sees it as fundamentally social in the Weberian sense. I take Realism to be a theory that explains power politics ultimately by reference to material forces, whether biological or technological, and as such its view is not fundamentally social. In order to keep alive the possibility of meaningful theoretical disagreement, therefore, it seems better to follow Iain Johnston's practice of calling power political behavior "realpolitik" rather than "Realism."[47] The Realist tradition contains much descriptive wisdom about realpolitik, but this does not entail the truth of its explanation for realpolitik.

What Realism-as-description shows is that when the Other is an enemy the Self is forced to mirror back the representations it has attributed to the Other. Thus, unlike most roles in social life, which are constituted by functionally differentiated "counter"-roles (teacher–student, master–slave, patron–client), the role of enemy is symmetric, constituted by actors being in the same position simultaneously. Self mirrors Other, becomes *its* enemy, in order to survive. This of course will confirm whatever hostile intentions the *Other* had attributed to the Self, forcing it to engage in realpolitik of its own, which will in turn reinforce the Self's perception of the Other, and so on. Realpolitik, in short, is a self-fulfilling prophecy: its beliefs generate actions that confirm those beliefs.[48] This is not to say that realpolitik is the sole cause of conflict, such that in its absence states would be friends, since if states really do want to conquer each other then realpolitik is as much effect as cause. The point is that whether or not states really are existential threats to each other is in one sense not relevant, since once a logic of enmity gets started states will behave in ways that *make* them existential threats, and thus the behavior itself becomes part of the problem. This gives enemy-images a homeostatic quality that sustains the logic of Hobbesian anarchies.

---

[47] Johnston (1995).   [48] Wendt (1992), Vasquez (1993), Alker (1996).

The logic of Hobbesian anarchy

Unlike foreign policy role theorists, who treat roles as qualities that states attribute to themselves and thus as properties of agents (what I would call role-*identities*), I have focused on the role attributed to the Other, and thus on role as a *position* in or property of a social structure. Like role theorists, however, I have so far treated enmity as an interaction- or micro-level phenomenon, as based on subjective images or perceptions. I did so partly for presentational reasons, but also because macro-level structures only exist in virtue of instantiations at the micro-level, which means that whatever logics the former have depend on actors acting in certain ways.

In most cases, however, micro-level role relationships are embedded in macro-level, *collective* representations. Collective representations have a life and logic of their own that cannot be reduced to actors' perceptions or behavior (chapter 4, pp. 150–165). As more and more members of a system represent each other as enemies, eventually a "tipping point"[49] is reached at which these representations take over the logic of the system. At this point actors start to think of enmity as a property of the *system* rather than just of individual actors, and so feel compelled to represent all Others as enemies simply because they are parts of the system. In this way the particular Other becomes Mead's "generalized Other,"[50] a structure of collective beliefs and expectations that persists through time even as individual actors come and go, and into the logic of which new actors are socialized. (The concepts of "discourse" and "hegemony" I take it have a similar, macro-level orientation.) It is in terms of positions within this structure that actors make attributions about Self and Other, rather than in terms of their actual qualities. The result is a logic of interaction based more on what actors know about their roles than on what they know about each other, enabling them to predict each other's behavior without knowing each other's "minds." This in turn generates emergent patterns of behavior at the macro-level. Collective representations are "frequency-dependent"[51] in that they depend for their existence on a sufficient number of representations and/or behaviors at the micro-level – the representation known as "Canada" only exists if enough people sustain

---

[49] Schelling (1978: 99–102); for a good illustration see Laitin (1998).
[50] Mead (1934: 154–156).   [51] Boyd and Richerson (1980: 100).

it – but as long as that number remains above the tipping point collective representations will be relatively autonomous from or supervene on ideas in the heads of individuals. The logic and tendencies of the Hobbesian anarchy emerge at this macro-level of analysis.

The logic of the Hobbesian anarchy is well known: the "war of all against all" in which actors operate on the principle of *sauve qui peut* and kill or be killed. This is the true "self-help" system (by which I mean to suggest that the anarchy described by Waltz is not that; see below), where actors cannot count on each other for help or even to observe basic self-restraint. Survival depends solely on military power, which means that increases in the security of A necessarily reduce that of B, who can never be sure that A's capabilities are defensive. Security is a deeply competitive, zero-sum affair, and security dilemmas are particularly acute not because of the nature of weapons – the offense–defense balance – but because of intentions attributed to others.[52] Even if what states really want is security rather than power their collective beliefs force them to *act* as if they are power-seeking. This structure generates four "tendencies," macro-level patterns that will get realized unless they are blocked by counter-vailing forces.[53]

The first is endemic and unlimited warfare. This does not mean that states will constantly be at war, since material considerations may suppress the manifestation of this tendency for a time, but as long as states collectively represent each other in Hobbesian terms, war may quite literally "at any moment occur."[54] A second is the elimination of "unfit" actors: those not adapted for warfare, and those too weak militarily to compete. This means, on the one hand, as Waltz argues, that we should see a tendency toward functional isomorphism, with all political entities becoming "like units" (states) with similar war-fighting capabilities.[55] On the other hand, however – something Waltz does not predict – we should also see a high death rate among weak states. Since their territories will be conquered by the strong, this will generate a corresponding tendency toward empire-building and re-duction in the overall number of political units – toward a concentration of power.[56] Partly counteracting this tendency is a third: states

---

[52] Herz (1950), Jervis (1978), Glaser (1997). If indeed they are even "dilemmas"; see Schweller (1996).
[53] This I take to be the Marxian understanding of tendencies; cf. Van Eeghan (1996).
[54] Waltz (1959: 232).   [55] Waltz (1979).   [56] Kaufman (1997: 117–123).

powerful enough to avoid elimination will balance each other's power.[57] However, in contrast to Waltz's view of balancing as the fundamental tendency of anarchy in general, the lack of inhibition and self-restraint in Hobbesian cultures suggests that balances of power there will be difficult to sustain, with the tendency toward consolidation being dominant in the long run. Finally, a Hobbesian system will tend to suck all of its members into the fray, making non-alignment or neutrality very difficult.[58] The principal exception will be states that are able to "hide" because of the material condition of geography (Switzerland in World War II), although geography's significance is itself subject to material changes in technology (nuclear weapons).

Although an ideal type, and perhaps never characteristic of the state of nature among individuals, the Hobbesian condition does describe significant portions of international history. International politics has often been characterized by endemic violence, isomorphic tendencies among units, a high rate of destruction and consolidation of units,[59] balancing when necessary, and little room for neutrality. This is significant given the cultural diversity of states systems, and lends support to the Realist view that in anarchy *plus ça change, plus c'est la même chose.* One can argue about how many of the past 5,000 years have been "Realist," but Mearsheimer's question is still important: why has this logic dominated international politics as often as it has?[60] I take up this question in chapter 7.

Three degrees of internalization

It is possible for a Hobbesian anarchy to have no culture at all. Here, all knowledge is private rather than shared. Hobbes' own, materialist portrayal of the state of nature and Bull's idea of "system" seem to be based on this assumption. The absence of shared culture has an interesting, perhaps counter-intuitive implication: the resulting warfare is not really "war" at all. Killing there may be aplenty, but it is akin to the slaughtering of animals, not war. War is a form of collective intentionality, and as such is only war if both sides *think* it is war.[61] Similarly, a balance of power in this context is not really a

---

[57] Waltz (1979).   [58] Cf. Wolfers (1962: 26–27).

[59] By one count, the world has gone from 600,000 autonomous political units in 1000 B.C. to about 200 today; see Carneiro (1978: 213–215).

[60] Mearsheimer's (1994/1995: 42).   [61] Searle (1995: 89).

"balance of power." Mechanical equilibrium there may be, but actors are not aware of it as such.

Individual human beings probably never lived in such a world because they are by nature group animals,[62] although it is not altogether unlike the situation facing infants, who have not yet acquired culture but get punished when they fail to follow its norms. States are by nature more solitary than people, however, and so in world politics systems of entirely private meanings have sometimes occurred. The archetype is the Hobbesian First Encounter, in which an aggressive state tries to conquer another, previously unknown state.[63] Huns emerging from the steppes to conquer and kill Romans, Mongols doing the same to medieval Europeans, Europeans colonizing non-Europeans, and so on are all examples of states operating in a world of private, domestically constituted meanings trying to conquer or enslave an Other.[64] The structure of these situations is still "social" in that they are based on ideas about the Other that each side takes into account, but these ideas are not shared and so do not form a culture. Neorealists would like anarchy to play an important causal role in explaining these Encounters, but in fact its role is only permissive. If the conquistadores had brought other meanings with them, like the Federation's "Prime Directive" of non-interference in the television show *Star Trek*, the results would have been quite different. There is nothing in anarchy as such that forces these situations to be Hobbesian, even if they often do take on such a structure; one can imagine Lockean and Kantian First Encounters as well.

These situations of pure private knowledge are not likely to last long. From the start of a First Encounter actors will be learning about each other and bringing their expectations into line, and they also have an incentive to communicate, if only to demand and arrange surrender. The fact that they do not recognize each other's right to life and liberty is nevertheless a powerful constraint on them ever forming a culture, since it means that they are as likely to kill the Other as share ideas with him. This constraint could be decisive for individuals, who can be killed quite easily. Because of their material nature as large organizations specializing in self-defense, however,

---

[62] On the implications of this point for "state of nature" theorizing see Alford (1994).

[63] See Schwartz, ed. (1994) for an introduction to First Encounters, and for discussion of their significance for IR, Inayatullah and Blaney (1996).

[64] Note that "private" and "domestic" here are relative to the target only, since many of these states formed their beliefs in states systems of their own.

states are much harder to "kill" than people and so the strict analogy to Hobbes' state of nature does not hold.[65] This resilience is relative, with weak states being vulnerable to elimination by the strong, but enemies that survive the initial clash of arms will be the tougher for it, and start forming a shared understanding of their condition, the Hobbesian culture.

In this culture states have shared knowledge of at least three things: (1) that they are dealing with other states, beings like themselves; (2) that these beings are their enemies and therefore threaten their life and liberty; and (3) how to deal with enemies – how to make war, communicate threats, arrange surrenders, balance power, and so on. What states now share, in short, are the norms of a realpolitik culture,[66] where power politics and self-help are not just behavioral regularities, as in nature, but a shared *understanding* about "how things are done." Killing is now "war": an institution, not in the sense of rules that reduce violence (in the Hobbesian case they do not), as in Bull's analysis,[67] but in the sense that everyone knows what war is and what it is about. Similarly, a mechanical equilibrium is now a "balance of power." Ironically, therefore, it is only with the emergence of a Hobbesian *culture* that "Realism" can emerge as a discourse about international politics.

This culture can be internalized to three degrees, which yield three pathways, and corresponding hypotheses, for how it may be realized: force (the traditional Realist hypothesis), price (Neoliberal or rationalist), and legitimacy (Idealist or constructivist). Although their outcomes are similar (a Hobbesian structure), their differences bear on a number of important theoretical and empirical issues: why states comply with Hobbesian culture, the quality of that compliance, its resistance to change, and ultimately the difference that it makes.

The First Degree hypothesis

When a cultural norm has been internalized only to this degree an actor knows what the norm is, but complies only because he is forced to, directly or by the threat of certain, immediate punishment that

---

[65] This – and the fact that Hobbes himself knew this – has been pointed out by a number of commentators; see, for example, Bull (1977: 46–51), Heller (1980), and Buzan (1991: 148–149).
[66] See Ashley (1987), who uses the term "community" rather than "culture" to make the point.
[67] Bull (1977: 184–199).

would force him. He is neither motivated to comply of his own accord, nor does he think that doing so is in his self-interest. He does it because he must, because he is coerced or compelled. His behavior is purely externally rather than internally driven – though compliance brought about by the *threat* of force adds a self-regulating element, and begins to blur the line with the Second Degree case (hence the qualifiers "certain" and "immediate" above). Given the external source of his behavior the quality of his compliance is low and requires constant pressure; remove the compulsion and he will break the norm. Even though he shares knowledge of the rules, he does not accept their implications for himself. Others are positioning him in a particular role, but he is contesting it. If he succeeds then he breaches the norm, if he fails then he is forced to comply. In this situation, in sum, it is private meanings plus material coercion rather than culture which does most of the explanatory work, which is how Realists tend to think about the difference that norms make.

This is one reason that states may conform to Hobbesian norms. It is fairly easy to see how this could happen to "nice," status quo states who would rather get along than conquer each other. A world of such states would only get into a Hobbesian situation in the first place if they mistakenly assumed the worst about each other's intentions, but uncertainty and risk-aversion could lead to just that. If so, they will feel compelled to engage in deep revisionist behavior even though they neither want to nor think it is in their self-interest, which in turn compels other states to do so as well. This is the familiar logic of the security dilemma, albeit a particularly acute one, which is a "dilemma" only because states are better off cooperating.[68] What is ultimately driving this logic is a collective representation of their condition as Hobbesian. Thus even though on one level material force is doing most of the work in explaining why these status quo states engage in realpolitik, it is coercion based on a shared idea which pushes the system in one direction, despite a distribution of interests that points in another.

Perhaps paradoxically, however, a system of revisionist, "Hitler" states may also be forced to comply with Hobbesian norms. The interest of these states is in conquering each other, at the limit in creating a world empire, and as such they are not better off cooperating. Although this distribution of interests means their

---

[68] Schweller (1996).

enmity is real rather than a chimera, which constitutes a very different reason for getting into the Hobbesian world than the world of nice states above (will to power rather than misperception), as long as they have internalized its culture only to the first degree Hitler states will be equally coerced by its logic. What they want is for other states to surrender, not fight back; realpolitik is not an end in itself, nor is it something they do out of self-interest. It is forced on them by the fact that other states represent them as an enemy and act accordingly.

The Westphalian system being a Lockean culture, neither of these exemplary First Degree Hobbesian situations explains much of recent Western history. What has happened instead are temporary regressions to a Hobbesian condition when a powerful state had an internal revolution and rejected Lockean norms altogether. The clearest examples are the French Revolution and subsequent Napoleonic Wars, which Bukovansky[69] argues created a (temporary) "state of nature" with the rest of Europe, and the rise of Hitler and World War II. In both cases exogenous changes in a few states led to a rejection of existing shared meanings in favor of private ones, and unlimited aggression in an effort to "share" the latter, which forced status quo states to comply with Hobbesian norms. (A similar story might be told about "rogue" or "pariah" states today.) Although in neither case would most of us admire the goals of the revisionists, at least in the Napoleonic case one could argue that forcing a Hobbesian logic on the existing dynastic system was necessary to destroy norms that had become corrupt, and as such was ultimately a basis for a historically progressive transformation of the system.

The Second Degree hypothesis

It is not easy to make a clean distinction between First and Second Degree internalization, between being forced to do something and doing it out of self-interest, especially if we allow merely the threat of force to count as coercion.[70] Yet in everyday life we are often called upon to make exactly this distinction and the result is seen as meaningful, notably in courts of law, where the conclusion that someone was coerced into a crime may exonerate them or at least reduce their sentence. Despite its difficulties, the distinction seems intuitive and important, and it is useful to make an effort to characterize it.

---

[69] Bukovansky (1999a).   [70] See Hurd (1999) for a nice try; cf. Krasner (1991).

The intuition turns on the idea of "choice." The First Degree case corresponds to situations in which most of us would be willing to say that actors had no choice but to follow a norm – even though it is an existential feature of the human condition that we always have *some* choice, to "just say no," even if that means certain death.[71] In the Second Degree case actors do have a meaningful choice, which implies the existence of a social or temporal space where actors are free from direct and immediate coercion. Second Degree internalization exists when actors in this space obey cultural norms not because they think the norms are legitimate (the Third Degree case), but because they think it is in their self-interest. Actors see an advantage to compliance in advancing an exogenously given interest, and as such their attitude toward the norm is instrumental, using it for their own purposes. Compared to the coercion case their compliance is more internally driven or *self-regulating*, and therefore likely to be of higher quality. Even without coercion they will tend to comply. But compared to the Third Degree case compliance is still more externally determined. Actors have no intrinsic interest in complying with norms, and to that extent still experience them as external constraints. Their compliance is "necessary," even though they benefit from it. Another way to put this is in terms of whether actors *accept* the implications of shared knowledge for themselves. In the First Degree case actors "share" culture in the sense that they "know" it, but do not accept its implications for their behavior. In the Second Degree case actors accept shared meanings and so there is now a more or less normalized culture, but the acceptance is purely instrumental. As soon as the costs of following the rules outweigh the benefits, actors should change their behavior.

At this stage of internalization actors begin to offer justifications for their behavior by reference to shared expectations.[72] In a Hobbesian culture these justifications will emphasize "necessity" and "raison d'état." Although they are not being directly coerced into practices of realpolitik and as such have the space to consider alternative courses of action, states all know that this is how the game is played and that it is only a matter of time before they are under attack again. They will therefore justify their own realpolitik practices with arguments like "everyone knows that if we had not conquered X, then Y would have,

---

[71] Carveth (1982: 213–215).
[72] On justifications as a guide to normative structure see especially Kratochwil (1989).

intolerably weakening our relative position," or "everyone knows that it is in war that the virtue of the nation is forged," or "everyone knows that if we had not attacked B, B would have attacked us, giving them the benefit of surprise." These arguments have meaning to other states because of shared ideas about how things are done. This is not to say that a state could not give meaning to such beliefs all by itself, just as a paranoid or schizophrenic can live in a world of private meanings, but then that is why we consider them paranoid or schizophrenic. We may hear their words and understand their literal meaning, but they are not "making sense" because they are not speaking a language we share. Similarly in a Hobbesian culture: not only do states have "Realist" beliefs, but these are justified and made intelligible by the fact that states all know they are necessary.

The shared knowledge that constitutes Lockean and Kantian cultures is to an important extent institutionalized in international law and regimes, with corresponding manifestations at the domestic level. By contrast, the violent and alienated nature of Hobbesian culture ensures that its norms are not likely to be formalized at the systemic level, and indeed its members might not even see them as norms, or themselves as forming a culture, at all. Their shared knowledge might be entirely "tacit."[73] If such a culture is institutionalized, therefore, it is likely to be at the *domestic* level only. If this domestic knowledge were purely private then we could not speak of a systemic culture, but if each member of the system operates under the same domestic constraints and at least tacitly knows this about the others, then we can speak in such terms.

As a general rule we can expect that any Hobbesian culture which has survived for more than a short time will be internalized at least to the Second Degree, since the costs to individual states of failing to accept the fact that they are in such a system could be fatal. Whether these cultures will always have Third Degree effects is less clear.

The Third Degree hypothesis

Sometimes people follow norms not because they think it will serve some exogenously given end but because they think the norms are legitimate and therefore *want* to follow them. To say that a norm is legitimate is to say that an actor fully accepts its claims on himself, which means appropriating as a subjectively held identity the role in

---

[73] On tacit knowledge see Pleasants (1996).

which they have been positioned by the generalized Other. In the Second Degree case actors "try on" identities that conform to role expectations but do so for only instrumental reasons, relating to them as if they were external objects. In the Third Degree case actors identify with others' expectations, relating to them as a part of themselves. The Other is now inside the cognitive boundary of the Self, constituting who it sees itself as in relation to the Other, its "Me." It is only with this degree of internalization that a norm really constructs agents; prior to this point their identities and interests are exogenous to it. Because it is constitutive of their identity, in turn, actors now have a stake in the norm that they did not before. Their behavior is interested, but not "self"-interested (chapter 5, pp. 238–243). The quality of their compliance will therefore be high, as will their resistance to normative change.

There is an apparent paradox in applying this reasoning to the Hobbesian culture which makes it a hard case for a constructivist analysis. The paradox concerns the peculiarities of the role of enemy, which dictates that an actor should try to take away the life and/or liberty of the very actors whose expectations they need to internalize to constitute their identities as enemies. How could actors have a stake in a culture the logical basis of which they are trying to destroy? What would it mean to internalize the role of enemy to this degree? On the surface the answer might seem to be for the posture of Self toward Other in enmity, deep revisionism, to become an interest rather than merely a strategy. Many states historically have had such an interest, of course, but this cannot be the answer to our question, since an interest in conquest is not the same thing as an interest in enmity, and indeed they are in some way opposed. An interest in deep revisionism is satisfied by conquest, an interest in enmity is not; deep revisionism seeks to remove the Other from the game, enmity needs the Other to constitute its identity; deep revisionism sees the Hobbesian culture as an obstacle to be overcome, enmity sees it as an end in itself. The posture toward the Other entailed by enmity, in other words, seems to vitiate internalizing a Hobbesian culture so deeply that it constitutes interests.

The solution to this problem depends on a material constraint, namely that states do not have enough power to "kill" each other. If states did have that power in a Hobbesian culture then they would exercise it, since that is what one must do to survive in such a world. Material constraints – notably, a balance of power or inadequate

273

military technology – can prevent this outcome. Given such a constraint, it is possible not only for enmity to be seen as necessary (the Second Degree case), but as legitimate, and with that legitimacy for states to appropriate the enemy identity as their own, with its corresponding interests. Power politics is now not just a means but an end in itself, a value constituted collectively as "right," "glorious," or "virtuous," and as a result states now *need* the Other to play the role of enemy as a site for their efforts to realize those values. What matters now is "fighting the good fight," just *trying* to destroy your enemies, not whether you succeed; indeed were you to succeed the result might be cognitive dissonance and uncertainty about who you are in the absence of your enemy – a phenomenon sometimes cited as a cause of US foreign policy drift after the Cold War.

Hobbesian culture has both causal and constitutive effects on the internalization of this identity. The causal effects concern the role that the culture plays in the production and reproduction of enemy identities over time. Causal effects presuppose that the explanans (identities and interests) exists independent of the explanandum (culture), and that interaction with the latter changes the former over time in a billiard ball, mechanistic sense. I address this side of identity formation in chapter 7. Because it assumes that Self and Other are independently existing, however, a causal orientation suggests that the resulting identities and interests are entirely actors' own, not intrinsically dependent on shared knowledge for their meaning. The constitutive effects of culture show that this is not right, that identities and interests depend conceptually or logically on culture in the sense that it is only in virtue of shared meanings that it is possible to think about who one is or what one wants in certain ways. Identity is here an effect of culture in the way that speech is an effect of language: in each case it is the structure of the latter, the grammar, that makes the former possible. The relation is one of logical necessity, not causal contingency, an internal rather than external relation. To say that a state has fully internalized a Hobbesian culture in this constitutive sense, therefore, is not to say that it has been affected in billiard ball fashion by something external to it, but that it is carrying the culture around in its "head," defining who it is, what it wants, and how it thinks. In the rest of this section I want to flesh this proposition out.

There are at least three ways in which states may need each other to be enemies, all of which might be considered forms of "adversary symbiosis."[74] Two are well known, but none to my knowledge has been used to argue that enemy identities are constituted by the culture of the international system. In each case the enemy has to have enough material power to avoid getting killed too easily, but the rest of the logic is thoroughly social.

The most conventional argument about adversary symbiosis concerns the military–industrial complex. Over time, interaction in a Hobbesian system tends to create domestic interest groups who profit from the arms race and therefore lobby national decision-makers not to reduce arms spending. Insofar as this lobbying is successful, these groups will help constitute a state identity that depends for its existence on an enemy Other. Some have suggested, for example, that the US and Soviet militaries had a common interest in sustaining the Cold War because of the benefits it generated for each. These benefits were greatest when the Other could be portrayed as an existential threat, and as such constituted an interest not only in exaggerating the perceived threat posed by the Other, but in acting in aggressive ways which exacerbated its reality. By projecting and acting on an expectation that the Other was supposed to be an enemy, each was encouraging him to take on that identity so that the Self could in turn maintain its own identity. To that extent the militaristic identity of each depended logically, not just causally, on meanings shared with an enemy-Other.

The second argument concerns "in-group solidarity," which concerns the role of enemies in enabling states to meet their national interests. In recent IR scholarship this argument has been made most interestingly, though in different forms, by Campbell[75] and Mercer.[76]

Working out of a postmodernist perspective, Campbell argues that the American state depends on a "discourse of danger" in which state elites periodically invent or exaggerate threats to the body politic in order to produce and sustain an "us" in distinction to "them," and thereby justify the existence of their state. On one level this hypothesis taps some of the same cultural mechanisms as the familiar "rally round the flag" phenomenon underlying the "diversionary theory of war," according to which weak governments divert internal dissent by engaging in external aggression.[77] What Campbell adds is the hypothesis that discourses of danger produce the distinction between

[74] Stein (1982).   [75] Campbell (1992).   [76] Mercer (1995).
[77] Levy (1988).

"internal" and "external" in the first place and as such constitute the whole idea of a distinct group on which the state's corporate identity depends. States' dependence on discourses of danger would seem to be a matter of degree, with the US perhaps at the high end of the spectrum, but state security always depends on an on-going process of differentiating Self from the Other, and it is reasonable to think that this process sometimes takes Hobbesian forms. In those cases who states are and what they want would depend on meanings shared with an enemy-Other.

In contrast to Campbell's focus on states' physical security needs, Mercer focuses on their self-esteem needs, but he too is dealing with the problem of in-group solidarity. As we saw in chapter 5, Mercer uses social identity theory to argue that like the members of any human group, the members of states tend to compare their group favorably to other states in order to enhance their self-esteem, and that this predisposes states to define their interests in egoistic terms. It is important to emphasize that this "in-group bias" does not in itself imply aggression or enmity,[78] but it does provide a cognitive resource for such behavior. If a shared understanding exists that this is how states are going to constitute each other, in turn, then states may find that enmity has value in itself, since by mobilizing in-group/out-group dynamics it can significantly bolster group self-esteem.

The third mechanism by which Hobbesian cultures may constitute interests, projective identification, is not generally recognized in IR scholarship and I offer it more tentatively than the others. In part this is because it comes out of psychoanalytic theory, specifically Melanie Klein's work on "object relations," about which some social scientists may be skeptical, and in part because of the difficulty of applying it to groups. However, there is today a growing body of psychoanalytic work on social theory in general,[79] and, led by Vamik Volkan and C. Fred Alford, on inter-group and international relations in particular,[80] and so it seems useful to consider its relevance to the story.

The projective identification thesis emphasizes the enemy's role as a site for displacing unwanted feelings about the Self. According to this

---

[78] Struch and Schwartz (1989).
[79] See, for example, Carveth (1982), Golding (1982), Alford (1989), and Kaye (1991).
[80] Volkan (1988), Alford (1994). See Moses (1982), Bloom (1990), Kristeva (1993), Cash (1996), and Sucharov (2000). Interestingly, Kaplan's (1957: 253–270) classic includes an appendix applying psychoanalytic ideas to the international system. (I thank Mike Barnett for bringing this to my attention.)

idea, individuals who, because of personal pathologies, cannot control potentially destructive unconscious fantasies, like feelings of rage, aggression, or self-hatred, will sometimes attribute or "project" them on to an Other, and then through their behavior pressure that Other to "identify" with or "act out" those feelings so that the Self can then control or destroy them by controlling or destroying the Other.[81] As in social identity theory this serves a self-esteem function, but here self-esteem needs are met not simply by making favorable comparisons with an Other but by trying to destroy him. A requirement of this process is therefore "splitting" the Self into "good" and "bad" elements, with the latter being projected on to the Other. Howard Stein saw such a process at work in the US during the Cold War: "[w]e do not relate to the Soviet Union as though it were separate, distinct, from ourselves; rather we act toward it as though it were an unruly, unacceptable part or aspect of ourselves."[82] This can in turn be a basis for the cultural constitution of enmity, since the split Self needs the Other to identify with its ejected elements, to collude with the Self, in order to justify destroying them via the Other. At first the Other might not cooperate or identify with this desire, in which case we would be dealing with chimerical enemy images like those that animated the Nazis, rather than a shared culture. If the Other projects *its* unwanted elements on to the Self, however, then each will be able to play the role the other needs, and their shared (if tacit or unconscious) knowledge to this effect will make their revisionist desires meaningful. Each will have a stake in the enemy-Other because it enables them to try to control or destroy parts of themselves to which they are hostile.

Even if this argument is accepted at the level of individuals, when applied to states it raises hard questions of anthropomorphism, operationalization, and falsification that I cannot address here. My point in floating it is not to assert its truth but to illustrate one more way in which a Hobbesian culture might constitute interests, and to remind us, *inter alia*, that human motivation may be more complicated than the usual assumption in IR of rational egoism. Moreover, it seems to capture certain features of "intractable conflicts"[83] in international politics that are less obviously accounted for by other explanations: chimerical enemies, irrational hatred, the inability to

---

[81] See Alford (1994: 48–56) for a good overview.   [82] Stein (1985: 250).
[83] Kriesberg, *et al.*, eds. (1989).

recognize the role that one's own aggression plays in conflict, and the enthusiasm with which people may go to war, suggesting a cathartic release of pent-up aggression or rage. All have quite natural explanations if what is going on in trying to kill the Other is killing part of the Self. The role that unconscious processes play in international politics is something that needs to be considered more systematically, not dismissed out of hand.

These three hypotheses all suggest ways in which the norms of the Hobbesian culture may constitute an interest in enmity, rather than merely regulating the behavior of actors whose enmity is constituted exogenously. Enmity here is constituted top–down, not bottom–up. Paradoxically, therefore, despite the greater depth of their polarization the relationship between enemies in this Third Degree case is more "intimate" than it is in less fully internalized Hobbesian cultures.[84] Having defined their identities and interests in terms of a shared systemic culture, enemies have become a group – albeit a dysfunctional one that has suppressed any sense of itself. Characterizing Hobbes' state of nature, Alford uses the psychoanalytic concept of a "regressed group" to describe this condition:

> The group seems like a bunch of autonomous individuals, but only because the members are in such a state of dedifferentiation that all they can know of the other is that he is other, his otherness constituting the threat that dedifferentiation defends against. Not as autonomy but as isolation is how individuality is experienced in the regressed group.[85]

This, I would suggest, is the ultimate deep structure of the Hobbesian world, not the Realist's combination of human nature plus anarchy.

This matters in the end for the possibility of change. It is often assumed that Realism's materialist approach inevitably leads to an emphasis on the impossibility of structural change under anarchy, and that an idealist approach must emphasize the plasticity of structure. In my view the opposite is true. The more deeply that a structure of shared ideas penetrates actors' identities and interests the more resistant to change it will be. No structure is easy to change, but a Hobbesian culture that constructs states as enemies will be a lot more resilient than one in which shared ideas matter as little as Realists say.

[84] On identity in intimate relationships see Blumstein (1991).
[85] Alford (1994: 87).

The Lockean culture

It is an interesting question how much of international history fits the Hobbesian mold. Judging from the violence and high death rate of states in the past it seems clear that world politics has *often* been Hobbesian, and some Realists might argue that it has always been so. It would make sense for enmity to dominate international history if new states systems are prone to starting out that way, since cultures are self-fulfilling prophecies which are resistant to change. This makes the modern, Westphalian states system all the more surprising, however, since it clearly is not Hobbesian. The death rate of states is almost nil; small states are thriving; inter-state war is rare and normally limited; territorial boundaries have "hardened";[86] and so on. Realists tend not to attach much significance to such changes,[87] and focus on continuities instead: wars still happen, power still matters. Yet to my mind the empirical record suggests strongly that in the past few centuries there has been a qualitative structural change in international politics. The kill or be killed logic of the Hobbesian state of nature has been replaced by the live and let live logic of the Lockean anarchical society.[88] In chapter 7 I explore one way of thinking about the causes of this change. Here I focus just on how the Lockean ideal type is constituted, and suggest that it is not as much a self-help system as we often assume.

Rivalry

The Lockean culture has a different logic from the Hobbesian because it is based on a different role structure, rivalry rather than enmity. Like enemies, rivals are constituted by representations about Self and Other with respect to violence, but these representations are less threatening: unlike enemies, rivals expect each other to act as if they recognize their sovereignty, their "life and liberty," as a *right*, and therefore not to try to conquer or dominate them. Since state sovereignty is territorial, in turn, this implies recognition of a right to some "property" as well. Unlike friends, however, the recognition among rivals does not extend to the right to be free from violence in disputes.

---

[86] Smith (1981).

[87] Buzan's (1991) distinction between "immature" and "mature" anarchies is an important exception.

[88] Bull (1977). On Locke's view of anarchy see Simmons (1989).

Moreover, some of these disputes may concern boundaries, and so rivalry could involve some territorial revisionism. The right to some property – enough to "live" – is acknowledged, but which property may be disputed, sometimes by force.

Underlying rivalry is a right to sovereignty.[89] In chapter 5 I argued that sovereignty is an intrinsic property of the states, like being six feet tall, and as such it exists even when there are no other states. This property becomes a "right" only when other states recognize it. Rights are social capacities that are conferred on actors by others' "permission" to do certain things.[90] A powerful state may have the material capability to defend its sovereignty against all comers, but even without that ability a weak state can enjoy its sovereignty if other states recognize it as a right. The reason for this is that a constitutive feature of having a right is self-limitation by the Other, his acceptance of the Self's enjoyment of certain powers. I take this to be implicit in what IR scholars call being "status quo" toward other states. The status quo may be enforced in the last instance by coercion, but as even Hobbes recognized a society based solely on force would not last long. Whether out of self-interest or the perceived legitimacy of its norms, the members of a well-functioning society must also restrain *themselves*. For Hobbes the role of the state was to institutionalize such self-restraint, not be a complete substitute for it.[91] Having a right depends on others' restraint, on being treated by them as an end in yourself rather than as merely an object to be disposed of as they see fit. Absent such restraint rights are nothing more than whatever a person can get away with, which is to say not "rights" at all.

When states recognize each other's sovereignty as a right then we can speak of sovereignty not only as a property of individual states, but as an *institution* shared by many states. The core of this institution is the shared expectation that states will not try to take away each other's life and liberty. In the Westphalian system this belief is formalized in international law, which means that far from being merely an epiphenomenon of material forces, international law is actually a key part of the deep structure of contemporary international politics.[92] Despite the absence of centralized enforcement, almost all

---

[89] On sovereignty as a right see Ruggie (1983a), Fain (1987), Baldwin (1992), Kratochwil (1995), and Reus-Smit (1997).

[90] Fain (1987: 134–160).   [91] Hanson (1984).

[92] Kocs (1994); see also Coplin (1965) and Slaughter (1995).

states today adhere to this law almost all of the time,[93] and it is increasingly considered binding (and therefore enforceable) even on states that have not agreed to its provisions.[94] Modern inter-state rivalry, in other words, is constrained by the structure of sovereign rights recognized by international law, and to that extent is based on the rule of law. Within that constraint, however, rivalry is compatible with the use of force to settle disputes, and as such the Lockean culture is not a complete rule of law system. What this comes down to in the end is the level of violence that states expect of each other. Rivals expect Others to use violence sometimes to settle disputes, but to do so within "live and let live" limits.

Realists might point out that states can never be "100 percent certain" about each other's intentions because they cannot read each other's minds or be sure they will not change,[95] and from this argue that since in an anarchy the costs of a mistake can be fatal states have no choice but to represent each other as enemies. This reasoning makes sense in a Hobbesian culture, but it is hard to see its force today, when almost all states *know* that almost all other states recognize their sovereignty. This knowledge is not 100 percent certain, but *no* knowledge is that. The question is whether states' knowledge about each other's intentions is sufficiently uncertain to warrant worst-case assumptions, and in most cases today the answer is no. This is precisely what one would expect in a culture based on the institution of sovereignty, which enables states to make reliable inferences about each other's status quoness even without access to their "minds." One could argue that policy-makers' complacency is irrational, that because of anarchy they *should* treat each other as enemies, but that actually seems far more irrational than acting on the basis of the vast experience which suggests otherwise. It would be crazy today for Norway and Sweden, Kenya and Tanzania, or almost any other dyad in the international system to represent each other as enemies; rivals perhaps, but not enemies. The exceptions (North and South Korea; Israeli and Palestinian radicals) highlight just how unusual enmity is today. Moreover, despite their Hobbesian inclinations this fact is not lost on most Realists. Waltz's assumption that states seek security rather than power would make little sense if states really did think that others were trying to conquer them. Anarchy may

---

[93] Henkin (1979: 47).   [94] Charney (1993).   [95] Mearsheimer (1994/1995: 10).

make the achievement of rivalry difficult, but even most Realists seem to think it is possible.

The implications of rivalry for the Self are less clear than they are of enmity because the Other's perceived restraint gives a state a choice. If the Other is an enemy then a state has little choice but to respond in kind. Not so with rivalry. Some states may consider an Other willing to restrain itself a "sucker," and respond by trying to "kill" it, as exemplified perhaps by Hitler's reaction to the Munich agreement. In this case there is an asymmetry in roles (one side sees rivalry, the other enmity), and the result will be a quick descent into a Hobbesian world. The ever-present possibility of such a descent is what motivates Realist "worst-caseism," but this does not happen very often in the modern world because other states' recognition of its sovereignty gives a state space to make another choice – to reciprocate. If it does then states enter the logic of rivalry.

Rivalry has at least four implications for foreign policy. The most important is that whatever conflicts they may have, states must behave in a status quo fashion toward each other's sovereignty. The second implication concerns the nature of rational behavior. Whereas enemies have to make decisions on the basis of high risk-aversion, short time horizons, and relative power, rivalry permits a more relaxed view. The institution of sovereignty makes security less "scarce," so risks are fewer, the future matters more, and absolute gains may override relative losses. If prospect theory defines rational behavior for enemies, then expected-utility theory does for rivals. This does not mean that states no longer worry about security, but their anxiety is less intense because certain pathways on the "game tree" – those involving their own "death" – have been removed. Third, relative military power is still important because rivals know that others might use force to settle disputes, but its meaning is different than it is for enemies because the institution of sovereignty changes the "balance of threat."[96] In the Hobbesian world military power dominates all decision-making, whereas in the Lockean it is less of a priority. Threats are not existential, and allies can be more easily trusted when one's own power is insufficient. Finally, if disputes do go to war, rivals will limit their own violence. In the Westphalian system these limits are expressed in Just War Theory and standards of civilization, which lays down the conditions under and extent to

[96] Walt (1987).

which states may use violence against each other. There is growing empirical evidence that these norms cause states to restrain themselves in modern warfare.[97] Enemies and rivals may be equally prone to violence, but a small difference in roles makes a big difference in its degree.

The logic of Lockean anarchy

So far I have talked about rivalry as an inter-psychological relationship, as a conjoining of subjective beliefs about the Self and the Other. If these beliefs change then so does the rivalry. It is important to acknowledge this level in the structure of rivalry because subjective perceptions are a micro-foundation for cultural forms. However, there is another, macro-, level in the organization of rivalry, in which "rival" is a preexisting position in a stock of shared knowledge that supervenes on the ideas of individual states. This is rivalry as a *collective* representation. Once rivalry acquires this status states will make attributions about each other's "minds" based more on what they know about the structure than what they know about each other, and the system will acquire a logic of its own. Practices of rivalry sustain this logic, such that if their frequency falls below the tipping point it will change, but until then the system will have a macro-structure that can be multiply realized at the micro-level. This structure, Bull's "anarchical society," generates four tendencies.

The first is that warfare is simultaneously accepted and constrained. On the one hand, states reserve and periodically exercise the right to use violence to advance their interests. War is accepted as normal and legitimate,[98] and could be just as common as in the Hobbesian anarchy. On the other hand, wars tend to be limited, not in the sense of not killing a lot of people, but of not killing *states*. Wars of conquest are rare, and when they do occur other states tend to act collectively to restore the status quo (World War II, Korean War, the Gulf War). This suggests that the standard definition of war in IR scholarship as "a conflict producing at least 1000 battle deaths" conflates two different social kinds, what Ruggie calls "constitutive" wars and "configurative" wars.[99] In constitutive wars, which dominate Hobbesian anar-

---

[97] See, for example, Ray (1989), Nadelmann (1990), Price (1995), and Tannenwald (1999).
[98] See Jochnick and Normand (1994).
[99] Ruggie (1993: 162–163). Ruggie makes a further distinction between configurative and positional wars.

chies, the type and existence of units is at stake; in configurative wars, which dominate Lockean anarchies, the units are accepted by the parties, who are fighting over territory and strategic advantage instead. The causes, dynamics, and outcomes of the two kinds of war should vary, and as such they should not be treated as one dependent variable.

Limited warfare underpins a second tendency, which is for the system to have a relatively stable membership or low death rate over time. Membership is key, since this tendency does not apply to states whose sovereignty is not recognized by the system, like the indigenous states of the Americas before the Conquest. Indeed, placing the fate of these unrecognized states next to that of recognized ones provides some of the strongest evidence for a structural difference between Lockean and Hobbesian anarchies. As David Strang[100] shows, since 1415 states recognized as sovereign by European states have a much higher survival rate than those that were not. In the modern era "micro" states like Singapore and Monaco – much weaker in relative terms than the Aztecs or Incas – are flourishing, and even "failed" states that lack empirical sovereignty manage to persist because international society recognizes their juridical sovereignty.[101] In all of these cases states survived for social not material reasons, because potential predators *let* them live. This indicates a world in which the weak are protected by the restraint of the strong, not a survival of the fittest.

A third tendency is for states to balance power. Waltz sees this as an effect of anarchy as such, but the argument here suggests that balancing is actually more of an effect of the mutual recognition of sovereignty. In the Hobbesian anarchy states balance if they must, but the lack of mutual recognition and resulting pressure to maximize power gives balancing a "knife's edge" quality, enabling a tendency toward concentrating power to dominate. If states think that others recognize their sovereignty, however, then survival is not at stake if their relative power falls, and the pressure to maximize power is much less. The institution of sovereignty in effect "arrests" the Hobbesian tendency toward concentration. In this situation balancing can paradoxically become a relatively stable source of order with respect to the many *non*-existential issues that may remain sources of violent conflict. This is not to deny that balancing

---

[100] Strang (1991).   [101] Jackson and Rosberg (1982).

also provides insurance against loss of sovereignty, which an unbalanced distribution of power in principle threatens, but in Lockean systems most states most of the time do not in fact need (nor do they have) this insurance because recognition makes it unnecessary.[102] It is precisely because balancing is *not* essential for survival, in other words, that it becomes a basis for order in the first place.

A final tendency is that neutrality or non-alignment becomes a recognized status. If states can resolve their differences then there is no necessity for them to compete militarily at all, since there is no longer a threat of revisionism. It may be difficult to achieve such a condition as long as states are prone to violence and security dilemmas, but assuming that conflicts can be resolved mutual indifference is a stable outcome in a live and let live system.

These tendencies suggest that the anarchy portrayed by Waltz is actually a Lockean rather than Hobbesian system. His analogy to markets, which presuppose institutions that ensure that actors do not kill each other,[103] his emphasis on balancing, his observation that modern states have a low death rate, and his assumption that states are security- rather than power-seeking are all things associated with the relatively self-restrained Lockean culture, not the war of all against all. In one sense this is not surprising, since Waltz's main concern, the Westphalian system, *is* a Lockean culture. Unfortunately, Waltz does not address the possibility that this culture has a different logic than the Hobbesian one with which Realism is often associated, nor the underlying social relations that generate this logic in the first place. This allows Neorealists to trade on the tough, hard-nosed rhetoric of "Realism" while presupposing the kinder, gentler world described by their critics. A Lockean culture, in short, is a condition of possibility for the truth of Neorealism.

Internalization and the Foucault effect

The institution of sovereignty is the basis of the contemporary international system. There have always been exceptions to its norms, which raise hard questions about the extent to which the system is

---

[102] On the role of mutual recognition as a basis for social order see Pizzorno (1991).

[103] See Nau (1994) for a good discussion of the ways in which the market analogy poses problems for Waltz's account.

Lockean,[104] but nevertheless almost all states today obey those norms almost all of the time, which poses even harder questions to any other interpretation of the system. In this section I consider how this widespread compliance should be explained. The three possibilities – coercion, self-interest, and legitimacy – reflect the three degrees to which sovereignty norms can be internalized. Different degrees may apply to different states, but taken in the aggregate they constitute three pathways by which a Lockean culture can be realized, and thus three answers to the question, "what difference does sovereignty make to the international system?" The answer to this question matters for explaining how rivalry works, and for predicting its stability. After briefly reviewing the First and Second Degree arguments I concentrate on the Third, and especially its constitutive aspects, which I suggest can be described together as a "Foucault Effect"[105] – the social constitution of "possessive individuals."

The First Degree, Realist explanation for the Lockean culture holds when states comply with sovereignty norms because they are forced to by the superior power of others. This power might be exercised directly, like the Allied Coalition's roll-back of Iraq's conquest of Kuwait, or indirectly, as in situations where the balance of power, dominance of defensive technology, or other material conditions make the costs of attempting conquest too high.[106] In either case, in order for coercion to explain compliance it must be the case that states neither want to comply of their own accord nor see it as in their self-interest. It must be against their will, which in effect means that they must have revisionist interests toward others' sovereignty. If this were not the case then while it may still be true that some states lack the material power to take away others' sovereignty, this would not explain their status quo behavior, since they do not want to change it in the first place. One cannot be coerced into not doing something one does not want to do.

Sometimes coercion is the explanation for compliance with sovereignty norms. Napoleon, Hitler, and Saddam Hussein would all have revised the life and liberty of other states had they not been prevented by superior power. In cases like these material forces do more explanatory work than shared ideas, since although "shared" in the

---

[104] See especially Krasner (1993, 1995/6). On the significance of exceptions to rules see Edgerton (1985).
[105] Burchell, *et al.*, eds. (1991).   [106] See Powell (1991), Liberman (1993).

sense of "commonly known," the institution of sovereignty is not shared in the sense of "accepted" by revisionist states. If this were true of most states in the system then a Lockean culture would quickly degenerate into a Hobbesian. Thus, even though the coercion explanation for compliance with sovereignty norms makes sense in the breach, it is ill-equipped to account for the long term stability of Lockean cultures, which depends on a critical mass of powerful states – enough to prevent the system from tipping into another logic – *not* trying to revise each other's sovereignty. The durability of the modern, Westphalian culture suggests that it has been internalized more deeply than Realism would predict.

The Second Degree, Neoliberal or rationalist, explanation holds when states comply with sovereignty norms because they think it will advance some exogenously given interest, like security or trade. As Barry Weingast[107] shows, sovereignty can be seen as a "focal point" or salient outcome around which expectations naturally converge, which reduces uncertainty in the face of multiple equilibria and enables states to coordinate their actions on mutually beneficial outcomes. In this way the institution of sovereignty exerts a causal or regulative effect on states, which is the usual focus of individualist analyses of institutions. One of the nice features of Weingast's article, however, is that it also reveals constitutive effects, at least on behavior (as opposed to identities and interests), namely the role that shared beliefs about what *counts* as a violation of sovereignty play in enabling the institution to work. In Europe before The Peace of Augsburg in 1555 trying to force another state to be Catholic counted as a legitimate action, and may have been applauded by other states for stamping out heresy. After that the identical physical behavior counted as a violation of a prince's right to determine the religion of his own subjects, and would have been deplored. It is such constitutive effects that make the causal effects of norms possible. Whether causal or constitutive, however, culture matters much more here than in the First Degree case, but still as an intervening variable between power and interest and outcomes.[108]

As with coercion, it is important to define the self-interest explanation narrowly enough that it does not become trivial. On the one hand, to say that states comply with sovereignty for self-interested reasons presupposes that they have enough social space for this to be

---

[107] Weingast (1995).   [108] Krasner (1983a).

a choice, so that their respect for others' sovereignty is due in part to a self-restraint which is missing in the coercion case. The institution is now achieving effects on states in part from the inside out, which is what internalization is all about. On the other hand, to count as self-interested the choice must still be made for consequentialist reasons, because the benefits for other interests outweigh the costs, and since these incentives are shaped by how other states are expected to react, to *that* extent the choice is still determined by the external situation. Norm violation remains a live option on the decision tree, and states are engaged in on-going calculations about whether choosing it would be in their interest. The institution of sovereignty is just one more object in the environment that distributes costs and benefits, so that whenever the cost–benefit ratio indicates that breaking its rules will bring a net benefit that is what states will do.[109] What this instrumental attitude rules out is obeying sovereignty norms because they are valued for their own sake. States are status quo toward each other's sovereignty not because they are status quo states, but because this serves some other purpose; status quoness is a strategy, not an interest. Indeed, the self-interest explanation seems to preclude any interest, status quo or revisionist, toward sovereignty itself. Revisionist interests are out because then compliance would be due to coercion, and status quo interests are out because then states would value the norms themselves. Self-interested states are *indifferent* to sovereignty norms, in other words, not in the sense that they do not care if such norms exist (they do, since this helps them advance other interests), but in the sense that they do not care, one way or the other, about the norms as such.

This brings us to the Third Degree or constructivist hypothesis. Instrumentalism may be the attitude when states first settle on sovereignty norms, and continue to be for poorly socialized states down the road. People are the same way. We obey the law initially because we are forced to or calculate that it is in our self-interest. Some people never get beyond that point, but this is not true for most of us, who obey the law because we accept its claims on us as legitimate.[110] Implicit in this legitimacy are identities as law-abiding citizens which lead us to define our interests in terms of the law's "interest." External norms have become a voice in our heads telling us that we *want* to follow them. The distinction between "interest" and

[109] See Krasner (1993, 1995/6).   [110] Tyler (1990); also see Hurd (1999).

"self"-interest is important here: our behavior is still "interested," in the sense that we are motivated to obey the law, but we do not treat the law as merely an object to be used for our own benefit. The costs and benefits of breaking the law do not figure in our choices because we have removed that option from our decision tree. The same thing happens in the fully internalized Lockean culture. Most states comply with its norms because they accept them as legitimate, because they identify with them and want to comply.[111] States are status quo not just at the level of behavior, but of interests as well, and as such are now more fully self-regulating actors.

As an example consider the question of why the US does not conquer the Bahamas. Coercion does not seem to be the answer, since probably no state could prevent the US from taking them, nor is there any evidence that the US has a revisionist desire to do so in the first place. The self-interest argument initially seems to do better: US policymakers might calculate that conquest would not pay because of the damage it would do to the US reputation as a law-abiding citizen, and because the US can achieve most of the benefits of conquest through economic dominance anyway. Both of these assumptions about the cost–benefit ratio are probably true, but there are two reasons to doubt that they explain US inaction. First, it is doubtful that US policymakers are making or even ever did make such calculations. It may be that respecting Bahamian sovereignty is in the self-interest of the US, but if this does not figure in its thinking then in what sense does it "explain" its behavior? Second, the definition of what counts as "paying" is shot through with cultural content. A state whose main goal was national or religious glory might not care very much about economic benefits or a reputation as law-abiding, and therefore define costs and benefits quite differently. Conquest "paid" for Nazi Germany and Imperial Japan,[112] at least initially, and the US was certainly willing to "pay" to conquer the Native Americans. Why would similar reasoning not apply to the Bahamas? The answer seems to be that the US has a status quo interest toward the Bahamas, but in order for this to be satisfying we also need to ask *why* it has this interest. My proposal is that it stems from having internalized sovereignty norms so deeply that the US defines its interests in terms of the norms, and regulates its own behavior accordingly. The US

---

[111] See Coplin (1965), Franck (1990), Kocs (1994), Koh (1997), and Hurd (1999).
[112] Liberman (1993).

perceives the norms as legitimate and therefore the Bahamas, as a party to those norms, has a right to life and liberty that the US would not even think of violating.

It seems to me that in the late twentieth century this is why most states follow international law. It also seems that most mainstream IR scholars, Neorealist and Neoliberal alike, must believe it as well, at least implicitly, since their work almost always assumes that the distribution of interests with respect to sovereignty is heavily biased toward the status quo. What the Bahamas Problem suggests, in other words, is that theories purporting to explain contemporary international politics solely by reference to coercion or self-interest in fact presuppose the legitimacy effects of the Lockean culture. That culture has become part of the background knowledge in terms of which modern states define their national interests.

I now want to argue that this tendency to take the culture's deepest effects for granted goes deeper, to the kinds of actors that get to have interests at all. Exogenously given in most rationalist models of international politics are four assumptions about the nature of state "individuals." These assumptions are generally good ones and I shall not dispute them. What I shall argue, rather, is that they are good because they are effects of a Lockean culture so deeply internalized today that we almost forget it is there. What I shall try to do, in other words, is endogenize rationalist assumptions about international politics to their cultural conditions of possibility.

The four constitutive effects I have in mind can be seen as aspects of a "Foucault Effect," the thesis that the self-regulating, possessive individual is an effect of a particular discourse or culture.[113] If the partly essentialist view of identity defended in chapter 5 is correct then this thesis cannot be taken too literally.[114] In the literal sense people are individuals in virtue of self-organizing biological structures that do not presuppose social relations. Although their internal structures are social rather than biological, the same principle applies to states. In both cases self-organization creates pre-social material individuals with intrinsic needs and dispositions. However, the Foucault Effect is not about the constitution of material individuality,

---

[113] In various forms this theory of individuation is found throughout holist social theory, back at least to Hegel. I use Foucault's name because his version (see especially 1979) is well known today (see also Pizzorno, 1991); the phrase 'Foucault Effect' is due to Burchell, *et al.*, eds. (1991).

[114] See Kitzinger (1992).

but about its meaning, the *terms* of individuality, not individuality per se. It is only in certain cultures that people are treated as intentional agents with identities, interests, and responsibility, the capacities most of us today associate with being an individual or person. The fact that human beings have these capacities naturally does not always mean they have them *socially*, and this matters for their life chances. Slaves, women, and racial "inferiors" were often held to different standards of conduct because they were not considered fully human, and so on. Conversely, the fact that animals do not seem to have such capacities naturally has not always prevented them from having them socially, as evidenced by the fact that in medieval Europe animals were often tried in courts of law and ex-communicated by the Church.[115] The hypothesis of the Foucault Effect, then, is that when moderns conceptualize and treat each other as "individuals," they are drawing on a particular, essentially liberal[116] discourse about what their bodies mean. This discourse makes material into social individuality, creating what we today understand as "rational actors," and, by extension, the possibility of theories that presuppose such creatures.

The Lockean culture individualizes states in a similar manner, although I shall argue that in doing so it paradoxically creates capacities for "other-help"[117] that the conventional, self-help assumption fails to see. The culture affects all four kinds of identities that the "individuals" of international politics can have – corporate, type, collective, and role (chapter 5). In what follows I describe these identity effects using the example of the Westphalian system. This example will affect the specifics of my narrative, but not its general structure.

The first individualizing effect of the Lockean culture is defining the criteria for membership in the system, which determines what kinds of "individuals" have standing and are therefore part of the distribution of interests. As we all know in the Westphalian system it is only states that have such standing; other kinds of individuals, whether biological or corporate, may increasingly be getting it, but this challenges the original constitution of this culture and will continue to be a long, hard fight. The dominance of states in the Westphalian system might be due to inherent competitive advantages in an anarchic world, in which case systemic culture would have little to do with it. However, as Hendrik Spruyt shows, it seems due more importantly to the fact that states recognized each other as the only

---

[115] Evans (1987).   [116] Pizzorno (1992).   [117] Mercer (1995).

kind of actor with standing, a fact which they eventually institutionalized by making empirical sovereignty the criterion for entry into international society.[118] Actors that fail this test are not recognized by the international system as "individuals," which makes it much more difficult for their interests to be realized. In this light the institution of sovereignty can be seen as a "structure of closure," exerting structural power that keeps certain kinds of players out of the game of international politics.[119] Interestingly, despite its much less forgiving character the Hobbesian culture is one in which any kind of individual can play, since there are no rules giving certain actors standing and others not. The Lockean culture pays for its relative tranquility with a less open membership policy.

On the surface this seems to be the ultimate self-help policy, since it suggests that the only way for actors to get recognized as members of the system is to *force* their way in, there being no other way to achieve exclusive authority over a territory but to expel other states. But the reality seems more complicated. Many states were only able to "exclude" others because more powerful states did not try to prevent their exclusion. In these cases empirical sovereignty seems to presuppose at least tacit recognition of juridical sovereignty rather than the other way around. This reversal of the official procedure is most obvious for failed states in Africa,[120] but it is true of many other Small Powers as well, who were only able to exclude Great Powers because the latter did not resist. The "self-help" here, in other words, is one that depends on the restraint of the powerful, which amounts to a passive form of "other-help." That might still be self-help in an interesting sense, but not in the ultimate sense of *sauve qui peut*.

This calls attention to the second constitutive effect of the Lockean culture, which is determining what kinds of *type* identities get recognized as individuals. To become a member of the Westphalian system it has never been enough merely to have the corporate identity of a state; within that category it has always been necessary also to conform to type identity criteria which define only certain *forms* of state as legitimate.[121] Historically these criteria were expressed in the "standard of civilization," a set of systemic norms requiring that states' political authority be organized domestically in a certain way,

---

[118] Spruyt (1994).
[119] Murphy (1984).; cf. Guzzini (1993), Onuf and Klink (1989).
[120] Jackson and Rosberg (1982).
[121] Bukovansky (1999a, b).

namely like the hierarchical, bureaucratic, and (initially) Christian and monarchical authority of European states.[122] In the eighteenth and nineteenth centuries many non-European polities were empirically sovereign, but because they did not organize their authority in this manner they were not considered civilized – and therefore to have sovereign rights. Norms of what counts as a legitimate type identity have since changed. It is no longer necessary for a state to be Christian or monarchical; now it is being a "nation-"state,[123] having the institutions of a "modern" state,[124] refraining from genocide, and, increasingly, being a "capitalist" and "democratic" state. In all these respects being part of Westphalian culture is not just a matter of a state's physical individuality, but of conforming the internal structure of this individuality to external norms about its proper form. As with other type identities, like being "left-handed," this internal structure is rooted in intrinsic features of material actors and as such is constitutionally exogenous to the international system (a state can be democratic all by itself), but its social meaning and consequences are *en*dogenous.

The third way in which Lockean culture constitutes states as individuals relates to their collective or social identities. In their interactions within the Lockean culture states tend to be self-interested, but this is not true when it comes to the Lockean culture itself. Part of what it means to fully internalize a culture is that actors identify with it and therefore feel a sense of loyalty and obligation to the group which the culture defines. The peculiar nature of the Lockean culture is such that states are individualized within this group, but because the culture also constitutes their identities relative to non-members – as "civilized" states, for example – they will have a stake or interest in the group which they would not have if its norms were less fully internalized. This social identity matters because it facilitates collective action against outsiders; when the group is threatened, its members will see themselves as a "we" that needs to act collectively, as a team, in its defense. What the fully internalized Lockean culture does, in other words, is give its members an expanded sense of Self that includes the group, and this group consciousness in turn creates a rudimentary capacity for other-help, not just in the passive sense of self-restraint but in the active sense of

---

[122] Gong (1984), Neumann and Welsh (1991).
[123] Barkin and Cronin (1994), Hall (1999).   [124] McNeely (1995), Meyer, *et al.* (1997).

being willing to come to each other's aid. This capacity is only rudimentary, however, because of the limited norms of the Lockean culture. It is only when the actual survival of members is threatened by outsiders, by rogue states, for example, that Lockean states' collective identity will become manifest. For fights within the group states are on their own.

This relates to the final effect of the Lockean culture, which is in a sense to obscure the preceding three effects and constitute states as "possessive" individuals instead. I take this to be an effect on states' role identities, and is a key basis for rivalry. According to C.B. MacPherson, possessive individualism is a distinctive feature of the *liberal* view of the individual.

> Its possessive quality is found in its conception of the individual as essentially the proprietor of his own person or capacities, owing nothing to society for them. The individual was seen neither as a moral whole, nor as a part of a larger social whole, but as an owner of himself. The relation of ownership, having become for more and more men the critical important relation determining their actual freedom and actual prospect of realising their full potentialities, was read back into the nature of the individual.[125]

Liberalism "desocializes" the individual, in other words, drawing a veil over his inherently social qualities and treating them as purely individual possessions instead. A consequence is that it becomes much more difficult to see why people should have any responsibility for each other's welfare, and thus to engage in collective action within the group. If people do not depend on each other for their identities then each is "his own man" and by implication owes nothing to his fellows except perhaps to leave them alone. Self-interest is thereby constituted as the appropriate relationship of Self to Other, which in effect *creates* the collective action problem,[126] but to do so it must forget the Self's dependence on the Other's recognition of his rights and identities. Thus, since that dependence could be threatened by being self-interested all the way down, liberalism arguably contains a deep tension between its legitimation of self-interest and the fact that individuals have an objective interest in the group which makes their

---

[125] MacPherson (1962: 3), quoted from Shotter (1990: 166).

[126] The effect of individualization on collective action is an old theme of Marxist scholarship (see Jessop, 1978; Poulantzas, 1978), and has also featured in more recent work on social movements (Pizzorno, 1991). For an application to the international system see Paros (1999).

individuality possible. This tension may underlie some of the worry today in the West about the erosion of community values in favor of individual self-interest.

As Ruggie has suggested, the Westphalian culture has a similar effect on states.[127] It constitutes states as the individuals with the right to play the game of international politics, but does so in a way that makes each state seem to be the sole proprietor and guardian of that right. Westphalian states are possessive individuals who do not appreciate the ways in which they depend on each other for their identity, being instead "jealous" of their sovereignty and eager to make their own way in the world. An important reason for this individualistic attitude may be the criterion for membership in international society itself, which encourages states to treat juridical sovereignty as an entitlement due them as a result of purely their own efforts to establish empirical sovereignty first. The effect of collective amnesia that juridical sovereignty is dependent on others is to constitute self-interest as the appropriate way to relate to each other, and self-help as its systemic corollary. Self-interest and self-help are not intrinsic attributes of states and anarchy, in other words, but effects of a particular conception of the individual. The role structure of rivalry feeds on this conception. Rivals know that they are members of a group in which individuals do not kill each other, but this collective identity is usually in the background of their interactions, which center instead on jealously protecting and advancing their own interests within that context. As we have seen, these efforts are mitigated by states' self-limiting behavior, as well as by the occasional reminder by threats from outside that they are in fact part of a group, and as such the system is not self-help all the way down. But whether this mutual dependence can in the long run survive an ideology of possessive individualism is not clear.

The suggestion that Westphalian states are afflicted with a possessive individualism stemming from collective amnesia about their social roots raises a concluding question about whether a Lockean culture could be compatible with a more "relational" individualism that acknowledged those roots. In social theory this question has been taken up especially by feminists, who have argued that the atomistic and egoistic view of the individual found in liberalism and its

---

[127] Ruggie (1983a).

rationalist off-shoots in social science is a gendered view rooted in the male experience.[128] Feminist IR scholars have used these arguments to critique the traditional view of state sovereignty, pointing toward the possibility of a relational view in which inter-state rivalry would be less intense and collective action more likely.[129]

Whether or not the Westphalian theory of sovereignty is intrinsically gendered is an important and challenging question that I cannot address here. It is clear that feminist critiques can be fruitfully applied to that theory, but less clear whether this is because gender has had a causal impact on Westphalian sovereignty, since there are structurally similar, non-feminist critiques of liberalism that come to many of the same conclusions, but do so via psychological, sociological, or anthropological evidence.[130] Whatever the causal roots of the possessive view of sovereignty might be, in turn, there is also the question of how a relational view would differ from the conception of individuality found in the fully internalized Kantian culture, which I consider in passing below.

The Third Degree Lockean culture is the basis for what we today take to be "common sense" about international politics: that a certain type of state is the main actor in the system, that these actors are self-interested individualists, that the international system is therefore in part a self-help system – but that states also recognize each other's sovereignty and so are rivals rather than enemies, that they have status quo interests which induce them to constrain their own behavior and cooperate when threatened from outside, and that the system is therefore in part an other-help system qualitatively different in its fundamental logic than the Hobbesian world of *sauve qui peut*. This common sense is the starting point for mainstream theorizing in IR, which tends to discount the importance of cultural variables. What I have tried to do is endogenize this starting point, to show that it depends on a particular cultural background which can be taken as given for certain purposes, but without which we cannot make sense of modern international politics. This matters for the larger argument of this book, in turn, because if today's common sense about international politics is a function of historically con-

---

[128] See, for example, DiStefano (1983), Scheman (1983), and England and Kilbourne (1990).

[129] Keohane (1988b), Tickner (1989), and several contributions to Peterson, ed. (1990).

[130] See, for example, Sandel (1982), Sampson (1988), Markus and Kitayama (1991), and Kitzinger (1992).

tingent shared ideas rather than the intrinsic nature of states or anarchy, then the question arises how that common sense might be transformed, and with it the cultural conditions of possibility for mainstream thinking.

The Kantian culture

Lockean assumptions have dominated Westphalian politics for the past three centuries. Hobbesianism has occasionally reared its head, but each time has been beaten back down by status quo states. This Lockean dominance is reflected in IR scholarship, which despite the deference given to "The Hobbesian Problem" has focused much more on the problems of getting along in a live and let live system than of surviving in a kill or be killed one. Yet since World War II the behavior of the North Atlantic states, and arguably many others, seems to go well beyond a Lockean culture. In such a culture we expect states sometimes to use force to settle disputes, yet no such violence has occurred in the North Atlantic region; and we also expect them to think individualistically about their security, yet these states have consistently operated as a security "team." The cause of these departures from Lockean norms might be structural in the Neorealist sense, namely a bipolar distribution of capabilities that temporarily suppressed intra-Western rivalries, which the collapse of the Soviet Union should now reignite.[131] There is another possible structural cause of these patterns, however, an idealist one, which is that a new international political culture has emerged in the West within which non-violence and team play are the norm, in which case there might not be any such return to the past. I will call this culture "Kantian" because Kant's *Perpetual Peace* is the most well-known treatment of it,[132] but in doing so I will remain agnostic about whether his emphasis on republican states is the only way to realize it. A world of republican states may be a sufficient condition for a Kantian culture, but we do not yet know if it is necessary. My sketch of this culture will be briefer than the others, especially on internalization, since the reader by now has got the basic idea.

---

[131] For example, Mearsheimer (1990a).
[132] See especially Hurrell (1990) and Huntley (1996).

Friendship

The Kantian culture is based on a role structure of friendship. Relative to "enemy," the concept of "friend" is undertheorized in social theory, and especially in IR, where substantial literature exists on enemy images but little on friend images, on enduring rivalries but little on enduring friendships, on the causes of war but little on the causes of peace, and so on. On the surface there seem to be good empirical and theoretical reasons for this imbalance. Enmity is a much bigger problem for international politics than friendship, and history suggests that few states remain friends for long anyway. Realists see this as evidence that the search for friendship in anarchy is utopian and even dangerous, and that the most we can hope for is that states will act on the basis of "interests" (rivalry?) rather than "passions" (enmity?).[133] Rationalists, in turn, have difficulty squaring friendship with a model of states as self-interested utility-maximizers. And then there is this gut feeling that thinking about states as "friends" simply takes anthropomorphism one step too far.

Yet there are also empirical and theoretical arguments pointing the other way. Statesmen today routinely refer to other states as friends. "Cheap talk" perhaps, but it is reflected in their behavior. The US and Britain are widely acknowledged to have a "special" relationship, and to a lesser degree the same can be said of many other dyads in today's international system, even France and Germany, whose recent behavior seems easier to explain by the logic of friendship than by enmity or rivalry. On the theoretical side, Schmitt[134] saw friendship as fully half, with enmity, of the deep structure of "the political," and Wolfers[135] too recognized the importance of enmity *and* amity in international relations. Finally, while it is important to take the problems of anthropomorphism seriously, if scholars are willing to treat states as enemies then it makes no sense to apply a different standard to "friend." For all these reasons, it seems time to begin thinking systematically about the nature and consequences of friendship in international politics.

As I shall use the term,[136] friendship is a role structure within which states expect each other to observe two simple rules: (1) disputes will

---

[133] Cf. Hirschman (1977), Williams (1998).   [134] Schmitt (1932/1976).
[135] Wolfers (1962).
[136] This treatment is tailored to the problem of national security; for a broader discussion see Badhwar, ed. (1993).

be settled without war or the threat of war (the rule of non-violence); and (2) they will fight as a team if the security of any one is threatened by a third party (the rule of mutual aid). Three points about these rules should be noted. First, the rules are independent and equally necessary. Non-violence could in principle be accompanied by in-difference to the fate of the Other (as when parties agree to "live in peace but go their separate ways"), while mutual aid against outsiders could be accompanied by force within the relationship (as in the "care" of the husband who beats his wife but protects her from violence by other men). Friendship exists when states expect each other to observe both rules. Second, friendship concerns national security only, and need not spill over into other issue areas. Non-violence and mutual aid impose limits on how other issues can be handled, but within those limits friends may have considerable conflict. Finally, and most importantly, friendship is temporally open-ended, in which respect it is qualitatively different from being "allies." Allies engage in the same basic behavior as friends, but they do not expect their relationship to continue indefinitely. An alliance is a temporary, mutually expedient arrangement within rivalry, or perhaps enmity, and so allies expect to eventually revert to a condition in which war between them is an option – and will plan accordingly. Friends may of course have a falling out, but their expectation up front is that the relationship will continue.

The logic of Kantian anarchy

The two rules of friendship generate the macro-level logics and tendencies associated with "pluralistic security communities" and "collective security." In their seminal work, Karl Deutsch and his associates defined a pluralistic security community as a system of states (hence "pluralistic") in which "there is real assurance that the members of that community will not fight each other physically, but will settle their disputes in some other way."[137] Real assurance here comes not from a Leviathan who enforces peace through centralized power (an "amalgamated" security community), but from shared knowledge of each other's peaceful intentions and behavior. As always this knowledge is not 100 percent certain, but neither is the

---

[137] Karl Deutsch, *et al.* (1957: 5). This work has recently been considerably deepened by Emanuel Adler and Michael Barnett, eds. (1998).

knowledge that a Leviathan will keep the peace, as the frequency of civil war attests.[138] The issue is one of probability, not possibility. War is always a logical possibility between states because the capacity for violence is inherent to their nature, but in a pluralistic security community war is no longer considered a legitimate way of settling disputes. This does not prevent conflicts from arising, but when they do arise they are handled by negotiation, arbitration, or the courts, even when the material cost of war to one or both parties might be low. The US and Canada have a variety of conflicts over fishing, trade, and the environment, for example, but the US does not consider violence as a means of getting its way, despite its overwhelming military power. What the shared knowledge that constitutes a security community does, in other words, is change the meaning of military power from its meaning in rivalry. In disputes among rivals relative military capabilities matter to outcomes because the parties know they might be used. In disputes among friends this is not the case, and other kinds of power (discursive, institutional, economic) are more salient.[139]

One way to think about the difference between a pluralistic security community and a collective security system is that the former concerns disputes within a group, while the latter concerns disputes between a group and outsiders (whether non-members or erstwhile members who have renounced the group's norms). Collective security is based on the principle of mutual aid,[140] or "all for one, one for all": when the security of any one member of the system is threatened by aggression all members are supposed to come to its defense even if their own individual security is not at stake.[141] The norm is one of "generalized" reciprocity, in which actors help each other even when there is no direct or immediate return, as there is in "specific" reciprocity.[142] When such a norm is functioning properly the dominant behavioral tendency will be one of multilateralism or other-help with respect to national security.[143] Because of this collective security is usually juxtaposed to the balance of power, which relies on the alternative principle of self-help. Self-help may lead states to form

---

[138] Indeed, Deutsch, *et al.* (1957) found that pluralistic security communities had a better track record of keeping the peace than states.

[139] See Bially (1998).   [140] Kropoktin (1914).

[141] See Claude (1962), Wolfers (1962), Kupchan and Kupchan (1991), and Downs, ed. (1994).

[142] Taylor (1982: 29), Keohane (1986a).   [143] Ruggie, ed. (1993).

alliances, which also involve collective action, but the difference between ally and friend makes for a qualitative difference between alliances and collective security. In an alliance states engage in collective action because they each feel *individually* threatened by the same threat. Their collaboration is self-interested and will end when the common threat is gone. Collective security is neither threat- nor time-specific. Its members pledge mutual aid because they see themselves as a single unit for security purposes *a priori*, no matter by whom, when, or whether they might be threatened. Their military capabilities therefore have a different meaning for each other than they do in an alliance. Parties to the latter know that their allies' capabilities might be used against them once their collaboration is over, and as such they pose a latent threat to each other which colors their choices, even if that threat is temporarily suppressed by the greater threat of external aggression. True "thinking like a team"[144] is impossible in such circumstances. In collective security states' capabilities have a different meaning. Far from being latent threats they are an asset to all, since each knows they will only be used on behalf of the collective.

In IR scholarship collective security has traditionally been defined as a universal system, such that anything short of global membership means that a balance of power and rivalry must be at work. This seems too restrictive. It is true that universal collective security is necessary for a Kantian culture *at the global level*. However, making collective security an all or nothing proposition obscures two important possibilities. One is that states may operate on an "all for one, one for all" basis within relatively autonomous regional sub-systems or security complexes, but not with outsiders.[145] Although this is not the case today, for example, within South America or the Indian subcontinent we can imagine states engaging in mutual aid even if they are not individually threatened. The other possibility is that even when a balance of power system dominates the global level, states within each bloc might collaborate not because they perceive the other bloc as a threat to their individual security, but because they believe in a team approach to security with the members of their bloc. The fact that the members of a bloc can be either rivals or friends also helps us explain change over time, as in the case of NATO, which may have formed initially as an alliance with the expectation that it would be

[144] Sugden (1993).   [145] See Downs and Iida (1994: 18–19); cf. Buzan (1991).

temporary, but seems to have become a collective security system with an expectation of permanence.[146] What constitutes collective security are the reasons for and open-endedness of collective action, not how universal it is.

To my knowledge there has been little work on the relationship between pluralistic security communities and collective security systems, perhaps in part because of the tendency to think of the latter as universal. The preceding discussion indicates that at least in theory they have different structures, with different logics and tendencies, which stem from the two rules of friendship. In practice, however, they tend to go together. Observing a rule of non-violence with a neighbor may remove a potential security threat, but by itself does little to protect from aggressive third parties the peaceful neighborhood of which both are part. Observing a rule of mutual aid, in turn, helps protect a state from those third parties, but will be hard to sustain if states insist on settling their own disputes by force. Taken individually, in other words, the two tendencies do not seem qualitatively different from the patterns associated with the logic of rivalry. Taken together, however, they do constitute a different pattern, and will tend to reinforce each other over time.

Internalization

The Kantian culture is susceptible to the same three degrees of internalization as its counterparts, which determine the pathway by which its norms are realized, its stability over time, and the plausibility of Neorealist, Neoliberal, and Idealist arguments in a given case.

Material coercion in IR tends to be associated with Realism, a defining feature of which (many might say) is the belief that a Kantian culture, of any degree of internalization, can never emerge in an anarchy. This kind of thinking underlies the diagonal thinking in figure 4, which would make the bad things in international life the province of materialist theories and the good things the province of idealist ones. Throughout this book I have argued that this is a problematic assumption. Whatever Realists might think about the likelihood of a Kantian culture, the materialist social theory on which

---

[146] Risse-Kappen (1996); cf. Kupchan and Kupchan (1991), Duffield (1992).

they characteristically rely should be as applicable to such a culture as to any other. The Kantian culture might be a hard case for materialists in the same way that the Hobbesian is for idealists, but it is not an impossible one.

Part of the Kantian culture, the pluralistic security community, is fairly easy to explain by material coercion, the argument being a simple extension of that used to explain compliance with the Lockean culture. In the latter states are prevented against their will from killing each other; now they are prevented from even attacking. This might be due to deterrence and/or sanctions by status quo states against revisionists (where these terms are now defined by acceptance not only of others' sovereignty, but of their right to be free from violence), but before such measures are even necessary revisionist states could be prevented from attacking simply by the expected costs of war. Economic interdependence, the fragility of modern civilization, and especially the spread of nuclear weapons could make even limited warfare irrational. This in turn suggests an interesting rationale for managed nuclear proliferation.[147]

Collective security poses a more serious challenge for a coercion theory. Here coercion has to explain not only non-violence but cooperation, and, moreover, do so in a way that distinguishes it from alliance behavior. If only a few states in a collective security system are reluctant cooperators then this might not be too difficult, since the majority could force them into burden sharing through a variety of formal and informal sanctions. But this leaves the cooperation of the majority, and with them the existence of the system, unexplained. To explain their cooperation in coercive, non-alliance terms we need factors that threaten them as a group rather than individually, and that are not seen as temporary. Two candidates might be the fear of planetary devastation due to environmental collapse or nuclear war.[148] Both would create functional imperatives for states to cooperate against their will on issues of national security.

It is easier, though ultimately still difficult, to explain compliance with the Kantian culture if it has been internalized to the Second Degree, which means that states follow its norms for reasons of individual self-interest. The principal difference from the First Degree case is that here states do not have a desire to violate the rules (i.e.

---

[147] See Mearsheimer (1990a), Waltz (1990).
[148] Weigert (1991), Deudney (1993).

their interests are not revisionist, even if they might engage in revisionist behavior), and thus they do not need to be coerced into complying against their will. However, unlike the Third Degree case they have no particular desire to follow the rules either; their behavior reflects a purely instrumental calculation about whether compliance will advance exogenous interests, rather than an interest one way or another in the rules as such.

The self-interest explanation for pluralistic security community is again an extension of that used to explain compliance with Lockean norms. The costs of violating the norm still figure in states' calculations, but rather than thwarting an interest in aggression they are now viewed indifferently as simply part of the incentive structure for different behaviors. Collective security is harder to explain with this account, since whereas non-violence might be a "dilemma of common aversions," mutual aid is a "dilemma of common interests"[149] and as such subject to the collective action problem. Inis Claude's classic critique of collective security highlights the difficulty of making such a system work when states are self-interested.[150] Nevertheless, one of the important contributions of Neoliberal scholarship has been to show that in certain conditions – low discount rates on future utility, small number of actors, the presence of institutions that lower uncertainty and transaction costs, and so on – egoistic states can overcome collective action problems. Most of this literature has focused on political economy, but some has addressed collective security.[151]

Rather than try to summarize this rich and extensive body of work, let me just note its implications for what I am calling friendship between states. When collective security norms are internalized only to the Second Degree, friendship is a *strategy*, an instrumentality, that states choose in order to obtain benefits for themselves as individuals. There is no identification of Self with Other, no equating national interests with international interests,[152] no sacrifice for the group except as necessary to realize their own, exogenous interests; all this is disallowed by a non-tautological definition of self-interest. At this degree of internalization, in other words, states have an impoverished conception of "friendship," one that most individuals might think

---

[149] Stein (1983).   [150] Claude (1962: 152–204).

[151] See, for example, Keohane (1984), Lipson (1984), Oye, ed. (1986), Martin (1992), and Downs, ed. (1994).

[152] Claude (1962: 199).

hardly worth the name. Yet they behave "as if" they were friends, coming to each other's aid when their security is threatened, and doing so with the shared expectation that this pattern will continue indefinitely. For egoistic states friendship might be nothing more than a hat that they try on each morning for their own reasons, one that they will take off as soon as the costs outweigh the benefits, but until that happens they will be friends in fact even if not in principle.

That said, few cultures will be stable in the long run if their members are engaged in an on-going calculation about whether compliance serves their individual interests. Given the relatively demanding obligations of friendship, this provides reason to doubt whether a Second Degree Kantian culture could ever consolidate at the international level. However, just as there is a lot more collective action in domestic life than the pure self-interest model leads us to expect, so it may be possible for states to mitigate their collective action problems by internalizing Kantian norms to a deeper level.

With the Third Degree of internalization states in the Kantian culture accept the claims it makes on their behavior as legitimate. As I am interpreting the concept of legitimacy, this means that states identify with each other, seeing each other's security not just as instrumentally related to their own, but as literally being their own. The cognitive boundaries of the Self are extended to include the Other; Self and Other form a single "cognitive region."[153] In chapter 5 I used the concept of collective identity to describe this phenomenon, but there are many cognates in the literature which would serve equally well: "we-feeling," "solidarity," "plural subject," "common in-group identity," "thinking like a team," "loyalty,"[154] and so on. All refer to a shared, super-ordinate identity that overlays and has legitimate claims on separate bodily identities. This identity creates collective interests, which means that not only are actors' choices interdependent, which is true even of egoists in game theory, but so are their interests.[155] International interests are now part of the national interest, not just interests that states have to advance in order to advance their separate national interests; friendship is a preference over an outcome, not just a preference over a strategy.[156] And this in turn helps generate other-help or altruistic behavior, which many

---

[153] Adler (1997a).
[154] See, respectively, Deutsch, *et al.* (1957), Markovsky and Chaffee (1995), Gilbert (1989), Gaertner, *et al.* (1993), Sugden (1993), Oldenquist (1982).
[155] Hochman and Nitzan (1985). [156] Powell (1994: 318).

students of social dilemmas have argued is often crucial to explaining the success of collective action in the real world.[157] It is important to note that this does not imply a necessarily zero-sum relationship with helping oneself, as the concepts of "other-help" and "altruism" might suggest, since collective identity is constituted by defining the welfare of the Self to *include* that of the Other, not by serving the Other's welfare to the exclusion of the Self's, which is a rather different thing (martyrdom perhaps). However, collective identity does imply a willingness when necessary to make sacrifices for the Other for his own sake, because he has legitimate claims on the Self. In the context of the Kantian culture, in other words, it implies that states must really be friends, not just act as if they are.

Identification with others is rarely total. Even at the level of individuals, who are by nature group animals, people routinely have both egoistic and collective motivations. This is emphasized in an interesting way by psychoanalytic social theorists, who stress the ambivalent nature of all internalizations because of the fear of "deindividuation," of being swallowed up by the needs of the group.[158] Resistance to internalization makes sense in light of evolutionary theory, since if individuals were predisposed to sacrifice themselves entirely to group needs they would probably not live long enough to reproduce themselves. The pull of egoism is likely to be even stronger for states, who as corporate beings are predisposed to favor the needs of their members over those of outsiders and thus are not inherently group "animals" (chapter 5). In the provision of collective security this tendency is likely to manifest itself in frequent arguments about free riding and burden sharing, which should they remain unresolved may undermine collective identities. Yet none of this vitiates the possibility of such identities, since actors are capable of having multiple group identifications at once. Americans may identify first with the United States, but typically will also identify to varying degrees with their home state, Canada, the West, and even mankind as a whole, which depending on the issue will affect their behavior accordingly. There is no reason to think the same would not be true of states, who may form a collective identity when it comes to physical security, yet be exceedingly individualistic or jealous of their

---

[157] See, for example, Lynn and Oldenquist (1986), Melucci (1989), Dawes, *et al.* (1990), Calhoun (1991), Morris and Mueller, eds. (1992), and Kramer and Goldman (1995).
[158] See Kaye (1991: 101) and Alford (1994: 87–88).

sovereignty when it comes to burden sharing, economic growth, cultural autonomy, or what have you. What social scientists should do is explore the tensions between different levels of group identification, not assume a priori that they do not exist.

Beyond the anarchy problematique?

It may be useful to conclude this discussion by pointing out that the Kantian culture calls into question two core assumptions of the anarchy problematique on which this chapter has been based, namely our traditional understandings of "anarchy" and "state." Waltz treated these terms as a dichotomy, with the state defined as centralized authority ("hierarchy") and anarchy as the absence of hierarchy, which means that the international system would by definition be an anarchy until there is a world government. More recently Helen Milner[159] and others have suggested that anarchy-hierarchy should be seen as a continuum rather than dichotomy, and interest has also emerged in the idea of "governance without government," which highlights ways in which anarchic systems may nonetheless be governed by institutions.[160] These are important conceptual innovations, but noteworthy also in that they do not directly challenge the traditional meanings of "anarchy" and "state." Making anarchy-hierarchy a continuum still assumes that anarchy is overcome to the extent that authority is centralized, and the literature on international governance has not argued that the system is not formally an anarchy.

There is no reason to question traditional understandings of concepts just for its own sake. However, in this case it may be useful because a distinctive feature of the Kantian anarchy is an at least de facto rule of law, which limits what states can legitimately do to advance their interests. Enforcement of these limits is not centralized, which may reduce the surety and swiftness with which violations are punished, but as long as most states have internalized them they will be seen as a legitimate constraint on their actions and enforced collectively. And since legitimate constraint or power is the basis for "authority," this raises the intriguing possibility that what the Kantian culture creates is *de*centralized authority – an "internationalization of political authority" in Ruggie's[161] words – an idea which has not been

---

[159] Milner (1991).   [160] Rosenau and Czempiel, eds. (1992), Young (1994).
[161] Ruggie (1983b).

developed in the literature. A decentralized authority structure does not seem to be an anarchy, if that is taken literally to mean "without rule," nor does it seem to be a state (or on a continuum of stateness, as the European Union arguably is) if that means *centralized* authority. What a Kantian culture based on the rule of law suggests, in other words, is that two dimensions are relevant to the constitution of anarchy/non-anarchy rather than the traditional one, namely the degree of centralization of power *and* the degree of authority enjoyed by the system's norms.[162] These dimensions are logically independent, as suggested even by the textbook definition of the state as a structure of "centralized authority," which if it is not to be redundant implies the possibility also of decentralized authority.

So dominant in contemporary consciousness is the assumption that authority must be centralized that scholars are just beginning to grapple with how decentralized authority might be understood. One possibility is Bull's idea of "neo-Medievalism," which given the problems posed by the concept of the "feudal state" has the advantage of leaving our traditional understanding of "state" intact.[163] Others have tried to rethink the concept of the state, with neo-Marxists opting for the idea of an "international state,"[164] and others for a "post-modern" state.[165] Recent work on constitutionalism in the EU also speaks to this problem,[166] and Arend Lijphart's[167] discussion of "consociationalism" may be relevant as well. I cannot address these possibilities here, but the question of how to think about a world that is becoming "domesticated"[168] but not centralized, about a world "after anarchy,"[169] is one of the most important questions today facing not only students of international politics but of political theory as well.[170]

Conclusion

Let me summarize the main points of the chapter, and then address a concluding question about time and progress.

There is no such thing as a "logic of anarchy" *per se*. The term

---

[162] Nau (1993); cf. Onuf and Klink (1989). [163] Bull (1977: 264–276).
[164] Cox (1987), Picciotto (1991), Wendt (1994), Caporaso (1996).
[165] Sorenson (1997); cf. Ruggie (1993). [166] Bellamy, *et al.*, eds. (1995).
[167] Lijphart (1977), Taylor (1990).
[168] Ashley (1987); see also Hanrieder (1978).
[169] Hurd (1999). [170] See Walker (1993), Held (1995).

"anarchy" itself makes clear why this must be so: it refers to an absence ("with*out* rule"), not a presence; it tells us what there is not, not what there is. It is an empty vessel, without intrinsic meaning. What gives anarchy meaning are the kinds of people who live there and the structure of their relationships. This is true even for Neorealism, which derives its conclusions about anarchy by assuming that the actors are states and therefore armed, that they are necessarily self-interested but not in a bad, inherently aggressive way, and that their interactions are structured mainly by material forces.[171] I have also taken states as my actors, while allowing their interests to vary. Crucially, however, I argued that the most important structures in which states are embedded are made of ideas, not material forces. Ideas determine the meaning and content of power, the strategies by which states pursue their interests, and interests themselves. (Note that this is not to say that ideas are more important than power and interest, but rather that they constitute them; see chapter 3.) Thus, it is not that anarchic systems have no structure or logic, but rather that these are a function of social structures, not anarchy. Anarchy is a nothing, and nothings cannot be structures.

Distributions of ideas are social structures. Some of these ideas are shared and some are not. I focused on the former, which make up the part of social structure known as culture. In this chapter, therefore, the shared ideas or culture of an anarchic system is its structure, although in reality there is more to its social structure than that. I proposed that anarchy can have at least three distinct cultures, Hobbesian, Lockean, and Kantian, which are based on different role relationships, enemy, rival, and friend. These structures and roles are instantiated in states' representations of Self and Other (role identities) and ensuing practices, but it is at the macro-level, relatively autonomous from what states think and do, that they acquire logics and tendencies that persist through time. Cultures are self-fulfilling prophecies that tend to reproduce themselves. Thus, even though defining the structure of the international system as a distribution of ideas calls our attention to the possibility that those ideas, and with them the "logic of anarchy," might change, it is no implication of this model that structural change is easy or even possible in given historical circumstances.

---

[171] As Robert Powell (1994: 315) puts it, "what have often been taken to be the implications of anarchy do not really follow from the assumption of anarchy. Rather, these implications result from other implicit and unarticulated assumptions about the states' strategic environment."

Much depends on how deeply states have internalized their shared culture. This can have three degrees, which generate three pathways by which cultures can be realized, coercion, self-interest, and legitimacy. Cultural forms reproduced primarily by coercion tend to be the least stable, those by legitimacy the most. In IR scholarship today these pathways are associated with competing theories, Neorealism, Neoliberalism, and Idealism? (constructivism), but since it is an empirical question which pathway realizes a given cultural form, all three theories have something to tell us. But it is important to emphasize that the question of how deeply a culture is internalized is unrelated to how conflictual it is. Against the tacit assumption in much of IR that more shared ideas equals more cooperation, I have argued that the concept of culture is analytically neutral between conflict and cooperation. A Hobbesian war of all against all can be as much a cultural form as Kantian collective security. Knowing which of these cultures dominates is the first thing we need to know about a particular anarchic system, and will enable us to make sense in turn of the role that power and interest play within it.

The key question that I have *not* addressed in this chapter is the question of process, of how the structures of international politics are reproduced and transformed by the practices of state (and non-state) agents. The discussion so far has been about structure, not process. I have shown that the structure of anarchy varies with changes in the distribution of ideas, but not how those changes and resulting structures are produced and sustained. I have not yet shown, in other words, that "anarchy is what states make of it." That is what I try to do in the next chapter. By way of transition, I want to end this chapter with a question that arises naturally from the way it was organized, which is whether I mean to suggest that cultures of international politics tend to evolve in a linear direction or progress over time. As figure 4 graphically suggests, this question of cultural "time" has two aspects, vertical and horizontal.[172]

The vertical question is whether with respect to a given culture there is a tendency for actors to internalize it more deeply over time, to move inevitably from First Degree internalization to Third.[173] My view here is a qualified yes. As cultural practices get routinized in the form of habits they get pushed into the shared cognitive background,

---

[172] I want to thank Jennifer Mitzen for first encouraging me to think about this question.
[173] On habit see Camic (1986), Rosenau (1986), and Baldwin (1988).

becoming taken for granted rather than objects of calculation. Other things being equal, therefore, the longer a practice has been in existence the deeper it will be embedded in the individual and collective consciousness. This generalization must be qualified, of course, by the fact that other things are never equal. Apart from exogenous shocks, if a norm comports with an actor's exogenously given needs or wants, for example, then it may be internalized very quickly; if it is at odds with those needs then it may be accepted only slowly. This is why I chose the term "degree" rather than "stage" to describe depths of internalization. Like third degree burns, in the right conditions norms can become internalized almost instantaneously. Although strictly speaking third degree burns have to go through first and second degree stages first, if the heat is high enough it is possible to speed up time and for all practical purposes skip stages. The same is true of socialization.

Perhaps the more provocative question about cultural time in international politics is the horizontal one of whether it is inevitable that anarchies will move from Hobbesian to Lockean to Kantian structures – a rather different "logic of anarchy" than Realists propose – which, on one definition at least, amounts to a question about the inevitability of "progress."[174] Here my feeling is that the answer must be no, but with a twist.

There is nothing in this chapter to suggest that there must be a progressive evolution in the political culture of the international system. The argument has not been "dialectical" in that sense; it has emphasized the fundamentally conservative nature of culture, not its progressivism. To be sure, the high death rate of the Hobbesian culture creates incentives to create a Lockean culture, and the continuing violence of the latter, particularly as the forces of destruction improve in response to its competitive logic, creates incentives in turn to move to a Kantian culture. But there is no historical necessity, no guarantee, that the incentives for progressive change will overcome human weaknesses and the countervailing incentives to maintain the status quo. The passage of time may simply deepen bad norms, not create good ones. Note that this is different from saying, as Realists are wont to do, that progress in international politics is impossible. In fact, it seems obvious that today's international system represents considerable progress over that of 500 or

---

[174] On progress in international relations see Adler and Crawford, eds. (1991).

even 1500 A.D.; progress there has been. The point is rather that it is contingent, not necessary.

The twist, however, is that even if there is no guarantee that cultural time in international politics will move forward, I do think one can argue that it will not move backward, unless there is a big exogenous shock. Once a Lockean culture has been internalized there is little chance of it degenerating into a Hobbesian one, and similarly for a Kantian into a Lockean. The historical trajectory of the franchise in democratic societies provides an instructive analogy. As Robert Goodin[175] points out, there are almost no cases of voting rights being (selectively) taken away after once being granted. The reason – and here I modify Goodin's more rationalistic explanation – is that once people have internalized the privilege of voting they will fight hard to keep it, making regression too costly. This adds to the traditional constraint of path dependency: not only is the future of a system shaped by the path it took in the past, but the option of "turning around" in the chosen path is closed off. A similar argument may apply to states. With each "higher" international culture states acquire *rights* – to sovereignty in the Lockean case, freedom from violence and security assistance in the Kantian – that they will be loathe to give up, whatever new institutions they may create in the future. This process may not survive exogenous shocks, like invasion (the barbarian invasion of Rome), or a revolution in the domestic constitution of member states (the American and French Revolutions). But with respect to its endogenous dynamic, the argument suggests that the history of international politics will be unidirectional: if there are any structural changes, they will be historically progressive. Thus, even if there is no guarantee that the future of the international system wil be better than its past, at least there is reason to think it will not be worse.

[175] Goodin (1992: 95–96).

7 Process and structural change

In chapter 6 I argued that the deep structure of an international system is formed by the shared understandings governing organized violence, which are a key element of its political culture. Three ideal type cultures were discussed, Hobbesian, Lockean, and Kantian, which are based on and constitute different role relationships between states: enemy, rival, and friend. The chapter focused on structure, mirroring the focus on agency in chapter 5. Little was said in either chapter about *process* – about how state agents and systemic cultures are sustained by foreign policy practices, and sometimes transformed. In this chapter I address these questions.

Although this discussion of process comes after my discussions of structure and agency, there is a sense in which it is prior to both. Structures and agents are both effects of what people *do*. Social structures do not exist apart from their instantiation in practices. As structures of a particular kind this is true also of corporate agents, but even individuals are just bodies, not "agents," except in virtue of social practices. Practices are governed by preexisting structures and entered into by preexisting agents, but the possibility of referring to either as "preexisting" presupposes a social process stable enough to constitute them as relatively enduring objects. Agents and structures are themselves processes, in other words, on-going "accomplishments of practice."[1] Ultimately this is the basis for the claim that "anarchy is what states make of it."

The import of this claim nevertheless depends partly on the ease and extent to which agents and structures can be changed. If process invariably *re*produces agents and structures in the same form then it

---

[1] Ashley (1988).

becomes relatively uninteresting: an essential part of the causal story yes, but one that can be safely bracketed for most purposes. This may explain the neglect of process by Neorealists,[2] who by treating the logic of anarchy as a constant are saying that it tightly constrains what states can make of it. I believe this skepticism about process is unwarranted, and an artifact of a materialist theory of structure that makes invisible what actually determines the logic of anarchy, its culture and role structure. Without culture Neorealists are left with a superficial definition of structural change as a change in the distribution of capabilities, which may affect interaction but not the logic of anarchy. This leads to the counter-intuitive conclusion that the end of the Cold War in 1989 was not a structural change, while the collapse of the Soviet Union in 1991 was (from bi- to multi- or unipolarity), despite the fact that Great Power behavior changed dramatically after 1989 but not after 1991. A cultural theory of structure yields the opposite conclusion. From now on when I say "structural change" I will mean "cultural change."

Once understood as a culture it is hard to sustain the argument that the deep structure of international politics has never changed. For much of international history states lived in a Hobbesian culture where the logic of anarchy was kill or be killed. But in the seventeenth century European states founded a Lockean culture where conflict was constrained by the mutual recognition of sovereignty. This culture eventually became global, albeit in part through a Hobbesian process of colonialism. In the late twentieth century I believe the international system is undergoing another structural change, to a Kantian culture of collective security. So far this change is limited mostly to the West, and even there it is still tentative, but a case can be made that change is happening. With each change the international system has achieved a qualitatively higher capacity for collective action, despite its continuing anarchic structure. States periodically have made something new of anarchy.

Constructivist social theory is often associated with the belief that change is easy. This claim might describe certain forms of constructivism,[3] but not the structuralist form I defend here. Like other constructivists I think it is important to show how social facts are constituted by shared ideas because this may reveal new possibilities

---

[2] For exceptions see Buzan, Jones, and Little (1993) and Snyder (1996).
[3] See, for example, Unger (1987).

for change, but I would also emphasize that these facts might not be malleable in some historical circumstances. Indeed, if anything, structural change should be quite difficult. As a self-fulfilling prophecy culture has natural homeostatic tendencies, and the more deeply it is internalized by actors the stronger those tendencies will be. Far from providing prima facie evidence for a constructivist approach, the fact of structural change in international politics actually poses a significant explanatory challenge. How can states make a new culture of anarchy when the structure of the existing one disposes them to reproduce it?

There are at least two ways to approach this question, which reflect different models of "what is going on" in the social process, and specifically of the extent to which the reproduction of agents is implicated within it. One treats agents as exogenous to process, the other treats them as endogenous.

The first I take to be the hard core of the rationalist approach to interaction, exemplified by game theory, which Jeffrey Legro aptly describes as involving an analytical "two-step": first there is an exogenous step of preference formation, and then a step of interaction between given actors, the outcome of which is determined by the expected value or price of different behaviors.[4] For any given level of analysis rationalism characteristically addresses only the second step, and to that extent treats identities and interests as "exogenously given." (I say "characteristically" because there have been interesting attempts to endogenize preferences within a rationalist framework.[5] These attempts implicitly abandon the two-step model and in effect switch to the second, constructivist approach to process.) However, it is important to note here that "exogenously given" does not mean, as some critics of rationalism have taken it to mean, that identities and interests are fixed or constant. Rationalism does not preclude changes of identity and interest, *as long as* this occurs in the first "step," before or outside the interaction being analyzed. A rationalist approach to the international system, for example, is compatible with the Liberal view that purely domestic changes (i.e. exogenous to interaction) can change state identities in ways that in turn change system structure.[6]

---

[4] Legro (1996). The assumptions of this approach are clearly laid out in Stigler and Becker's (1977) classic essay.

[5] See, for example, Elster (1982), Cohen and Axelrod (1984), Raub (1990), Becker (1996), and Clark (1998).

[6] For example, Moravcsik (1997).

What "exogenously given" *does* mean, however, is that identities and interests are not seen as being continuously in process in or sustained by interaction itself. In the analysis of interaction they are constants, not processes or outcomes, even if they change outside interaction. With respect to the purely systemic causes of structural change, therefore, rationalism directs us to treat states as given (usually as egoists), and to focus on how their behavior changes in response to changing prices in the environment.

The second, constructivist approach to process, exemplified I think by symbolic interactionism, assumes that more is "going on" in interaction than the adjustment of behavior to price. The reproduction of agents, of their identities and interests, is also at stake. In interaction states are not only trying to get what they want, but trying to sustain the conceptions of Self and Other which generate those wants. Agents themselves are on-going effects of interaction, both caused and constituted by it. The difficulty of sustaining these effects varies. Some identities are easy to reproduce while others are hard. But even when identities and interests do not change during interaction, on this view their very stability is endogenous to interaction, not exogenous. From the interactionist perspective, therefore, the assumption of exogenously given agents is a reification, an abstracting away from those aspects of the interaction process that create agents' taken-for-grantedness.[7] This reification is sometimes useful, since preferences are sometimes stable and we may not be interested in their origins. But whenever we treat identities and interests as given, we should regard this as a methodological bracketing of the process by which they are produced, and not let it become a tacit ontology. To understand this process we need to show how identities and interests are a continuing outcome of interaction, always in process, not show them only as an input.

What we have, then, are two meta-hypotheses for thinking about structural change in international politics. If different levels of institutionalized collective action are the effects, and measures, of structure, then one hypothesis is that through interaction states with given interests are finding that elusive mix of incentives and sanctions which enables them to cooperate in spite of the free rider problem.[8]

---

[7] See Mead (1934), Hewitt (1976, 1989), McCall and Simmons (1978), and Stryker (1980).

[8] On just how far this starting point can get us, see especially Taylor and Singleton (1993) and Hardin (1995a, b).

The other hypothesis is that through interaction states are creating new interests which make them less vulnerable to the free rider problem in the first place. To give this difference content we need to stipulate what kinds of interests the rationalist model will take as given. Although thin rational choice theory does not require an assumption of egoism or self-interest, in practice it is often thickened that way (chapter 3). This is particularly true in IR where Realism has long held sway, since self-interest is a foundational assumption of Realism. The difference between the two hypotheses can now be seen to concern the givenness of the "Self" in "self-interest." The rationalist model is saying that the boundaries of the Self are not at stake in and therefore do not change in interaction, so that in learning to cooperate states do not come to identify with each other. The constructivist model is saying that the boundaries of the Self are at stake in and therefore may change in interaction, so that in cooperating states can form a collective identity. If that is actually "what is going on" then the rationalist hypothesis – and in this case also Realism – will predict too little change, understate its robustness, and misdescribe how it occurs. These are the conclusions of a growing number of studies outside of IR,[9] but within IR the mainstream practice is generally to assume the truth of the rationalist model and not address its rivals.[10] Since the rationalist model is well developed, in this chapter I focus on clarifying an interactionist alternative, with a view toward subsequent comparison.[11]

The chapter is organized into three main parts. Drawing on interactionist social theory, in the first section I develop a general, evolutionary model of identity formation, showing how identities are produced and reproduced in the social process.[12] In the next section I argue that structural change in international politics involves collective identity formation. Putting these two sections together, I then advance a simple causal theory of collective identity formation under anarchy, containing four "master" variables that can be realized in multiple ways in real world international systems: interdependence, common fate, homogenization, and self-restraint.

Finally, it should be noted that the argument of the chapter assumes

---

[9] See, for example, Melucci (1989), Calhoun (1991), Howard (1991), Morris and Mueller, eds. (1992), and Kramer, *et al.* (1995).

[10] Though see Harsanyi (1969) and Keohane (1984: 109–132).

[11] Also see Barnett (1998), who draws on Goffman (1969).

[12] Kowert and Legro (1996: 469) argue that constructivists currently lack such a theory.

that states are purposive actors to which we can legitimately apply the anthropomorphic concepts of social theory like identity, interest, and intentionality. For a defense of this assumption I refer the reader to chapter 5.

Two logics of identity formation

All structural theories presuppose a theory of the social process that underlies structure. Although he does not refer to it as such, Waltz's theory is found in *Theory of International Politics* (pp. 74–77), where he discusses two mechanisms by which "structure affects behavior," competition and socialization. Competition affects behavior by rewarding those who produce goods efficiently and punishing those who do not, and socialization does so by rewarding and punishing for conformity to social norms.

Waltz's theory of process is not well developed, and seems ambiguous as between the rationalist and constructivist accounts sketched above. His use of the Darwinian idea of natural selection to describe the effects of competition suggests a construction argument, since types of units rather than just behavior are at stake in selection, and his interest in socialization, a staple of sociological discourse, points in the same direction. However, there are also important respects in which Waltz does not see states as constructed. In contrast to a thick view of socialization that would treat norms as affecting identities and interests, like rationalists he offers a thin one which treats them as only affecting behavior. His treatment of competition is similarly ambivalent. Waltz assumes that states are "self-regarding" before they start interacting (p. 91), which means that egoistic identities exist *prior* to natural selection, and he also notes that states today have a very low death rate (p. 95), which means there cannot be much selection of units going on in the first place (see below). Notwithstanding his avowed structuralism the dominant metaphors in Waltz's book are economic rather than sociological, and in economics it is characteristic to treat agents as given in the social process rather than as its effects.

Some of the ambiguity in Waltz's account could perhaps be cleared up by simply distinguishing more explicitly between the behavioral and construction effects of process. In this section I attempt to do that by building an interactionist model of the social process that focuses on how identities and interests are constructed – as a "dependent variable" – and relating this to its more behavioral, game-theoretic cousin. However, the real problem in Waltz's theory of process is the materialist ontology of structure on which it is predicated, which by suppressing the social dimension of structure makes it difficult to see socialization as having anything but behavioral effects (chapter 3, pp. 101–102). The idealist ontology of structure that I sketched in earlier chapters at least admits the possibility of construction effects and as such is a prerequisite for a more full-bodied, constructivist approach to socialization. Thus, although this section and chapter are concerned primarily with the debate between constructivists and rationalists about agency and structure (the y-axis in figure 1), the debate between materialists and idealists (the x-axis) figures as an important backdrop.

An "evolutionary" approach provides a useful over-arching frame for integrating these two issues. To count as evolutionary a theory must meet three criteria.[13] (1) It must explain the movement of a variable over time. Here this is state identities regarding security (enemy, rival, friend), and so the unit of change is a trait, rather than a species on the one hand or behavior on the other. In contrast to Hendrik Spruyt's impressive study of the transition to a state-centric world from one populated also by city-states and leagues (different "species"),[14] the fact that states dominate the contemporary world system is not at issue in my account. Since identities and interests are cognitive phenomena I am talking about what Emanuel Adler has called "cognitive evolution," within a single species.[15] (2) It must specify a means for generating variation in the dependent variable, and a mechanism for winnowing the effects of that variation on the population. In nature variation comes from genetic mutation; here it comes from unit-level changes in the structure of state-society relations and from the strategic choices of foreign policy decision-makers. The nature of the winnowing process is my main focus below. (3) Finally, it must incorporate inertial tendencies that stabilize these changes in the population. Here this is provided by states' commitments to their identities, reinforced by institutional structures at the domestic and international level.

The core of any evolutionary model is the process by which variations generated at the unit-level (changes in state identity and interest) are winnowed at the macro- or population-level (the inter-

---

[13] See Nelson (1995: 54) and Florini (1996: 369).   [14] Spruyt (1994).

[15] Adler (1991).

national system). In nature there is only one winnowing mechanism: natural selection. In society a second family of mechanisms exists and is usually much more powerful: cultural selection. Natural and cultural selection form two causal pathways through which identities may evolve, the "two logics" in the title of this section. (Notice that the logics are materialist and idealist, *not* rationalist and constructivist.) The differences between them parallel those between Waltz's competition and socialization, but the terminology of natural and cultural selection avoids some problematic connotations of Waltz's language,[16] and also enables us to exploit the debate in sociobiology about their relative importance, which ultimately concerns the role of ideas and material forces in social evolution.[17] Like Neorealists, orthodox "Darwinians" are materialists who minimize the role of ideas by arguing that cultural forms must be adaptive in a genetic sense. And like Institutionalists, heterodox "Lamarckians" are idealists who highlight the importance of ideas by pointing to the variability of cultural forms under similar material conditions. Most Lamarckians do not deny a role for natural selection, and so favor a "dual inheritance" or "co-evolutionary" model of social evolution (genetic and cultural) rather than a complete cultural reductionism,[18] but it is a model in which cultural selection does most of the explanatory work. The "ideas *almost* all the way down" position taken in chapter 3 is of this kind. Social scientists are overwhelmingly Lamarckian in their outlook (Neorealists excepted), including many who have developed evolutionary models of their subjects.[19]

The discussion that follows is organized around the distinction between natural and cultural selection (and thus materialist versus idealist approaches to process), but once having dealt with natural selection relatively quickly I will concentrate on articulating a constructivist approach to cultural selection and its relationship to rationalism, with particular attention to the mechanism of social learning. To illustrate the discussion I use as an example the evolution

---

[16] Specifically, the connotation that natural selection ("competition") is conflictual and cultural selection ("socialization") cooperative. In my view both kinds of selection can be conflictual, and both cooperative.

[17] See, for example, Campbell (1975), Boyd and Richerson (1985), and Wilson and Sober (1994); for applications to economics see Hirshleifer (1978) and Witt (1991).

[18] On the co-evolutionary model see especially Boyd and Richerson (1985).

[19] Notably Nelson and Winter (1982) and Spruyt (1994). "Organizational ecology" represents a more Darwinian approach to social evolution; see Hannan and Freeman (1989) and Singh and Lumsden (1990).

of the egoistic, competitive ideas about Self and Other that constitute the identity of enemy. This will go part way toward answering Mearsheimer's question about why international systems historically have been prone to Hobbesianism,[20] and set the stage for the discussion in the following sections about how states have escaped such a world.

Natural selection

Natural selection occurs when organisms that are relatively poorly adapted to the competition for scarce resources in an environment fail to reproduce and are replaced by the better adapted. The metaphor of a "survival of the fittest" is often used to describe this process, but it can be misleading insofar as it suggests that the strong kill off the weak. Natural selection is not about a war of all against all, but about differential reproductive success. This can be used to explain the evolution of species (states vs. city-states) or of traits (identities and interests) within a species, but the mechanism is the same, the reproductive success of organisms. Traits are selected through the fates of the organisms who carry them, not through the selection of traits as such. Moreover, as Waltz points out in his discussion of competition, natural selection does not require cognition, rationality, or intentionality, and to that extent it is a material process that operates behind the backs of actors.[21] Learning and socialization are not part of it, since characteristics acquired during an organism's lifetime cannot be reproduced by its genes.

Sociobiologists traditionally have argued that natural selection favors egoists on the grounds that they will defeat altruists in the competition for scarce resources. On this view – which some sociobiologists are now challenging (see below) – human evolution "should have produced *homo economicus.*"[22] A parallel story can be told about the evolution of egoistic states, but to do so we need to take care to avoid two problems.

One is the common Realist assumption that states are by definition, by their intrinsic constitution, self-interested. Waltz reveals the problem when he says (p. 91) that states are self-regarding at the *start* of their interaction, *before* they form states systems. If this were

---

[20] Mearsheimer (1994/5: 10).   [21] Waltz (1979: 76–77).
[22] Boyd and Richerson (1980: 101); cf. Witt (1991).

true then we could not use natural selection in the international system to explain their egoism, since it is not something that can vary independently of being a state. States being egoists by definition is like people having 42 chromosomes, which as a constitutive, exogenously given feature of being human cannot be selected for in human relationships. Natural selection may favor the evolution of egoists, but we can only see this if we conceptualize the relationship between egoism and its hosts as contingent rather than necessary. This makes added sense if we recall that self-interest is not a function of simply trying to meet one's needs (and thus part of human nature), but of doing so in a particular *way*, by treating the Other instrumentally (chapter 5, p. 240). This means that self-interest is not an intrinsic property of actors, like being six feet tall, but a relational one constituted by a particular identity toward an Other. One cannot be an egoist all by oneself. The most that could be a constitutive feature of the state, therefore, is a predisposition to adopt egoistic identities, not those identities as such.

This relates to a second problem, which has emerged recently with the growing interest in IR in social identity theory.[23] The experimental findings supporting this theory strongly suggest that states may indeed have a predisposition to be self-interested, since the members of human groups almost always show favoritism toward each other in dealing with the members of out-groups. This is an important finding that clearly bears on an evolutionary explanation for Hobbesian anarchies. However, it does not in itself explain such an outcome, since a tendency toward in-group bias is not the same thing as a tendency toward inter-group aggression,[24] the latter being a key feature of Hobbesian cultures, nor does it preclude competing groups from forming a "common in-group" or collective identity.[25] Even if social identity theory is true it does not follow that anarchies will necessarily have self-help cultures.

That said, social identity theory does give us reason to think that, all other things being equal, in the beginning of an anarchic system natural selection is more likely to produce a self-help than other-help culture, which will then become a self-sustaining logic. When states first form states systems they do so in a context free of institutional constraints. This does not force them to be self-interested, but given

---

[23] See especially Mercer (1995). [24] Struch and Schwartz (1989).
[25] Gaertner, *et al.* (1993).

the natural tendency toward in-group favoritism, in such a world any states which, because of domestic "genetic" variation, happen to adopt aggressive, egoistic identities will tend to prosper at the expense of those which do not. The result over time is "one bad apple spoils the barrel": in a pre-institutional anarchy the population of identities and interests will be dragged down to the level of the most self-interested actors, because there is "nothing to prevent it."[26] That something like this may have occurred in international history is supported by Robert Carneiro's estimate that in 1000 B.C. there were 600,000 independent political units in the world, and today there are only about 200.[27] A lot of states obviously failed to reproduce, and an inability to play power politics as well as others probably had something to do with it. As a materialist argument, I take this to be the explanation for the evolution of egoism and Hobbesian culture which is most consistent with Realism, and it seems a good one. Cultural selection may also play a role, but in a world without shared ideas the material logic of natural selection is likely to be powerful, and once it has locked in a culture deviant states will be under pressure to conform.

While natural selection may help explain the emergence of Hobbesian identities 3,000 years ago, however, it is of only marginal relevance to explaining state identities today. The problem, as Timothy McKeown has pointed out,[28] is that because natural selection operates via reproductive success, in order for it to work survival must be difficult, which for modern states it manifestly is not. When survival is difficult there is a tight coupling between changes in the environment and the fates of different kinds of units, such that the unfit get replaced. When survival is easy changes in the environment have little effect on reproductive success, enabling inefficient and unfit actors to survive. Since the advent of the Westphalian system in 1648 the death rate for its members has fallen dramatically, despite continuing warfare and inequalities of power. Small Powers have thrived and Great Powers like Germany and Japan that seemed to "commit suicide" have been "reincarnated." In one of the few instances since World War II when one state was in danger of losing its "life" to another, the aggressor (Iraq) was overwhelmed by a coalition of states from all over the globe, most of whom had no egoistic stake in Kuwait.

Realists might explain this ease of survival in terms of the material

---

[26] Waltz (1959: 188).   [27] Carneiro (1978: 213).   [28] McKeown (1986: 53).

fact that states are harder to "kill" than individuals. That seems partly right. But it does not explain the survival of weak states in an anarchy of the strong or of defeated states in an anarchy of the victorious, nor does it explain why the survival rate of modern states differs from that of pre-modern. As I argued in chapter 6, it seems more likely that the low death rate of modern states is due to the institution of sovereignty, in which states recognize each other as having rights to life, liberty, and property, and as a result limit their own aggression. As sociobiologists have pointed out, institutions often have the effect of protecting the weak from the strong, which attenuates the relevance of natural selection to social life and creates a basic difference between "natural economy" and "political economy."[29] Whatever the explanation, however, in contemporary international politics there seems to be a great deal of "slack," or, conversely, little "selection pressure,"[30] in the relationship between competition and state survival. If this slack continues, and there is every reason to think it will (both the Realist and Institutionalist explanations for state survival are likely to remain operative), natural selection will not be an important factor in the evolution of state identities in the future. Whatever might explain such changes, it will not be because egoistic states were driven to extinction by a failure to adapt.

Cultural selection

Cultural selection is an evolutionary mechanism involving "the transmission of the determinants of behavior from individual to individual, and thus from generation to generation, by social learning, imitation or some other similar process."[31] I take this to be equivalent to what sociologists (and Waltz) call "socialization." Rather than working behind the backs of actors through reproductive failure, cultural selection works directly through their capacities for cognition, rationality, and intentionality.[32]

I shall examine two mechanisms of cultural selection, imitation and social learning. These can be used in rationalist fashion to explain behavior given identities and interests, or in constructivist fashion to explain identities and interests themselves. In that way the concept of

---

[29] Hirshleifer (1978).   [30] Witt (1985: 382).   [31] Boyd and Richerson (1980: 102).
[32] On the differences between this and natural selection in the case of foreign policy see Levy (1994: 298–300).

cultural selection or socialization raises, in a way that natural selection does not, the question of whether a rationalist or constructivist approach is best, but it does not prejudge the answer. What divides the two approaches is how deep the effects of imitation and learning are thought to go, or how deeply social norms get internalized, which is an empirical question, not that they involve cultural selection. Since the rationalist approach is well known I will focus on articulating a constructivist one, with particular reference to learning.

Imitation

Identities and interests are acquired by imitation when actors adopt the self-understandings of those whom they perceive as "successful," and as such imitation tends to make populations more homogeneous. Although perhaps difficult to distinguish in practice, intuitively there seem to be at least two kinds of success: "material" success is a function of acquiring power or wealth, while "status" success is a function of prestige.[33] The former can be a source of the latter, but there also seem to be forms of prestige that are unrelated to material success – being a good husband, a good role model, a good teacher, and so on. The differences between these kinds of success would be worth exploring further, but of more interest to me here is that both presuppose standards of measurement, and no matter how natural these might seem to people in a given time and place, standards are in fact always constituted by shared understandings that vary by cultural context. In American society today it is difficult to define material success in terms other than making lots of money, yet in medieval Europe it was often more important to live a virtuous and God-fearing life, and those who made money were seen as crude and venal. In international politics we usually define material success as having and using power, yet the standards for what counts as power and its legitimate use have varied widely. There was once a day when conquering other states was considered glorious and virtuous; today such behavior is constitutive of "pariahs" and "rogues." Within a culture standards of success may be objective social facts over which actors have little control, but that does not make such facts natural.

Although natural selection seems to provide a compelling explanation in theory for the evolution of Hobbesian anarchies, imitation may actually play a more important role in practice because it can have

---

[33] Florini (1996: 375).

much faster effects on a population. Whereas natural selection can change a population's characteristics only over many generations, imitation can do so as quickly as an idea's success can be demonstrated, certainly within the span of a single generation. Thus, with respect to material success, seeing the fate of altruists in anarchy at the hands of egoists, states not yet in danger of extinction might decide that the only way to survive is to fight fire with fire and adopt realpolitik identities themselves. And on the status side, once Hobbesian norms have become dominant the idea may take hold collectively that success in war is a matter not only of life and death but of prestige and virtue, creating a reason beyond its survival value for states to imitate those who embody the standard. Because neither depends on reproductive success, both ideas could take over a new anarchic system very quickly once Hobbesian identities have gotten a foothold. The result is a "Realist" outcome [*sic*], but one generated by a mechanism quite unlike the natural selection dynamic emphasized by Darwinians, namely a Lamarckian process in which the sharing of ideas is central. Once a Hobbesian culture has been internalized in a population, in turn, the speed with which imitation could change that population may slow considerably, since new ideas now have to overcome entrenched older ones, but imitation is likely to remain a much faster mechanism of evolution than natural selection. Support for this suggestion is found in the work of John Meyer and his colleagues, who have documented a rapid and increasing homogenization of state forms in the late twentieth century in the absence of material incentives linked to reproductive success.[34] This finding speaks most directly to the debate between materialists (Darwinians) and idealists (Lamarckians) in IR, but insofar as the homogenization concerns not just behavior but also identities then it bears on the issue between rationalists and constructivists as well.[35]

Social learning

Social learning is a second mechanism of cultural selection, and the one of primary interest to me here. As with imitation the depth of its effects can vary. Rationalist models often lack a dynamic element, but when they do incorporate learning they generally emphasize its

---

[34] For example, Meyer (1980), Thomas, *et al.* (1987), Boli and Thomas (1997), and Meyer, *et al.* (1997); a similar point is made within organizational theory by Dobbins (1994: 137).

[35] See Finnemore (1996b) for a good overview.

behavioral effects, treating identities and interests as constant and focusing on how the acquisition of new information about the environment enables actors to realize their interests more effectively. Learning sometimes goes no deeper than these behavioral effects ("simple" learning), but constructivist approaches highlight the possibility that learning may also have construction effects on identities and interests ("complex" learning).[36] Although there have been interesting attempts to explore this possibility within a game-theoretic approach to interaction,[37] game theory was not designed for this task and so its relevant conceptual repertoire is relatively underdeveloped. In contrast, the symbolic interactionist tradition rooted in the work of George Herbert Mead has a rich framework for thinking about how identities and interests are learned in social interaction. In what follows I use an interactionist framework, and specifically "identity theory" (an attempt to translate interactionism into testable propositions),[38] to construct a simple model of complex learning, with the evolution of egoistic identities again as an example.[39]

To summarize up front: the basic idea is that identities and their corresponding interests are learned and then reinforced in response to how actors are treated by significant Others. This is known as the principle of "reflected appraisals" or "mirroring" because it hypothesizes that actors come to see themselves as a reflection of how they think Others see or "appraise" them, in the "mirror" of Others' representations of the Self. If the Other treats the Self as though she were an enemy, then by the principle of reflected appraisals she is likely to internalize that belief in her own role identity *vis-à-vis* the Other. Not all Others are equally significant, however, and so power and dependency relations play an important role in the story.

---

[36] The distinction between simple and complex learning is from Nye (1987). Haas (1990) captures the same difference in distinguishing "adaptation" and "learning."

[37] See the citations in note 5 above.

[38] Identity theory was first articulated as such by Sheldon Stryker (1980, 1987, 1991); see also McCall and Simmons (1978), Burke (1991), and Howard and Callero, eds. (1991). Note that "identity theory" is not the same thing as "social identity theory"; for a comparison of the two theories – from the standpoint of the latter – see Hogg, *et al.* (1995).

[39] More so than with natural selection and imitation, there are important doubts about the applicability of learning theory to corporate beings like states (e.g., Levy, 1994). This question has been addressed by students of organizational learning; for a sampling of opinion see Argyris and Schon (1978), Levitt and March (1988), and Dodgson (1993).

A useful way to begin unpacking this summary is to divide the problem into two issues, what actors bring with them to interaction, and how they learn identities once they get there. To simplify I assume two actors, Ego and Alter (an interactionist convention), meeting in a First Encounter, a world without shared ideas. While unrealistic for most applications, the latter assumption will help highlight the crucial role played in identity formation by how actors treat each other, and also to show that part of what is "going on" in the production and reproduction of culture is the production and reproduction of identities. The base model can be readily extended to situations in which culture already exists.

Ego and Alter are not blank slates, and what they bring to their interaction will affect its evolution. They bring two kinds of baggage, material in the form of bodies and associated needs, and representational in the form of some a priori ideas about who they are. The materiality of individuals' bodies is a function of biology, while that of states' "bodies" is a function of shared ideas supervening on biology. But the effect is the same: exogenously given, self-organizing facts – personal and corporate identities – that act upon and resist the world. These identities have reproduction requirements or basic needs that actors must satisfy if they are to survive. In chapter 3 I stipulated the needs of people as physical and ontological security, self-esteem, sociation, and transcendence, and in chapter 5 I gave the needs of states as physical security, autonomy, economic well-being, and collective self-esteem. None of these needs is inherently egoistic, but actors will resist learning identities that conflict with them and to that extent they impose a material constraint on identity-formation processes. At the same time, however, basic needs are also relatively uninteresting for our purposes here because they are the same for all members of a given species, and therefore predict no variation in identities and interests. If we want to explain why some learning creates egoistic identities and other learning creates collective ones, we need to look beyond basic needs to actors' representational baggage.

By assumption Alter and Ego do not share representations, but they are still likely to bring with them to their Encounter preconceived ideas about who they are that assign tentative roles and form the starting point for their interaction. Those ideas were no doubt formed in social interaction with other actors prior to the Encounter, but they are exogenous here. However, roles are internally related, so that by assigning one to the Self an actor at least implicitly assigns one to the Other. For analytical purposes we can distinguish two aspects of this process, "role-taking" and "altercasting."[40] Role-taking involves choosing from among the available representations of the Self who one will be, and thus what interests one intends to pursue, in an interaction. In a First Encounter actors have considerable freedom in choosing how to represent themselves (as conqueror, explorer, trader, proselytizer, civilizer, and so on), whereas in most real life situations role-taking is significantly constrained by preexisting shared under-standings (when I step in front of a classroom I could in theory take the role of opera singer, but that would be costly). However, it is an important feature of the interactionist model that even in the latter case role-taking is seen at some level as a *choice*, of a "Me" by the "I," no matter how unreflective that choice might be in practice.[41] In this voluntarist aspect symbolic interactionism converges with recent rationalist scholarship on identity formation, which also emphasizes the volitional character of the process.[42]

By taking a particular role identity Ego is at the same time "casting" Alter in a corresponding counter-role that makes Ego's identity mean-ingful. One cannot be a trader without someone to trade with, a proselytizer without a convert, or a conqueror without a conquest. In situations where knowledge is shared, representations of Alter will often correspond to how Alter represents himself, allowing interaction to proceed relatively smoothly. When I go into the classroom I represent those in front of me as "students," and since they generally share this view of themselves we can get on with the class. In a First Encounter such a congruence of representations is less likely to occur, and so the potential for conflict is higher.

On the basis of their representations of Self and Other, Alter and Ego each construct a "definition of the situation."[43] The accuracy of these definitions is not important in explaining action (though it is in explaining outcomes). It is a core tenet of interactionism that people

---

[40] On the former see Turner (1956) and Schwalbe (1988), and on the latter Weinstein and Deutschberger (1963). While both concepts have their origins in symbolic interac-tionism, I believe that much the same ideas are conveyed by structuralist concepts like "interpellating" and "positioning." On these latter see Althusser (1971), Doty (1996), and Weldes (1999).

[41] See Mead (1934), Franks and Gecas (1992), and Rosenthal (1992).

[42] See, for example, Hardin (1995a), Fearon (1997), and Laitin (1998).

[43] See Mead (1934), Stebbins (1967), and Perinbanayagam (1974). The concepts of "frame" and "problem representation" get at a similar idea.

act toward objects, including other actors, on the basis of the meaning those objects have for them,[44] and these meanings stem from how situations are understood. "If men define situations as real, they are real in their consequences." Normally situation descriptions are embedded in culture and therefore shared. When I enter the checkout line at the grocery store the cashier and I will probably both define the situation in similar ways. In a First Encounter this generally will not be the case. The resulting uncertainty may affect behavior, particularly by inducing caution about physical security, as Realists would emphasize, but the only way for actors to accomplish their goals is to try to bring their respective understandings into line, to communicate. Having looked at what actors bring to interaction from the outside, this brings us to the second question of what happens to their identities and interests once they get there.

A social act might be broken down into four scenes. Scene One: based on its a priori definition of the situation Ego engages in some action. This constitutes a signal to Alter about the role that Ego wants to take in the interaction and the corresponding role into which it wants to cast Alter. Ego is trying to "teach" its definition of the situation to Alter.[45] Scene Two: Alter ponders the meaning of Ego's action. Many interpretations are possible because there are no shared understandings and behavior does not speak for itself. Alter's interpretation is guided by its own, a priori definition of the situation, as well as by whatever information was contained in Ego's signal that cannot be assimilated to that definition. Dissonant information embodies the reality constraint that Ego poses for Alter. Alter could ignore this information, but that could be costly depending on power relationships. If Alter revises his ideas because of Ego's action then learning (simple or complex) has occurred. Let us assume Alter learned something. Scene Three: based on his new definition of the situation, Alter engages in an action of his own. As with Ego, this constitutes a signal about the role that Alter wants to take and the corresponding role into which it wants to cast Ego. Scene Four: Ego interprets Alter's action and prepares his response. As with Alter, this interpretation reflects prior situation descriptions and any learning in response to dissonant information. Assuming that one has not killed

---

[44] Blumer (1969: 2).

[45] On teaching as an important element in interaction see Finnemore (1996a: 12–13, 64–65).

the other, Alter and Ego will now repeat this social act until one or both decide that the interaction is over. In so doing they will get to know each other, changing a distribution of knowledge that was initially only privately held (a mere social structure) into one that is at least partly shared (a culture).

Power relations play a crucial role in determining the direction in which this evolution unfolds. In order for an interaction to succeed, in the sense that actors bring their beliefs enough into line that they can play the same game, each side tries to get the other to see things its way. They do so by rewarding behaviors that support their definition of the situation, and punishing those that do not. Power is the basis for such rewards and punishments, although what counts as power depends on definitions of the situation.[46] If Ego wants to interact with Alter on the basis of trader identities, the fact that it has nuclear weapons may be of little value in bringing this about. Given its context-specificity, however, having more power means Ego can induce Alter to change its definition of the situation more in light of Ego's than vice-versa. In this light, then, as Karl Deutsch put it, power can be seen as "the ability to afford not to learn."[47] This ability will vary from case to case and dyad to dyad. Not all Others are "significant" Others. But where there is an imbalance of relevant material capability social acts will tend to evolve in the direction favored by the more powerful.

The underlying logic here is the self-fulfilling prophecy: by treating the Other as if he is supposed to respond a certain way Alter and Ego will eventually learn shared ideas that generate those responses, and then by taking those ideas as their starting point they will tend to reproduce them in subsequent interactions. Identities and interests are not only learned in interaction, in other words, but *sustained* by it. The mass of relatively stable interactions known as "society" depends on the success of such self-fulfilling prophecies in everyday life.[48] Although he does not distinguish between the behavioral and construction effects of interaction, this idea is nicely captured by what Morton Deutsch calls "the crude law of social relations": "[t]he characteristic processes and effects elicited by any given type of social relation tend also to induce that type of social relation,"[49] to which we

---

[46] Baldwin (1979).   [47] Deutsch (1966: 111).
[48] See Krishna (1971), Kukla (1994), and chapter 4, pp. 184–189.
[49] Deutsch (1983: 7).

might add "mediated by power relations." From the "Crude Law" can be drawn the conclusion that the most important thing in social life is how actors represent Self and Other. These representations are the starting point for interaction, and the medium by which they determine who they are, what they want, and how they should behave. Society, in short, is "what people make of it," and as corporate "people" this should be no less true of states in anarchical society.

Which brings us to the question of how states might learn the egoistic conceptions of security that underpin Hobbesian cultures. We have already shown how states might become egoists through natural selection and imitation. They might also do so through learning. The key is how Alter and Ego represent themselves in the beginning of their encounter, since this will determine the logic of the ensuing interaction. *If* Ego casts Alter in the role of an object to be manipulated for the gratification of his own needs (or, equivalently, takes the role of egoist for himself), then he will engage in behavior that does not take Alter's security needs into account in anything but a purely instrumental sense. If Alter correctly reads Ego's "perspective" he will "reflect" Ego's "appraisal" back on himself, and conclude that he has no standing or rights in this relationship. This will threaten Alter's basic needs, and as such rather than simply accept this positioning Alter will adopt an egoistic identity himself (egoism being a response to the belief that others will not meet one's needs), and act accordingly toward Ego. Eventually, by repeatedly engaging in practices that ignore each other's needs, or practices of power politics, Alter and Ego will create and internalize the shared knowledge that they are enemies, locking in a Hobbesian structure. The self-fulfilling prophecy here, in other words, is "Realism" [sic] itself.[50] If states start out thinking like "Realists" then that is what they will teach each other to be, and the kind of anarchy they will make.

In this narrative there are at least two things "going on" that game theorists and interactionists would agree on. The first is that actors revise their definitions of the situation based on new information, that they learn. Whether this updating process is Bayesian, as often assumed by game theorists, or hampered by cognitive or psychological constraints does not matter here; what matters is that both approaches are compatible with learning of some sort. The second

---

[50] See Wendt (1992), Vasquez (1993), Alker (1996: 184–206). For a more general model of the effects of conflict strategies on images of the Other see Kaplowitz (1984, 1990).

point of agreement is that part of what is being produced in this learning process is an ability to see oneself from the standpoint of the Other. Interactionists call this "taking the perspective" of the Other, and for game theorists it is essential to the "I know that you know that I know . . ." regress that constitutes common knowledge. Given that in IR shared knowledge is often associated with cooperation and friendship, it is important to note that this is not the same thing as "empathy." Perspective-taking is about being able to anticipate others' reactions to the Self, which requires an ability to see the Self through their eyes. Empathy is about experiencing the Other's feelings and welfare as if they were one's own, about identifying with him, which is different. In some cases perspective-taking may lead to empathy, but in others it may not. Saying that the emergence of shared knowledge is associated with the emergence of a capacity for perspective-taking says nothing about the nature of that knowledge. Enemies perspective-take just as much as friends.

It is important to emphasize areas of overlap between the rationalist and constructivist approaches to interaction because there is a tendency for proponents of each to assume either that they face a zero-sum situation in which only one side can be right, or that they are simply talking about different things, such as "strategic" versus "communicative" action. My approach is instead to try to reconcile the two approaches as capturing different aspects of a single kind of interaction, with game theory being subsumed – I will argue – as an instance or special case of interactionism. Recognizing that game theory can accommodate learning and perspective-taking is essential to such a synthesis.

However, it is equally important to recognize the differences between the two accounts of what is going on in interaction, and in particular about how deep the effects of interaction go in constructing the Self. Two differences are apparent, one causal and one constitutive.

The causal difference concerns the question of stasis and change in identities and interests. The characteristic rationalist assumption, usually made a priori, is that learning and perspective-taking do not change who actors are or what they want, just their ability to achieve their wants in a given social context (simple learning). The interactionist assumption is that learning and perspective-taking may also change identities and interests (complex learning). This is where the concepts of "reflected appraisals" and "mirroring" come in. Over time, as Alter and Ego mutually adjust to the representations of Self and Other conveyed in each other's actions, their ideas about who they are and what they want will come to reflect the appraisals of the Other, at first perhaps for instrumental reasons, but increasingly internalized. In some cases, or over certain time spans, there might be no such change of identity and interest, in which case a game-theoretic model will be useful. But in the interactionist view whether or not such changes have occurred is an empirical question that needs to be investigated, not assumed away a priori. By asking for such an investigation, moreover, interactionism leads to a different view even of those cases where interaction does *not* change identities and interests. Unlike the rationalist model's assumption that who agents are is not at stake in interaction, interactionism emphasizes that even when the ideas that constitute identities and interests are not changing, they are being continually *reinforced* in interaction. The reproduction of seemingly "given" agents, of stasis in conceptions of Self and Other, in other words, is itself an on-going effect of interaction.

This relates to the other difference between the two approaches, which concerns the constitutive effects of coming to share representations of Self and Other. Rationalist approaches to these representations focus on actors' beliefs about what kind of other actors are involved in an interaction, on actors' "types." Ego perceives Alter as a "proselytizer," for example, and thus also believes, through perspective-taking, that Alter perceives Ego as a potential "convert." This makes sense as far as it goes, but implicit in this way of thinking is a tacit essentialist assumption that what the object of perception is, and this includes the identity of the Self as an object of the Other's perception, does not depend on perceptions. Representations are treated as passive with respect to the constitution of their objects, not active. They are "about" independently existing phenomena, not "productive" of those phenomena. The problem facing rational actors, therefore, is making sure that they perceive other actors, and other actors' perceptions of them, *correctly*. This is similar to how beliefs are handled in the literature on misperception in foreign policy, which is often seen as antithetical to rationalism.[51] Here too the objects of perception are treated as existing independently of the

---

[51] See, for example, Jervis (1976, 1988), Stein (1982), and Little and Smith, eds. (1988); cf. Wagner (1992).

representations of others, and the problem is therefore how to explain, and help actors avoid, mistakes in perceiving what things really are. We might call this a "sociology of error" approach to representations.

In the constructivist view there is more going on in the learning of shared ideas than this. Constructivism emphasizes that Ego's ideas about Alter, right or wrong, are not merely passive perceptions of something that exists independent of Ego, but actively and on-goingly *constitutive* of Alter's role vis-à-vis Ego. Through her representational practices Ego is saying to Alter, "you *are* an X (trader; convert; conquest), I expect you to act like an X, and I will act toward you as if you were an X." To that extent who Alter is, in this interaction, depends on who Ego *thinks* Alter is. The same is true for Ego's own role identity vis-à-vis Alter, which is a function of Ego's beliefs about Alter's beliefs about Ego. Role-identities are the meanings that actors attribute to themselves when seeing themselves as an object, that is, from the perspective of the Other. When Ego takes the perspective of Alter in an attempt to anticipate Alter's behavior, therefore, she is constituting or positioning herself in a particular way. To that extent who Ego is, in this interaction, is not independent of who Ego thinks Alter thinks Ego is. Now, these self-understandings are in one sense inside Ego's own head, but they only become meaningful in virtue of Alter confirming them, which is to say in virtue of social relations (chapter 4, pp. 173–178). Smith can stipulate her identity as "the President" any time she likes, but unless others share this idea she cannot *be* the President, and her ideas about herself will be meaningless.[52] What this means is that in initially forming shared ideas about Self and Other through a learning process, and then in subsequently reinforcing those ideas causally through repeated interaction, Ego and Alter are at each stage jointly defining who each of them is. This joint constitution of identity is ultimately difficult to reconcile with the methodological individualism that underlies both rational choice theory and the misperceptions literature, which holds that thought, and thus identity, is ontologically prior to society.

---

[52] For discussion of how actors deal with conflicts between their own expectations of Self and the expectations they believe others hold for them see Troyer and Younts (1997).

Summary

In this section I used mostly symbolic interactionist ideas to develop a constructivist model of the social process, with special reference to the evolution of identities and interests. The model engaged both materialist and rationalist alternatives. Whereas materialists tend to privilege natural selection as the dominant logic of identity formation, I privileged cultural selection. Natural selection may be more fundamental at some level, since cultural selection must ultimately be adaptive for organisms' reproduction, a principle which I think also holds for states. However, the key insight of the Lamarckian, "dual inheritance" approach is that even if this is true cultural selection may still explain most of the variance in cultural forms, and create the parameters within which natural selection operates. Whether this is true for the egoistic state identities that have so often been a feature of international history I do not know, but I gave some reasons for thinking that both natural and cultural selection mechanisms could have been at work in their evolution. Within the framework of cultural selection, in turn, I sketched a simple model of how identities are formed by imitation and social learning, with special reference to the latter. What distinguishes this model from its rationalist counterpart is a different conception of what is going on or at stake when actors interact, namely the production and reproduction of identities and interests versus strategic choices on the basis of given identities and interests. The two models are not mutually exclusive, at least not if the rationalist model is taken to be a special case of the constructivist, but they do call attention to different aspects of the social process.

Collective identity and structural change

If structures are always in process then a theory of structural change must explain why their instantiating processes change. In the beginning of this chapter I identified two approaches to this task. The rationalist strategy treats identities and interests as exogenously given and constant, and focuses on the factors shaping actors' expectations about each other's behavior. Structural change occurs when the relative expected utility of normative vs. deviant behavior changes. The constructivist strategy treats identities and interests as endogenous to interaction and thus a dependent variable in process. Structural change occurs when actors redefine who they are and what they want. The strategies are not mutually exclusive, but they are different, with different ideas about what is going on in structural change and what causes it to happen.

From a constructivist perspective the mark of a fully internalized culture is that actors identify with it, have made it, the generalized Other, part of their understanding of Self. This identification, this sense of being part of a group or "we," is a social or collective identity that gives actors an interest in the preservation of their culture. Collective interests mean that actors make the welfare of the group an end in itself, which will in turn help them overcome the collective action problems that beset egoists. When their culture is threatened well-socialized actors will tend instinctively to defend it. Actors are still rational, but the unit on the basis of which they calculate utility and rational action is the group.

This picture departs considerably from the self-interest model of social life – which in eschewing group sentiment altogether is actually quite an extreme model – but it is important to emphasize the limits of collective identity. One is that collective identities are relationship specific. The fact that Germany identifies with France's security says nothing about its attitude toward Brazil. Second, the scope and behavioral implications of a collective identity depend on the purposes for which it is constituted, and are in that sense issue- or threat-specific. In Lockean culture states identify with each other's survival, so that "death threats" to one are seen as threats to all, but this does not extend to identification with each other's security more generally because in many respects it is still a self-help culture. In the Kantian culture the scope of identification is broader and as such should generate collective action in response to any military threat, not just death threats. Third, even within a relationship and issue covered by a collective identity, it will often be in tension with egoistic identities. Total identification, to the point of sacrificing one's basic needs for the Other, is rare. Individuals want to meet their basic needs, which compete to varying degrees with the needs of groups, and this predisposes them to worry about being engulfed by the latter. The same is true of groups relative to other groups. Identification is usually ambivalent, involving an on-going tension between desires for individuation and assimilation.[53] In all three respects, the fact that

---

[53] For different perspectives see Brewer (1991), Kaye (1991: 101), Wartenberg (1991), and Levitas (1995).

internalizing a culture involves the formation of a collective identity should not blind us to the possibility that egoistic identities may still be important. The picture here is one of "concentric circles" of identification,[54] in which the nature and effects of collective identity vary from case to case, not one of altruism across the board.

Notwithstanding these limits, the main point I want to make here is that because the structure of any internalized culture is associated with a collective identity, a change in that structure will involve a change in collective identity, involving the breakdown of an old identity and the emergence of a new. Identity change and structural change are not equivalent, since identity formation happens ultimately at the micro-level and structural change happens ultimately at the macro, but the latter supervenes on the former.[55] Given this connection and my concern in this chapter with process, in what follows I shall approach the problem of structural change as a problem of collective identity formation.

The problem is a generic one whose solutions in different contexts will probably have much in common. Whether we are talking about workers, citizens, or states, the constitutive requirement of collective identity formation is the same, namely redefining the boundaries of Self and Other so as to constitute a "common in-group identity" or "we-feeling." Intuitively it seems that there could only be so many ways to do this, or at least that certain factors might be present in many cases. This suggests that studies outside of IR should be relevant to thinking about collective identity formation in international politics,[56] although the fact of anarchy makes the problem uniquely difficult in ways that other fields have not had to consider. Moreover, the generality of the problem also suggests that a model of collective identity formation in anarchy should be relevant to *any* international system. Like many Realists, therefore, I intend my model to be trans-historical and trans-cultural in its applicability.

Nevertheless, for purposes of discussion I shall take a Lockean culture as my starting point and focus on how it might be transformed into a Kantian culture. In effect, I ask how and why might the dominant role in the system can be transformed from that of rival to

---

[54] Lasswell (1972), Linklater (1990).

[55] On supervenience and micro-foundations see chapter 4, pp. 152–157.

[56] See, for example, Tajfel, ed. (1982), Turner, *et al.* (1987), Morris and Mueller, eds. (1992), Gaertner, *et al.* (1993), Brewer and Miller (1996), and Turner and Bourhis (1996).

that of friend. I narrow my focus in this way because this is the problem faced by the international system today. Whether or not international politics has been Hobbesian for most of history, states managed to escape that culture some years ago. The challenge now is to broaden the limited identification of the Lockean culture into the fuller identification of the Kantian culture. Narrowing scope has the additional virtue of permitting a significant economy of presentation. I argued above that identities evolve through two kinds of selection, natural and cultural. Yet once states create a Lockean culture natural selection becomes relatively unimportant because states no longer die out. Today weak, incompetent, and even failed states manage to reproduce themselves without difficulty, because other states recognize their sovereignty. Thus, while there may be a role for natural selection in the evolution of a Kantian culture, I shall not address it here. This will allow me to concentrate on cultural selection, but may also limit the extent to which the model can be applied to the transformation of Hobbesian cultures, where natural selection is more important.

Structural change is difficult. The term "structure" itself makes it clear why this must be so, since it calls attention to patterns or relationships that are relatively stable through time. If things were constantly changing then we could not speak of their being structured at all. In this light the longevity of the Hobbesian culture in international politics is no surprise; like any culture it is a self-fulfilling prophecy that once in place will tend to reproduce itself. This tendency has both "internal" and "external" sources. Internal sources of stability refer to factors within actors that make them not want change. Ultimately this is rooted in the human need for ontological security, which creates a generalized preference for order and predictability, but of more concrete importance is the internalization of roles in identities, which generates subjective commitments to objective positions in society.[57] We can see this at work in the Lockean culture, in which states define their interests by reference to the role of rival because this is "how things are done." As long as feedback from the system stays within an acceptable range relative to their national interests they will be unlikely to question this identity, giving their behavior a "cybernetic" quality instead.[58] External sources of

---

[57] On identity commitment see Foote (1951), Becker (1960), Stryker (1980), and Burke and Reitzes (1991).
[58] See Steinbruner (1974) and Burke (1991).

structural stability are factors in the system that inhibit change even if actors want it. Institutions like sovereignty and the balance of power are one example, which reward certain practices and punish others. But even if some actors succeed in overcoming these incentives at the micro-level, states face the additional external constraint that cultures are macro-level phenomena which become unstable only when enough important actors change their behavior that a tipping point is crossed. It is not enough for Germany and France to transcend rivalry; other Great Powers must as well before the structure of the system as a whole will turn. For both internal and external reasons, therefore, cultures have an intrinsically conservative quality which ensures that structural change will be the exception, not the rule.

Structural change is also path dependent. Collective identity formation in international politics takes place not on a tabula rasa but against a cultural background in which the dominant response to changes in the environment has been egoistic, whether in the extreme form of enmity or the milder form of rivalry. The path from the "here" of self-help to the "there" of collective security must tap into and transform that disposition. This is not inevitable. Egoism is deeply entrenched in international life, so much so that the idea of states becoming "friends" can easily seem naive. Even if the pressure to become friends is strong, as I think it increasingly is, egoistic identity commitments might not give way. The evolution of identities is a dialectic of actual and possible selves,[59] and there are no guarantees that the weight of the past will be overcome.

Yet it remains the case that identities are always in process, always contested, always an accomplishment of practice. Sometimes their reproduction is relatively unproblematic because contestation is low, in which case taking them as given may be analytically useful. But in doing so we should not forget that what we take to be given is in fact a *process* that has simply been sufficiently stabilized by internal and external structures that it *appears* given. A methodology should not become a tacit ontology. This is particularly important to remember in considering the evolution of collective identities, since their egoistic counterparts are themselves only sustained by practices. States may be very committed to egoistic identities, and the cultures that constitute them may be quite resilient, but this does not change the fact that they are continuously in process. When states engage in

---

[59] Markus and Nurius (1986).

egoistic foreign policies, therefore, more is going on than simply an attempt to realize given selfish ends. They are also instantiating and reproducing a particular conception of who they are.

In thinking about the evolution of collective identities I have already set natural selection aside, which is not very important in a world where states no longer die out. I now want to also set aside the cultural selection mechanism of imitation. This is not because of any presumed unimportance. Indeed, one of the important patterns in the contemporary international system, the tendency of many Third World and former communist states to adopt the institutional and ideological attributes of Western states, seems to be largely explained by imitation.[60] However, this tendency presupposes the prior existence of a collective identity to which states are trying to gain membership, in this case "the West" or "modernity," which is what I am trying to explain in the first place. In bracketing imitation I do not mean to discount its importance in the way that I did natural selection, but the following discussion nevertheless concentrates on social learning.

The interactionist model of how identities are learned centers on the mechanism of reflected appraisals. Actors learn to see themselves as a reflection of how they are appraised by significant Others. The key variable here is how the Other treats or "casts" the Self, weighted by power and dependency relations. Identities must still be "taken" by the Self, an issue to which rational choice theory speaks, but the emphasis in interactionism is on the representational practices of the Other that structure the choices of the Self, not on those choices themselves.

The kind of representational practice that produces enemies is known as realpolitik, which involves treating others in self-interested terms, casting them as if they were nothing but objects, without standing or rights, to be killed, conquered, or left alone as one sees fit. At the other end of the spectrum, the kind of representational practice that produces friends might be called "prosocial," which involves treating others as if one not only respected their individual security concerns but also "cared" for them, a willingness to help them even when this serves no narrowly self-interested purpose. In treating Alter in this way Ego is casting Alter in the role of friend, and, given the

---

[60] The work of John Meyer and his colleagues is especially interesting in this regard; see the references in note 34 above.

symmetry of the role, taking the same role for himself. Ego's effort may be misunderstood. Alter may mistake offers of security assistance as a trick. Since the logic of reflected appraisals turns on how actors *think* they are appraised, the potential for noise in the relationship between the role cast by the Other and that taken by the Self is important. But with persistence a prosocial security policy should eventually be able to communicate Ego's desire that Alter be its friend. Of course, Alter might want no such thing and resist Ego's overtures. Just because someone wants to be your friend does not mean you want to be *theirs* – you might simply see them as a sucker. Everything depends, therefore, on how committed Alter is to his previous identity, and on how much power each has. A powerful state engaging in prosocial policies will have more impact on the identities of weak states than vice-versa. But in the end the evolution of social interaction is conditioned less by power than by the purposes to which it is put. Treating an Other prosocially, "as if" he were a friend, reflects the kind of purpose most likely to create collective identities, and as such is ultimately what we need to explain.

It might be objected that this argument is circular because prosocial behavior is not only a cause of collective identity but an *effect*. That is true, but I think the circularity is benign. The "Crude Law of Social Relations" is recursive: by engaging in certain practices agents produce and reproduce the social structures that constitute and regulate those practices and their associated identities. Even though agents and social structures are mutually constitutive and co-deter-mined, the mechanism through which this occurs, the first cause of social life, is what actors *do*. "We are – or become – what we do." Actors can do things even if they do not already have the identities which those practices will eventually create. States might initially engage in prosocial policies for egoistic reasons, for example (and indeed, in a Lockean structure this is exactly what we would expect), but if sustained over time such policies will erode egoistic identities and create collective ones.

In what follows I examine four causal mechanisms or "master variables" that could explain why states in a Lockean world would engage in prosocial security policies and thereby spur collective identity formation. The phrase "master variables" is meant to call attention to the possibility that these mechanisms can be instantiated concretely in different ways. Kant, for example, argued that repub-lican states would create a "Kantian culture". I agree with that claim, but there might be other pathways to the same effect – Islamic states, socialist states, "Asian Way" states, and so on. What I want to leave open, in other words, is the possibility that a Kantian culture is *multiply realizable*. Treating the problem of collective identity formation under anarchy as a problem of social theory rather than just of late twentieth century international politics helps us do that by shifting our attention away from the particular, perhaps currently dominant sufficient conditions emphasized by Kant and Kantians and toward more general, necessary conditions that are not reducible to those particularities. In the event, much of Kant's reasoning about why republicanism would lead to "perpetual peace" is replicated below, but he leaves the social theory underlying his argument implicit and as a result does not help us think about alternative ways of realizing the same effects. I do not know if such alternatives would work in practice, but it is a possibility that should not be foreclosed a priori.

Master variables

The master variables are interdependence, common fate, homogeneity, and self-restraint. There may be others as well, but I shall not address them here. All four have been discussed to varying degrees by IR scholars, but in contemporary IR not often with an eye toward collective identity formation. Earlier work by regional integration theorists like Karl Deutsch, Ernst Haas, and the neofunctionalists are the main exceptions to this generalization and as such what follows might be seen as part of the social theory backdrop to their ideas.[61] Usually the emphasis in IR is on how the variables cause cooperation among egoists, which takes egoistic identities as given. In my view the real significance of these variables is to undermine egoistic identities and help create collective ones.

I take the variables to be of two kinds. The first three (inter-dependence, common fate, and homogeneity) are active or efficient causes of collective identity. The last (self-restraint) is an enabling or permissive cause. All four may be present in a given case, and the more that are present the more likely collective identity formation will occur. But all that is necessary for it to occur is one efficient cause

---

[61] Deutsch (1954), Deutsch, *et al.* (1957), Haas (1964). For an overview of neofunction-alism see Tranholm-Mikkelsen (1991), and for recent extensions of Deutsch's ideas see Adler and Barnett, eds. (1998).

combined with self-restraint. Self-restraint therefore plays a key role in the story, more so than I think has often been recognized. In Liberal IR scholarship self-restraint has emerged as an important cause of the democratic peace, but that involves states merely refraining from a practice (war), not working together. Building on this result, I argue that self-restraint has deeper effects, enabling states to solve the fundamental problem of collective identity formation: overcoming the fear of being engulfed by the Other.

Interdependence

Actors are interdependent when the outcome of an interaction for each depends on the choices of the others. Although interdependence is often used to explain cooperation, it is not confined to cooperative relationships; enemies can be as interdependent as friends. In order to cause collective identity, interdependence must be objective rather than subjective, since once a collective identity exists actors will experience each other's gains and losses as their own, as "inter-dependent," by definition. The relationship between subjective inter-dependence and collective identity is constitutive rather than causal. The problem is changing objective into subjective interdependence, what Kelley and Thibaut call the "given" pay-off matrix into the "effective" one, the latter being a "psychological transformation" that represents objective interdependence as one of subjective, collective identity.[62] What I want to explore is how and why such a trans-formation may come about.

Keohane and Nye distinguish two aspects of interdependence, "sensitivity" and "vulnerability."[63] Sensitivity measures the degree to which changes in one actor's circumstances affect other actors, which captures the extent to which outcomes for individual actors are jointly controlled.[64] Vulnerability measures the costs an actor would incur from ending a relationship. When either is highly asymmetric we speak of dependence not interdependence. Sensitivity seems closer to the core meaning of interdependence, but vulnerability is a key factor in how states will respond. Vulnerable states are more likely to accept high levels of sensitivity than invulnerable ones. Interdependence is a matter of degree, depending on the "dynamic density" of interactions

---

[62] Kelley and Thibaut (1978: 16–20); also see Kramer, *et al.* (1995: 365–366).
[63] Keohane and Nye (1989: 12–16, passim).   [64] Kroll (1993: 331).

in a context; higher density implies greater interdependence.[65] But interdependence is also issue-specific and not always fungible, which means that increases in one issue area, like the economy, might not spill over into other areas like security.

Interdependence has received extensive attention in IR scholarship, especially among Liberals.[66] Most of this scholarship has focused in rationalist fashion on the consequences of interdependence for behavior; less has focused on its identity effects.[67] The behavioral approach is nicely illustrated by Robert Axelrod's now classic study of the "evolution of cooperation" in an iterated Prisoner's Dilemma game.[68] Using a computer tournament, Axelrod showed how interdependence can be exploited over time by a reciprocal, Tit-for-Tat strategy to generate stable cooperation despite the incentives to defect (and indeed, he showed that such a strategy would dominate all others). Increases in interdependence should reinforce this effect.

The force of this conclusion depends on its assumptions. Axelrod assumed that actors value the future today and expect to continue interacting. Realists argue that both assumptions are problematic in anarchy, and that Axelrod also assumes, implicitly, that actors seek absolute rather than relative gains, which is equally a problem. These objections have generated much useful discussion.[69] But I am more interested here in two other, less often discussed assumptions that give the model a "behavioral" cast. One is that communication is non-verbal. The "actors" in his tournament are strategies, not people, and as such they cannot talk or negotiate their way to cooperative outcomes. The other assumption is that actors do not engage in complex learning. Axelrod recognizes that people may internalize new definitions of their interests, but this is not his main narrative, which assumes continued egoism and simple learning. These two assumptions constitute a "hard case" and as such give his model greater generality; it can explain cooperation among pigeons as much as people. If actors can learn to cooperate without talking or changing

---

[65] On density of interactions as a factor in international relations see Ruggie (1983a), Buzan, Jones, and Little (1993), and Barkdull (1995); cf. Durkheim (1933/1984: 200–225).

[66] In addition to Keohane and Nye (1989) see, for example, Baldwin (1980), Stein (1989), and Kroll (1993).

[67] On the latter see Lasswell (1972), Crawford (1991), and Ruggie (1993).

[68] Axelrod (1984).

[69] See Grieco (1990), Powell (1991), Snidal (1991), and Baldwin, ed. (1993).

their interests, then the potential for cooperation is probably even greater when these assumptions are relaxed. By the same token, however, these assumptions may underestimate prospects for cooperation in the real world, and/or misrepresent how and why it occurs.

A constructivist approach would relax these assumptions.[70] Let me start with the second, which concerns the effect of cooperative behavior on egoistic identities. As emphasized above, egoistic identities are not intrinsic, exogenously given features of human agency but social terms of individuality that need to be constantly reproduced through practice. When people choose to "defect" in a social dilemma they are simultaneously choosing to reproduce the egoistic identities that constitute that dilemma. And conversely for prosocial behavior: by choosing to cooperate in a social dilemma Ego implicitly takes a collective identity, acting "as if" he cares for Alter, even if this is initially for selfish reasons, and signals to Alter, "I expect you to do the same in return" (altercasting). If Alter reciprocates then Ego's tentative new identity will be reinforced, leading to further cooperation and, over time, an internalization of collective identity on both sides. On the "we are what we do" theory of social interaction, in other words, by acting as if it had a new identity and teaching the Other what it must do to help sustain that identity, each actor erodes his previous identity and learns to see himself in the mirror of the Other, changing his conception of who he is. This is complex learning, the creation not just of regulative norms for given identities but of constitutive norms for new identities. To the extent that complex learning is going on in interaction, interdependence will have deeper effects than Axelrod's narrative would suggest.

The other assumption of the narrative that I want to relax is that all communication is non-verbal. In the real world most human communication takes place discursively. Since this is one of the most important things that distinguishes us from other animals, it seems unnecessary – notwithstanding the virtues of the hard case – to limit our theories about why people cooperate to theories that can also explain why pigeons cooperate. Unlike pigeons human beings can grasp interdependence symbolically, and on that basis engage in "ideological labor" – talk, discussion, education, myth-making, and so on – to create a shared representation of the interdependence and the "we" that it constitutes, before anyone has made any behavioral

---

[70] An earlier version of this argument appears in Wendt (1994).

decisions at all.[71] This assumes that someone had the bright idea of portraying the situation as one of interdependence in the first place, for which there is no guarantee, but if leadership is present and a discourse begins about what "we" should do, a collective can form much more quickly than through non-verbal communication, leading to "swift trust."[72] Indeed, unlike non-verbal communication, where trust that others will not exploit one's collective role-taking can emerge only after a long period of cooperative behavior, in a discursive process trust can to some extent be forged beforehand, "generat[ing] the very behaviour which might logically seem to be its precondition."[73] This has been called "elicitative" trust, since actors elicit cooperation from others by communicating that it is *expected*.[74] Reflected appraisals are driving this process, since part of what is involved in the discursive constitution of a We is representing Self and Other in ways that will generate prosocial behaviors that will reinforce the collective role each identity takes. By the same token, however, if in a discursive process actors represent each other in conflictual or competitive terms then no such identity will emerge. This is the logic of the self-fulfilling prophecy: if people form a shared representation of themselves and the world, then it becomes that way for them.

Reflected appraisals have deeper and faster effects on identities as dependency rises, which means that the transformation of interdependence into collective identity will be affected by the density of interaction. One consequence of this, well known from rationalist work on collective action, is that it becomes more difficult to form a collective as the number of actors rises, since rising numbers are generally associated with thinner relationships.[75] This will be particularly true for non-verbal communication, since as actors multiply it becomes harder to engage in the targeted reinforcement crucial to the success of Tit-for-Tat, but even discursive effects will be weakened if relationships are thin. Since interdependence varies across dyads, this puts a premium on what happens where it is highest, in what Deutsch, *et al.* called "core areas," around which concentric circles of

---

[71] The phrase "ideological labor" is due to Stuart Hall (1986). On the implications of ideological labor for collective action and identity see Ellingson (1995), Fearon (1998), and with reference to IR, Haas, ed. (1992), Shore (1996), and Mitzen (2000). On the coercive potentials of talk see Bially (1998).

[72] Meyerson, *et al.* (1995).   [73] Gambetta (1988: 234).

[74] Kramer, *et al.* (1995: 374).   [75] Ibid.: (358, 364).

identification might then develop.[76] In the security issue area these might be called "primary" security dilemmas like France–Germany and India–Pakistan. As pairs of "significant" Others go, in turn, so go prospects for collective identity in the system as a whole. Indeed, even if ties to peripheral actors are thin, if core actors can form collective identities this may have demonstration effects that lead to imitation of the core, exploiting what Mark Granovetter has called "the strength of weak ties."[77]

Realist critics of the thesis that interdependence promotes cooperation have pursued two main tracks, arguing either that the degree of interdependence in international politics is low or relatively constant,[78] or that even if it is high or increasing it will not bring states together. Since the former is an empirical issue that does not challenge the logic of the theory, let me conclude this discussion by focusing on the latter.

The objection is that the ability of interdependence to induce cooperation and collective identity formation is constrained by a fear of exploitation. As interdependence increases actors become more vulnerable to each other and thus have more objective reason for insecurity. This might not be a crippling problem in domestic politics where security is guaranteed by the state, but in a self-help system actors can count only on themselves, and as such must be particularly concerned to minimize threats to their autonomy.[79] At the limit this means assuming the worst about others lest trusting them gets you stabbed in the back, but even states who think in terms of probabilities rather than worst-case possibilities will tend to discount the long-term benefits of cooperation, minimize their dependency on others, and worry about relative gains – all of which make it difficult to engage in the prosocial practices necessary to forge collective identities.[80]

Fear of exploitation is a genuine concern in anarchy, and is why interdependence is not a sufficient condition for collective identity formation among states. States will cooperate only if they can overcome this fear, which interdependence alone does not ensure. Yet in fact they do overcome it: if fear of exploitation were a decisive

---

[76] Deutsch, *et al.* (1957).   [77] Granovetter (1973).

[78] Waltz (1979: 120–160), Thomson and Krasner (1989).

[79] "Resource dependence" theorists have argued that all organizations, not just states, seek to minimize their dependency on each other (e.g., Pfeffer and Salancik, 1978). For a constructive critique of this proposition see Oliver (1991).

[80] Grieco (1988).

constraint then modern states would not cooperate nearly as much as they do. I believe this stems in important part from the fact that international politics today has a Lockean rather than Hobbesian culture, which reduces the self-help character of the system (chapter 6, p. 292) and thus the costs of being exploited. Even if their cooperation is exploited states will rarely find their survival at stake. Moreover, this Lockean culture is thoroughly internalized in the community of states, which means that states have little *interest* in exploiting others to the fullest extent possible. States limit their exploitation of each other not because they are forced to or believe it is in their self-interest, but because they want to and other states know this. As we will see below, knowing that other states will restrain *themselves* is a key condition enabling states to realize the positive effects of interdependence.

Common fate

Actors face a common fate when their individual survival, fitness, or welfare depends on what happens to the group as a whole.[81] As with interdependence, this can only cause collective identity if it is an objective condition, since subjective awareness of being "in the same boat" is constitutive of collective identity, not a cause. Having a common fate can sometimes be good, as in the case of individuals who receive money from a class-action lawsuit, but in international politics it is often bad, typically being constituted by an external threat to the group. The threat may be social, like that which Nazi Germany posed to other European states, or material, like the threat of ozone depletion or nuclear war. Because they are easily confused it is important to note that common fate is not the same thing as interdependence.[82] Interdependence means that actors' choices affect each other's outcome, and as such implies interaction. Common fate has no such implication. Even though they did not all interact with each other, Native Americans suffered a common fate at the hands of Europeans, who constituted them as a group by representing them as savages and treating them accordingly. Interdependence stems from the interaction of two parties; common fate is constituted by a third party which defines the first two as a group.

Common fate arguments are common in IR, especially among

---

[81] Sterelny (1995: 171); also see Campbell (1958).   [82] Turner and Bourhis (1996: 38).

Realists, who use them to explain alliances. Perceiving a common threat posed by growing German power in the late nineteenth century, in 1893 France and Russia changed their foreign policy from hostility to alliance. Like rationalists, Realists usually assume that this affects only behavior, not identity. France and Russia remained egoists, and had the common threat receded either might have found it useful to abandon the alliance, as Italy did in 1915 its alliance with Germany. The hypothesis that actors remain egoists in common fate situations may in some cases be borne out, particularly in the early stages of cooperation. But in other cases actors will form collective identities.

How and why might common fate have this effect? An interesting answer has been developed by some sociobiologists, which bears a look given their unimpeachable credentials as "Realists" about human nature. Sociobiologists have long sought to explain altruism, the fact of which in nature and society they correctly see as a challenge to their model of individuals as inherently selfish. Like Axelrod's model, the traditional sociobiological explanation focuses on specific reciprocity (an interdependence argument), which pre-serves classical evolutionary theory's emphasis on the gene or individual as the unit of selection.[83] More recently, however, others have argued that selection may work on various "levels" or "vehi-cles," constituted by the common fate of their elements.[84] "Group selection" theory hypothesizes that in inter-group competition groups of altruists will have an evolutionary advantage over groups of egoists because the former can more easily generate collective action and need to devote fewer resources to policing their members. Humans have always competed in groups, and it makes sense that we would have evolved psychological mechanisms that permit "team play" for this purpose.[85]

One might think that Realists in IR would have little difficulty accepting the notion of hierarchical selection, since they too are interested in selection at the level of the group (the state), which affects individuals through their common fate as its subjects. Social identity theory, for example, with which Mercer tries to justify the Realist assumption of group egoism and self-help, proposes that

[83] See Trivers (1971).
[84] For example, Wilson (1989), Hodgson (1991), Wilson and Sober (1994), Sterelny (1995).
[85] Wilson and Sober (1994: 601); cf. Sugden (1993).

individuals' identities *within* groups are collective rather than egoistic.[86] Collective identification among states is simply one more level of group organization to which selection processes might be applied. Despite the intuitive appeal of group selection theory, however, when applied to states it runs afoul of the dominant assumption in IR that states are inherently selfish. Realists and rationalists alike overwhelmingly assume that states will shirk collective responsibilities whenever they can, so that groups will only form if they offer selective incentives to their members, or if "principals" invest substantial resources in policing "agents."[87] These models have become quite sophisticated, but their premise – that states are always egoistic – is on any nontrivial definition of self-interest demonstrably false. We can try to avoid this problem by assuming that states act "as if" they are always egoistic, on the grounds that this is a hard case, but if the point is to explain how and why they *really do* form collectives this move is unsatisfying. In real life states cooperate much more than they have to, and group selection by common fate seems to help explain this fact.

There is a problem here, however: the fact that altruism is beneficial for a group does not explain how its members become altruistic. Common fate is an objective condition, collective identity a subjective one, and there is no guarantee that the one will lead to the other – it could simply lead to a mentality of "every man for himself." This illustrates a general problem about altruism acknowledged by group selection theorists: altruism involves a tension between levels of selection. Even if a group of altruists will do better than a group of egoists in the competition *between* groups, egoists will do better than altruists *within* the group.[88] What we need, therefore, is a mechanism that explains how common fate at the group-level becomes collective identity at the unit-level. Without this we are left with an inadequate functionalist explanation of collective identity. Michael Hechter has criticized earlier group selection theories of solidarity on just these grounds.[89] The Hobbesian solution, which Realists might invoke at this stage to justify their own assumption of collective identity within groups, emphasizes the socializing effects of state power on indi-

---

[86] Mercer (1995).
[87] See Olson (1965), Moe (1984), Hechter (1987); cf. Taylor and Singleton (1993).
[88] Wilson and Sober (1994: 598).
[89] Hechter (1987: 24–25); also see Pettit (1993: 158–163).

viduals' identities.[90] But this solution is not available at the international level.

In thinking about mechanisms other than state power it is useful to return to the discussion above of how behavioral and discursive mechanisms work under interdependence. A behavioral mechanism, defined as non-verbal communication, is likely to be less effective under common fate than under interdependence because the incentives to cooperate are more oblique, stemming indirectly from a third party rather than from the conditions of interaction itself. The difficulty is manifest in the animal kingdom, where common fate is often not sufficient to induce cooperation. If this barrier can be surmounted, however, then non-verbal cooperative behavior, repeated over and over again, will undermine egoistic identities and internalize the cooperative relationship in collective identities. By taking a collective identity on an at least "as if" basis, repeated cooperation leads to habits of thought which motivate actors to cooperate even if the objective source of common fate disappears (NATO after 1991?) – i.e., not just because of the transaction costs of abandoning a cooperative regime, but because they *want* to.

Nevertheless, given the significant hurdles that common fate poses for behavioral approaches to cooperation it is fortunate that human beings rarely communicate through non-verbal behavior alone. In contrast to interdependence, the positive potential of which can be realized with little or no symbolic representation, because common fate is constituted by third parties a symbolic representation of the situation as one of common fate is almost necessary. Sometimes this representation is easy to come by, as in cases where an aggressor threatens the survival of two states simultaneously. Facing extinction, it is natural for the defenders to frame their situation as one of common fate on the principle that "the enemy of my enemy is my friend," and on the basis of that representation to constitute themselves as a We who should work together, even if their own behavior is not otherwise interdependent. In cases where the threat is less acute, however, much more ideological labor may be necessary before actors can represent themselves as having a common fate. One thinks here of the difficulties faced today in getting states to take seriously the threat of global warming, or of Tecumseh's travels in the early nineteenth century throughout the Ohio River Basin trying to con-

---

[90] Hanson (1984).

vince other Native Americans that they faced a common fate at the hands of the whites and should band together as a result. As these examples indicate, in situations that do not have sufficient salience the emergence of perceptions of common fate may depend on "entrepreneurs" and/or "epistemic communities"[91] who take the lead in reframing how actors understand themselves. Such leadership is not always present.

Even when leadership is present, however, common fate is not a sufficient condition for collective identity formation because as with interdependence, actors may fear exploitation by others in the collective, particularly in anarchy. History is replete with examples where distrust or hostility prevented states who faced a common threat from working together, permitting aggressors to divide and rule them. Believing that those with whom one might cooperate will exhibit self-restraint is therefore an important condition for the foregoing logic to take hold.

Homogeneity

A final efficient cause of collective identity formation is homogeneity or alikeness. Organizational actors can be alike in two relevant senses, in their corporate identities and their type identities (chapter 5, pp. 224–227).[92] The first refers to the extent to which they are isomorphic with respect to basic institutional form, function, and causal powers. In their corporate identity the primary actors in contemporary world politics are "like units": states, understood as centralized authority structures with a territorial monopoly on the legitimate use of organized violence. Non-state actors increasingly matter in world politics, but they have tenuous standing in what remains a state-centric, "inter-national," system. The second kind of homogeneity concerns type variation within a given corporate identity. In the case of states the variation is in how their political authority is organized domestically, in their regime type. Along this dimension the units of today's world system are considerably less alike. Democracy and capitalism may be increasingly dominant ways of constituting state

---

[91] See Haas, ed. (1992).
[92] A complicating factor is that common fate can also be seen as a kind of homogeneity, in that actors experience like outcomes; see Turner and Bourhis (1996: 38–39).

authority in the late twentieth century, but they are far from universal. Homogeneity in both senses matters for collective identity formation.

As above it is important to distinguish between objective and subjective issues. The concept of collective identity presupposes that members categorize themselves as being alike along the dimensions that define the group, and as such the perception of homogeneity helps *constitute* collective identity. The *causal* relationship, therefore, must be between "objective" homogeneity and its subjective categorization. (Where objective homogeneity comes from is an important question, with natural selection and imitation probably playing a big role, but I shall not address it here.)[93] The hypothesis would be that increases in objective homogeneity cause actors to recategorize others as being like themselves. Categorizing others as being similar to oneself is not the same thing as identifying with them, but it fosters the latter in two ways.

One, indirect, effect is to reduce the number and severity of conflicts that can otherwise arise from differences of corporate and type identity. The argument here is a second-image one that as Fred Halliday shows goes back at least to Edmund Burke.[94] Many wars stem from the transposition of domestic institutions or values into foreign policies that conflict with the foreign policies of other states *because* they have different institutions or values. Capitalist states have conflicts with socialist ones in part because the former are constituted to seek open markets and the latter to seek closed ones. Conflicts arise between democratic and authoritarian states because their domestic norms of conflict resolution are different. Huntington's "clash of civilizations" thesis also seems to operate on the assumption that heterogeneity breeds conflict. And so on. This is not to dismiss the possibility that states might learn to live peacefully with diversity, nor is it to suggest that like units will have no conflicts. It is only to say that internal differences may be one source of external conflict. Other things being equal, therefore, the reduction of those differences will increase the coincidence of states' interests,[95] and that in turn promotes collective identity formation by reducing the rationale for egoistic identities, which respond to a belief that others will not care for the Self.

[93] See especially Spruyt (1994) and Meyer, *et al.* (1997).
[94] Halliday (1992); cf. Bukovansky (1999a).
[95] Note that coincident interests are not the same thing as collective interests; cf. Keohane (1984: 51–52).

The other effect of homogeneity is more direct. Collective identity presupposes that actors see each other as like themselves along the dimensions that constitute them as a group. The collective identity constituting "France" is a function of people representing each other as sharing the attributes and commitments deemed essential to being "French." The causal theory of knowledge underlying scientific realism suggests that homogenization will help create this representation because over time our theories about the world will be conditioned by its reality (see chapter 2, pp. 57–60). And that growing correspondence of reality and perception will in turn tend to produce prosocial behavior, on the grounds that "if they are just like us then we should treat them accordingly." This has been clearly understood by state elites, who through education, immigration, and language policies have tried to create "imagined communities" of people who share objective attributes and as a result come to see themselves as being alike, and different than the members of other states.[96] A comparable if more decentralized process of homogenization helped create contemporary international society: in order to be seen as a member of this society states had to have a number of domestic attributes that were initially characteristic primarily of European states.[97] To be sure, whether another state has certain attributes is partly in the eye of the beholder and thus subject to debate, as Ido Oren's interesting work on the classification of "democratic" states shows.[98] But the fact that objective reality does not strictly determine our perceptions does not mean there is *no* relationship between the two. In the scientific realist view observation is theory-laden, not theory-*determined*, and objective reality imposes varying degrees of cost on those who would ignore it altogether.

Apart from the potential for slack between objective reality and its subjective representation, homogenization is not a sufficient condition for collective identity formation for two other reasons. First, as actors become alike along some dimensions they may differentiate themselves along other, even trivial, ones in a "narcissism of small differences." This possibility stems from the nature of groups. Groups exist to meet their members' needs, and so if those needs are threatened they will be prone to a defensive response. Usually the

---

[96] Anderson (1983).
[97] See Bull (1977: 22–52), Gong (1984), and Neumann and Welsh (1991: 347–348).
[98] Oren (1995).

threat comes in the form of another group pursuing interests opposed to the interests of the group (in effect, from heterogeneity), but *homo*geneity can also be a threat because the existence of any group as a distinct entity requires a cognitive boundary separating it from other groups ("difference").[99] Homogenization erodes the objective basis for that boundary and thereby calls into question the group's raison d'être. Inventing or problematizing new sources of group differentiation shores up the boundary between the group Self and the Other. This need for difference does not have to lead to aggression or disrespect toward other groups (to "Othering"), and need not block the formation of a collective identity on other issues. But it does weaken the relationship between homogenization and prosocial behavior, even in the Lockean culture where recognition of group individuality is a fundamental norm. This makes the *Other's* response to homogenization crucial, since if it shows self-restraint there is less danger the group Self will feel its identity is threatened.

A second reason why homogenization may fail to produce collective identity is that as actors become more alike there is less potential for a division of labor between them. A division of labor increases the extent to which actors are interdependent and suffer a common fate, both of which we have seen can be causes of collective identity formation. Homogeneous actors lack "natural" functional complementarities and as such will have less incentive to create a sense of community, particularly if they are relatively self-sufficient actors like states. In this light we can see that, while facilitating prosocial behavior by making it easier to see each other as like themselves, the historical process which culminated in the dominance of states over non-state actors in international politics also reduced the need for prosocial behavior, and may even have positively discouraged it by creating units predisposed by nature to resist interdependence and functional specialization. This conclusion needs to be tempered by the fact that homogeneity of identity is at least in principle compatible with differentiation of function, and even facilitates the latter by enabling actors to see themselves as members of the same group within which they can then establish functional differentiation. Nevertheless, states are not intrinsically dependent upon one another in the manner of capitalist and worker or master and slave, and this means

---

[99] Cf. Barth (1969), Tajfel, ed. (1982), and Connolly (1991).

that any division of labor will only be able to emerge after the fact of homogenization.

In sum, there is little theoretical reason to think that a convergence of corporate and even type identities will in itself generate prosocial security policies and thus collective identity. And there is much evidence to the contrary. European monarchies were very homogeneous and fought wars for centuries; only when facing the common threat of domestic revolution did their homogeneity become a basis for collective action in the Concert of Europe.[100] Socialist states fared little better in the absence of Soviet hegemony. Despite a common language, religion, and pan-Arab ideology, Arab states have shown little unity, especially after they consolidated territorial sovereignty.[101] Nevertheless, it would be a mistake to dismiss homogeneity altogether as a cause of collective identity formation, as some skeptics have done.[102] Even if in theory one can imagine a community of infinite diversity, in practice communities require *some* consensus on values and institutions. Other things being equal, homogeneity facilitates that consensus by reducing conflict and increasing the ability to see Self and Other as members of the same group. Other things may not be equal, of course, but that does not vitiate its contribution to our story. It just means that contribution must be understood in relation to other causal mechanisms.

Self-restraint

Interdependence, common fate, and homogeneity are efficient causes of collective identity formation and thus structural change. As they increase actors have more incentive to engage in prosocial behavior, which erodes egoistic boundaries of the Self and expands them to include the Other. This process can only proceed, however, if actors can overcome their fear of being engulfed, physically or psychically, by those with whom they would identify. All actors have basic needs – national interests in the case of states – stemming from the reproduction requirements of their internal constitution, which they must meet to survive. Notwithstanding its potential benefits, identifying with other actors poses a threat to this effort, since it means giving others' needs standing alongside one's own, and the two will often be at least

---

[100] Schroeder (1993).   [101] Barnett (1995, 1998).
[102] For example, Neumann (1996: 166).

partly in conflict. What is best for the group is not always best for the individual. In order to get past this threat, which is the source of egoism and "Realism," actors must trust that their needs will be respected, that their individuality will not be wholly submerged by or sacrificed to the group. Creating this trust is the fundamental problem of collective identity formation, and is particularly difficult in anarchy, where being engulfed can be fatal. The variables discussed so far do not solve this problem, and even intensify it by increasing the temptation to identify with others.

The traditional solution to the problem of trust is external constraint by a third party. In domestic politics this is found in the coercive power of the state. In international politics Great Powers may sometimes play such a role for Small Powers, but hierarchy is not an option overall. However, alternative sources of external constraint can be found in military technology and in security institutions. When defensive technology has a significant (and known) advantage,[103] or when offensive technology is dominant but unuseable, as with nuclear weapons under Mutual Assured Destruction, then states are constrained from going to war and thus, ironically, may be willing to trust each other enough to take on a collective identity. Although Realists have not generally made the latter inference, it follows naturally from arguments about the benefits of a "unit veto" system created through managed nuclear proliferation.[104] Institutions, in turn, are an external constraint when they are internalized only to the first or second "degree" (chapter 6), which is to say that states obey their norms only when they are forced to or calculate that it is in their self-interest. Since we are talking here about collective identity with respect to security, the relevant norms are those of the pluralistic security community – respect for sovereignty and non-violent dispute resolution.[105] The former constrains states from killing each other, the latter from even attacking each other. Neither is a norm of mutual aid, which is what the Kantian culture's collective security system requires,[106] but by

---

[103] Jervis (1978).
[104] On unit veto systems see Kaplan (1957), and on the potential benefits of managed nuclear proliferation Waltz (1990); cf. Deudney (1993).
[105] The creation of norms is relatively more difficult in the security than economic issue area; see Lipson (1984).
[106] As Hechter (1987: 23) points out, mutual aid norms constitute collective identity, not cause it, and as such we cannot invoke them to explain the latter without tautology.

reducing states' fear of exploitation the one set of norms can facilitate the emergence of the other.

Military technology and weakly internalized security regimes may provide functionally equivalent substitutes for the constraining power of Leviathan, assuaging states' concerns about being engulfed and thereby helping them achieve the benefits of a collective identity. But they are an imperfect and temporary solution at best because they do not address the problem of trust directly. As *external* constraints, they do not reassure states that others will refrain from looking for ways to get around the constraints (by investing in technologies designed to break a military stalemate, for example), or that others will not violate a regime's norms if an opportunity to do so presents itself (always a problem in anarchy). With only external constraints, in other words, states must constantly worry that others may at some point "break out" and engulf them, and that makes identification with them difficult, because they cannot be trusted *on their own* to respect the needs of the Self. This problem inhibits collective identity formation even under a Leviathan, which Hobbes understood could not create society through coercion and self-interest alone, and is obviously even more serious in anarchy. It is partly for this reason that Norbert Elias argues that self-control is the essence of civilization.[107] External constraints may play a role in initiating the building of trust, but collective identity implies giving over to the Other at least some responsibility for the care of the Self, and that will generally require something more.

That something more is a belief that the Other will constrain *itself* in the demands it makes on the Self. If actors believe that others have no desire to engulf them, nor would do so out of self-interested opportunism, then it will be easier to trust that in identifying with them their own needs will be respected, even in the absence of external constraints. In the terms introduced earlier, by conveying respect for Alter's *per se* individuality, Ego's self-restraint enables Alter to give up his egoistic *terms* of individuality in favor of identification with Ego. By holding ourselves back, in short, we make it possible for others to step forward and identify with us, enabling us in turn to identify with them. This does not by itself generate collective identity, since without positive incentives to identify self-restraint may simply lead to

---

[107] Elias (1982); for further discussion of Elias' work as it might pertain to IR see Mennell (1989) and van Krieken (1989).

indifference. But given those incentives – provided by the other master variables – self-restraint plays a key role in enabling them to be realized. Perhaps paradoxically, then, we might say that self-restraint is the ultimate basis for collective identity and friendship, that the latter are rooted fundamentally not in acts of cooperation, though these too are essential, but in respecting each other's difference.

The key problem with this logic, as emphasized by Realists, is our inability to read others' minds and thus uncertainty about whether they will in fact restrain themselves in the absence of third party constraints. This problem is especially serious in a self-help system where the costs of a mistaken inference can be fatal. Yet despite our limited telepathic abilities, in point of fact human beings do manage to make correct inferences about each other's – even strangers' – intentions, much, even most, of the time. Society would be impossible if this were not the case. Helping us make such inferences is one of the main things that culture, shared knowledge, is for. Moreover, we manage this feat even when there is no external constraint forcing the subject of our inferences to behave in a certain way. When Bahamian foreign policymakers wake up each morning, they *know* that the United States is not going to conquer them, not because they think the US will be deterred by superior power, nor because they think that on that day the US will calculate that violating the norms of sovereignty is not in its self-interest, but because they know that the US will restrain *itself*. Like all knowledge this belief is not 100 percent certain, but it is reliable enough that we would think it irrational for the Bahamians to act on any other basis. Not all inferences in international politics are this reliable, of course, but that is not the point. The point is that much of the time states do, in fact if not literally, read each other's minds, enabling them to trust that others will of their own accord respect their individuality and needs.

Given the empirical reality that states often know that others will be self-limiting, the question becomes, "how do states acquire this knowledge?" (Note the question is not "how do states become self-limiting?," although that is part of it, but "how do other states know that they are self-limiting?") Three answers suggest themselves.

One possibility is if through repeated compliance states gradually internalize the institution of the pluralistic security community to the third degree. Even if states initially comply with this institution for reasons of coercion or self-interest, continuing adherence over time will tend to produce conceptions of identity and interest which presuppose its legitimacy, making compliance habitual or second nature.[108] External constraints become internal constraints, so that social control is achieved primarily through self-control.[109] Reciprocity is important in this context, since it is through this mechanism that states teach each other that following the rules is worthwhile. This explains only how states become self-limiting, not how they know that others are self-limiting. However, by observing each other's habitual compliance, especially if it is accompanied by foreign policy rhetoric that does not complain about the rules, states gradually learn that others have no desire to break the rules nor are likely to seize opportunities for doing so, and as such can be trusted to respect the needs of the Self.

Creating trust this way is a slow process. It may be the only way if states think that the sole reason why others are complying with norms is out of coercion or self-interest, but this is not always the case. A second pathway, therefore, often identified with Liberal IR theory, is via domestic politics. For reasons of cognitive consistency, habit, and/ or societal pressure, and if the international environment permits, states will tend to externalize or transpose domestic ways of doing things – resolving conflict, organizing economic relationships, obser-ving the rule of law, and so on – in their foreign policy behavior.[110] Many domestic practices are not conducive to self-limitation in foreign policy, but some are, the most well-established case being democracy. Whether the cause lies in its culture or its institutions, it appears to be the case that democratic states are strongly predisposed by their internal constitutional structure to limit the instruments they use in their disputes with each other to peaceful means.[111] Although the evidence is more ambiguous, I believe a similar claim could be made about capitalist states at an advanced or late stage in their development, when significant fractions of capital have become multi-national.[112] As before, this explains only self-limitation and not trust that others are self-limiting. However, given their predispositions

[108] On the role of habit in social life see Camic (1986), Rosenau (1986), Baldwin (1988), and Hodgson (1997).
[109] See Mead (1925), Elias (1982), and Hurd (1999).
[110] See especially Lumsdaine (1993), Rosenberg (1994), and Bukovansky (1999b); on the transposition of norms in social theory see Sewell (1992).
[111] Russett (1993).
[112] On the implications of the internationalization of capital for the state see Murray (1971), Cocks (1980), Duvall and Wendt (1987), Picciotto (1991), and Shaw (1997).

democratic states tend to observe security community norms almost naturally, in effect achieving "instant" third degree internalization without having to go through a long process of reciprocal learning.[113] Whereas in the reciprocal learning pathway the internalization of norms of mutual trust starts from scratch and proceeds "top–down," in the domestic politics pathway the norms are in a sense already internalized, and need only be revealed as such to other states through their foreign policy.

A third pathway to self-restraint may work where the others fail: *self-binding*.[114] Self-binding tries to allay Alter's anxiety about Ego's intentions through unilateral initiatives, with no expectation of specific reciprocity. Since in a self-help system the problem for such an initiative is that it may be seen as self-serving, the challenge is to make one's gestures toward the Other credible by imposing visible sacrifices on oneself. For example, one could unilaterally give up certain technologies (as the Ukraine did with nuclear weapons), or withdraw from occupied lands (as the Soviets did from Eastern Europe and Afghanistan), or institute domestic constitutional constraints on the use of force abroad (as in postwar Germany and Japan), or subordinate one's foreign policy to the collective (as Germany has in important ways done in the EU).[115] Of course, self-sacrificing actions like these only make sense if a state believes it will not be badly damaged as a result, which is precisely the kind of belief hardest to come by in self-help systems (hence the security "dilemma"). Thus, as a precondition for self-binding it may be necessary for a state to revise downward, on its own, its estimate of the threats its faces. As a result of such an examination it might realize that nuclear "sufficiency" is enough to deter aggression rather than parity or superiority, or that Alter is not as hostile as was previously thought, or that his hostility is contingent on Ego's own actions. The last possibility is particularly interesting, since it involves recognizing and then ending one's own contribution to the self-fulfilling prophecy that underlies the security dilemma, which requires a critical look at the "Me" from the standpoint of the "I."[116]

---

[113] The systemic aspects of the democratic peace hypothesis are addressed by Risse-Kappen (1995).

[114] On self-binding see Elster (1979) and Maoz and Felsenthal (1987); cf. Deudney (1995).

[115] Unilateral initiatives also played an important role in the Israeli–Egyptian rapprochement in the late 1970s; see Kelman (1985).

[116] See Frankfurt (1971), Christman (1980), and Rosenthal (1992).

We tend not to expect such reflexivity from states, but an important exception was the effort of Soviet New Thinkers to "take away the Western excuse for being afraid of the Soviet Union" by engaging in unilateral peace initiatives. One might argue that postwar Japanese and especially German foreign policies display a similar self-awareness about the importance of self-restraint.

It will be hard to sustain a strategy of self-binding over the long run if Others never reciprocate, and to that extent its success will eventually depend on the emergence of shared norms of self-restraint. Nevertheless, in thinking about the causes of self-restraint it is important to recognize self-binding as a distinct strategy because in a sense it has fewer preconditions than the others. It is more likely to succeed in conflictual relationships where relative gains seeking rather than positive reciprocity is the rule, in asymmetric relationships where a hegemon has little incentive to reciprocate the actions of small powers, and in the absence of states that are predisposed for internal, domestic reasons toward peace. Like the discursive construction of collective identity under common fate, in other words, self-binding may be able to create trust before the conditions that it is normally thought to require exist.

In sum, self-restraint is not an active cause of collective identity because it says nothing about the willingness to help others. Indeed, by strengthening the principle of "respect for difference" it ironically injects a further reason beyond self-interest for non-intervention in other states' lives, making mutual aid even harder to justify. However, by helping to constitute a security community self-restraint also reduces states' anxieties about being engulfed if they give the Other some responsibility for the care of the Self, enabling the positive incentives provided by the other master variables to work. In the sociobiological terms above, it reduces the tension between levels of selection: by lowering the likelihood of within-group selection against altruists, self-restraint favors the selection of altruists in between-group competition. Self-restraint generates collective identity only in conjunction with the other factors in the model, but its role in that combination is essential.

Discussion

Collective identity formation among states takes place against a cultural background in which egoistic identities and interests are initially dominant, and as such there will be resistance to the process all along the way. This is not unique to international politics. Individuals will resist forming groups if this threatens the fulfillment of their personal needs, and groups will resist forming higher groups if this threatens the fulfillment of group needs. Collective identities are rarely perfect or total. In most situations the best that can be expected is concentric circles of identification, where actors identify to varying degrees with others depending on who they are and what is at stake, while trying to meet their individual needs as well. On the other hand, the fact that states will resist collective identity formation does not mean it can never be created.

Egoistic identities are themselves only sustained by particular kinds of interaction, and the factors adduced in this section will put these under a lot of stress.[117] This stress on egoistic identities has sometimes been so great that states have merged their bodies in a new *corporate* identity (the US in 1789, Germany in 1871; the European Union today?), which is a logical endpoint of the processes described above. But collective identity formation does not depend on transcending anarchy. The fact that France and Germany have become friends has dramatically altered the European landscape, and there have been equally radical identity changes in the Cold War, Middle East, and elsewhere. States will always seek to preserve their individuality, but this does not preclude them from making the *terms* of their individuality more collective.

As an approach to explaining structural change in international politics the discussion in this section is nevertheless incomplete in two important senses. These limits highlight the fact that what I have done is explore only one relatively self-contained module in a larger causal chain, not offered a complete theory of structural change.

One limit is that I did not address the question of how the master variables might be instantiated, i.e., what causes them to go up or down. This silence was useful, since it leaves open the possibility that the variables are multiply realizable, which encourages us not to settle prematurely on liberal democracy as the only pathway to a Kantian culture. But as a result I said relatively little about domestic factors, which are likely to be crucial for any pathway. Capitalist states are more likely to be interdependent than communist ones, democratic states more likely to show self-restraint than fascist ones, and so on.

[117] Burke (1991).

Exploring these considerations would take my argument in a Liberal direction; in important ways my theory of international politics is a Liberal theory. However, it should not be concluded from this that systemic theorizing about international politics can be *reduced* to domestic factors, any more than biology can be reduced to chemistry or chemistry to physics. Wholes are always dependent on their parts, but this relationship will in most cases be one of supervenience, not reduction (chapter 4, pp. 155–156), for various reasons: because the same systemic property (here, master variable) may be multiply realizable at the unit-level; because the extent to which a given unit-level attribute can affect the system depends on its distribution and frequency in the system; and because the interaction of parts often has unintended consequences. Understanding how the master variables are affected by unit-level factors is essential to a complete model of state identity formation in international politics, but understanding how those variables themselves work is a relatively autonomous theoretical problem, and as such a distinct component in that larger model.

The other sense in which the discussion is incomplete as a study of structural change is that it focused entirely on the logic of identity-formation at the micro-level, which does not in itself explain structural change at the *macro*-level. (Unlike Neorealists I have argued that there are also structures at the micro-level, changes in which are linked to identity changes, but these are not at issue here.) To be sure, given that the structure of an internalized culture and the collective identities of its agents are mutually constitutive, a change in the one implies a change in the other. But there is still a gap between cultural change and identity change because cultural change requires not only that identities change, but that their frequency and distribution cross a threshold at which the logic of the structure tips over into a new logic. A Lockean culture with 200 members will not change just because two of its members acquire a Kantian identity, unless perhaps they are also its only superpowers, in which case other states may follow suit. In order to explain structural change, therefore, we have to explain not just individual identity changes but collective or aggregate identity changes, and these are often subject to frequency-dependency effects. "The presence of such effects means that individual changes depend on whether, and with which frequency, the same changes have already occurred in others. This can give rise to typical features of non-linear dynamics – abrupt change and hysteresis."[118] By not addressing the causes of such aggregate effects (imitation and natural selection might play important roles here), I have left a crucial element in the explanation of structural change unspecified. But even though the logic of collective identity formation on which I have focused is not sufficient to explain structural change at the macro-level, it is an essential micro-foundation.

Conclusion

This chapter looked at the process of international politics, complementing the studies of agency and structure in chapters 5 and 6. Looking at process is important because it is only through the interaction of state agents that the structure of the international system is produced, reproduced, and sometimes transformed. The logic of that interaction at a given moment will reflect the characteristics of state agents and the systemic structures in which they are embedded, but the process of interacting adds an irreducible and potentially transformative element which must be studied on its own terms.

I discussed two models of "what's going on" in the social process. They differ about what exactly it *is* that is thought to be in process, and thus about what is at stake when actors interact. What I defined as the rationalist model assumes that what is at stake are behavioral choices only. The identities and interests (properties) of the agents who make these choices are not themselves assumed to be in process, but given. The social process consists of interlocking actions seeking to satisfy identities and interests by adjusting behavior to changing incentives in the environment. The constructivist model assumes that agents themselves are in process when they interact. Their properties rather than just behaviors are at stake. Agents still choose behaviors in response to incentives, and so this model does not preclude the rationalist model, but the assumption is made that more is actually going on in those choices than just the squaring of means to ends: actors are also instantiating and reproducing identities, narratives of who they are, which in turn constitute the interests on the basis of which they make behavioral choices.

Understood in this way, there is no contradiction between ration-

[118] Witt (1991: 568).

alist and constructivist models of the social process. Each concentrates on a different aspect of process, but in the larger scheme of things there is no reason to suppose that both behavior and properties would not vary. To that extent the choice between the two models is primarily an analytical or methodological one, a function of what question we are interested in. This suggests that it would be useful to know the "scope conditions" for when each model's assumptions hold.[119] Rationalist models would be most useful when it is plausible to expect that identities and interests will not change over the course of an interaction, and constructivist models would be most useful when we have reason to think they will change. Since change is more likely the longer our time frame, this suggests a temporal division of labor: rationalism for today and tomorrow, constructivism for the *longue durée*. And it might also suggest that since relative stability of identity and interest seems more nearly the norm, the rationalist model should be used as a "baseline" case against which the constructivist model should be judged. Although one might argue just the opposite on the grounds that we need precisely to problematize identities and interests *first* to know if the scope conditions for rationalist models (i.e. stable identities) hold.

From an analytical standpoint there is much to commend this framing of the relationship between the two models. Each is useful for answering certain questions, and these questions are not mutually exclusive. From an ontological standpoint, however, a large issue remains: either agents are themselves at stake in, or endogenous to, the social process or they are not. If they are endogenous, then even if they are relatively stable for some period of time, allowing us to bracket their construction while pursuing behavioral questions, the fact remains that more will actually be going on in the social process than just making behavioral choices. What will also be going on is the on-going production and reproduction of modes of subjectivity, since modes of subjectivity are themselves processes that need to be reproduced in order for agents to exist at all. Thus, unless rationalists are prepared to argue that identities *really are* exogenous to the social process, which probably few would do, then we are left with rationalism as a methodological convenience, not an ontology. The rationalist model isolates an important moment in the social process, a moment of perfect subjectivity when actors choose actions on the

---

[119] Jepperson, Wendt, and Katzenstein (1996: 71), Checkel (1998: 346).

basis of identities and interests which are for an instant given. But in making those choices actors are simultaneously reproducing themselves as "givens," which only a constructivist approach can grasp.

An important reason for emphasizing the processual character of identities and interests is that it helps call into question the privileged status in IR of the assumption that states are motivated by self-interest or egoism. I have argued that on any non-trivial definition of self-interest states would not be seen as purely self-interested much of the time, yet IR scholars almost always assume that they are. This assumption comes from Realism, not rational choice theory. Thin rational choice theory does not take a stand on the content of actors' desires or beliefs, and so can accommodate a wide range of motivational assumptions. Realism, however, does take a stand: whatever states are up to, it must be out of self-interest. Realism is one thick theory of state interest.

If the assumption that states are always and inherently self-interested were a true description of an independently existing reality, then it makes sense to marry Realism to a rationalist model of process. But I have claimed that the Realist theory of state interests in fact naturalizes or reifies a particular culture and in so doing helps reproduce it. Since the social process is how we get structure – structure is carried in the heads of agents and is instantiated in their practices – the more that states think like "Realists" the more that egoism, and its systemic corollary of self-help, becomes a self-fulfilling prophecy. As economist Robert Frank puts it:

> (O)ur beliefs about human nature help shape human nature itself. What we think about ourselves and our possibilities determines what we aspire to become; and it shapes what we teach our children, both at home and in the schools. Here the pernicious effects of the self-interest theory have been more disturbing. It tells us that to behave morally is to invite others to take advantage of us. By encouraging us to expect the worst in others, it brings out the worst in us: dreading the role of chump, we are often loath to heed our nobler instincts.[120]

Realism's commitment to self-interest participates in creating and reifying self-help worlds in international politics. To that extent Realism is taking an at least implicit stand not only on what international life is, but on what it *should* be; it becomes a normative as

[120] Frank (1988: xi).

well as a positive theory. Making the constructivist move of seeing egoism as always at stake in the social process helps us see that self-interest is not some external *deus ex machina* driving the international system, but itself an on-going product of the system. If self-interest is not sustained by practice it will die out. The possibility of structural change is born out of that fact.

Conclusion

The subject of this book was the ontology of international life. Ontology is not something that most IR scholars spend much time thinking about. Nor should they. The primary task of IR social science is to help us understand world politics, not to ruminate about issues more properly the concern of philosophers. Yet even the most empirically minded students of international politics must "do" ontology, because in order to explain how the international system works they have to make metaphysical assumptions about what it is made of and how it is structured. This is true of all explanatory endeavors, not just IR: "[n]o science can be more secure than the unconscious metaphysics which tacitly it presupposes."[1] This is because human beings do not have direct, unmediated access to the world. All observation is theory-laden, dependent on background ideas, generally taken as given or unproblematic, about what kinds of things there are and how they are structured. We depend on these ontological assumptions particularly when the objects of our inquiry are not observable, as in IR. The problem comes with the fact that in so conditioning our perceptions, ontologies inevitably influence the content of our substantive theories. In this book I tried to show that Neorealism's problematic conclusions about international politics stem from its underlying materialist and individualist ontology, and that by viewing the system in idealist and holist terms we could arrive at a better understanding.

The dominant ontology today in mainstream theories of international politics is materialist. IR social scientists usually turn first to

---

[1] The quote is from Alfred North Whitehead; I do not know its source. I took it from Myers (1983), who used it for his own frontispiece.

material forces, defined as power and interest, and bring in ideas only to mop up residual unexplained variance. This approach is clearest in Neorealism, but Neoliberalism seems to be based on it as well. I have defended an idealist or social ontology. In my view such an ontology should not deny or obscure the fact that culture supervenes on nature, and as such I rejected the "ideas *all* the way down" thesis that might be associated with a thicker, more radical constructivism. But neither should idealism be reduced to the proposition that ideas matter only to the extent that power and interest do not. The key is to reclaim power and interest from materialism by showing how their content and meaning are constituted by ideas and culture. Having stripped power and interest explanations of their implicit ideational content we see that relatively little of international life is a function of material forces as such. It therefore makes more sense to begin our theorizing about international politics with the distribution of ideas, and especially culture, in the system, and then bring in material forces, rather than the other way around. The importance of this ultimately lies in perceived possibilities for social change. Although there is no 1:1 correspondence between positions in the idealism–materialism debate and beliefs about the ease of social change, showing that seemingly material conditions are actually a function of how actors think about them opens up possibilities for intervention that would otherwise be obscured.

A concern with how power and interest are constituted by ideas is shared by the phenomenological tradition in the study of foreign policy decision-making, which might be likened to a "subjectivist" approach to ideas because of its emphasis on individual perceptions. It would be interesting to explore what, if anything, a more self-consciously constructivist approach might add to this approach,[2] but my concern in this book has been with international politics, not foreign policy. This raises the question of how the ideas held by state agents relate to the ideas that make up the structure of the international system.

The dominant ontology in mainstream theories of international politics for thinking about this "agent–structure problem" is methodological individualism, particularly as expressed in rational choice and game theory. Individualism holds that social structures supervene on the properties and interactions of independently existing, preconsti-

---

[2] See Weldes (1999); cf. Herrmann and Fischerkeller (1995).

tuted agents, like states. I argued that this view actually is compatible with two propositions that it often neglects and to which it is often thought to be opposed: that social systems like the international system contain macro-level structures; and that these structures might have causal effects on ("socially construct") the identities and interests of state agents. But what an individualist ontology cannot see is that agents might be *constituted* by social structures, that the nature of states might be bound up conceptually with the structure of the states system. That is the distinctive claim of a holist or structuralist ontology, which I defended in this book. Given an idealist frame of reference, this comes down to the proposition that the ideas held by individual states are given content or meaning by the ideas which they share with other states – that state *cognition* depends on states systemic *culture*. Accepting this point matters for questions of theory and method, since it means that in analyzing what states think it makes sense to start with the culture of the international system and work top–down, rather than start with unit-level perceptions and work bottom–up. IR scholars should think more like structural anthropologists than economists or psychologists.[3] And idealism and holism also matter for questions of change, since the more deeply that states have internalized the culture of the states system the more difficult it will be to change.

In sum, the ontology of international life that I have advocated is "social" in the sense that it is through ideas that states ultimately relate to one another, and "constructionist" in the sense that these ideas help define who and what states are.

It is widely held that a constructivist ontology is incompatible with the positivist epistemology of natural science, and requires a special, interpretivist or post-positivist epistemology instead. Drawing on a realist philosophy of science I have argued against that view. There is nothing in the intellectual activity required to explain processes of social construction that is epistemologically different than the intellectual activity engaged in by natural scientists. Scientists in both domains are concerned with explaining why one thing leads to another, and with understanding how things are put together to have the causal powers that they do. The fact that the objects of these activities are material in the one case (natural kinds) and ideational in the other (social kinds) may call for different methods of inquiry – we

---

[3] See Weldes, *et al.*, eds. (1999).

cannot interview bacteria, or figure out what someone is thinking by doing a cell culture – but methods are not epistemologies. The epistemic authority of *any* scientific study, whether using interpretive or positivist methods, depends on publicly available evidence and the possibility that its conclusions might in some broad sense be falsified. If there is no such evidence or if a study is non-falsifiable, then it might still be interesting as a form of art, self-expression, or revelation, but it is not an effort to know the world through "science." This point is not lost on post-positivists, who despite their epistemological relativism, generally play by the rules of science in their empirical practice. They are tacit realists.

One argument of this book, therefore, is that social scientists should not be as worried about epistemology as many today seem to be. The point is to explain the world, not to argue about how we can know it. Epistemology generally will take care of itself in the hurly-burly of scientific debate.

Still, a valuable lesson comes out of post-positivist critiques of social science: not that we should reject science, but that we should see that two kinds of questions are necessary to the scientific enterprise, causal and constitutive. Causal questions inquire into the antecedent conditions or mechanisms that generate independently existing effects; this is generally what we want to know when we ask "why?" something happened or "how?" a process works. Constitutive questions inquire into the conditions of possibility that make something what it is or give it the causal powers that it has, and as such they are interested in relationships of conceptual, not natural necessity; this is what we want to know when we ask "how is X possible?" or, simply, "what is X?" A full understanding of a phenomenon requires answers to both kinds of question, but they can be answered relatively independently of each other.

There is no reason that someone asking a causal question cannot take things as given which a constitutive perspective would problematize, any more than it is necessary for someone asking a constitutive question to follow up with a causal one. Neither question is better or more important than the other. Both, moreover, are *explanatory*. Constitutive questions are in part requests for descriptions, but so are some causal questions ("how does this engine work?"). And answering constitutive questions often requires constructing theories, particularly when – as in IR – we are dealing with unobservables. Constitutive theories explain important facts. The double-helix model is an answer to the question of how DNA is constituted, and it seems odd to say that it does not "explain" cell behavior, or that rational choice theory's model of how rational actors are constituted does not "explain" human behavior. Finally, as these examples make clear, the distinction between causal and constitutive questions transcends the natural–social science divide. Natural and social scientists alike ask both kinds of questions. This allows us to recast the epistemological polemics about whether the social sciences should become social physics into a more productive discussion of the logics and differences between two kinds of question that are asked throughout the sciences.

Distinguishing between causal and constitutive questions and positioning both in the realm of IR social science is important partly just because they are different. It also serves an important purpose for the sociology of knowledge in IR.

Mainstream IR, like political science more generally, is oriented overwhelmingly toward causal questions. Constitutive inquiries are hardly recognized as a distinct, let alone valid, part of science. Asking causal questions is of course good. Social kinds, including the state and states system, are in one sense objective facts or things that relate to each other in a causal way, just like things in nature. However, social kinds are as much processes as they are things. And in treating them as if they were "things" it is important to see that we are also reifying them, taking a snapshot of them apart from the processes by which they are sustained. Temporary reification is useful, and indeed we must bracket or take for granted certain processes simply to go about daily life. But permanent reification is problematic. Over-privileging a naturalistic, causal approach to social life leaves us susceptible to forgetting that social kinds are *social*, made of ideas instantiated in practice. And since these ideas are after all *our* ideas, if we forget that social kinds are social then we forget that we are their makers or authors. As a result, rather than experiencing social systems voluntaristically, as artifacts of our design and intent, we experience them deterministically, as if they were forces of nature pressing upon us, as much in our control as the wind and the rain. Causal or "problem-solving" theory gives us some control over problems within these naturalized social worlds, but it does not help us call into question their underlying assumptions.

Constitutive or critical theory reminds us that social kinds like the international system are ideas authored by human beings. By asking how social kinds are put together to have the causal powers that they do, constitutive questions show us the role that our own practices play in sustaining the seemingly objective social facts – the "logic of anarchy" – in front of us. And it may also suggest new ways of putting things together. Constitutive theorizing does not in itself guarantee that society will try to rethink its social kinds, but it does make possible this kind of critical thinking. Gorbachev's New Thinking was a deep, conceptual reassessment of what the US–Soviet relationship "was." It was constitutive theorizing, at the lay level, and based on it the Soviets were able to end, unilaterally and almost overnight, a conflict that seemed like it had become set in stone. It may be that objective conditions were such that the Soviets "had" to change their ideas about the Cold War, but that does not change the fact that in an important sense those ideas *were* the Cold War, and as such changing them by definition changed the reality.

By highlighting the role our practices play in sustaining social kinds, therefore, constitutive theorizing enhances our collective capacity for critical self-reflection or "reflexivity."[4] This gives us perspective on our social environment and helps us to overcome any false sense of determinism. It also opens up the possibility of thinking self-consciously about what direction to go in. Reflexive rethinking is only possible in social, not natural kinds. Purely material structures cannot engage in second-order reflection on themselves because they are not ideas. At the individual level to varying degrees we all think reflexively, and as the example of Soviet New Thinking suggests even states are capable of doing so. The question is this: can the states *system* achieve reflexivity? If the international system is at base a structure of ideas, then can that structure achieve "self-awareness," and what are the implications if it does? To some extent this has already happened. Not only do modern states see themselves as a We bound by certain rules, but since at least the Congress of Vienna in 1815 they have been evolving a collective, second-order awareness of how that collective identity functions, and of what is required to keep it orderly.[5] This emerging collective self-consciousness is found and expressed in the "public sphere" of international society, an emerging space where states appeal to public reason to

[4] See Kohut (1985: 209–11).
[5] Schroeder (1993); on international governance see Rosenau and Czempiel, eds. (1992) and Young (1994).

hold each other accountable and manage their joint affairs.[6] The emergence of an international public sphere signals the emergence of a joint awareness, however embryonic at this stage, of how their own ideas and behavior make the logic of anarchy a self-fulfilling prophecy.

With that joint awareness comes a potential for self-intervention designed to change the logic and bring international society under a measure of rational control. In individuals we might call this "therapy" or "character planning";[7] in social systems like international society it would be called "constitutional design," "engineering", or "steering".[8] The effort to design institutions that would steer the evolution of international society in certain directions would no doubt itself have unintended consequences,[9] not least because the international system is an anarchy and so suffers all the problems of "heterocephaly." But at least in a reflexive system there is a possibility of design and collective rationality that does not exist in a reified system.

The possibility of collective reflexivity at the international level highlights the fact that the problem with Realism is not its state-centrism. The states systemic project is not inherently reactionary or incapable of generating progress. The problem with Realism is its individualist and materialist ontology of structure, not the fact that it focuses exclusively on states. By reconceptualizing the structure of the system in holist and especially idealist terms we make it possible to ask constitutive questions that might lead to progress in the system's evolution. We need not think only around the state but can think in and through it.

A design orientation toward international life suggests two concluding points. One is the importance of dialogue between IR and the fields of Political Theory and Normative IR, which until recently has been kept very limited by the domestic orientation of most Political Theory and the marginalization of normative questions in IR by

[6] On the idea of an international public sphere in this sense see Lynch (1999), Mitzen (2000). For more cosmopolitan conceptions of the public sphere see Bohmann and Lutz-Bachmann, eds. (1997).

[7] Elster (1983b); Bovens (1992).

[8] See Buchanan (1990), Horowitz (1991), Goodin, ed. (1996), Soltan and Elkin, eds. (1996), and Luhmann (1997).

[9] Which raises an interesting question about the relationship between intentional design and the more unconscious processes of systemic evolution that I explored in chapter 7. For a good introduction to this question see Vanberg (1994).

Realism.[10] To be sure, in order to realize its objectives a science of design must be concerned importantly with explanatory or positive questions; it must be a science, attuned to what will work, how, and why. But within those parameters, there will usually be many institutional choices. These choices are fundamentally normative: "design for *what*?" How should we balance the rights of individuals, groups, and states in designing international orders? How should we ensure that transnational power structures are democratically accountable? How should considerations of inter-generational equity figure in these questions? Positive IR by definition is not set up to answer such questions; as such it offers incomplete guidance about what we should do. Political Theory and Normative IR may not have the answers, but they are at least set up to ask the questions. In fact, what is needed is for the two to work together, since positive IR brings to the table an awareness of the institutional realities and path dependencies of the existing system which is necessary to avoid utopianism in the pursuit of normative goals.[11] As such, a reflexive, design orientation gives students of facts and students of values in world politics something to talk about, in a way that the materialist orientation of Realism does not.

This leads to the other question, which is about the relationship of theory and practice. Different kinds of knowledge have different uses. One way to define "Realism" is the view that the culture of international life does not depend on what states do, and IR scholars should therefore take that culture as given – reify it – and focus on helping states do the best that they can within it. The kind of knowledge produced by this theory is useful for solving problems within the existing system, but not for changing the system itself. The result is that problem-solving theory has the practical effect in the real world of helping to reproduce the status quo, and in this way Realism, despite its claim of objectivity, becomes a normative as well as scientific theory. "Idealism," then, would be the view that the culture of international life does depend on what states do – that anarchy is what states make of it – and that IR should therefore focus on showing how states create that culture and so might transform it. The knowledge produced by reflexive or critical theory is generally

---

[10] For signs that a conversation between the two fields is gathering steam see Connolly (1991), Held (1995), Linklater (1998), and Onuf (1998); cf. Wight (1966).

[11] Booth (1991) and Goodin (1995) are thoughtful meditations on the problem of combining ideals and reality.

more useful for changing the world than working within it. Both kinds of knowledge are scientific, but to different normative ends. Ultimately, then, the question becomes what is IR *"for"*?[12] This is not a question that can be answered by social scientists alone, but by helping us to become reflexive Idealism at least gives us a choice.

[12] See Wendt (1999).

Bibliography

Abbott, Andrew (1995) "Things of boundaries," *Social Research*, 62, 857–883.

Abrams, Dominic and Michael Hogg, eds. (1990) *Social Identity Theory*, New York: Harvester Wheatsheaf.

Abrams, Philip (1988) "Notes on the difficulty of studying the state," *Journal of Historical Sociology*, 1, 58–89.

Achen, Christopher (1989) "When is a state with bureaucratic politics representable as a unitary rational actor?" manuscript presented at the 1989 International Studies Association meeting, London.

Adler, Emanuel (1991) "Cognitive evolution: A dynamic approach for the study of international relations and their progress," in E. Adler and B. Crawford, eds., *Progress in Postwar International Relations*, New York: Columbia University Press, pp. 43–88.

(1997a) "Imagined (security) communities: Cognitive regions in international relations," *Millennium*, 26, 249–277.

(1997b) "Seizing the middle ground: Constructivism in world politics," *European Journal of International Relations*, 3, 319–363.

Adler, Emanuel and Michael Barnett, eds. (1998) *Security Communities*, Cambridge: Cambridge University Press.

Adler, Emanuel and Beverly Crawford, eds. (1991) *Progress in Postwar International Relations*, New York: Columbia University Press.

Adler, Paul and Bryan Borys (1993) "Materialism and idealism in organizational research," *Organization Studies*, 14, 657–679.

Agnew, John (1994) "The territorial trap: The geographical assumptions of international relations theory," *Review of International Political Economy*, 1, 53–80.

Alcoff, Linda (1993) "Foucault as epistemologist," *The Philosophical Forum*, 25, 95–124.

Alexander, C. Norman and Mary Glenn Wiley (1981) "Situated activity and identity formation," in M. Rosenberg and R. Turner, eds., *Social Psychology*, New York: Basic Books, pp. 269–289.

Alford, C. Fred (1989) *Melanie Klein and Critical Social Theory*, New Haven: Yale University Press.

Bibliography

(1994) *Group Psychology and Political Theory,* New Haven: Yale University Press.
Alker, Hayward (1996) *Rediscoveries and Reformulations,* Cambridge: Cambridge University Press.
Allison, Graham (1971) *The Essence of Decision,* Boston: Little, Brown.
Almond, Gabriel (1988) "The return to the state," *American Political Science Review,* 82, 853–74.
Almond, Gabriel and Sidney Verba (1963) *Civic Culture,* Boston: Little, Brown.
Althusser, Louis and Etienne Balibar (1970) *Reading Capital,* London: New Left Books.
(1971) "Ideology and ideological state apparatuses," in Althusser, *Lenin and Philosophy and Other Essays,* New York: Monthly Review Press, pp. 127–186.
Anderson, Benedict (1983) *Imagined Communities,* London: Verso.
Andrews, Bruce (1975) "Social rules and the state as a social actor," *World Politics,* 27, 521–540.
Antholis, William (1993) "Liberal democratic theory and the transformation of sovereignty," Ph.D. dissertation, Yale University.
Antony, Michael (1993) "Social relations and the individuation of thought," *Mind,* 102, 247–61.
Archer, Margaret (1982) "Morphogenesis versus structuration: On combining structure and action," *British Journal of Sociology,* 33, 455–483.
(1995) *Realist Social Theory: The Morphogenetic Approach,* Cambridge: Cambridge University Press.
Argyris, Chris and Donald Schon (1978) *Organizational Learning: A Theory of Action Perspective,* Reading, MA: Addison-Wesley.
Ashley, Richard (1983) "Three modes of economism," *International Studies Quarterly,* 27, 463–496.
(1984) "The poverty of neorealism," *International Organization,* 38, 225–286.
(1987) "The geopolitics of geopolitical space: Toward a critical social theory of international politics," *Alternatives,* 12, 403–434.
(1988) "Untying the sovereign state: A double reading of the anarchy problematique," *Millennium,* 17, 227–262.
Atterton, Peter (1994) "Power's blind struggle for existence: Foucault, genealogy, and Darwinism," *History of the Human Sciences,* 7, 1–20.
Augoustinos, Martha and John Michael Innes (1990) "Towards an integration of social representations and social schema theory," *British Journal of Social Psychology,* 29, 213–231.
Axelrod, Robert (1984) *The Evolution of Cooperation,* New York: Basic Books.
Bach, Kent (1975) "Analytic social philosophy – basic concepts," *Journal for the Theory of Social Behaviour,* 5, 189–214.
Bach, Robert (1982) "On the holism of a world system perspective," in T. Hopkins and I. Wallerstein, eds., *World-Systems Analysis,* Beverly Hills: Sage, pp. 159–180.
Badhwar, Neera Kapur, ed. (1993) *Friendship: A Philosophical Reader,* Ithaca: Cornell University Press.

Baldwin, David (1979) "Power analysis and world politics," *World Politics*, 31, 161–194.

(1980) "Interdependence and power: A conceptual analysis," *International Organization*, 34, 471–506.

Baldwin, David, ed. (1993) *Neorealism and Neoliberalism*, New York: Columbia University Press.

Baldwin, John (1988) "Habit, emotion, and self-conscious action," *Sociological Perspectives*, 31, 35–58.

Baldwin, Thomas (1992) "The territorial state," in H. Gross and R. Harrison, eds., *Jurisprudence: Cambridge Essays*, Oxford: Clarendon Press, pp. 207–230.

Barkdull, John (1995) "Waltz, Durkheim, and international relations: The international system as an abnormal form," *American Political Science Review*, 89, 669–680.

Barkin, Samuel and Bruce Cronin (1994) "The state and the nation: Changing norms and the rules of sovereignty in international relations," *International Organization*, 48, 107–130.

Barnes, Barry (1988) *The Nature of Power*, Oxford: Polity Press.

Barnett, Michael (1993) "Institutions, roles, and disorder: The case of the Arab states system," *International Studies Quarterly*, 37, 271–296.

(1995) "Sovereignty, nationalism, and regional order in the Arab states system," *International Organization*, 49, 479–510.

(1998) *Dialogues in Arab Politics: Negotiations in Regional Order*, New York: Columbia University Press.

Bar-Tal, Daniel (1990) *Group Beliefs*, New York: Springer-Verlag.

Bartelson, Jens (1995) *A Genealogy of Sovereignty*, New York: Cambridge University Press.

Barth, Frederik, ed. (1969) *Ethnic Groups and Boundaries*, Boston: Little, Brown.

Bates, Robert, Rui J.P. de Figueiredo Jr., and Barry Weingast (1998) "The politics of interpretation: Rationality, culture, and transition," *Politics and Society*, 26, 221–256.

Becker, Gary (1996) *Accounting for Tastes*, Cambridge, MA: Harvard University Press.

Becker, Howard (1960) "Notes on the concept of commitment," *American Journal of Sociology*, 66, 32–40.

Bellamy, Richard *et al.*, eds. (1995) *Democracy and Constitutional Culture in the Union of Europe*, London: Lothian Foundation Press.

Benjamin, Roger and Raymond Duvall (1985) "The capitalist state in context," in Benjamin, ed., *The Democratic State*, Lawrence: University of Kansas Press, pp. 19–57.

Ben-Menahem, Yemima (1990) "The inference to the best explanation," *Erkenntnis*, 33, 319–344.

Bentley, Arthur (1908) *The Process of Government*, Chicago: University of Chicago Press.

Bibliography

Benton, Ted (1981) "Objective interests and the sociology of power," *Sociology*, 15, 161–184.

Berger, Peter and Thomas Luckmann (1966) *The Social Construction of Reality*, New York: Anchor Books.

Bernecker, Sven (1996) "Davidson on first-person authority and externalism," *Inquiry*, 39, 121–139.

Bhargava, Rajeev (1992) *Individualism in Social Science*, Oxford: Clarendon Press.

Bhaskar, Roy (1979) *The Possibility of Naturalism*, Atlantic Highlands, NJ: Humanities Press.

(1986) *Scientific Realism and Human Emancipation*, London: Verso.

Bially, Janice (1998) "The power politics of identity," Ph.D. dissertation, Yale University.

Biersteker, Thomas and Cynthia Weber, eds. (1996) *State Sovereignty as Social Construct*, Cambridge: Cambridge University Press.

Bilgrami, Akeel (1992) *Belief and Meaning*, Oxford: Blackwell.

Bilmes, Jack (1986) *Discourse and Behavior*, New York: Plenum Press.

Bimber, Bruce (1994) "Three faces of technological determinism," in M. Smith and L. Marx, eds., *Does Technology Drive History?*, Cambridge, MA: MIT Press, pp. 79–100.

Biro, John (1992) "In defence of social content," *Philosophical Studies*, 67, 277–293.

Bloom, William (1990) *Personal Identity, National Identity, and International Relations*, Cambridge: Cambridge University Press.

Bloor, David (1983) *Wittgenstein: A Social Theory of Knowledge*, New York: Columbia University Press.

Blum, Alan and Peter McHugh (1971) "The social ascription of motives," *American Sociological Review*, 36, 98–109.

Blumer, Herbert (1969) "The methodological position of symbolic interactionism," in Blumer, *Symbolic Interactionism: Perspective and Method*, Englewood Cliffs, NJ: Prentice-Hall, pp. 1–60.

Blumstein, Philip (1991) "The production of selves in personal relationships," in J. Howard and P. Callero, eds., *The Self-Society Dynamic*, Cambridge: Cambridge University Press, pp. 305–322.

Bohman, James and Matthias Lutz-Bachmann, eds. (1997) *Perpetual Peace: Essays on Kant's Cosmopolitan Ideal*, Cambridge, MA: MIT Press.

Boli, John and George Thomas (1997) "World culture in the world polity: A century of international non-governmental organization," *American Sociological Review*, 62, 171–190.

Booth, Ken (1991) "Security in anarchy: Utopian realism in theory and practice," *International Affairs*, 67, 527–545.

Bovens, Luc (1992) "Sour grapes and character planning," *Journal of Philosophy*, 89, 57–78.

Boyd, Richard (1979) "Metaphor and theory change," in A. Ortony, ed., *Metaphor and Thought*, Cambridge: Cambridge University Press, pp. 356–408.

(1984) "The current status of scientific realism," in J. Leplin, ed., *Scientific Realism*, Berkeley: University of California Press, pp. 41–82.

(1989) "What realism implies and what it does not," *Dialectica*, 43, 5–29.

(1990) "Realism, approximate truth, and philosophical method," in C. Wade Savage, ed., *Scientific Theories*, Minneapolis: University of Minnesota Press, pp. 355–391.

(1991) "Realism, anti-foundationalism and the enthusiasm for natural kinds," *Philosophical Studies*, 61, 127–148.

(1992) "Constructivism, realism, and philosophical method," in J. Earman, ed., *Inference, Explanation, and Other Frustrations*, Berkeley: University of California Press, pp. 131–198.

Boyd, Robert and Peter Richerson (1980) "Sociobiology, culture and economic theory," *Journal of Economic Behavior and Organization*, 1, 97–121.

(1985) *Culture and the Evolutionary Process*, Chicago: University of Chicago Press.

Breakwell, Glynis and David Canter, eds. (1993) *Empirical Approaches to Social Representations*, Oxford: Clarendon Press.

Brewer, Marilynn (1991) "The social self: On being the same and different at the same time," *Personality and Social Psychology Bulletin*, 17, 475–482.

Brewer, Marilynn and Norman Miller (1996) *Intergroup Relations*, New York: Brooks/Cole.

Brooks, Stephen (1997) "Dueling realisms," *International Organization*, 51, 445–477.

(2000) "The globalization of production and international security," Ph.D. dissertation, Yale University.

Brown, James (1994) *Smoke and Mirrors: How Science Reflects Reality*, London: Routledge.

Bruce, Steve and Roy Wallis (1983) "Rescuing motives," *The British Journal of Sociology*, 34, 61–71.

Buchanan, James (1990) "The domain of constitutional economics," *Constitutional Political Economy*, 1, 1–18,

Bueno de Mesquita, Bruce (1981) *The War Trap*, New Haven: Yale University Press.

(1985) "Toward a scientific understanding of international conflict: A personal view," *International Studies Quarterly*, 29, 121–136.

Bueno de Mesquita, Bruce, Stephen Krasner, and Robert Jervis (1985) "Symposium: Methodological foundation of the study of international conflict," *International Studies Quarterly*, 29, 119–154.

Bukovansky, Mlada (1997) "American identity and neutral rights from independence to the War of 1812," *International Organization*, 51, 209–243.

(1999a) "The altered state and the state of nature: The French Revolution in international politics," *Review of International Studies*, 25, 197–216.

(1999b) "Ideas and power politics: the American and French Revolutions in international politics," book manuscript, Dartmouth College.

Bibliography

Bull, Hedley (1977) *The Anarchical Society*, New York: Columbia University Press.

Bunge, Mario (1993) "Realism and antirealism in social science," *Theory and Decision*, 35, 207–235.

Burchell, Graham, Colin Gordon, and Peter Miller, eds. (1991) *The Foucault Effect*, London: Harvester.

Burge, Tyler (1979) "Individualism and the mental," in P. French, *et al.*, eds., *Midwest Studies in Philosophy*, vol. IV, Minneapolis: University of Minnesota Press, pp. 73–121.

(1986) "Individualism and psychology," *The Philosophical Review*, 95, 3–45.

(1989) "Wherein is language social?" in A. George, ed., *Reflections on Chomsky*, Oxford: Blackwell, pp. 175–91.

Burke, Peter (1980) "The Self: Measurement requirements from an interactionist perspective," *Social Psychology Quarterly*, 43, 18–29.

(1991) "Identity processes and social stress," *American Sociological Review*, 56, 836–849.

Burke, Peter and Donald Reitzes (1991) "An identity theory approach to commitment," *Social Psychology Quarterly*, 54, 239–251.

Buzan, Barry (1991) *People, States, and Fear*, Boulder: Lynne Rienner, 2nd edn.

(1993) "From international system to international society: Structural realism and regime theory meet the English school," *International Organization*, 47, 327–352.

Buzan, Barry, Charles Jones, and Richard Little (1993) *The Logic of Anarchy*, New York: Columbia University Press.

Buzan, Barry and Richard Little (1994) "The idea of 'international system': Theory meets history," *International Political Science Review*, 15, 231–255.

Calhoun, Craig (1991) "The problem of identity in collective action," in J. Huber, ed., *Macro-Micro Linkages in Sociology*, Beverly Hills: Sage Publications, pp. 51–75.

Callero, Peter (1986) "Toward a Meadian conceptualization of role," *The Sociological Quarterly*, 27, 343–358.

Camic, Charles (1986) "The matter of habit," *American Journal of Sociology*, 91, 1039–1087.

Campbell, David (1992) *Writing Security*, Minneapolis: University of Minnesota Press.

Campbell, Donald (1958) "Common fate, similarity, and other indices of the status of aggregates of persons as social entities," *Behavioral Science*, 3, 14–25.

(1975) "On the conflicts between biological and social evolution and between psychology and moral tradition," *American Psychologist*, 30, 1103–1126.

Caporael, Linnda, *et al.* (1989) "Selfishness examined: Cooperation in the absence of egoistic incentives," *Behavioral and Brain Sciences*, 12, 683–699.

Caporaso, James (1996) "The European Union and forms of state: Westphalian, regulatory or post-modern?" *Journal of Common Market Studies*, 34, 29–52.

Carlsnaes, Walter (1992) "The agency-structure problem in foreign policy analysis," *International Studies Quarterly*, 36, 245–270.

Carneiro, Robert (1978) "Political expansion as an expression of the principle of competitive exclusion," in R. Cohen and E. Service, eds., *Origins of the State*, Philadelphia: Institute for the Study of Human Issues, pp. 205–223.

Carnoy, Martin (1984) *The State and Political Theory*, Princeton: Princeton University Press.

Carr, Edward Hallett (1939/1964) *The Twenty Years' Crisis, 1919–1939*, New York: Harper Torchbooks.

Carrier, Martin (1991) "What is wrong with the miracle argument?" *Studies in History and Philosophy of Science*, 22, 23–36.

(1993) "What is right with the miracle argument: Establishing a taxonomy of natural kinds," *Studies in History and Philosophy of Science*, 24, 391–409.

Carveth, Donald (1982) "Sociology and psychoanalysis: The Hobbesian problem revisited," *Canadian Journal of Sociology*, 7, 201–230.

Cash, John (1996) *Identity, Ideology and Conflict: The Structuration of Politics in Northern Ireland*, Cambridge: Cambridge University Press.

Cederman, Lars-Erik (1994) "Unpacking the national interest: An analysis of preference aggregation in ordinal games," in P. Allan and C. Schmidt, eds., *Game Theory and International Relations*, London: Edward Elgar, pp. 50–73.

(1997) *Emergent Actors in World Politics*, Princeton: Princeton University Press.

Charney, Jonathon (1993) "Universal international law," *American Journal of International Law*, 87, 529–551.

Chase-Dunn, Christopher (1981) "Interstate system and capitalist world-economy: One logic or two?" *International Studies Quarterly*, 25, 19–42.

Checkel, Jeffrey (1998) "The constructivist turn in international relations theory," *World Politics*, 50, 324–348.

Christman, John (1988) "Constructing the inner citadel: Recent work on the concept of autonomy," *Ethics*, 99, 109–124.

Churchland, Paul and Clifford Hooker, eds. (1985) *Images of Science*, Chicago: University of Chicago Press.

Clark, Austen (1994) "Beliefs and desires incorporated," *Journal of Philosophy*, 91, 404–425.

Clark, William (1998) "Agents and structures: Two views of preferences, two views of institutions," *International Studies Quarterly*, 42, 245–270.

Claude, Inis (1962) *Power and International Relations*, New York: Random House.

Clinton, W. David (1986) "The national interest: Normative foundations," *Review of Politics*, 48, 495–519.

Cocks, Peter (1980) "Towards a Marxist theory of European integration," *International Organization*, 34, 1–40.

Cohen, G.A. (1978) *Karl Marx's Theory of History: A Defense*, Princeton: Princeton University Press.

Cohen, Joshua (1995) "Samuelson's operationalist-descriptivist thesis," *Journal of Economic Methodology*, 2, 53–78.

Cohen, Michael and Robert Axelrod (1984) "Coping with complexity: The adaptive value of changing utility," *American Economic Review*, 74, 30–42.

Coleman, James (1982) *The Asymmetric Society*, Syracuse: Syracuse University Press.

Connerton, Paul (1989) *How Societies Remember*, Cambridge: Cambridge University Press.

Connolly, William (1983) "The import of contests over 'interests'," in Connolly, *The Terms of Political Discourse*, Princeton: Princeton University Press, pp. 46–83.

(1991) *Identity/Difference*, Ithaca: Cornell University Press.

Cook, Thomas and Donald Campbell (1986) "The causal assumptions of quasi-experimental practice," *Synthese*, 68, 141–180.

Coplin, William (1965) "International law and assumptions about the state system," *World Politics*, 17, 615–634.

Copp, David (1980) "Hobbes on artificial persons and collective actions," *The Philosophical Review*, 89, 579–606.

Cortell, Andrew and James Davis (1996) "How do international institutions matter? The domestic impact of international rules and norms," *International Studies Quarterly*, 40, 451–478.

Coulter, Jeff (1983) *Rethinking Cognitive Theory*, London: Macmillan.

(1989) *Mind in Action*, Cambridge: Polity Press.

(1992) "Bilmes on 'internal states'," *Journal for the Theory of Social Behaviour*, 22, 239–251.

Cox, Robert (1986) "Social forces, states and world orders: Beyond international relations theory," in R. Keohane, ed., *Neorealism and its Critics*, New York: Columbia University Press, pp. 204–254.

(1987) *Production, Power, and World Order*, New York: Columbia University Press.

Crawford, Beverly (1991) "Toward a theory of progress in international relations," in E. Adler and B. Crawford, eds., *Progress in Postwar International Relations*, New York: Columbia University Press, pp. 438–468.

Crawford, James (1979) *The Creation of States in International Law*, Oxford: Clarendon Press.

Cross, Charles (1991) "Explanation and the theory of questions," *Erkenntnis*, 34, 237–60.

Cummins, Robert (1983) *The Nature of Psychological Explanation*, Cambridge, MA: MIT Press.

Cummiskey, D. (1992) "Reference failure and scientific realism: A response to the meta-induction," *British Journal for the Philosophy of Science*, 43, 21–40.

Currie, Gregory (1984) "Individualism and global supervenience," *British Journal for the Philosophy of Science*, 35, 345–358.

(1988) "Realism in the social sciences: Social kinds and social laws," in R.

Nola, ed., *Relativism and Realism in Science*, Kluwer Academic Publishers, pp. 205–227.

Da Fonseca, Eduardo Giannetti (1991) *Beliefs in Action: Economic Philosophy and Social Change*, Cambridge: Cambridge University Press.

D'Amico, Robert (1992) "Defending social science against the postmodern doubt," in S. Seidman and D. Wagner, eds., *Postmodernism and Social Theory*, Oxford: Blackwell, pp. 137–155.

D'Andrade, Roy (1984) "Cultural meaning systems," in R. Shweder and R. LeVine, eds., *Culture Theory: Essays on Mind, Self, and Emotion*, Cambridge: Cambridge University Press, pp. 88–119.

  (1992) "Schemas and motivation," in R. D'Andrade and C. Strauss, eds., *Human Motives and Cultural Models*, Cambridge: Cambridge University Press, pp. 23–44.

  (1995) *The Development of Cognitive Anthropology*, Cambridge: Cambridge University Press.

D'Andrade, Roy and Claudia Strauss, eds. (1992) *Human Motives and Cultural Models*, Cambridge: Cambridge University Press.

Dant, Tim (1996) "Fetishism and the social value of objects," *The Sociological Review*, 44, 495–516.

Davidson, Donald (1963) "Actions, reasons, and causes," *Journal of Philosophy*, 60, 685–700.

Davies, James (1991) "Maslow and theory of political development," *Political Psychology*, 12, 389–430.

Dawes, Robyn *et al.* (1990) "Cooperation for the benefit of us – not me, or my conscience," in J. Mansbridge, ed., *Beyond Self-Interest*, Chicago: University of Chicago Press, pp. 97–110.

Day, Timothy and Harold Kincaid (1994) "Putting inference to the best explanation in its place," *Synthese*, 98, 271–295.

De Jong, Huib Looren (1997) "Some remarks on a relational concept of mind," *Theory and Psychology*, 7, 147–172.

D'Entreves, Alexander (1967) *The Notion of the State*, Oxford: Clarendon Press.

  (1973) "The state," in P. Wiener, ed., *Dictionary of the History of Ideas*, New York: Scribner, pp. 312–318.

Denis, Claude (1989) "The genesis of American capitalism: An historical inquiry into state theory," *Journal of Historical Sociology*, 2, 328–356.

Dennett, Daniel (1987) *The Intentional Stance*, Cambridge, MA: MIT Press.

Denzau, Arthur and Douglass North (1994) "Shared mental models: Ideologies and institutions," *Kyklos*, 47, 3–31.

Dessler, David (1989) "What's at stake in the agent-structure debate?" *International Organization*, 43, 441–473.

  (1991) "Beyond correlations: Toward a causal theory of war," *International Studies Quarterly*, 35, 337–355.

Deudney, Daniel (1993) "Dividing realism: Structural realism versus security materialism on nuclear security and proliferation," *Security Studies*, 1, 7–37.

Bibliography

(1995) "The Philadelphian system: Sovereignty, arms control, and the balance of power in the American states-union, circa 1787–1861," *International Organization*, 49, 191–228.

(1999) "Geopolitics as theory: Historical security materialism," manuscript, Johns Hopkins University.

Deutsch, Karl (1954) *Political Community at the International Level*, Garden City, NY: Doubleday and Company, Inc.

(1963) *The Nerves of Government: Models of Political Communication and Control*, New York: Free Press.

(1968) *The Analysis of International Relations*, Englewood Cliffs, NJ: Prentice-Hall, Inc.

Deutsch, Karl, et al. (1957) *Political Community and the North Atlantic Area*, Princeton: Princeton University Press.

Deutsch, Morton (1983) "The prevention of World War III: A psychological perspective," *Political Psychology*, 4, 3–31.

Devitt, Michael (1991) "Aberrations of the realism debate," *Philosophical Studies*, 61, 43–63.

Devitt, Michael and Kim Sterelny (1987) *Language and Reality*, Cambridge, MA: MIT Press.

Dewey, John (1926) "Corporate personality," *Yale Law Journal*, 35, 655–673.

Dews, Peter (1984) "Power and subjectivity in Foucault," *New Left Review*, 144, 72–95.

Dickinson, John (1927) "A working theory of sovereignty, Part I," *Political Science Quarterly*, 42, 524–548.

DiMaggio, Paul (1997) "Culture and cognition," *Annual Review of Sociology*, 23, 263–287.

DiStefano, Christine (1983) "Masculinity as ideology in political theory: Hobbesian man considered," *Women's Studies International Forum*, 6, 633–644.

Dobbin, Frank (1994) "Cultural models of organization: The social construction of rational organizing principles," in D. Crane, ed., *The Sociology of Culture*, Oxford: Blackwell, pp. 117–141.

Dodgson, Mark (1993) "Organizational learning: A review of some literatures," *Organization Studies*, 14, 375–394.

Doty, Roxanne Lynn (1996) *Imperial Encounters*, Minneapolis: University of Minnesota Press.

(1997) "Aporia: A critical exploration of the agent-structure problematique in international relations theory," *European Journal of International Relations*, 3, 365–392.

Douglas, Mary (1986) *How Institutions Think*, Syracuse: Syracuse University Press.

Downs, George, ed. (1994) *Collective Security Beyond the Cold War*, Ann Arbor: University of Michigan Press.

Downs, George and Keisuke Iida (1994) "Assessing the theoretical case against collective security," in Downs, ed., *Collective Security Beyond the Cold War*, Ann Arbor: University of Michigan Press, pp. 17–39.

Doyal, Len and Ian Gough (1984) "A theory of human needs," *Critical Social Policy*, 6–38.

Doyle, Michael (1983) "Kant, liberal legacies, and foreign affairs, Parts I and II," *Philosophy and Public Affairs*, 12, 205–235 and 323–353.

Dray, William (1959) "'Explaining what' in history," in P. Gardiner, ed., *Theories of History*, Glencoe, IL: Free Press, pp. 403–408.

Duffield, John (1992) "International regimes and alliance behavior: Explaining NATO conventional force levels," *International Organization*, 46, 819–855.

Dunne, Timothy (1995) "The social construction of international society," *European Journal of International Relations*, 1, 367–389.

Dupre, John (1993) *The Disorder of Things*, Cambridge, MA: Harvard University Press.

Durkheim, Emile (1898/1953) "Individual and collective representations," in *Sociology and Philosophy*, D. Pocock, trans., Glencoe: Free Press, pp. 1–34.

(1933/1984) *The Divisions of Labor in Society*, New York: Free Press.

Duvall, Raymond and Alexander Wendt (1987) "The international capital regime and the internationalization of the state," manuscript, University of Minnesota.

Edgerton, Robert (1985) *Rules, Exceptions, and Social Order*, Berkeley: University of California Press.

Edwards, Derek, Malcolm Ashmore, and Jonathan Potter (1995) "Death and furniture: The rhetoric, politics and theology of bottom line arguments against relativism," *History of the Human Sciences*, 8, 25–49.

Elias, Norbert (1982) *The Civilizing Process*, New York: Pantheon.

Ellingson, Stephen (1995) "Understanding the dialectic of discourse and collective action," *American Journal of Sociology*, 101, 100–144.

Elman, Colin (1996) "Why *not* Neorealist theories of foreign policy?" *Security Studies*, 6, 7–53.

Elster, Jon (1979) *Ulysses and the Sirens*, Cambridge: Cambridge University Press.

(1982) "Sour grapes – utilitarianism and the genesis of wants," in A. Sen and B. Williams, eds., *Utilitarianism and Beyond*, Cambridge: Cambridge University Press, pp. 219–238.

(1983a) *Explaining Technical Change*, Cambridge: Cambridge University Press.

(1983b) *Sour Grapes*, Cambridge: Cambridge University Press.

(1989) *The Cement of Society*, Cambridge: Cambridge University Press.

Elster, Jon, ed. (1986) *The Multiple Self*, Cambridge: Cambridge University Press.

Emirbayer, Mustafa (1997) "Manifesto for a relational sociology," *American Journal of Sociology*, 103, 281–317.

Emmet, Dorothy (1976) "'Motivation' in sociology and social anthropology," *Journal for the Theory of Social Behaviour*, 6, 85–104.

England, Paula and Barbara Stanek Kilbourne (1990) "Feminist critiques of the separative model of self," *Rationality and Society*, 2, 156–171.

Escobar, Arturo (1995) *Encountering Development*, Princeton: Princeton University Press.

Esser, Hartmut (1993) "The rationality of everyday behavior," *Rationality and Society*, 5, 7–31.

Evans, E. (1987) *The Criminal Prosecution and Capital Punishment of Animals*, London: Faber.

Fain, Haskell (1987) *Normative Politics and the Community of Nations*, Philadelphia: Temple University Press.

Fairclough, Norman (1992) *Discourse and Social Change*, Oxford: Polity Press.

Farr, Rob and Serge Moscovici, eds. (1984) *Social Representations*, Cambridge: Cambridge University Press.

Fay, Brian (1975) *Social Theory and Political Practice*, London: Allen and Unwin.

(1986) "General laws and explaining human behavior," in D. Sabia and J. Wallulis, eds., *Changing Social Science*, Albany: State University of New York Press, pp. 103–128.

Fearon, James (1997) "What is identity (as we now use the word)?" manuscript, University of Chicago.

(1998) "Deliberation as discussion," in J. Elster, ed., *Deliberative Democracy*, Cambridge: Cambridge University Press, pp. 44–68.

Feigl, Herbert (1970) "The 'orthodox' view of theories," in M. Radner and S. Winokur, eds., *Minnesota Studies in the Philosophy of Science*, vol. IV, Minneapolis: University of Minnesota Press, pp. 3–16.

Fentress, James and Chris Wickham (1992) *Social Memory*, Oxford: Blackwell.

Ferejohn, John (1991) "Rationality and interpretation," in K. Monroe, ed., *The Economic Approach to Politics*, New York: Harper-Collins, pp. 279–305.

Ferguson, Yale and Richard Mansbach (1991) "Between celebration and despair: Constructive suggestions for future international theory," *International Studies Quarterly*, 35, 363–386.

Fine, Arthur (1984) "The natural ontological attitude," in J. Leplin, ed., *Scientific Realism*, Berkeley: University of California Press, pp. 83–107.

Finley, David, Ole Holsti, and Richard Fagen (1967) *Enemies in Politics*, Chicago: Rand McNally.

Finnemore, Martha (1996a) *National Interests in International Society*, Ithaca: Cornell University Press.

(1996b) "Norms, culture, and world politics: insights from sociology's institutionalism," *International Organization*, 50, 325–347.

Fiorina, Morris (1995) "Rational choice and the new(?) institutionalism," *Polity*, 28, 107–115.

Fischer, Markus (1992) "Feudal Europe, 800–1300: Communal discourse and conflictual practices," *International Organization*, 46, 427–466.

Florini, Ann (1996) "The evolution of international norms," *International Studies Quarterly*, 40, 363–389.

Foote, Nelson (1951) "Identification as the basis for a theory of motivation," *American Sociological Review*, 16, 14–21.

Foucault, Michel (1979) *Discipline and Punish*, New York: Vintage Books.
   (1980) *Power/Knowledge*, New York: Pantheon.
   (1982) "The subject and power," *Critical Inquiry*, 8, 777–795.
Fowler, Michael and Julie Bunck (1996) "What constitutes the sovereign state?" *Review of International Studies*, 22, 381–404.
Franck, Thomas (1990) *The Power of Legitimacy Among Nations*, Oxford: Oxford University Press.
Frank, Robert (1988) *Passions with Reason*, New York: Norton.
Frankfurt, Harry (1971) "Freedom of the will and the concept of a person," *Journal of Philosophy*, 68, 5–20.
Franks, David and Viktor Gecas (1992) "Autonomy and conformity in Cooley's self-theory: The looking-glass self and beyond," *Symbolic Interaction*, 15, 49–68.
Frege, Gottlob (1892/1993) "On sense and reference," in A. Moore, ed., *Meaning and Reference*, Oxford: Oxford University Press, pp. 23–42.
French, Peter (1984) *Collective and Corporate Responsibility*, New York: Columbia University Press.
Freudenburg, William, Scott Frickel, and Robert Gramling (1995) "Beyond the nature/society divide: Learning to think about a mountain," *Sociological Forum*, 10, 361–392.
Frey, Frederick (1985) "The problem of actor designation in political analysis," *Comparative Politics*, 17, 127–152.
Friedman, Kenneth (1982) "Is inter-theoretic reduction feasible?" *British Journal for the Philosophy of Science*, 33, 17–40.
Friedman, Milton (1953) "The methodology of positive economics," in Friedman, *Essays in Positive Economics*, Chicago: University of Chicago Press.
Fukuyama, Francis (1989) "The end of history?" *The National Interest*, 16, 3–18.
Gaertner, Samuel *et al.* (1993) "The common ingroup identity model: Recategorization and the reduction of intergroup bias," in W. Stroebe and M. Hewstone, eds., *European Review of Social Psychology*, 4, 1–26.
Gambetta, Diego (1988) "Can we trust trust?" in Gambetta, ed., *Trust*, Oxford: Blackwell, pp. 213–237.
Garfinkel, Alan (1981) *Forms of Explanation*, New Haven: Yale University Press.
Geanakoplos, John (1992) "Common knowledge," *Journal of Economic Perspectives*, 6, 53–82.
Geanakoplos, John, David Pearce, and Ennio Stacchetti (1989) "Psychological games and sequential rationality," *Games and Economic Behavior*, 1, 60–79.
George, Alexander (1979) "Case studies and theory development," in P. Lauren, ed., *Diplomacy*, New York: Free Press, pp. 43–68.
George, Alexander and Robert Keohane (1980) "The concept of national interests: Uses and limitations," in George, *Presidential Decisionmaking in Foreign Policy*, Boulder: Westview, pp. 217–238.
George, Alexander and Timothy McKeown (1985) "Case studies and theories

of organizational decision making," in R. Coulam and R. Smith, eds., *Advances in Information Processing in Organizations*, vol. II, Greenwich: JAI Press, pp. 21–58.

Geser, Hans (1992) "Towards an interaction theory of organizational actors," *Organization Studies*, 13, 429–451.

Giddens, Anthony (1979) *Central Problems in Social Theory*, Berkeley: University of California Press.

  (1982) *Profiles and Critiques in Social Theory*, Berkeley: University of California Press.

  (1984) *The Constitution of Society*, Berkeley: University of California Press.

  (1985) *The Nation-State and Violence*, Berkeley: University of California Press.

Gilbert, Margaret (1987) "Modelling collective belief," *Synthese*, 73, 185–204.

  (1989) *On Social Facts*, Princeton: Princeton University Press.

  (1994) "Durkheim and social facts," in W. Pickering and H. Martins, eds., *Debating Durkheim*, London: Routledge, pp. 86–109.

Gill, Stephen, ed. (1993) *Gramsci, Historical Materialism and International Relations*, Cambridge: Cambridge University Press.

Gilpin, Robert (1981) *War and Change in World Politics*, Cambridge: Cambridge University Press.

  (1986) "The richness of the tradition of political realism," in R. Keohane, ed., *Neorealism and its Critics*, New York: Columbia University Press, pp. 301–321.

Glaser, Charles (1997) "The security dilemma revisited," *World Politics*, 50, 171–201.

Glass, J. and W. Johnson (1988) "Metaphysics, MSRP and economics," *British Journal for the Philosophy of Science*, 39, 313–329.

Glennan, Stuart (1996) "Mechanisms and the nature of causation," *Erkenntnis*, 44, 49–71.

Goffman, Erving (1969) *Strategic Interaction*, Philadelphia: University of Pennsylvania Press.

Golding, Robert (1982) "Freud, psychoanalysis, and sociology: Some observations on the sociological analysis of the individual," *British Journal of Sociology*, 33, 545–562.

Goldstein, Judith (1993) *Ideas, Interests, and American Trade Policy*, Ithaca: Cornell University Press.

Goldstein, Judith and Robert Keohane, eds. (1993) *Ideas and Foreign Policy*, Ithaca: Cornell University Press.

Goldstein, Judith and Robert Keohane (1993) "Ideas and foreign policy: An analytical framework," in Goldstein and Keohane, eds., *Ideas and Foreign Policy*, Ithaca: Cornell University Press, pp. 3–30.

Gong, Gerritt (1984) *The Standard of 'Civilization' in International Society*, Oxford: Clarendon Press.

Goodin, Robert (1992) *Motivating Political Morality*, Oxford: Blackwell.

(1995) "Political ideals and political practice," *British Journal of Political Science*, 25, 37–56.

Goodin, Robert, ed. (1996) *The Theory of Institutional Design*, Cambridge: Cambridge University Press.

Goodman, Nelson (1978) *Ways of Worldmaking*, Indianapolis: Hackett Publishing Co.

Gottmann, Jean (1973) *The Significance of Territory*, Charlottesville: University of Virginia Press.

Gourevitch (1978) "The second image reversed: The international sources of domestic politics," *International Organization*, 32, 881–912.

Granovetter, Mark (1973) "The strength of weak ties," *American Journal of Sociology*, 78, 1360–1380.

Green, Donald and Ian Shapiro (1994) *Pathologies of Rational Choice Theory*, New Haven: Yale University Press.

Greenblatt, Stephen (1991) *Marvellous Possessions: The Wonder of the New World*, Chicago: University of Chicago Press.

Greenwood, John (1990) "Two dogmas of neo-empiricism: The 'theory-informity' of observation and the Quine-Duhem thesis," *Philosophy of Science*, 57, 553–574.

(1991) *Relations and Representations*, London: RKP.

(1994) "A sense of identity: Prolegomena to a social theory of personal identity," *Journal for the Theory of Social Behaviour*, 24, 25–46.

Gregory, Derek and John Urry, eds. (1985) *Social Relations and Spatial Structures*, New York: St. Martins Press.

Grieco, Joseph (1988) "Anarchy and the limits of cooperation: A realist critique of the newest liberal institutionalism," *International Organization*, 42, 485–508.

(1990) *Cooperation Among Nations*, Ithaca: Cornell University Press.

Gulick, Edward (1955) *Europe's Classical Balance of Power*, New York: Norton.

Gunnell, John (1975) *Philosophy, Science, and Political Inquiry*, General Learning Press.

Guzzini, Stefano (1993) "Structural power: The limits of neorealist analysis," *International Organization*, 47, 443–478.

Haas, Ernst (1964) *Beyond the Nation-State*, Stanford: Stanford University Press.

(1983) "Words can hurt you; or, who said what to whom about regimes," in S. Krasner, ed., *International Regimes*, Ithaca: Cornell University Press, pp. 23–59.

(1990) *When Knowledge is Power*, Berkeley: University of California Press.

Haas, Peter, ed. (1992) "Knowledge, power, and international policy coordination," *International Organization*, 46, 1–390.

Hacking, Ian (1983) *Representing and Intervening*, Cambridge: Cambridge University Press.

(1986) "Making up people," in T. Heller, *et al.*, eds., *Reconstructing Individualism*, Stanford: Stanford University Press, pp. 222–236.

(1991) "A tradition of natural kinds," *Philosophical Studies*, 61, 109–126.

Bibliography

Haines, Valerie (1988) "Social network analysis, structuration theory and the holism-individualism debate," *Social Networks*, 10, 157–182.

Halbwachs, Maurice (1992) *On Collective Memory*, ed. Lewis Coser, Chicago: University of Chicago Press.

Hall, Rodney Bruce (1999) *National Collective Identity: Social Constructs and International Systems*, New York: Columbia University Press.

Hall, Stuart (1977) "Re-thinking the 'base-and-superstructure' metaphor," in J. Bloomfield, *et al.*, eds., *Class, Hegemony, and Party*, London: Lawrence and Wishart, pp. 43–71.

  (1986) "The problem of ideology – Marxism without guarantees," *Journal of Communication Inquiry*, 10, 28–44.

Halliday, Fred (1992) "International society as homogeneity: Burke, Marx, Fukuyama," *Millennium*, 21, 435–461.

Hannan, Michael and John Freeman (1989) *Organizational Ecology*, Cambridge, MA: Harvard University Press.

Hanrieder, Wolfram (1978) "Dissolving international politics: Reflections on the nation-state," *American Political Science Review*, 72, 1276–1287.

Hanson, Donald (1984) "Thomas Hobbes' 'highway to peace'," *International Organization*, 38, 329–354.

Hardin, Russell (1995a) "Self-interest, group identity," in A. Breton, *et al.*, eds., *Nationalism and Rationality*, Cambridge: Cambridge University Press, pp. 14–42.

  (1995b) *One for All: The Logic of Group Conflict*, Princeton: Princeton University Press.

Harding, Alan (1994) "The origins of the concept of the state," *History of Political Thought*, 15, 57–72.

Harre, Rom (1986) *Varieties of Realism*, Oxford: Blackwell.

Harsanyi, John (1969) "Rational-choice models of political behavior vs. functionalist and conformist theories," *World Politics*, 21, 513–538.

Hasenclever, Andreas, Peter Mayer, and Volker Rittberger (1997) *Theories of International Regimes*, Cambridge: Cambridge University Press.

Haslam, Nick (1998) "Natural kinds, human kinds, and essentialism," *Social Research*, 65, 291–314.

Haslett, D. (1990) "What is utility?" *Economics and Philosophy*, 6, 65–94.

Haugeland, John (1978) "The nature and plausibility of cognitivism," *The Behavioral and Brain Sciences*, 2, 215–226.

Hausman, Daniel (1995) "Rational choice and social theory: A comment," *Journal of Philosophy*, 92, 96–102.

Hawkes, Terence (1977) *Structuralism and Semiotics*, Berkeley: University of California Press.

Hechter, Michael (1987) *Principles of Group Solidarity*, Berkeley: University of California Press.

Hedstrom, Peter and Richard Swedberg (1996) "Social mechanisms," *Acta Sociologica*, 39, 281–308.

Held, David (1995) *Democracy and the Global Order*, Stanford: Stanford University Press.

Heller, Mark (1980) "The use and abuse of Hobbes: The state of nature in international relations," *Polity*, 13, 21–32.

Hellman, Geoffrey (1983) "Realist principles," *Philosophy of Science*, 50, 227–249.

Helman, Gerald and Steven Ratner (1992/3) "Saving failed states," *Foreign Policy*, 89, 3–20.

Hempel, Carl and Felix Oppenheim (1948) "Studies in the logic of explanation," *Philosophy of Science*, 15, 135–175.

Henderson, David (1994) "Accounting for macro-level causation," *Synthese*, 101, 129–156.

Henkin, Louis (1979) *How Nations Behave*, 2nd edn, New York: Council on Foreign Relations.

Henriques, Julian *et al.* (1984) *Changing the Subject: Psychology, Social Regulation and Subjectivity*, London: Methuen.

Herrmann, Richard and Michael Fischerkeller (1995) "Beyond the enemy image and spiral model: Cognitive-strategic research after the Cold War," *International Organization*, 49, 415–450.

Herz, John (1950) "Idealist internationalism and the security dilemma," *World Politics*, 2, 157–180.

Hewitt, John (1976) *Self and Society: A Symbolic Interactionist Social Psychology*, Boston: Allyn and Bacon.

   (1989) *Dilemmas of the American Self*, Philadelphia: Temple University Press.

Hirschman, Albert (1977) *The Passions and the Interests*, Princeton: Princeton University Press.

Hirshleifer, Jack (1978) "Natural economy versus political economy," *Journal of Social and Biological Structures*, 1, 319–337.

   (1985) "The expanding domain of economics," *American Economic Review*, 75, 53–68.

Hirst, Paul (1977) "Economic classes and politics," in A. Hunt, ed., *Class and Class Structure*, London: Lawrence and Wishart, pp. 125–154.

Hobbs, Jesse (1994) "A limited defense of the pessimistic induction," *British Journal for the Philosophy of Science*, 45, 171–191.

Hochman, Harold and Shmuel Nitzan (1985) "Concepts of extended preference," *Journal of Economic Behavior and Organization*, 6, 161–176.

Hodgson, Geoffrey (1991) "Hayek's theory of cultural evolution," *Economics and Philosophy*, 7, 67–82.

   (1997) "The ubiquity of habits and rules," *Cambridge Journal of Economics*, 21, 663–84.

Hogg, Michael, Deborah Terry, and Katherine White (1995) "A tale of two theories: A critical comparison of identity theory with social identity theory," *Social Psychology Quarterly*, 58, 255–269.

Bibliography

Hollis, Martin (1987) *The Cunning of Reason,* Cambridge: Cambridge University Press.

(1994) *The Philosophy of Social Science,* Cambridge: Cambridge University Press.

Hollis, Martin and Steve Smith (1990) *Explaining and Understanding International Relations,* Oxford: Clarendon Press.

Hollis, Martin and Robert Sugden (1993) "Rationality in action," *Mind,* 192, 1–35.

Holsti, Kal (1970) "National role conceptions in the study of foreign policy," *International Studies Quarterly,* 14, 233–309.

Holt, Jim (1996) "Whose idea is it, anyway? A philosopher's feud," *Lingua Franca,* January/February, 29–39.

Homans, George (1990) "Rational-choice theory and behavioral psychology," in C. Calhoun, *et al.,* eds., *Structures of Power and Constraint,* Cambridge: Cambridge University Press, pp. 77–89.

Honneth, Axel (1996) *The Struggle for Recognition,* Cambridge, MA: MIT Press.

Horgan, Terence (1993) "From supervenience to superdupervenience," *Mind,* 102, 555–586.

Horowitz, Amir (1996) "Putnam, Searle, and externalism," *Philosophical Studies,* 81, 27–69.

Horowitz, Donald (1991) *A Democratic South Africa? Constitutional Engineering in a Divided Society,* Berkeley: University of California Press.

Howard, Judith (1991) "From changing selves toward changing society," in J. Howard and P. Callero, eds., *The Self-Society Dynamic,* Cambridge: Cambridge University Press, pp. 209–237.

(1994) "A social cognitive conception of social structure," *Social Psychology Quarterly,* 57, 210–227.

Howard, Judith and Peter Callero, eds. (1991) *The Self-Society Dynamic,* Cambridge: Cambridge University Press.

Howe, R. (1994a) "A social-cognitive theory of desire," *Journal for the Theory of Social Behaviour,* 24, 1–23.

(1994b) "The cognitive nature of desire," *The Southern Journal of Philosophy,* 32, 179–194.

Hudson, Robert (1994) "Background independence and the causation of observations," *Studies in History and Philosophy of Science,* 25, 595–612.

Humberstone, I. (1987) "Wanting as believing," *Canadian Journal of Philosophy,* 17, 49–62.

Hume, David (1740/1978) *A Treatise of Human Nature,* Oxford: Clarendon Press.

(1748/1988) *An Enquiry Concerning Human Understanding,* Buffalo: Prometheus Books.

Hunt, Shelby (1994) "A realist theory of empirical testing: Resolving the theory-ladenness/objectivity debate," *Philosophy of the Social Sciences,* 24, 133–158.

Huntington, Samuel (1993) "The clash of civilizations?" *Foreign Affairs*, Summer, 22–49.

Huntley, Wade (1996) "Kant's third image: Systemic sources of the liberal peace," *International Studies Quarterly*, 40, 45–76.

Hurd, Ian (1999) "Legitimacy and authority in international politics," *International Organization*, 53, 379–408.

Hurrell, Andrew (1990) "Kant and the Kantian paradigm in international relations," *Review of International Studies*, 16, 183–205.

Hutchins, Edwin (1991) "The social organization of distributed cognition," in L. Resnick, *et al.*, eds., *Perspectives on Socially Shared Cognition*, Washington DC: American Psychological Association.

Ikenberry, G. John and Charles Kupchan (1990) "Socialization and hegemonic power," *International Organization*, 44, 283–315.

Inayatullah, Naeem and David Blaney (1996) "Knowing encounters: Beyond parochialism in international relations theory," in Y. Lapid and F. Kratochwil, eds., *The Return of Culture and Identity in IR Theory*, Boulder: Lynne Rienner, pp. 65–84.

Jackson, Frank and Philip Pettit (1990) "In defence of folk psychology," *Philosophical Studies*, 59, 31–54.

(1992) "In defense of explanatory ecumenism," *Economics and Philosophy*, 8, 1–21.

(1993) "Structural explanation in social theory," in D. Charles and K. Lennon, eds., *Reduction, Explanation, and Realism*, Oxford: Oxford University Press, pp. 97–131.

Jackson, Robert and Carl Rosberg (1982) "Why Africa's weak states persist: The juridical and the empirical in statehood," *World Politics*, 35, 1–24.

James, Alan (1986) *Sovereign Statehood*, London: Allen and Unwin.

(1993) "System or society?" *Review of International Studies*, 19, 269–288.

Jencks, Christopher (1990) "Varieties of altruism," in J. Mansbridge, ed., *Beyond Self-Interest*, Chicago: University of Chicago Press, pp. 53–67.

Jepperson, Ronald, Alexander Wendt, and Peter Katzenstein (1996) "Norms, identity, and culture in national security," in P. Katzenstein, ed., *The Culture of National Security*, New York: Columbia University Press, pp. 33–75.

Jervis, Robert (1970) *The Logic of Images in International Relations*, New York: Columbia University Press.

(1976) *Perception and Misperception in International Politics*, Princeton: Princeton University Press.

(1978) "Cooperation under the security dilemma," *World Politics*, 30, 167–214.

(1988) "Realism, game theory, and cooperation," *World Politics*, 40, 317–349.

Jessop, Bob (1978) "Capitalism and democracy: The best possible political shell?" in G. Littlejohn, *et al.*, eds., *Power and the State*, New York: St. Martins, pp. 10–51.

(1982) *The Capitalist State*, New York: New York University Press.

(1990) *State Theory*, University Park, PA: Pennsylvania State University Press.

Jochnick, C. and R. Normand (1994) "The legitimization of violence," *Harvard International Law Journal*, 35, 49–95.

Johnson, Doyle Paul (1990) "Security versus autonomy motivation in Anthony Giddens' concept of agency," *Journal for the Theory of Social Behaviour*, 20, 111–130.

Johnston, Alastair Iain (1995) *Cultural Realism: Strategic Culture and Grand Strategy in Chinese History*, Princeton: Princeton University Press.

Jost, John (1995) "Toward a Wittgensteinian social psychology of human development," *Theory and Psychology*, 5, 5–25.

Jussim, Lee (1991) "Social perception and social reality: A reflection-construction model," *Psychological Review*, 98, 54–73.

Kahneman, Daniel and Carol Varey (1991) "Notes on the psychology of utility," in J. Elster and J. Roemer, eds., *Interpersonal Comparisons of Well-Being*, Cambridge: Cambridge University Press, pp. 127–163.

Kaplan, Morton (1957) *System and Process in International Politics*, New York: Wiley.

Kaplowitz, Noel (1984) "Psychopolitical dimensions of international relations: The reciprocal effects of conflict strategies," *International Studies Quarterly*, 28, 373–406.

(1990) "National self-images, perception of enemies, and conflict strategies," *Political Psychology*, 11, 39–82.

Katzenstein, Peter, ed. (1996) *The Culture of National Security*, New York: Columbia University Press.

Kaufman, Stuart (1997) "The fragmentation and consolidation of international systems," *International Organization*, 51, 173–208.

Kaye, Howard (1991) "A false convergence: Freud and the Hobbesian problem of order," *Sociological Theory*, 9, 87–105.

Keat, Russell and John Urry (1982) *Social Theory as Science*, 2nd edn, London: RKP.

Kegley, Charles (1993) "The neoidealist moment in international studies? Realist myths and the new international realities," *International Studies Quarterly*, 37, 131–146.

Kegley, Charles, ed. (1995) *Controversies in International Relations Theory: Realism and the Neoliberal Challenge*, New York: St. Martin's Press.

Kelley, Harold and John Thibaut (1978) *Interpersonal Relations: A Theory of Interdependence*, New York: Wiley.

Kelman, Herbert (1985) "Overcoming the psychological barrier: An analysis of the Egyptian-Israeli peace process," *Negotiation Journal*, 1, 213–234.

Keohane, Robert (1984) *After Hegemony*, Princeton: Princeton University Press.

(1986a) "Reciprocity in international relations," *International Organization*, 40, 1–27.

(1986b) "Theory of world politics: Structural realism and beyond," in R. Keohane, ed., *Neorealism and its Critics*, New York: Columbia University Press, pp. 158–203.

(1988a) "International institutions: Two approaches," *International Studies Quarterly*, 32, 379–396.

(1988b) "International relations theory: Contributions of a feminist standpoint," *Millennium*, 18, 245–253.

(1990) "International liberalism reconsidered," in J. Dunn, ed., *The Economic Limits to Modern Politics*, Cambridge: Cambridge University Press, pp. 165–194.

Keohane, Robert, ed. (1986) *Neorealism and its Critics*, New York: Columbia University Press.

Keohane, Robert and Lisa Martin (1995) "The promise of institutionalist theory," *International Security*, 20, 39–51.

Keohane, Robert and Joseph Nye (1989) *Power and Interdependence*, 2nd edn, Glenville, IL: Scott Foresman.

Kimura, Masato and David Welch (1998) "Specifying 'interests': Japan's claim to the Northern Territories and its implications for international relations theory," *International Studies Quarterly*, 42, 213–243.

Kincaid, Harold (1986) "Reduction, explanation, and individualism," *Philosophy of Science*, 53, 492–513.

(1988) "Supervenience and explanation," *Synthese*, 77, 251–281.

(1993) "The empirical nature of the individualism-holism dispute," *Synthese*, 97, 229–247.

(1996) *Philosophical Foundations of the Social Sciences*, Cambridge: Cambridge University Press.

King, Gary, Robert Keohane, and Sidney Verba (1994) *Designing Social Inquiry*, Princeton: Princeton University Press.

Kitcher, Philip (1993) *The Advancement of Science*, Oxford: Oxford University Press.

Kitzinger, Celia (1992) "The individuated self concept: A critical analysis of social-constructionist writing on individualism," in G. Breakwell, ed., *Social Psychology of Identity and the Self Concept*, Surrey University Press, pp. 251–250.

Klotz, Audie (1995) *Protesting Prejudice: Apartheid and the Politics of Norms in International Relations*, Ithaca: Cornell University Press.

Kocs, Stephen (1994) "Explaining the strategic behavior of states: International law as system structure," *International Studies Quarterly*, 38, 535–556.

Koh, Harold (1997) "Why do nations obey international law?" *Yale Law Journal*, 106, 2599–2659.

Kohut, Heinz (1985) "Creativeness, charisma, group psychology," in Kohut, *Self-Psychology and the Humanities*, New York: Norton, pp. 171–211.

Kornblith, Hilary (1993) *Inductive Inference and its Natural Ground*, Cambridge, MA: MIT Press.

Kowert, Paul and Jeffrey Legro (1996) "Norms, identity, and their limits: A theoretical reprise," in P. Katzenstein, ed., *The Culture of National Security*, New York: Columbia University Press, pp. 451–497.

Kramer, Roderick, Marilynn Brewer, and Benjamin Hanna (1995) "Collective trust and collective action," in R. Kramer and T. Tyler, eds., *Trust in Organizations*, Thousand Oaks: Sage, pp. 357–389.

Kramer, Roderick and Lisa Goldman (1995) "Helping the group or helping yourself? Social motives and group identity in resource dilemmas," in D. Schroeder, ed., *Social Dilemmas*, New York: Praeger, pp. 49–67.

Krasner, Stephen (1978) *Defending the National Interest*, Princeton: Princeton University Press.

(1983a) "Structural causes and regime consequences: Regimes as intervening variables," in S. Krasner, ed., *International Regimes*, Ithaca: Cornell University Press, pp. 1–21.

(1983b) "Regimes and the limits of realism," in Krasner, ed., *International Regimes*, Ithaca: Cornell University Press, pp. 355–368.

(1991) "Global communications and national power: Life on the Pareto frontier," *World Politics*, 43, 336–366.

(1993) "Westphalia and all that," in J. Goldstein and R. Keohane, eds., *Ideas and Foreign Policy*, Ithaca: Cornell University Press, pp. 235–264.

(1995/6) "Compromising Westphalia," *International Security*, 20, 115–151.

Krasner, Stephen, ed. (1983) *International Regimes*, Ithaca: Cornell University Press.

Kratochwil, Friedrich (1982) "On the notion of 'interest' in international relations," *International Organization*, 36, 1–30.

(1986) "Of systems, boundaries, and territoriality," *World Politics*, 39, 27–52.

(1989) *Rules, Norms, and Decisions*, Cambridge: Cambridge University Press.

(1993) "The embarrassment of changes: Neo-realism as the science of realpolitik without politics," *Review of International Studies*, 19, 63–80.

(1995) "Sovereignty as *dominium*: Is there a right to humanitarian intervention?" in G. Lyons and M. Mastanduno, eds., *Beyond Westphalia*, Baltimore: Johns Hopkins University Press, pp. 21–42.

Kratochwil, Friedrich and John Ruggie (1986) "International organization: A state of the art on an art of the state," *International Organization*, 40, 753–775.

Kreps, David (1990) "Corporate culture and economic theory," in J. Alt and K. Shepsle, eds., *Perspectives on Positive Political Economy*, Cambridge: Cambridge University Press, pp. 90–143.

Kriesberg, Louis *et al.*, eds. (1989) *Intractable Conflicts and their Transformation*, Syracuse: Syracuse University Press.

Kripke, Saul (1971) "Identity and necessity," in M. Munitz, ed., *Identity and Individuation*, New York: New York University Press, pp. 135–164.

Krishna, Daya (1971) " 'The self-fulfilling prophecy' and the nature of society," *American Sociological Review*, 36, 1104–1107.

Kristeva, Julia (1993) *Nations Without Nationalism*, New York: Columbia University Press.

Kroll, John (1993) "The complexity of interdependence," *International Studies Quarterly*, 37, 321–348.

Kroon, Frederick (1985) "Theoretical terms and the causal view of reference," *Australasian Journal of Philosophy*, 63, 143–166.

Kropotkin, Petr (1914) *Mutual Aid: A Factor of Evolution*, Boston: Porter Sargent Publishers.

Kuhn, Thomas (1962) *The Structure of Scientific Revolutions*, Chicago: University of Chicago Press.

Kukla, Andre (1994) "The structure of self-fulfilling and self-negating prophecies," *Theory and Psychology*, 4, 5–33.

Kupchan, Charles and Clifford Kupchan (1991) "Concerts, collective security, and the future of Europe," *International Security*, 16, 114–161.

Kusch, Martin (1997) "The sociophilosophy of folk psychology," *Studies in History and Philosophy of Science*, 28, 1–25.

Laffey, Mark and Jutta Weldes (1997) "Beyond belief: Ideas and symbolic technologies in the study of international relations," *European Journal of International Relations*, 3, 193–237.

Lagueux, Maurice (1994) "Friedman's 'instrumentalism' and constructive empiricism in economics," *Theory and Decision*, 37, 147–174.

Laitin, David (1998) *Identity in Formation: The Russian-Speaking Populations in the Near Abroad*, Ithaca: Cornell University Press.

Lakatos, Imre (1970) "Falsification and the methodology of scientific research programmes," in I. Lakatos and A. Musgrave, eds., *Criticism and the Growth of Knowledge*, Cambridge: Cambridge University Press, pp. 91–196.

Lamborn, Alan (1997) "Theory and the politics in world politics," *International Studies Quarterly*, 41, 187–214.

Lancaster, Sandra and Margaret Foddy (1988) "Self-extensions: A conceptualization," *Journal for the Theory of Social Behaviour*, 18, 77–94.

Lane, Ruth (1996) "Positivism, scientific realism and political science," *Journal of Theoretical Politics*, 8, 361–382.

Lapid, Yosef (1989) "The third debate: On the prospects of international theory in a post-positivist era," *International Studies Quarterly*, 33, 235–254.

Lapid, Yosef and Friedrich Kratochwil, eds. (1996) *The Return of Culture and Identity in IR Theory*, Boulder: Lynne Rienner.

Larkins, Jeremy (1994) "Representations, symbols, and social facts: Durkheim and IR theory," *Millennium*, 23, 239–264.

Lasswell, Harold (1972) "Future systems of identity in the world community," in C. Black and R. Falk, eds., *The Future of the International Legal Order*, vol. IV, Princeton: Princeton University Press, pp. 3–31.

Latsis, Spiro (1972) "Situational determinism in economics," *The British Journal for the Philosophy of Science*, 23, 207–245.

Bibliography

Laudan, Larry (1981) "A confutation of convergent realism," *Philosophy of Science*, 48, 19–49.

Layder, Derek (1990) *The Realist Image in Social Science*, London: Macmillan.

Layne, Christopher (1993) "The unipolar illusion: Why new great powers will rise," *International Security*, 17, 5–51.

Lebow, Richard Ned (1981) *Between Peace and War*, Baltimore: Johns Hopkins University Press.

(1998) "Beyond parsimony," *European Journal of International Relations*, 4, 31–66.

Lebow, Richard Ned and Thomas Risse-Kappen, eds. (1995) *International Relations Theory and the End of the Cold War*, New York: Columbia University Press.

Lebow, Richard Ned and Janice Stein (1989) "Rational deterrence theory: I think, therefore I deter," *World Politics*, 41, 208–224.

Legro, Jeffrey (1996) "Culture and preferences in the international cooperation two-step," *American Political Science Review*, 90, 118–137.

Leplin, Jarrett (1984) "Introduction," in Leplin, ed., *Scientific Realism*, Berkeley: University of California Press, pp. 1–7.

(1988) "Is essentialism unscientific?" *Philosophy of Science*, 55, 493–510.

Levine, Andrew, Elliott Sober, and Erik Olin Wright (1987) "Marxism and methodological individualism," *New Left Review*, 162, 67–84.

Levitas, Ruth (1995) "We: Problems in identity, solidarity and difference," *History of the Human Sciences*, 8, 89–105.

Levitt, Barbara and James March (1988) "Organizational learning," *Annual Review of Sociology*, 14, 319–340.

Levy, Jack (1988) "The diversionary theory of war: A critique," in M. Midlarsky, ed., *Handbook of War Studies*, London: Unwin Hyman, pp. 259–288.

(1994) "Learning and foreign policy: Sweeping a conceptual minefield," *International Organization*, 48, 279–312.

(1997) "Prospect theory, rational choice, and international relations," *International Studies Quarterly*, 41, 87–112.

Lewis, David (1969) *Convention: A Philosophical Study*, Cambridge, MA: Harvard University Press.

Lewis, J. David (1979) "A social behaviorist interpretation of the Meadian 'I'," *American Journal of Sociology*, 85, 261–287.

Leydesdorff, Loet (1993) "Is society a self-organizing system?" *Journal of Social and Evolutionary Systems*, 16, 331–349.

Liberman, Peter (1993) "The spoils of conquest," *International Security*, 18, 125–153.

Lijphart, Arend (1977) *Democracy in Plural Societies*, New Haven: Yale University Press.

Linklater, Andrew (1990) "The problem of community in international relations," *Alternatives*, 15, 135–153.

(1998) *The Transformation of Political Community: Ethical Foundations of the Post-Westphalian Era*, Columbia, SC: University of South Carolina Press.

Lipson, Charles (1984) "International cooperation in economic and security affairs," *World Politics*, 37, 1–23.

Lipton, Peter (1991) *Inference to the Best Explanation*, London: Routledge.

Little, Daniel (1991) *Varieties of Social Explanation*, Boulder: Westview.

(1993) "On the scope and limits of generalizations in the social sciences," *Synthese*, 97, 183–207.

Little, Richard and Steve Smith, eds. (1988) *Belief Systems in International Relations*, Oxford: Blackwell.

Loar, Brian (1985) "Social content and psychological content," in R. Grimm and D. Merrill, eds., *Contents of Thought*, Tucson: University of Arizona Press, pp. 99–110.

Long, David and Peter Wilson, eds. (1995) *Thinkers of the Twenty Years' Crisis: Inter-War Idealism Reassessed*, Oxford: Clarendon Press.

Luhmann, Niklas (1990) *Essays on Self-Reference*, New York: Columbia University Press.

(1997) "The control of intransparency," *Systems Research and Behavioral Science*, 14, 359–371.

Lumsdaine, David (1993) *Moral Vision in International Politics*, Princeton: Princeton University Press.

Lynch, Marc (1999) *State Interests and Public Spheres: The International Politics of Jordan's Identity*, New York: Columbia University Press, forthcoming.

Lynn, Michael and Andrew Oldenquist (1986) "Egoistic and nonegoistic motives in social dilemmas," *American Psychologist*, 41, 529–534.

MacPherson, C.B. (1962) *The Political Theory of Possessive Individualism*, Oxford: Clarendon Press.

Majeski, Stephen and David Sylvan (1998) "Modeling theories of constitutive relations in politics," manuscript, University of Washington.

Mandelbaum, Maurice (1955) "Societal facts," *British Journal of Sociology*, 6, 305–317.

Manicas, Peter and Alan Rosenberg (1985) "Naturalism, epistemological individualism and the 'strong programme' in the sociology of knowledge," *Journal for the Theory of Social Behaviour*, 15, 76–101.

Mann, Michael (1979) "Idealism and materialism in sociological theory," in J. Freiberg, ed., *Critical Sociology: European Perspectives*, New York: Irvington Publishers, pp. 97–119.

(1984) "The autonomous power of the state: Its origins, mechanisms and results," *European Journal of Sociology*, 25, 185–213.

(1993) "A theory of the modern state," chapter 3 in *The Sources of Social Power*, vol. II, Cambridge: Cambridge University Press, pp. 44–91.

Maoz, Zeev and Dan Felsenthal (1987) "Self-binding commitments, the inducement of trust, social choice, and the theory of international cooperation," *International Studies Quarterly*, 31, 177–200.

Markova, Ivana (1982) *Paradigms, Thought, and Language*, New York: Wiley.

Markovsky, Barry and Mark Chaffee (1995) "Social identification and solidarity," in Markovsky, *et al.*, eds., *Advances in Group Processes*, vol. XII, Greenwich, CT: JAI Press, pp. 249–270.

Markus, Hazel and Shinobu Kitayama (1991) "Culture and the self: Implications for cognition, emotion, and motivation," *Psychological Review*, 98, 224–253.

Markus, Hazel and Paula Nurius (1986) "Possible selves," *American Psychologist*, 41, 954–969.

Martin, Lisa (1992) *Coercive Cooperation: Explaining Multilateral Economic Sanctions*, Princeton: Princeton University Press.

Maryanski, Alexandra and Jonathan Turner (1992) *The Social Cage: Human Nature and the Evolution of Society*, Stanford: Stanford University Press.

Mathien, Thomas (1988) "Network analysis and methodological individualism," *Philosophy of the Social Sciences*, 18, 1–20.

Maxwell, Grover (1962) "The ontological status of theoretical entities," in H. Feigl and G. Maxwell, eds., *Minnesota Studies in the Philosophy of Science*, vol. III, Minneapolis: University of Minnesota Press, pp. 3–27.

Maynard, Douglas and Thomas Wilson (1980) "On the reification of social structure," in S. McNall and G. Howe, eds., *Current Perspectives in Social Theory*, vol. I, Greenwich: JAI Press, pp. 287–322.

McCall, George and Jerry Simmons (1978) *Identities and Interactions*, New York: Free Press.

McCullagh, C. Behan (1991) "How objective interests explain actions," *Social Science Information*, 30, 29–54.

McKeown, Timothy (1986) "The limitations of 'structural' theories of commercial policy," *International Organization*, 40, 43–64.

McMullin, Ernan (1978) "Structural explanation," *American Philosophical Quarterly*, 15, 139–147.

(1984a) "A case for scientific realism," in J. Leplin, ed., *Scientific Realism*, Berkeley: University of California Press, pp. 8–40.

(1984b) "Two ideals of explanation in natural science," in P. French *et al.*, eds., *Midwest Studies in Philosophy*, vol. IX, Minneapolis: University of Minnesota Press, pp. 205–220.

McNeely, Connie (1995) *Constructing the Nation-State*, Westport: Greenwood Press.

Mead, George Herbert (1925) "The genesis of the self and social control," *International Journal of Ethics*, 35, 251–277.

(1934) *Mind, Self, and Society*, Chicago: University of Chicago Press.

Mearsheimer, John (1990a) "Back to the future: Instability in Europe after the Cold War," *International Security*, 15, 5–56.

(1990b) "Why we will soon miss the Cold War," *The Atlantic*, 266, 35–50.

(1994/1995) "The false promise of international institutions," *International Security*, 19, 5–49.

Mellor, D. (1982) "The reduction of society," *Philosophy*, 57, 51–75.

Melucci, Alberto (1989) *Nomads of the Present*, London: Hutchinson.

Mennell, Stephen (1989) "Humanity as a whole," in *Norbert Elias*, Oxford: Blackwell, chapter 9.

Mercer, Jonathan (1995) "Anarchy and identity," *International Organization*, 49, 229–252.

Meyer, John (1977) "The effects of education as an institution," *American Journal of Sociology*, 83, 55–77.

(1980) "The world polity and the authority of the nation-state," in A. Bergesen, ed., *Studies of the Modern World-System*, New York: Academic Press, pp. 109–137.

Meyer, John *et al.* (1997) "World society and the nation-state," *American Journal of Sociology*, 103, 144–181.

Meyerson, Debra, Karl Weick, and Roderick Kramer (1995) "Swift trust and temporary groups," in R. Kramer and T. Tyler, eds., *Trust in Organizations*, Thousand Oaks: Sage, pp. 166–195.

Miller, Arthur (1991) "Have incommensurability and causal theory of reference anything to do with actual science? – Incommensurability, no; causal theory, yes," *International Studies in the Philosophy of Science*, 5, 97–108.

Milner, Helen (1991) "The assumption of anarchy in international relations theory: A critique," *Review of International Studies*, 17, 67–85.

Mitchell, Sollace (1983) "Post-structuralism, empiricism and interpretation," in S. Mitchell and M. Rosen, eds., *The Need for Interpretation*, London: Athlone Press, pp. 54–89.

Mitchell, Timothy (1991) "The limits of the state," *American Political Science Review*, 85, 77–96.

Mitzen, Jennifer (2000) "Managing anarchy: The emergence and consolidation of the international public sphere," Ph.D. dissertation, University of Chicago.

Moe, Terry (1979) "On the scientific status of rational models," *American Journal of Political Science*, 23, 215–243.

(1984) "The new economics of organization," *American Journal of Political Science*, 28, 739–777.

Monroe, Kristen (1996) *The Heart of Altruism*, Princeton: Princeton University Press.

Moore, A., ed. (1993) *Meaning and Reference*, Oxford: Oxford University Press.

Moravcsik, Andrew (1997) "Taking preferences seriously: A liberal theory of international politics," *International Organization*, 51, 513–553.

Morgan, David and Michael Schwalbe (1990) "Mind and self in society: Linking social structure and social cognition," *Social Psychology Quarterly*, 53, 148–164.

Morgenthau, Hans (1946) *Scientific Man vs. Power Politics*, Chicago: University of Chicago Press.

(1948/1973) *Politics Among Nations*, 5th edn, New York: Knopf.

Morris, Aldon and C. Mueller, eds. (1992) *Frontiers in Social Movement Theory*, New Haven: Yale University Press.

Morrow, James (1994) "Modeling the forms of international cooperation: Distribution versus information," *International Organization*, 48, 387–423.

Morse, Jennifer (1997) "Who is rational economic man?" *Social Philosophy and Policy*, 14, 179–206.

Moses, Rafael (1982) "The group self and the Arab-Israeli conflict," *International Review of Psycho-Analysis*, 9, 55–65.

Most, Benjamin and Harvey Starr (1984) "International relations theory, foreign policy substitutability, and 'nice' laws," *World Politics*, 36, 383–406.

Moul, William (1973) "The level of analysis problem revisited," *Canadian Journal of Political Science*, 6, 494–513.

Mouzelis, Nicos (1989) "Political transitions in Greece and Argentina: Toward a reconceptualization of Marxist political theory," *Comparative Political Studies*, 21, 443–466.

Müller, Harald (1993) "The internalization of principles, norms, and rules by governments," in V. Rittberger, eds., *Regime Theory and International Relations*, Oxford: Oxford University Press, pp. 361–388.

Murphy, Raymond (1984) "The structure of closure: A critique and development of the theories of Weber, Collins, and Parkin," *British Journal of Sociology*, 35, 547–567.

(1995) "Sociology as if nature did not matter: An ecological critique," *British Journal of Sociology*, 46, 688–707.

Murray, Robin (1971) "The internationalization of capital and the nation state," *New Left Review*, 67, 84–109.

Musgrave, Alan (1985) "Realism versus constructive empiricism," in P. Churchland and C. Hooker, eds., *Images of Science*, Chicago: University of Chicago Press, pp. 197–221.

(1988) "The ultimate argument for scientific realism," in R. Nola, ed., *Relativism and Realism in Science*, Dordrecht: Kluwer Academic Publishers, pp. 229–252.

Myers, Milton (1983) *The Soul of Modern Economic Man*, Chicago: University of Chicago Press.

Nadelmann, Ethan (1990) "Global prohibition regimes: The evolution of norms in international society," *International Organization*, 44, 479–526.

Nagel, Ernest (1961) *The Structure of Science*, Indianapolis: Hackett.

Nau, Henry (1993) "Identity and international politics," manuscript, George Washington University.

(1994) "Why markets and international politics differ," manuscript, George Washington University.

Nelson, Alan (1984) "Some issues surrounding the reduction of macroeconomics to microeconomics," *Philosophy of Science*, 51, 573–594.

(1990) "Are economic kinds natural?" in C.W. Savage, ed., *Scientific Theories*, Minneapolis: University of Minnesota Press, pp. 102–135.

Nelson, Richard (1995) "Recent evolutionary theorizing about economic change," *Journal of Economic Literature*, 33, 48–90.

Nelson, Richard and Sydney Winter (1982) *An Evolutionary Theory of Economic Change*, Cambridge, MA: Harvard University Press.

Nemedi, Denes (1995) "Collective consciousness, morphology, and collective representations," *Sociological Perspectives* 38, 41–56.

Neufeld, Mark (1995) *The Restructuring of International Relations Theory*, Cambridge: Cambridge University Press.

Neumann, Iver (1996) "Collective identity formation: Self and other in international relations," *European Journal of International Relations*, 2, 139–174.

Neumann, Iver and Jennifer Welsh (1991) "The Other in European self-definition: An addendum to the literature on international society," *Review of International Studies*, 17, 327–348.

New, Caroline (1995) "Sociology and the case for realism," *Sociological Review*, 43, 808–827.

Niiniluoto, Ilkka (1980) "Scientific progress," *Synthese*, 45, 427–462.

Niou, Emerson and Peter Ordeshook (1994) "Less filling, tastes great: The Realist–Neoliberal debate," *World Politics*, 46, 209–234.

Nola, Robert (1994) "Post-modernism, a French cultural Chernobyl: Foucault on power/knowledge," *Inquiry*, 37, 3–43.

Nordlinger, Eric (1981) *On the Autonomy of the Democratic State*, Cambridge, MA: Harvard University Press.

Nye, Joseph (1987) "Nuclear learning and U.S.-Soviet security regimes," *International Organization*, 41, 371–402.

Oldenquist, Andrew (1982) "Loyalties," *Journal of Philosophy*, 79, 173–193.

Olick, Jeffrey and Joyce Robbins (1998) "Social memory studies," *Annual Review of Sociology*, 24, 105–140.

Oliver, Christine (1991) "Network relations and loss of organizational autonomy," *Human Relations*, 44, 943–961.

Ollman, Bertel (1971) *Alienation: Marx's Conception of Man in Capitalist Society*, Cambridge: Cambridge University Press.

Olson, Mancur (1965) *The Logic of Collective Action*, Cambridge, MA: Harvard University Press.

O'Neill, John (1994) "Essentialism and the market," *The Philosophical Forum*, 26, 87–100.

(1995) " 'I gotta use words when I talk to you': A response to death and furniture," *History of the Human Sciences*, 8, 99–106.

Onuf, Nicholas (1989) *World of Our Making*, Columbia, SC: University of South Carolina Press.

(1995) "Levels," *European Journal of International Relations*, 1, 35–58.

(1998) *The Republican Legacy in International Thought*, Cambridge: Cambridge University Press.

Onuf, Nicholas & Frank Klink (1989) "Anarchy, authority, rule," *International Studies Quarterly*, 33, 149–174.

Oren, Ido (1995) "The subjectivity of the 'democratic' peace: Changing U.S. perceptions of Imperial Germany," *International Security*, 20, 147–184.

Bibliography

Orren, Karen (1995) "Ideas and institutions," *Polity*, 28, 97–101.
Oye, Kenneth, ed. (1986) *Cooperation under Anarchy*, Princeton: Princeton University Press.
Palan, Ronen and Brook Blair (1993) "On the idealist origins of the realist theory of international relations," *Review of International Studies*, 19, 385–399.
Paros, Laura (1999) "The prison-house of sovereignty," *Alternatives*, forthcoming.
Pasic, Sujata (1996) "Culturing international relations theory," in Y. Lapid and F. Kratochwil, eds., *The Return of Culture and Identity in IR Theory*, Boulder: Lynne Rienner, pp. 85–104.
Peacocke, Christopher (1993) "Externalist explanation," *Proceedings of the Aristotelian Society*, 93, 203–230.
Perinbanayagam, R. (1974) "The definition of the situation: An analysis of the ethnomethodological and dramaturgical view," *Sociological Quarterly*, 15, 521–541.
(1985) *Signifying Acts: Structure and Meaning in Everyday Life*, Carbondale: Southern Illinois University Press.
Peterson, M.J. (1997) "The multiple knowledge bases of the study of international relations," manuscript, University of Massachusetts-Amherst.
Peterson, V. Spike, ed. (1992) *Gendered States*, Boulder: Lynne Rienner.
Pettit, Philip (1993) *The Common Mind*, Oxford: Oxford University Press.
Pfeffer, Jeffrey and Gerald Salancik (1978) *The External Control of Organizations*, New York: Harper and Row.
Picciotto, Sol (1991) "The internationalization of the state," *Capital and Class*, 43, 43–62.
Pizzorno, Alessandro (1991) "On the individualistic theory of social order," in P. Bourdieu and J. Coleman, eds., *Social Theory for a Changing Society*, Boulder: Westview, pp. 209–231.
(1992) "Foucault and the liberal view of the individual," in T. Armstrong, ed., *Michel Foucault Philosopher*, Harvester Press, pp. 204–211.
Platts, Mark (1991) *Moral Realities*, London: RKP.
Pleasants, Nigel (1996) "Nothing is concealed: De-centering tacit knowledge and rules from social theory," *Journal for the Theory of Social Behaviour*, 26, 233–255.
Poggi, Gianfranco (1990) *The State: Its Nature, Development and Prospects*, Stanford: Stanford University Press.
Porpora, Douglas (1983) "On the post-Wittgensteinian critique of the concept of action in sociology," *Journal for the Theory of Social Behaviour*, 13, 129–146.
(1989) "Four concepts of social structure," *Journal for the Theory of Social Behaviour*, 19, 195–211.
(1993) "Cultural rules and material relations," *Sociological Theory*, 11, 212–229.
Poulantzas, Nicos (1975) *Classes in Contemporary Capitalism*, London: New Left Books.

(1978) *State, Power, Socialism*, London: Verso.

Powell, Robert (1991) "Absolute and relative gains in international relations theory," *American Political Science Review*, 85, 1303–1320.

(1994) "Anarchy in international relations theory: The neorealist-neoliberal debate," *International Organization*, 48, 313–344.

Pratkanis, Anthony and Anthony Greenwald (1985) "How shall the self be conceived?" *Journal for the Theory of Social Behaviour*, 15, 311–329.

Price, Richard (1995) "A genealogy of the chemical weapons taboo," *International Organization*, 49, 73–104.

Putnam, Hilary (1975) *Mind, Language, and Reality*, Cambridge: Cambridge University Press.

(1978) *Meaning and the Moral Sciences*, London: RKP.

Radnitsky, G. and P. Bernholz, eds. (1986) *Economic Imperialism*, New York: Paragon House.

Rappaport, Steven (1995) "Economic models and historical explanation," *Philosophy of the Social Sciences*, 25, 421–441.

Raub, Werner (1990) "A general game-theoretic model of preference adaptations in problematic social situations," *Rationality and Society*, 2, 67–93.

Rawls, John (1955) "Two concepts of rules," *Philosophical Review*, 64, 3–32.

Ray, James Lee (1989) "The abolition of slavery and the end of international war," *International Organization*, 43, 405–441.

Reus-Smit, Christian (1997) "The constitutional structure of international society and the nature of fundamental institutions," *International Organization*, 51, 555–589.

(1999) *The Moral Purpose of the State*, Princeton: Princeton University Press.

Rieber, Robert, ed. (1991) *The Psychology of War and Peace: The Image of the Enemy*, Plenum Press.

Ringmar, Erik (1996) "On the ontological status of the state," *European Journal of International Relations*, 2, 439–466.

Risse-Kappen, Thomas (1995) "Democratic peace – warlike democracies? A social constructivist interpretation of the liberal argument," *European Journal of International Relations*, 1, 491–518.

(1996) "Collective identity in a democratic community: The care of NATO," in P. Katzenstein, ed. *The Culture of National Security*, Ithaca: Cornell University Press, pp. 357–399.

Rosenau, James (1986) "Before cooperation: Hegemons, regimes, and habit-driven actors in world politics," *International Organization*, 40, 849–894.

Rosenau, James and Ernst-Otto Czempiel, eds. (1992) *Governance without Government: Order and Change in World Politics*, Cambridge: Cambridge University Press.

Rosenberg, Alexander (1985) "Prospects for the elimination of tastes from economics and ethics," *Social Philosophy and Policy*, 2, 48–68.

(1992) *Economics – Mathematical Politics or Science of Diminishing Returns?* Chicago: University of Chicago Press.

Bibliography

(1995) *Philosophy of Social Science*, 2nd edn, Boulder: Westview Press.

Rosenberg, Justin (1994) *The Empire of Civil Society*, London: Verso.

Rosenberg, Morris (1981) "The self-concept: Social product and social force," in M. Rosenberg and R. Turner, eds., *Social Psychology*, New York: Basic Books, pp. 593–624.

Rosenthal, Sandra (1992) "Free selves, enriched values, and experimental method: Mead's pragmatic synthesis," *International Philosophical Quarterly*, 32, 79–93.

Rouse, Joseph (1987) *Knowledge and Power*, Ithaca: Cornell University Press.

Ruben, David-Hillel (1985) *The Metaphysics of the Social World*, London: RKP.

Rubinstein, David (1977) "The concept of action in the social sciences," *Journal for the Theory of Social Behaviour*, 7, 209–236.

(1981) *Marx and Wittgenstein: Social Praxis and Social Explanation*, London: RKP.

(1986) "Wittgenstein and social science," in S. Shanker, ed., *Ludwig Wittgenstein: Critical Assessments*, vol. IV, London: Croom Helm, pp. 290–311.

Ruggie, John (1983a) "Continuity and transformation in the world polity," *World Politics*, 35, 261–285.

(1983b) "International regimes, transactions, and change: Embedded liberalism in the postwar economic order," in S. Krasner, ed., *International Regimes*, Ithaca: Cornell University Press, pp. 195–232.

(1993) "Territoriality and beyond: Problematizing modernity in international relations," *International Organization*, 47, 139–174.

Ruggie, John, ed. (1993) *Multilateralism Matters*, New York: Columbia University Press.

Runciman, David (1997) *Pluralism and the Personality of the State*, Cambridge: Cambridge University Press.

Russett, Bruce (1993) *Grasping the Democratic Peace*, Princeton: Princeton University Press.

Sabini, John and Jay Schulkin (1994) "Biological realism and social constructivism," *Journal for the Theory of Social Behaviour*, 24, 207–217.

Sack, Robert (1986) *Human Territoriality*, Cambridge: Cambridge University Press.

Sampson, Edward (1988) "The debate on individualism: Indigenous psychologies of the individual and their role in personal and societal functioning," *American Psychologist*, 43, 15–22.

Sandel, Michael (1982) *Liberalism and the Limits of Justice*, Cambridge: Cambridge University Press.

Sandelands, Lloyd and Lynda St. Clair (1993) "Toward an empirical concept of group," *Journal for the Theory of Social Behaviour*, 23, 432–458.

Sartori, Giovanni (1989) "The essence of the political in Carl Schmitt," *Journal of Theoretical Politics*, 1, 63–75.

Satz, Debra and John Ferejohn (1994) "Rational choice and social theory," *Journal of Philosophy*, 92, 71–87.

Sayer, Andrew (1984) *Method in Social Science: A Realist Approach*, London: Hutchinson.

(1997) "Essentialism, social constructionism, and beyond," *Sociological Review*, 45, 453–487.

Schelling, Thomas (1960) *The Strategy of Conflict*, Cambridge, MA: Harvard University Press.

(1978) *Micromotives and Macrobehavior*, New York: W.W. Norton.

(1984) "Self-command in practice, in policy, and in a theory of rational choice," *American Economic Review*, 74, 1–11.

Scheman, Naomi (1983) "Individualism and the objects of psychology," in S. Harding and M. Hintikka, eds., *Discovering Reality*, Dordrecht: Reidel, pp. 225–244.

Schlagel, Richard (1984) "A reasonable reply to Hume's skepticism," *British Journal for the Philosophy of Science*, 35, 359–374.

Schmidtz, David (1995) *Rational Choice and Moral Agency*, Princeton: Princeton University Press.

Schmitt, Carl (1932/1976) *The Concept of the Political*, New Brunswick: Rutgers University Press.

Schmitt, Frederick, ed. (1994) *Socializing Epistemology*, Lanham, MD: Rowman and Littlefield.

Schneider, Susan and Reinhard Angelmar (1993) "Cognition in organizational analysis: Who's minding the store?" *Organization Studies*, 14, 347–374.

Schofield, Norman (1996) "Rules, equilibrium, beliefs, and social mathematics," in D. Braybrooke, ed., *Social Rules*, Boulder: Westview, pp. 233–248.

Schroeder, Paul (1993) "The transformation of political thinking, 1787–1848," in R. Jervis, ed., *Coping with Complexity in the International System*, Boulder: Westview, pp. 47–70.

(1994) "Historical reality and neorealist theory," *International Security*, 19, 108–149.

Schueler, G.F. (1995) *Desire*, Cambridge, MA: MIT Press.

Schutz, Alfred (1962) *Collected Papers, volume 1: The Problem of Social Reality*, The Hague: Martinus Nijhoff.

Schwab, George (1987) "Enemy or foe: A conflict of modern politics," *Telos*, 72, 194–201.

Schwalbe, Michael (1988) "Role taking reconsidered: Linking competence and performance to social structure," *Journal for the Theory of Social Behaviour*, 18, 411–436.

(1991) "The autogenesis of the self," *Journal for the Theory of Social Behaviour*, 21, 269–295.

Schwartz, Stephen, ed. (1977) *Naming, Necessity, and Natural Kinds*, Ithaca: Cornell University Press.

Schwartz, Stuart, ed. (1994) *Implicit Understandings*, Cambridge: Cambridge University Press.

Schweller, Randall (1993) "Tripolarity and the Second World War," *International Studies Quarterly*, 37, 73–103.

(1994) "Bandwagoning for profit: Bringing the revisionist state back in," *International Security*, 19, 72–107.

(1996) "Neorealism's status quo-bias: What security dilemma?" *Security Studies*, 5, 90–121.

Schweller, Randall and David Priess (1997) "A tale of two realisms: Expanding the institutions debate," *Mershon International Studies Review*, 41, Supplement 1, 1–32.

Scott, Andrew (1967) *The Functioning of the International Political System*, New York: Macmillan.

Searle, John (1969) *Speech Acts*, Cambridge: Cambridge University Press.

(1983) *Intentionality: An Essay in the Philosophy of Mind*, Cambridge: Cambridge University Press.

(1990) "Collective intentions and actions," in P. Cohen, J. Morgan, and M. Pollack, eds., *Intentions in Communication*, Cambridge, MA: MIT Press, pp. 401–415.

(1995) *The Construction of Social Reality*, New York: Free Press.

Sen, Amartya (1977) "Rational fools: A critique of the behavioural foundations of economic theory," *Philosophy and Public Affairs*, 6, 317–344.

Sensat, Julius (1988) "Methodological individualism and Marxism," *Economics and Philosophy*, 4, 189–219.

Sewell, William (1992) "A theory of structure: Duality, agency, and transformation," *American Journal of Sociology*, 98, 1–29.

Shapiro, Ian and Alexander Wendt (1992) "The difference that realism makes: Social science and the politics of consent," *Politics and Society*, 20, 197–223.

Sharrock, W. and D. Watson (1984) "What's the point of 'rescuing motives'?" *British Journal of Sociology*, 35, 435–451.

Shaw, Martin (1997) 'The state of globalization: Towards a theory of state transformation," *Review of International Political Economy*, 4, 497–513.

Shore, Chris (1996) "Transcending the nation-state? The European Commission and the (re)-discovery of Europe," *Journal of Historical Sociology*, 9, 473–496.

Shotter, John (1990) "Social individuality versus possessive individualism: The sounds of silence," in I. Parker and J. Shotter, eds., *Deconstructing Social Psychology*, London: RKP, pp. 155–169.

Shweder, Richard (1991) *Thinking Through Cultures*, Cambridge, MA: Harvard University Press.

Simmons, John (1989) "Locke's state of nature," *Political Theory*, 17, 449–470.

Singer, J. David (1961) "The level-of-analysis problem in international relations," in K. Knorr and S. Verba, eds., *The International System*, Princeton: Princeton University Press, pp. 77–92.

Singh, Jitendra and Charles Lumsden (1990) "Theory and research in organizational ecology," *Annual Review of Sociology,* 16, 161–195.

Skocpol, Theda (1995) "Why I am an historical institutionalist," *Polity,* 28, 103–106.

Slaughter, Anne-Marie (1995) "International law in a world of liberal states," *European Journal of International Law,* 6, 503–538.

Slovic, Paul (1995) "The construction of preference," *American Psychologist,* 50, 364–371.

Smith, Anthony (1981) "States and homelands: The social and geopolitical implications of national territory," *Millennium,* 10, 187–202.

(1989) "The origins of nations," *Ethnic and Racial Studies,* 12, 340–367.

Smith, David (1996) "The social construction of enemies: Jews and the representation of evil," *Sociological Theory,* 14, 203–240.

Smith, Michael (1987) "The Humean theory of motivation," *Mind,* 96, 36–61.

Smith, Rogers (1995) "Ideas, institutions, and strategic choice," *Polity,* 28, 135–140.

Smith, Steve (1983) "War and human nature," in I. Forbes and S. Smith, eds., *Politics and Human Nature,* London: Frances Pinter, pp. 164–179.

(1995) "The self-images of a discipline: A genealogy of international relations theory," in K. Booth and S. Smith, eds., *IR Theory Today,* Cambridge: Polity Press, pp. 1–37.

Snidal, Duncan (1991) "Relative gains and the pattern of international cooperation," *American Political Science Review,* 85, 701–726.

Snyder, Glenn (1996) "Process variables in neorealist theory," *Security Studies,* 5, 167–192.

Snyder, Glenn and Paul Diesing (1977) *Conflict Among Nations,* Princeton: Princeton University Press.

Snyder, Richard, H.W. Bruck, and Burton Sapin (1954) *Decision-Making as an Approach to the Study of International Politics,* Princeton: Princeton University Press.

Soltan, Karol and Stephen Elkin, eds. (1996) *The Constitution of Good Societies,* University Park, PA: Pennsylvania State University Press.

Sondermann, Fred (1977) "The concept of the national interest," *Orbis,* 21, 121–138.

Sorensen, Georg (1997) "An analysis of contemporary statehood: Consequences for conflict and cooperation," *Review of International Studies,* 23, 253–269.

Spiro, Melford (1987) "Collective representations and mental representations in religious symbol systems," in B. Kilborne and L. Langness, eds., *Culture and Human Nature: Theoretical Papers of Melford Spiro,* Chicago: University of Chicago Press, pp. 161–184.

Spruyt, Hendrik (1994) *The Sovereign State and its Competitors,* Princeton: Princeton University Press.

Srubar, Ilja (1993) "On the limits of rational choice," *Rationality and Society,* 5, 32–46.

413

Bibliography

Stebbins, R. (1967) "A theory of the definition of the situation," *Canadian Review of Sociology and Anthropology*, 4, 148–164.

Stein, Arthur (1983) "Coordination and collaboration: Regimes in an anarchic world," in S. Krasner, ed., *International Regimes*, Ithaca: Cornell University Press, pp. 115–140.

(1989) "Governments, economic interdependence, and international cooperation," in P. Tetlock, *et al.*, eds., *Behavior, Society, and International Conflict*, vol. III, Oxford: Oxford University Press, pp. 241–324.

(1990) *Why Nations Cooperate*, Ithaca: Cornell University Press.

Stein, Howard (1982) "Adversary symbiosis and complementary group dissociation," *International Journal of Intercultural Relations*, 6, 55–83.

(1985) "Psychological complementarity in Soviet-American relations," *Political Psychology*, 6, 249–261.

Steinbruner, John (1974) *The Cybernetic Theory of Decision*, Princeton: Princeton University Press.

Sterelny, Kim (1995) "Understanding life: Recent work in philosophy of biology," *British Journal for the Philosophy of Science*, 46, 155–183.

Stigler, George and Gary Becker (1977) "De gustibus non est disputandum," *American Economic Review*, 67, 76–90.

Stinchcombe, Arthur (1991) "The conditions of fruitfulness of theorizing about mechanisms in social science," *Philosophy of the Social Sciences*, 21, 367–388.

Strang, David (1991) "Anomaly and commonplace in European political expansion: Realist and institutional accounts," *International Organization*, 45, 143–162.

Strawson, Galen (1987) "Realism and causation," *The Philosophical Quarterly*, 37, 253–277.

Struch, Naomi and Shalom Schwartz (1989) "Intergroup aggression: Its predictors and distinctness from in-group bias," *Journal of Personality and Social Psychology*, 56, 364–373.

Stryker, Sheldon (1980) *Symbolic Interactionism: A Social Structural Version*, Menlo Park, CA: The Benjamin/Cummings Publishing Company.

(1987) "Identity theory: Developments and extensions," in K. Yardley and T. Honess, eds., *Self and Identity: Psychosocial Perspectives*, New York: Wiley, pp. 89–103.

(1991) "Exploring the relevance of social cognition for the relationship of self and society: Linking the cognitive perspective and identity theory," in J. Howard and P. Callero, eds., *The Self-Society Dynamic*, Cambridge: Cambridge University Press, pp. 19–41.

Stryker, Sheldon and Anne Statham (1985) "Symbolic interaction and role theory," in G. Lindzey and E. Aronson, eds., *Handbook of Social Psychology*, vol. I, New York: Random House, pp. 311–378.

Sucharov, Mira (2000) "The international self: Israel and the Palestinians, 1948–1995," Ph.D. dissertation, Georgetown University.

Suganami, Hidemi (1990) "Bringing order to the causes of war debates," *Millennium*, 19, 19–35.

Sugden, Robert (1991) "Rational choice: A survey of contributions from economics and philosophy," *The Economic Journal*, 101, 751–785.

   (1993) "Thinking as a team: Towards an explanation for nonselfish behavior," *Social Philosophy and Policy*, 10, 69–89.

Swales, John and Priscilla Rogers (1995) "Discourse and the projection of corporate culture: The mission statement," *Discourse and Society*, 6, 223–242.

Swidler, Ann (1986) "Culture in action: Symbols and strategies," *American Sociological Review*, 51, 273–286.

Sylvan, David and Barry Glassner (1983) "Is statistical inference appropriate to structuralism?" *Quality and Quantity*, 17, 69–86.

   (1985) *A Rationalist Methodology for the Social Sciences*, Oxford: Blackwell.

Tajfel, Henri, ed. (1982) *Social Identity and Intergroup Relations*, Cambridge: Cambridge University Press.

Tannenwald, Nina (1996) "Dogs that don't bark: The United States, the role of norms and the non-use of nuclear weapons since 1945," Ph.D. dissertation, Cornell University.

   (1999) "The nuclear taboo: The United States and the normative basis of nuclear non-use," *International Organization*, 53, forthcoming.

Taylor, Charles (1971) "Interpretation and the sciences of man," *Review of Metaphysics*, 25, 3–51.

Taylor, Michael (1982) *Community, Anarchy and Liberty*, Cambridge: Cambridge University Press.

   (1989) "Structure, culture and action in the explanation of social change," *Politics and Society*, 17, 115–162.

Taylor, Michael and Sara Singleton (1993) "The communal resource: Transaction costs and the solution of collective action problems," *Politics and Society*, 21, 195–214.

Taylor, Paul (1990) "Consociationalism and federalism as approaches to international integration," in A.J.R. Groom and P. Taylor, eds., *Frameworks for International Cooperation*, New York: St. Martins, pp. 172–184.

Teller, Paul (1986) "Relational holism and quantum mechanics," *British Journal for the Philosophy of Science*, 37, 71–81.

Teske, Nathan (1997) "Beyond altruism: Identity-construction as moral motive in political explanation," *Political Psychology*, 18, 71–91.

Thomas, George *et al.* (1987) *Institutional Structure: Constituting State, Society, and the Individual*, Beverly Hills: Sage.

Thomas, William and Dorothy Swain Thomas (1928) *The Child in America*, New York: Knopf.

Thomson, Janice (1994) *Mercenaries, Pirates, and Sovereigns: State-Building and Extraterritorial Violence in Early Modern Europe*, Princeton: Princeton University Press.

   (1995) "State sovereignty in international relations: Bridging the gap between theory and empirical research," *International Studies Quarterly*, 39, 213–234.

Bibliography

Thomson, Janice and Stephen Krasner (1989) "Global transactions and the consolidation of sovereignty," in E.-O. Czempiel and J. Rosenau, eds., *Global Changes and Theoretical Challenges*, Lexington: Lexington Books, pp. 195–219.

Tickner, Ann (1993) *Gender in International Relations*, New York: Columbia University Press.

Tilly, Charles (1985) "War making and state making as organized crime," in P. Evans, *et al.*, eds., *Bringing the State Back In*, Cambridge: Cambridge University Press, pp. 169–191.

(1990) *Coercion, Capital, and European States, AD 990–1990*, Oxford: Blackwell.

Tranholm-Mikkelsen, Jeppe (1991) "Neo-functionalism: Obstinate or obsolete?" *Millennium*, 20, 1–22.

Trivers, Robert (1971) "The evolution of reciprocal altruism," *Quarterly Review of Biology*, 46, 35–57.

Troyer, Lisa and C. Wesley Younts (1997) "Whose expectations matter? The relative power of first- and second-order expectations in determining social influence," *American Journal of Sociology*, 103, 692–732.

Truman, David (1951) *The Governmental Process*, New York: Knopf.

Tuomela, Raimo (1989) "Collective action, supervenience, and constitution," *Synthese*, 80, 243–266.

Turner, John and Penelope Oakes (1986) "The significance of the social identity concept for social psychology with reference to individualism, interactionism, and social influence," *British Journal of Social Psychology*, 25, 237–252.

Turner, John and Richard Bourhis (1996) "Social identity, interdependence and the social group: A reply to Rabbie *et al.*," in W. Peter Robinson, ed., *Social Groups and Identities*, Oxford: Butterworth Heinemann, pp. 25–63.

Turner, John, *et al.* (1987) *Rediscovering the Social Group*, Oxford: Blackwell.

Turner, Jonathon (1988) *A Theory of Social Interaction*, Stanford: Stanford University Press.

Turner, Ralph (1956) "Role-taking, role standpoint, and reference group behavior," *American Journal of Sociology*, 61, 316–328.

Turner, Stephen (1983, 1984) "Durkheim as a methodologist – Collective forces, causation, and probability," *Philosophy of the Social Sciences*, 13, 425–450, and 14, 51–71.

Tyler, Tom (1990) *Why People Obey the Law*, New Haven: Yale University Press.

Unger, Roberto (1987) *False Necessity: Anti-Necessitarian Social Theory in the Service of Radical Democracy*, Cambridge: Cambridge University Press.

Vanberg, Viktor (1994) *Rules and Choice in Economics*, London: Routledge.

van Eeghen, Piet-Hein (1996) "Towards a methodology of tendencies," *Journal of Economic Methodology*, 3, 261–284.

van Fraassen, Bas (1980) *The Scientific Image*, Oxford: Clarendon Press.

van Krieken, Robert (1989) "Violence, self-discipline and modernity: Beyond the 'civilizing process'," *Sociological Review*, 37, 193–218.

416

Vasquez, John (1993) *The War Puzzle*, Cambridge: Cambridge University Press.

(1995) "The post-positivist debate: Reconstructing scientific enquiry and international relations theory after Enlightenment's fall," in K. Booth and S. Smith, eds., *IR Theory Today*, Cambridge: Polity Press, pp. 217–240.

(1997) "The realist paradigm and degenerative versus progressive research programs," *American Political Science Review*, 91, 899–913.

Vincent, Andrew (1983) "The Hegelian state and international politics," *Review of International Studies*, 9, 191–205.

(1989) "Can groups be persons?" *Review of Metaphysics*, 42, 687–715.

Volkan, Vamik (1988) *The Need to Have Enemies and Allies*, Northvale, NJ: Jason Aronson, Inc.

von Wright, Georg (1971) *Explanation and Understanding*, Ithaca: Cornell University Press.

Wagner, R. Harrison (1992) "Rationality and misperception in deterrence theory," *Journal of Theoretical Politics*, 4, 115–141.

Walker, R.B.J. (1987) "Realism, change, and international political theory," *International Studies Quarterly*, 31, 65–86.

(1993) *Inside/Outside: International Relations as Political Theory*, Cambridge: Cambridge University Press.

Walker, Stephen (1992) "Symbolic interactionism and international politics: Role theory's contribution to international organization," in M. Cottam and C. Shih, eds., *Contending Dramas: A Cognitive Approach to International Organizations*, New York: Praeger, pp. 19–38.

Walker, Stephen, ed. (1987) *Role Theory and Foreign Policy Analysis*, Durham: Duke University Press.

Wallerstein, Immanuel (1974) *The Modern World-System I*, New York: Academic Press.

Walsh, D.M. (1998) "Wide content individualism," *Mind*, 107, 625–651.

Walt, Stephen (1987) *The Origins of Alliances*, Ithaca: Cornell University Press.

(1998) "International relations: One world, many theories," *Foreign Policy*, 110, 29–46.

Waltz, Kenneth (1959) *Man, the State, and War*, New York: Columbia University Press.

(1979) *Theory of International Politics*, Boston: Addison-Wesley.

(1986) "Reflections on *Theory of International Politics*: A response to my critics," in R. Keohane, ed., *Neorealism and its Critics*, New York: Columbia University Press, pp. 322–346.

(1990) "Nuclear myths and political realities," *American Political Science Review*, 84, 731–745.

Walzer, Michael (1984) "Liberalism and the art of separation," *Political Theory*, 12, 315–330.

Wartenberg, Thomas (1991) "Social movements and individual identity," *The Philosophical Forum*, 22, 362–382.

Watson, Adam (1992) *The Evolution of International Society*, London: Routledge.

Bibliography

Weber, Max (1978) *Economy and Society*, Berkeley: University of California Press.
Weigert, Andrew (1991) "Transverse interaction: A pragmatic perspective on environment as Other," *Symbolic Interaction*, 14, 353–363.
Weingast, Barry (1995) "A rational choice perspective on the role of ideas: Shared belief systems and state sovereignty in international cooperation," *Politics and Society*, 23, 449–464.
Weinstein, Eugene and Paul Deutschberger (1963) "Some dimensions of altercasting," *Sociometry*, 26, 454–466.
Weldes, Jutta (1989) "Marxism and methodological individualism," *Theory and Society*, 18, 353–386.
　(1996) "Constructing national interests," *European Journal of International Relations*, 2, 275–318.
　(1999) *Constructing National Interests: The U.S. and Missiles in Cuba*, Minneapolis: University of Minnesota Press.
Weldes, Jutta *et al.*, eds. (1999) *Cultures of Insecurity: States, Communities, and the Production of Danger*, Minneapolis: University of Minnesota Press.
Wellman, Barry and S. D. Berkowitz, eds. (1988) *Social Structures: A Network Approach*. Cambridge: Cambridge University Press.
Wendt, Alexander (1987) "The agent-structure problem in international relations theory," *International Organization*, 41, 335–370.
　(1992) "Anarchy is what states make of it: The social construction of power politics," *International Organization*, 46, 391–425.
　(1994) "Collective identity formation and the international state," *American Political Science Review*, 88, 384–396.
　(1995) "Constructing international politics," *International Security*, 20, 71–81.
　(1998) "On constitution and causation in international relations," *Review of International Studies*, 24, special issue, 101–117.
　(1999) "'What is IR for?': Notes toward a post-critical view," in R. Wyn Jones and R. Tooze, eds., *Critical Theory and World Politics*, Boulder: Lynne Rienner, forthcoming.
Wendt, Alexander and Michael Barnett (1993) "Dependent state formation and Third World militarization," *Review of International Studies*, 19, 321–347.
Wendt, Alexander and Raymond Duvall (1989) "Institutions and international order," in E.-O. Czempiel and J. Rosenau, eds., *Global Changes and Theoretical Challenges*, Lexington: Lexington Books, pp. 51–73.
Wendt, Alexander and Daniel Friedheim (1995) "Hierarchy under anarchy: Informal empire and the East German state," *International Organization*, 49, 689–722.
Wendt, Alexander and Ian Shapiro (1997) "The misunderstood promise of realist social theory," in K. Monroe, ed., *Contemporary Empirical Political Theory*, Berkeley: University of California Press, pp. 166–187.
Wiggins, David (1985) "Claims of need," in T. Honderich, ed., *Morality and Objectivity*, London: RKP, pp. 149–202.

Wight, Colin (1996) "Incommensurability and cross-paradigm communication: 'What's the frequency Kenneth'?" *Millennium*, 25, 291–319.

Wight, Martin (1966) "Why is there no international theory?" in H. Butterfield and M. Wight, eds., *Diplomatic Investigations*, London: Allen and Unwin, pp. 17–34.

(1991) "The three traditions of international theory," in G. Wight and B. Porter, eds., *International Theory: The Three Traditions*, Leicester: Leicester University Press, pp. 7–24.

Wildavsky, Aaron (1994) "Why self-interest means less outside of a social context," *Journal of Theoretical Politics*, 6, 131–159.

Williams, Michael (1998) "Identity and the politics of security," *European Journal of International Relations*, 4, 204–225.

Wilson, David (1989) "Levels of selection: An alternative to individualism in biology and the human sciences," *Social Networks*, 11, 257–272.

Wilson, David and Elliott Sober (1994) "Reintroducing group selection to the human behavioral sciences," *Behavioral and Brain Sciences*, 17, 585–608.

Wilson, Robert (1995) *Cartesian Psychology and Physical Minds: Individualism and the Sciences of the Mind*, Cambridge: Cambridge University Press.

Witt, Ulrich (1985) "Economic behavior and biological evolution: Some remarks on the sociobiology debate," *Journal of Institutional and Theoretical Economics*, 141, 365–389.

(1991) "Economics, sociobiology, and behavioral psychology on preferences," *Journal of Economic Psychology*, 12, 557–573.

Wolfers, Arnold (1962) *Discord and Collaboration*, Baltimore: Johns Hopkins University Press.

Wohlforth, William (1994/5) "Realism and the end of the Cold War," *International Security*, 19, 91–129.

Wood, Ellen Meiksins (1981) "The separation of the economic and the political in capitalism," *New Left Review*, 127, 66–95.

Wrong, Dennis (1961) "The oversocialized conception of man in modern sociology," *American Sociological Review*, 26, 183–193.

(1994) *The Problem of Order: What Unites and Divides Society*, Cambridge, MA: Harvard University Press.

Yee, Albert (1996) "The causal effects of ideas on policies," *International Organization*, 50, 69–108.

Young, Oran (1994) *International Governance: Protecting the Environment in a Stateless Society*, Ithaca: Cornell University Press.

Zakaria, Fareed (1998) *From Wealth to Power: The Unusual Origins of America's World Role*, Princeton: Princeton University Press.

Zerubavel, Eviatar (1997) *Social Mindscapes: An Invitation to Cognitive Sociology*, Cambridge, MA: Harvard University Press.

Zurn, Michael (1997) "Assessing state preferences and explaining institutional choice: The case of intra-German trade," *International Studies Quarterly*, 41, 295–320.

Index

Note: **Bold** page numbers refers to figures. Footnotes have not been indexed.

CAMBRIDGE STUDIES IN INTERNATIONAL RELATIONS